REWRITING INDIE CINEMA

FILM AND CULTURE SERIES

FILM AND CULTURE

A series of Columbia University Press

Edited by John Belton

For the list of titles in this series, see pages 339–341.

REWRITING INDIE CINEMA

IMPROVISATION, PSYCHODRAMA, *and the* SCREENPLAY

J. J. MURPHY

Columbia University Press
New York

Columbia University Press
Publishers Since 1893
New York   Chichester, West Sussex
cup.columbia.edu
Copyright © 2019 Columbia University Press

Library of Congress Cataloging-in-Publication Data
Names: Murphy, J. J., 1947– author.
Title: Rewriting indie cinema : improvisation, psychodrama,
and the screenplay / J. J. Murphy.
Description: New York : Columbia University Press, [2018] |
Series: Film and culture | Includes bibliographical references and index.
Identifiers: LCCN 2018041901| ISBN 9780231191968 (cloth : alk. paper) |
ISBN 9780231191975 (paperback : alk. paper) | ISBN 9780231549592 (e-book)
Subjects: LCSH: Independent films—United States—History and criticism. |
Motion picture plays, American—History and criticism.
Classification: LCC PN1993.5.U6 M79 2018 | DDC 791.430973—dc23
LC record available at https://lccn.loc.gov/2018041901

Columbia University Press books are printed on permanent
and durable acid-free paper.

Printed in the United States of America

Cover design: Noah Arlow
Cover image: *Tangerine* (2015). Courtesy of Sean Baker

TO GEORGE AND PAMELA HAMEL
AND FAMILY, WITH DEEP GRATITUDE,
FOR MAKING THIS BOOK POSSIBLE.

CONTENTS

ACKNOWLEDGMENTS

On a very hot Friday afternoon in July of 2016, I sat with six women and two men (another woman would join us the next day) for the start of a four-day residence on psychodrama in the small town of Highland, New York. After introductions by each member of the group, the psychodramatist had us gather on the original stage that J. L. Moreno had built in 1936. Each group member was asked to discuss the psychodrama she or he would like to enact in the session. Using a sociometric technique, which involved each member placing a hand on someone's shoulder and then reading the flow of energy within the group, the various participants collectively chose the person whose drama they wished to see. To my utter surprise, the group chose me, even though I was the only person who had never done psychodrama before. Through a strange series of events, my scholarly research for this book had led to this moment of finding myself in the spotlight among a group of strangers.

The genesis of this book has its roots in a keynote address that I gave at the first Screenwriting Research Network (SRN) conference in Leeds, England, which I eventually revised into an article for the *Journal of Screenwriting*. It was equally sparked by watching J. L. Moreno's psychodramas on television as a kid in the New York City area. The psychodramas were intense sessions of group psychotherapy. I remember my mother's dismay at discovering what I was watching. Whatever age I was, she didn't think it was an appropriate program. This didn't prevent me from viewing it subsequently; I simply kept the volume down. I find it fascinating how seemingly random early experiences end up shaping the direction of people's lives in profound ways. When I saw my first Warhol film as a college student, a light bulb went off inside my head. The same thing happened with Moreno, although it took me many years to grasp this connection more fully.

Like all films, books are a form of collaboration. Scott MacDonald's pioneering work on William Greaves was crucial to this project. Louise Archambault was an invaluable source of information and a major resource. She helped me set up interviews with Jonathan Gordon, as well as Shannon Baker and Audrey Henningham, the two principal performers in William Greaves's *Symbiopsychotaxiplasm: Take 2½*. I also appreciate the psychodramatists who generously gave of their time to speak with me at some length: Robert Siroka, Marcia Karp, John Nolte, Jim Sacks, and Nan Nally-Seif. It was John Nolte who first encouraged me to do psychodrama if I wanted to understand it fully. Kate Merkle also shared her knowledge of psychodrama. I also interviewed several filmmakers: Sean Baker, Sam Fleischner, James Solomon, and Spencer Parsons. I am grateful to Bianca Hunter for her willingness to discuss her performance in *Bad Lieutenant* and to Lawrence Michael Levine for discussing *The Zone*. The book would not be nearly as informative without the input from these interviews. Special thanks to Sean Baker for providing the image from *Tangerine* for the book cover.

Thanks to my film area colleagues: Kelley Conway, Jeff Smith, Lea Jacobs, Maria Belodubrovskaya, Ben Singer, Vance Kepley, David Bordwell, and Kristin Thompson. David Bordwell was kind enough to read a very early version of the book. His astute and detailed comments led me to rethink and restructure it. He also suggested the perfect publisher. Mike King proofread and provided insightful suggestions on the manuscript. I also owe appreciation to Kelley Conway for her valuable feedback, as well as John Powers, Richard Neupert, and Jim Healy. I owe special thanks to my graduate student, Matt Connolly, who served as a research assistant on this project, transcribed many of the interviews, and checked footnotes. Erica Moulton provided critical feedback and suggestions on final revisions. Kait Fyfe assisted me in selecting and making stills for the book. Linda Lucey went beyond the call of duty to help me navigate the funding for the various grants that I received. Brandon Colvin, Amy Sloper, Erik Gunneson, Peter Sengstock, and Mary Rossa were supportive of this research project in invaluable ways.

Little did I know, when I accepted the invitation to give the keynote at the first SRN Conference, that the scholars I would subsequently meet through the organization would profoundly influence my subsequent research and thinking about the screenwriting studies. These scholars include: Ian Macdonald, Kathryn Millard, Steven Maras, Steven Price, Eva Novrup Redvall, Adam Ganz, Jill Nelmes, Alex Munt, Jule Selbo, and Paul Wells.

On a personal level, the pressures of writing a book affect a person in all kinds of ways. There is an antisocial component in having to focus one's energies so intently on the work at hand. I feel lucky that my loving partner of many years, Nancy Mladenoff, who spends long hours painting in her studio, remains so understanding.

I owe a debt of gratitude to Philip Leventhal, my editor, and John Bolton, the series editor, at Columbia University Press. I could not have nicer or more supportive editors. I am very grateful to Philip for his engagement and good advice throughout the process. My thanks also go to the production supervisors, Kat Jorge at Columbia and Ben Kolstad at Cenveo. It was a pleasure to work with such a capable team during the production phase of the book. Some of this material appeared in various forms in three articles that I wrote for the *Journal of Screenwriting* as well as a chapter on mumblecore I wrote for Geoff King's edited volume, *A Companion to American Indie Film* (Wiley Blackwell, 2016).

The start of this project was funded by a summer research grant from the office of the Vice Chancellor for Research and Graduate Education at UW-Madison. A series of Hamel Family Faculty Research Grants also aided the research. At the crucial stage of the project, I received a Vilas Life Cycle Grant (WISELI) from UW-Madison. Jennifer Sheridan went out of her way to be of assistance in helping me apply for funding and in administering this award. A huge debt of appreciation goes to all my department colleagues who selected me to receive the Hamel Family Distinguished Chair in Communication Arts in 2015. This prestigious award gave me tremendous resources to pursue research on this project. It is an extreme honor to hold a chair named for the Hamel Family. George and Pamela Hamel are incredibly special people. They have not only supported my professorship, but they have given generously to the Department of Communication Arts and UW-Madison throughout the years. I dedicate this book to the Hamels with gratitude and affection.

REWRITING INDIE CINEMA

INTRODUCTION

Across the Spectrum:

From Improvisation to Psychodrama

On a quiet summer morning in 1968, the actor Rip Torn whacked Norman Mailer over the head with a hammer. As the men wrestled to the ground, Mailer tried to bite Torn's ear off. Eyes bulging, Torn began to strangle the director, who groaned and gasped for air, in front of witnesses and Mailer's family. As the well-built actor locked his muscular arms around the director's heavyset body, Mailer's wife, Beverly Bentley, pulled Torn's hair and pummeled him with her hands while two bystanders desperately tried to separate the bloodied combatants. Mailer's young children wailed in the background, crying out, "Daddy! Daddy!"

The fracas appears in Mailer's *Maidstone* (1970). This real-life drama is the most compelling scene in this fictional film. It wasn't scripted or staged. Torn did not pretend to strike the director with a hammer; he drew blood, which led to a vicious fight that caused Mailer's wife to become enraged and his young children to bawl hysterically. *Rewriting Indie Cinema* deals with such issues: the scripted and the unscripted, fiction and nonfiction, and the differences between them. This book grew out of my previous two: *Me and You and* Memento *and* Fargo: *How Independent Screenplays Work* and *The Black Hole of the Camera: The Films of Andy Warhol,* as well as my own filmmaking and experience of teaching narrative filmmaking. In these situations, I have become acutely aware of the relationship between what is written in a script and what might actually be occurring on set. What are the limits of the script? What are the limits of performance? What happens when a filmmaker chooses not to employ a traditional screenplay?

Rewriting Indie Cinema analyzes the shifting role of the screenplay throughout the history of modern American independent cinema. It attempts to shed light not only on industrial practice but, more importantly, on viable alternative approaches to scripting. My examination of American indie cinema from the perspective of the script and its impact on performance reveals tensions between two distinct practices. One strand remains firmly rooted in the primacy of the screenplay as an essential element of dramatic film production—the legacy of classical Hollywood production practices and, in the realm of independent cinema, such major institutions as the Sundance Institute and the PBS-backed American Playhouse series. The other practice moves away from the traditional screenplay through a variety of alternative creative forms: sketches, notes, outlines, treatments, storyboards, diagrams, photographs, or short stories.

Following the introduction of sound, the industrial model of the dialogue-driven screenplay became the standard convention for narrative cinema. A traditional screenplay allows studio executives, producers, and financial backers to exert control over the film they are making. As a result, the screenplay becomes a blueprint for all members on the production team. Norman Mailer, who directed three indie feature films—*Beyond the Law* (1968), *Wild 90* (1968), and *Maidstone*—describes the inevitable fixation on the screenplay during a production, even for a director, because, as he acknowledges, "It is all he can finally depend upon." Mailer asserts, "Given the fundamental, nay, even organic, confusion on a movie set over what everybody is really doing, the company has to pool all differences and be faithful to the script even when the script has lost any relation to the original conception, and has probably begun to constrict the real life which is beginning to emerge on the set."[1]

This book looks at two different major periods in American independent cinema. In the late 1950s and 1960s, American filmmakers were intent on creating a new type of narrative cinema that would counter the kinds of films produced by Hollywood. Dubbed the New American Cinema, these filmmakers began to experiment with alternative approaches to narrative in an effort to distinguish their work from the mainstream, much like the French New Wave did in France. Morris Engel, Ruth Orkin, and Ray Ashley's *Little Fugitive* (1953) was followed by Lionel Rogosin's *On the Bowery* (1956), Alfred Leslie and Robert Frank's *Pull My Daisy* (1959), Ron Rice's *The Flower Thief* (1960), and John Cassavetes's *Shadows* (1958, 1959), and later *Faces* (1968) and *Husbands* (1970). Works by Kent Mackenzie, Andy Warhol, Shirley Clarke, Norman Mailer, William Greaves, and Barbara Loden also came to embody this new cinema.

In the new century, indie filmmakers once again experimented with many of the same strategies, spurred on by the advent of digital technology. Despite achieving commercial success, Gus Van Sant became disenchanted with the industrial approach, which he found too limiting. *Gerry* (2002), *Elephant* (2003), *Last Days* (2005), and *Paranoid Park* (2007) helped set a new precedent for this second wave of unconventional scripting practices. Younger filmmakers associated with mumblecore made microbudget films about their peers that drew inspiration from the work of the New American Cinema. These filmmakers included Joe Swanberg who made *Hannah Takes the Stairs* (2007), which featured Greta Gerwig, and *Nights and Weekends* (2008), which they created together. Other notable films by Ronald Bronstein, Josh and Benny Safdie, Matthew Porterfield, Sean Baker, and Nathan Silver attempted to push boundaries by refusing to accept traditional methods of making films. In both periods discussed, indie filmmakers reacted against Hollywood and Hollywood performance styles. What made these indie films distinctive? Why did the filmmakers make such choices? Why did this type of filmmaking appear at these particular junctures?

In their efforts to develop an alternative narrative practice in the late 1950s and throughout the 1960s, American independent filmmakers were keenly aware of the drawbacks of the industrial model, especially in relying on a script. As Steven Maras notes, the idea of screenwriting as a strictly autonomous activity has wide-ranging implications because it "takes the script out of its production context and potentially reinforces a fracture between conception and execution that impacts on the way we might imagine creativity and expression, and think about the medium."[2] In place of the traditional screenplay, I argue, indie narrative filmmakers employed two major strategies that attempt to shift the emphasis from the written page to performance: improvisation and psychodrama.

IMPROVISATION AND PSYCHODRAMA

Anthony Frost and Ralph Yarrow define improvisation as "the skill of using bodies, space, imagination, objects and all human resources to generate or to reformulate a coherent physical expression of an idea, a situation and a character (even, perhaps, a text); to do this spontaneously, in response to the immediate stimuli of one's environment, without preconceptions."[3] Within the context of cinema, improvisation refers to a more spontaneous form of acting—a performance that unfolds in the moment, either in rehearsal or production, or during both. One assumption is that improvisation contrasts with the prescripted or the highly staged, largely due to the fact that it forces the performer in a dramatic film to move away from a preconceived notion of how a fictional character should be played.

In discussing cinematic improvisation, Virginia Wright Wexman suggests, "What the directors who work in collaboration with actors seem to be striving for is the sense of discovery that comes from the unexpected and unpredictable in human behavior."[4] Improvisation, however, has many variations. It creates a broad spectrum of options for the filmmaker. It can be viewed as moving from the scripted and rehearsed to the impromptu or the ad-libbed. The breadth of the spectrum provides a wide range of the possibilities for the many different forms of improvisation that can occur. As we shall see, this partially explains why the discussion of improvisation within cinema often becomes problematic and confused. While improvisation is often linked to comedy, because my focus is on its connection to psychodrama, I will only be concentrating on its use in dramatic films.

The dominance of the written script overshadows earlier examples of improvisation in cinema, including those found in the silent era. As Steven Price notes:

In the pre-feature film era, studios such as Selig and Edison left space in their scene outlines for improvised action during location shooting, and the records of story conferences involving slightly later film-makers such as Mack Sennett show that improvisation was a feature not only of the working process, but in some cases was also visible within the scripts themselves.[5]

In the sound era, filmmakers outside the United States—Jean Renoir, Roberto Rossellini, and Jacques Rivette, among others—also made use of improvisation in their films.[6]

Yet improvisation has a much longer and sustained history in theater, where it dates back at least to the commedia dell'arte in sixteenth-century Italy. In the United States, improvisation came to the fore with The Compass, a group founded by David Shepherd and Paul Sills in Chicago in the 1950s; the theater games of Viola Spolin; and later Sills's Second City. The Compass officially began on July 15, 1955, with the intention of altering conventional theater by changing its basic structure and the nature of acting through the creation of theater that was based on the techniques of improvisation.

One of the implicit goals of The Compass was to eliminate the playwright and to make the actors the key element in the theatrical production. According to Spolin, "The material and substance of scene improvisation are not the work of any one person or any one writer but came out of the cohesion of player acting upon player."[7] Spolin developed her ideas about improvisation in the late 1930s, and her observations of the productions of The Compass led to her book *Improvisation for the Theater*, written in 1963. It proved to be groundbreaking, especially in its efforts to democratize acting, which is evident in its first sentences: "Everyone can act. Everyone can improvise. Anyone who wishes to can play in the theater and learn to be 'stageworthy.' "[8]

There were, however, earlier precedents for modern improvisation in other countries in the early part of the twentieth century, namely, the work of Konstantin Stanislavsky in Russia, J. L. Moreno in Austria, and Jacques Copeau in France.[9] Stanislavsky, the cofounder and director of the Moscow Art Theatre, no doubt has had the greatest impact on performance in America. He espoused strong naturalism and largely defined the "expressive-realist" acting style that dominates film acting, which aims to be "true to life" rather than "stagy."[10] Stanislavsky's ideas influenced Lee Strasberg, who cofounded the Group Theatre in 1931 and twenty years later became the director of the famed Actors Studio. He was associated with the technique known as "Method acting," which used "affective memory" to help actors identify with the roles they were playing. Strasberg employed improvisation both as part of the training of actors as well as in rehearsals.[11] Method acting gained prominence because it was a technique used by a number of actors—most notably, Marlon Brando and James Dean—who went on to become major stars.

It was actually J. L. Moreno, however, who had the most radical ideas for transforming theater. Moreno believed that traditional theater was, in effect, "dead."[12] As a result, the actors were merely going through the motions because they "have had to give up their initiative and their spontaneity."[13] He reconceived theater as abandoning written plays in favor of a spontaneous acting out of dramas from everyday life that were improvised on stage and engaged the audience directly. He called his theatrical group "Stegreiftheater." Moreno developed the idea of the "Living Newspaper" to improvise situations from current events. Sawyer asserts that "Moreno's 1922 group may have been the first professional theater to perform without a script, improvising dialogue on stage in front of a paying audience."[14] Moreno's theater group began to draw large audiences and achieved a certain degree of popular success. In 1924, Moreno also published a short book, entitled *Das Stegreiftheater*, translated as *The Theatre of Spontaneity*, in which he elaborated upon his views on the subject.[15]

Less a systematic investigation of the subject than a bold polemic, *The Theatre of Spontaneity* is a critical text for understanding Moreno's ideas regarding spontaneity and improvisation and the role they can play in therapy. In it, Moreno emphasizes that his ultimate goal was for a person to be able to achieve a "spontaneously creative self."[16] For him, spontaneity and creativity are inextricably linked or twin concepts, but they are by no means identical in the sense that you could have one without the other. Spontaneity is key to creative behavior, or, in Moreno's words, "The first character of the creative act is its spontaneity."[17] After Moreno immigrated to America in 1925, he began to have informal sessions of what became known as "Impromptu Theatre," which had its first public production at Carnegie Hall on April 5, 1931. The reviews, however, were negative, causing Moreno to believe that the press and public were too conservative and too tied to tradition to accept the radical idea of a wholly spontaneous theater.[18]

Despite the fact that his work has been largely ignored within cinema studies, Moreno turns out to be a key figure. He laid the foundation for practices of improvisation while creating another important tradition, psychodrama. Moreno's interest eventually shifted from spontaneity and improvisation in a theatrical context to a therapeutic framework.

In 1925 a man named George, the husband of one of Moreno's sponta-neous performers, Barbara, complained about his wife's behavior. Moreno had Barbara play the role of a streetwalker being harassed by a man on stage. Her role enabled her to vent feelings of extreme anger, which led to improvement in their personal relationship. Moreno later asked George to join her on stage to recreate various incidents from their own personal lives. This experiment is generally recognized as the genesis of modern-day psychodrama.[19] Audiences were profoundly affected by Moreno's psychodramas, and they responded enthusiastically to this new change in direction. According to John Nolte, "Moreno contended that the audi-ence was more moved by the Barbara and George dramas because they recognized that what they were watching was real, the genuine experience of the actors, not just talented players creating dramas spontaneously."[20]

In cinema, the term "psychodrama" has a number of different mean-ings. In *Visionary Film*, P. Adams Sitney used it to describe a certain strain of short, symbolic avant-garde films of the 1940s and 1950s that dealt with intense psychological issues, such as Maya Deren and Alexander Hammid's *Meshes of the Afternoon* (1943) and Kenneth Anger's *Fireworks* (1947).[21] When applied to narrative cinema, it often broadly refers to a film that privileges the psychological aspect of a character as its most distinctive aspect. My use of the term "psychodrama" throughout the book, however, pertains specifically to the form of group psychother-apy developed by Moreno, who used theater as a means for patients to reenact troubling episodes from their lives in a public setting. According to Peter Felix Kellermann, these personal experiences include "memo-ries of specific happenings in the past, unfinished situations, inner dra-mas, fantasies, dreams, preparations for future risk-taking situations, or unrehearsed expressions of mental states in the here and now."[22] Zerka Moreno, who collaborated with her husband during his life and became the leading exponent of his work after his death more than forty years ago, defined psychodrama in much simpler terms, referring to it as "a form of improvisational theater of your own life."[23]

The fact that Moreno's initial experiments in improvisation with Ste-greiftheater led him to discover psychodrama demonstrates their implicit connection. Although Moreno stumbled upon role playing as a theatrical technique, he immediately grasped its therapeutic benefit. In 1936, he began using psychodrama with patients at a sanitarium in Beacon, New

York, where he built a specially designed stage to explore how it could be used to assist people to live in the moment. In the 1960s, Moreno's public sessions of psychodrama in Manhattan brought him greater notoriety among actors and directors from theater and film who were interested in how it could be used to enhance and liven performance within a dramatic context.

Because psychodrama directly involves the personal lives of the performers, it can be viewed as an extreme version of improvisation. In looking at films that employ the technique of psychodrama, I am particularly interested in filmic situations that push dramatic interaction to the point where the boundary between the fictional character and the performer's life is erased, and where the thin line between what viewers perceive as fiction and actuality blurs or breaks down entirely. As a result, both the performer and the viewer experience a heightened sense of reality. In terms of the spectrum of improvisation, psychodrama is on the opposite end from the rehearsed. Thus, when it occurs within a dramatic film, psychodrama tends to be a cinema of extreme psychological states.

Moreno differentiates between three different forms of psychodrama: the spontaneous, the planned, and the rehearsed.[24] In the first instance, Moreno explains that, although extemporaneous to a degree, some elements, such as the nature of the conflict, are at least partially planned and the session is nevertheless guided by a director who is orchestrating the psychodrama with the help of "auxiliary egos," namely, other actors. The planned psychodrama, on the other hand, is "extemporaneous at the moment of presentation," but it can nevertheless involve extensive preparation in advance.[25] He also outlines permutations that the planned psychodrama might take, which involve what he terms "degrees" of partial planning. For instance, it is possible that the subjects have not been privy to the advance planning, so they will be taken by surprise by certain unexpected developments in what transpires.

Moreno's final category, the "rehearsed" psychodrama, differs significantly from the previous two. He explains, "There is a difference between planning and rehearsing. The rehearsed form gives an accurate reproduction of what has been co-produced by the entire group previous to the performance itself. Nothing new is created in the moment of presentation."[26] The rehearsed psychodrama can be written in advance, including the dialogue, and given to a subject or patient to be acted out with other auxiliary egos or actors. Yet Moreno insists, "The acting out of a play idea of an individual playwright with the assistance of the cast, finally writing and rehearsing it with them, is *not* psychodrama. Similarly a psychological drama 'written' by a playwright [such] as Ibsen or O'Neill is not psychodrama."[27]

Moreno's distinction between a rehearsed psychodrama and a nonpsychodrama is both subtle and significant. In his example of a rehearsed psychodrama, what is to be performed might be written out in advance, but for the subject or patient (the protagonist) experiencing it, he or she remains in the present moment in the unfolding of the scripted event. On the other hand, an actor in an Ibsen or O'Neill play is merely performing what has already been rehearsed. There is no opportunity for the actor to experience a transformative moment in the same sense as someone might in a rehearsed psychodrama.

Moreno's discussion of the three different categories of psychodrama— the spontaneous, the planned, and the rehearsed—is also relevant to the discussion of improvisation. Andy Warhol, Norman Mailer, William Greaves, and Joe Swanberg would be examples of filmmakers who come closest to the first category in more fully embracing the "spontaneous," but even they usually engage, at least partially, in the second category by including some type of planning in advance. When Lionel Rogosin initially attempted to shoot *On the Bowery* off the cuff, it quickly resulted in his wasting a lot of footage, forcing him to create a brief story outline.

Australian filmmaker and theorist Kathryn Millard points out, "As a creative methodology, improvisation is process-orientated and privileges collaboration. Far from requiring no preparation, improvisation most often occurs within a loosely prepared structure."[28] As a result, most filmmakers who use improvisation tend to rely on some form of a treatment or outline. John Cassavetes, the filmmaker most often associated with improvisation, was actually dismissive of the totally spontaneous, which he referred to as "ad-libbing." For him, an ad-libbed or impromptu response never had the depth of characterization that he sought to achieve through written scripts and extensive rehearsal with his actors.

Moreno, on the other hand, places the highest value on spontaneity. Viola Spolin, who became one of the most influential teachers of improvisational acting, was strongly influenced by Moreno. In her book, *Improvisation for the Theater*, she contends:

> Through spontaneity we are re-formed into ourselves. It creates an explosion that for the moment frees us from handed-down frames of reference, memory choked with old facts and information and undigested theories and techniques of other people's findings. Spontaneity is the moment of personal freedom when we are faced with a reality and see it, explore it and act accordingly. In this reality the bits and pieces of ourselves function as an organic whole. It is the time of discovery, of experiencing, of creative expression.[29]

For Spolin, acting involves creating an environment for a performer to be able to access "intuitive knowledge" and achieve spontaneity.

THE SPONTANEOUS, THE PLANNED, AND THE REHEARSED

Rewriting Indie Cinema looks at both improvisation and psychodrama within the framework of the history of American independent cinema. Using the categories set out by Moreno—the spontaneous, the planned, and the rehearsed—I examine how improvisation and psychodrama have shaped the history of American independent cinema from the mid-1950s to the present. Whether filmmakers use a screenplay or an alternative form, such as an outline or treatment, will have bearing on both improvisation and psychodrama. Obviously, the less that is scripted in advance— the more a filmmaker moves away from a traditional screenplay—the more opportunity there is to use improvisation in the process of making the film. But the issue turns out be a great deal more complex, as Cassavetes's use of improvisation will demonstrate. Kathryn Millard argues:

> All writing involves elements of both improvisation and composition, and where any individual project belongs on this axis is simply a matter of degree. Films involving a high degree of improvisation with performers, for example, feature fully written scripts as often as brief scenarios.

The critical difference between an industrial screenplay model and one which values improvisation is not simply whether a script pre-dates production. Rather, it is the degree to which the screenplay remains open to new material throughout production.[30]

Millard's caution suggests that whatever the scripting process, it becomes even more important whether the production process itself remains open or closed. Most filmmakers who use improvisation, including Cassavetes, favor a process that remains open to whatever is occurring in the moment.

Whether there is a rehearsal process or workshop sessions involving the actors proves to be another critical factor in the equation. Although he started with a lengthy screenplay, Cassavetes used the rehearsal process to develop his characters, providing the strongest example of the "rehearsed" category. On the other end of the spectrum is a filmmaker like Joe Swanberg who works from an outline—often a single page—and partially discovers the film during the process of making it by collaborating with performers playing versions of themselves. This strategy is often employed effectively when filmmakers are working with nonprofessionals or "first-time actors," which is the term that Sean Baker prefers to use.

Of necessity, virtually all films, including those of Warhol when he stopped relying on scenarios, involve some form of preplanning, which again comes down to a matter of degree. In terms of being rehearsed, planned, or spontaneous, improvised films run the gamut. They display variation within and between the categories, and sometimes all three are employed within a single film, such as in Cassavetes's *Husbands* or Sean Baker's *Tangerine* (2015).

Why did a trend toward unscripted performance emerge in American independent cinema in the 1950s and 1960s? In dispensing with or moving away from reliance on a traditional screenplay, a confluence of factors drew American independent filmmakers toward improvisation. These included financial, technological, aesthetic, cultural, and political considerations. Hollywood at the time was largely a closed system in which producers exhibited financial and bureaucratic control over production. This was often done through means of the screenplay, which tended to govern most facets of the overall production.

Using a script as the basis for a production meant a filmmaker who was operating independently from the studio system needed performers who could make the written lines seem believable. Professional actors were too expensive to hire, and the type of acting found in Hollywood films was more stylized and dominated by stars and seasoned character actors. With the exception of Cassavetes, the early indie filmmakers were neither screenwriters nor actors. As a result, it makes practical sense that independent filmmakers would seek other options. Morris Engel, Ruth Orkin, and Ray Ashley used an ordinary child to explore Coney Island; Lionel Rogosin made the inhabitants of Manhattan's Bowery his subjects; Robert Frank and Alfred Leslie used other artists, such as poets, painters, and musicians; Kent Mackenzie turned to American Indians living in a Los Angeles neighborhood; Ron Rice cast the poet Taylor Mead; and even Cassavetes, a somewhat well-known professional actor, relied on his acting students or nonprofessionals rather than industry peers in making his debut film, *Shadows*.

Shifts in technology, too, contributed to the use of unscripted performance. The sudden availability of lightweight, portable 16 mm cameras and Nagra sound recorders allowed individuals outside the industry to make films more cheaply. It also gave them greater flexibility to shoot with small crews, which, in turn, gave them greater liberty to experiment and approach productions more spontaneously. Forsaking a reliance on the script and turning toward such methods as improvisation became an aesthetic decision born out of necessity. On a fundamental level, filmmakers were also reacting against what they perceived as the regimentation implied by a traditional script.

The shift from an emphasis on the written page to the performer had other implications. The movement away from preplanning toward improvisation placed greater emphasis on the human body. What was occurring in film was not an isolated gesture but an expression of a larger movement that was occurring within all the arts in America. In poetry, for instance, Allen Ginsberg used his own breath to determine the rhythmic lines of his poems. In painting, Jackson Pollock used his body to express his feelings on the canvas. As Daniel Belgrad insists, "Indeed, an accurate understanding of American intellectual and cultural life in the postwar decades depends on recognizing the existence of a coherent aesthetic of spontaneity and its social significance."[31]

The emphasis on spontaneity and improvisation formed a subversive discourse against the prevailing corporate liberalism of the postwar period. Its force could be felt in avant-garde art of the period as well as in subcultural movements such as the Beats and the counterculture. According to Belgrad:

> Spontaneity's challenge to the existing social order was founded on a belief in the value of the unconscious mind as the locus of possibilities denied legitimacy within the prevailing ideology. Writers, artists, and musicians hoped that the spontaneous work of art might serve as a communication from the "open" realm of the unconscious to the ideologically restricted world of consciousness.[32]

For indie filmmakers at the time, an interest in shifting the emphasis from the written script to the performer, from the preconceived to the improvised, shared a similar impetus.

THE RETURN OF THE SCREENPLAY
IN INDIE FILMMAKING

This book traces the use of improvisation and psychodrama back to the emergence of the New American Cinema and follows its trajectory up to the present, where improvisation has become far more commonplace due to the advent of digital technology. This has allowed filmmakers to make films much more cheaply—even with an adapted iPhone 5s, which Sean Baker used to shoot *Tangerine*. My decision to follow an historical approach stems from a desire to demonstrate how performance has been central to how independent filmmakers have developed alternative methods of scripting in opposition to industrial Hollywood practice. I am interested in providing a sense of the continuity of these ideas and practices by tracking how the use of both improvisation and psychodrama has unfolded over time.

In many ways, I will argue, improvisation and various versions of psychodrama defined independent cinema as an alternative practice in the late 1950s and the decade of the 1960s. Narrative features that employed these techniques, however, eventually lost momentum. By the time Barbara Loden made the semi-improvised *Wanda* in 1970, her film never received the recognition it deserved. Following the demise of the Film-makers Distribution Center in 1968, Jonas Mekas, the main champion of spontaneity and improvisation, had given up on narrative filmmaking entirely and redirected his energies toward creating Anthology Film Archives in 1970. This institution became dedicated to preserving what Mekas considered to be a canon of past cinematic achievements.

Without its major figurehead, indie cinema splintered into various factions, but narrative feature filmmaking seemed to suffer the most. There were notable exceptions in the 1970s, namely, the theory-based work of avant-garde dancer Yvonne Rainer, the politically engaged films of Jon Jost, the eccentric features by Mark Rappaport, the exploitation films of Paul Morrissey and John Waters, and the subversive horror of David Lynch's *Eraserhead* (1977). Charles Burnett made *Killer of Sheep* in 1977, which extended the earlier realist tradition of the New American Cinema, but it languished in obscurity for several years before it was finally rediscovered and screened at a number of major film festivals.

This state of affairs stemmed largely from the fact that there was not the proper infrastructure to sustain independent narrative filmmaking. An indigenous indie cinema was not economically viable without the necessary institutional changes and developments that occurred in the mid and late 1970s. These include: the creation of the Association of Independent Video and Filmmakers (AIVF) in 1975; the establishment of first Utah/ U.S. Film Festival (1978), which later became the Sundance Film Festival; and an American indie sidebar at the 1979 New York Film Festival, cosponsored by the Independent Feature Project (IFP). Within a short time, there were two other important developments: the PBS American Playhouse series, which would provide funding and showcase independent feature work, as well as Robert Redford's Sundance Institute, a laboratory workshop experience specifically targeted to independents with more commercial ambitions.

The creation of such institutions nourished independent filmmaking, but it also sparked a return to the more traditional screenplay that contrasts sharply with the innovations of New American Cinema improvisation. The Sundance Institute opened its doors in the summer of 1981, with the goal to provide a remedy for the two perceived weaknesses of most independent narrative projects: direction of actors and the screenplay.[33] The Institute was intended as a place for independent filmmakers to develop such skills under the tutelage of industry professionals. The early scripts selected tended to be highly personal, regional, and multicultural stories, such as Gregory Nava and Anna Thomas's *El Norte* (1983), the only project from the first Sundance Institute workshop to achieve a successful commercial release.

Both *El Norte* and Robert M. Young's *The Ballad of Gregorio Cortez* (1982) received financing from American Playhouse, which began in 1980, with Lindsay Law as its executive producer.[34] The purpose of the series was to provide a forum for the kinds of voices ordinarily neglected by both mainstream television and film. Besides giving independent features much-needed funding and exposure on public television, American Playhouse developed the innovative strategy of granting its feature film projects the option of a theatrical window before they aired on television. With other public funding sources extremely limited, American Playhouse played an important role in helping to bankroll independent productions while allowing the director to maintain creative control over the project. American Playhouse had a budget of $20 million for the 1985–1986 season, which made it the single largest funding source for independent filmmakers.[35] In its fifteen-year existence, American Playhouse helped finance and produce a number of critically acclaimed independent films.

Despite being backed by neither American Playhouse nor the Sundance Lab, Jim Jarmusch's low-budget *Stranger Than Paradise* (1984) played at the Cannes Film Festival and grossed over $2.4 million, managing to usher in a new era in indie cinema. Jarmusch used a treatment rather than a traditional script, but this turned out to be an anomaly. Most other indie success stories at the time, such as the films of John Sayles, Spike Lee, David Lynch, and Joyce Chopra, were scripted. The influence of Sundance Film Institute and American Playhouse ultimately inaugurated a period where filmmakers who happened to be strong screenwriters— Hal Hartley, Steven Soderbergh, Gus Van Sant, Quentin Tarantino, Todd Haynes, and Todd Solandz—began to dominate the independent scene. As an indication of this, the screenplays of these filmmakers were published as part of the marketing of their films.

Box office success stories, like Soderbergh's *sex, lies and videotape* (1989) and Tarantino's *Pulp Fiction* (1994), raised questions as to whether independent film represented a viable alternative to the mainstream industry. This phenomenon made the screenplay even more important to obtain financing, especially for filmmakers trying to attract name performers. Jon Jost declared indie cinema dead in 1989, largely due to the demise of 16 mm film and the fact that he believed a number of independent filmmakers were already selling out.[36] In 1995, Ted Hope, one of the partners of the independent film company Good Machine also believed indie cinema had become coopted by the mainstream.[37] Indie cinema, however, proved resilient. Two major trends emerged in the new century. Gus Van Sant, who had made successful Hollywood films based on screenplays, became disillusioned working within the confines of the industry. He decided to abandon the traditional script in favor of formal narrative experimentation in a series of films, beginning with *Gerry*. The pendulum toward unscripted performance swung back even more decisively with the development of mumblecore.

THE REDISCOVERY OF UNSCRIPTED PERFORMANCE

Mumblecore began under the radar with Andrew Bujalski's *Funny Ha Ha* in 2002, but it took a couple of years for the significance of the film to register. The movement gained traction at the 2005 SXSW Film Festival when a group of young filmmakers, of which Bujalski and Joe Swanberg turned out to be its major figures, began to make films that drew on the subcultural roots of Richard Linklater's *Slacker* (1991) and the early improvised work of Cassavetes, causing the group of diverse filmmakers to be referred to, among other monikers, as "Slackavetes." Bujalski shot *Funny Ha Ha* and his subsequent film *Mutual Appreciation* (2005) on 16 mm, but the rise of digital technology and computerized editing systems began to have a profound effect by allowing young filmmakers to make films both quickly and cheaply, and with more freedom to experiment. As a result, a number of feature filmmakers, epitomized by those associated with mumblecore, began to eschew traditional scripts in favor of improvisation and structured improvisation, and some discovered psychodrama.

Prior to the advent of mumblecore, there were occasional improvised films in the intervening years. Cassavetes continued to produce work in the 1970s and into the 1980s, but his trajectory became considerably more commercial. Allison Anders made the improvised *Border Radio* (1987), set in the punk scene in Los Angeles, and Rob Nilsson made *Heat and Sunlight* (1987) without the benefit of a script. Even though Nilsson's film was awarded the Grand Jury Prize at the 1988 Sundance Film Festival, the film had little impact in an environment that privileged the importance of a screenplay. The only film that exerted any sort of influence was Richard Linklater's *Slacker* (1991), which used structured improvisation to mine a subcultural phenomenon—young people hanging out in the Austin, Texas area.

With the exception of two films by Abel Ferrara, *Bad Lieutenant* (1992) and *Dangerous Game* (1993), which featured Harvey Keitel, psychodrama virtually disappeared in the period after Mailer made *Maidstone* in 1970. The advent of low-cost digital technology, however, brought both improvisation and psychodrama to the forefront once again in the new century. These techniques have become quite commonplace among contemporary indie filmmakers today, especially those working with micro-budgets. Yet, as this book makes clear, there is a long and rich tradition to this type of experimentation, even if the practitioners themselves are not always fully aware of their heritage.

REVOLT AND RESURGENCE

The initial section of the book focuses on the rise of an alternative film practice, where indie filmmakers reacted against the hegemony of Hollywood. The first chapter establishes the beginning of the New American Cinema. Jonas Mekas, the editor of *Film Culture* and a critic for the *Village Voice*, became the leading promoter for spontaneity and improvisation, and what he termed "plotless cinema." I look at early examples of improvisation by such filmmakers as Morris Engel, Lionel Rogosin, Alfred Leslie and Robert Frank, Ron Rice, and John Cassavetes. Cassavetes's *Shadows* became a landmark in the early use of improvisation, even though he released a second version of the film in which certain scenes were scripted.

These early pioneers experimented with a variety of improvisation techniques in order to give their films a greater sense of realism. I recognize that such terms as "real," "reality," and "realism" are relative and mutable concepts, which are contingent on a number of different factors, including history, culture, and technology. Their cinematic representations have been routinely critiqued as the constructs they are. When applied to performance, the same holds true. As Colin Counsell notes, "Realistic acting is the mode *deemed* realistic by its viewing culture, the style whose distinct repertoire of conventional signs—whose particular kind of artificiality— is agreed to signify the 'real.'"[38]

The second chapter explores the work of John Cassavetes, which has proven to be enormously influential on subsequent American indie filmmakers using improvisation, even if the methods he developed were idiosyncratic. His approach was developed over a nearly thirty-year career in which he directed twelve features, most notably *Shadows, Faces, Husbands, Minnie and Moskowitz* (1971), *A Woman Under the Influence* (1974), *Opening Night* (1977), and *Love Streams* (1984). Cassavetes was always refining his techniques, but they were firmly rooted in a written script and developed in the rehearsal process.

The third chapter looks at early attempts by filmmakers outside the discourse of the New American Cinema to mine cinematic realism within specific locales. Kent Mackenzie, Barbara Loden, and Charles Burnett made films about marginalized people that dealt with issues of race and class. Mackenzie did not have a screenplay but used an outline in making *The Exiles* (1961), a fictional film that documented a day in the life of displaced American Indians living in the Bunker Hill section of Los Angeles. In making *Wanda* (1970), which was set in the coal mining region of northeastern Pennsylvania, Loden started with a script. Working with a small crew, she was forced to rely on improvisatory techniques due to casting nonprofessional performers and having to obtain locations for shooting on short notice. In *Killer of Sheep*, Burnett turned his camera on his own South Central neighborhood in Los Angeles in an attempt to document it within a fiction film using a very short script.

In a cinematic context, intense improvisation can often skip over the divide between the fictional and the real. Chapter 4 explores early experiments that use versions of psychodrama, such as Jonas Mekas's filmed version of The Living Theatre's production of *The Brig* (1964). Andy Warhol's films provide the first extensive employment of the technique in indie cinema by creating pressure situations that he devised for his superstars beforehand. Influenced by Warhol's *Screen Tests*, Shirley Clarke's *Portrait of Jason* (1967) begins as a documentary-like interview with a gay black man named Jason Holliday (i.e., Aaron Payne) who spins fantastical yarns about his life as a hustler, houseboy, and frustrated performer. Clarke and Carl Lee, the other interviewer, eventually attempt to break through Holliday's multilayered persona, causing the film to transform into psychodrama, while also raising questions about the veracity of everything the viewer has witnessed.

Norman Mailer used a version of psychodrama in the first three films he made. By playing one of the main characters in each film, Mailer uses the technique, which Mouëllic refers to as "directing from the inside" in an attempt to provoke something to happen.[39] A threat of violence hangs over *Beyond the Law*, *Wild 90*, and *Maidstone*, which unintentionally wound up providing one of the most powerful and compelling examples of psychodrama in the history of cinema. The scene, which transpires over eight excruciating minutes, packs a wallop because it is not a simulation but an actual unscripted event that has been captured by the camera and was ultimately included by Mailer as part of the film.

As chapter 5 makes clear, any form of acting based on intense personal experience has the potential to be pushed into the realm of psychodrama. Two films by African American director William Greaves, *Symbiopsychotaxiplasm: Take One* (1968–1971) and *Take 2½* (2005), are central to any understanding of psychodrama. Greaves attended and participated in Moreno's psychodrama sessions and listed the renowned psychiatrist as one of the main influences on *Take One*. Greaves's two *Symbio* films are the only narrative feature films that employed a licensed psychodramatist, Marcia Karp, to work with his actors.

As the sixth chapter indicates, psychodrama reemerged briefly in the early 1990s. Abel Ferrara used a version of it in *Bad Lieutenant*, in which Harvey Keitel, in the midst of a bitter divorce, took Method acting to extreme limits in portraying a drug-addicted cop on a downward spiral. In *Dangerous Game*, Keitel plays a director who is a shooting a film about a marriage on the rocks that is so deeply personal it confuses the boundaries between the staged and the real for those involved in the production, including Madonna. The pop star, whose company financed the film, also becomes the unwitting victim of a film-within-a-film that Ferrara managed to turn into a psychodramatic situation.

The chapter on the Ferrara–Keitel films provides a bridge to the section on contemporary indie cinema in the new century. Chapter 7 examines a number of films by Gus Van Sant that use a minimal script or outline rather than a traditional screenplay. After making a number of highly successful Hollywood films, Van Sant became disillusioned with industrial practice, which he believed had become overly restrictive in terms of his own style of filmmaking. As a result, he experimented with alternative forms of scripting—some quite radical—in *Gerry*, *Elephant*, *Last Days*, and *Paranoid Park*, which the director adapted from a teen novel into a short script through an unconventional method.

Joe Swanberg is considered one of the leading figures of the influential movement known as mumblecore. As chapter 8 demonstrates, his large output best exemplifies the use of the spontaneous form of improvisation on a sustained level, even though one can find numerous exceptions— examples of planning and staging—in his films. Unlike Cassavetes, Swanberg does not use a traditional written screenplay. Instead, his early films depended on his nonprofessional cast to provide their own dialogue. This worked largely because Swanberg cast performers to play versions of themselves.

Mumblecore films are not the only recent indie films that use improvisation. The ninth chapter looks at the work of Matthew Porterfield, Sam Fleischner, and Sean Baker who employ various degrees of improvisation within their films, as well as a concern for place as an essential scripting element. For example, Fleischner's *Stand Clear of the Closing Doors* (2013), set in Rockaway Beach, Queens, was constrained by Hurricane Sandy, forcing the filmmaker to rely on improvisation even more than he expected. To complicate matters further, much of the film takes place on the New York subway, which made directorial "control" virtually impossible. Baker used improvisatory techniques in *Take Out* (2004), *Prince of Broadway* (2008), and *Tangerine*. In some ways, the trajectory of his films shows a movement from the spontaneous toward the rehearsed. His use of what he terms a "scriptment"—a cross between a script and treatment—embodies a unique form of alternative scripting.[40]

Chapter 10 examines the rediscovery of psychodrama in films by other contemporary filmmakers: Ronald Bronstein, Josh and Benny Safdie, and Nathan Silver. For instance, Bronstein collaborated with Josh and Benny Safdie in making *Heaven Knows What* (2014). The film was based on the life story of Arielle Holmes, a nineteen-year-old heroin addict, whom Josh Safdie cast from the streets of Manhattan. The filmmakers actually used psychodrama as an inducement for her to reenact her own life story on film. Nathan Silver, who rejects the use of traditional scripts, experimented with his own brand of psychodrama in five features to date, most notably in *Stinking Heaven* (2015), where the technique of performers recreating past traumatic experiences for the camera was borrowed directly from Moreno's work.

How does scriptless filmmaking overlap or differ from documentary? The films discussed in chapter 11 attempt to blur the boundary between fiction and documentary. Robert Greene's *Actress* (2014) provides an unusual example. In making an observational documentary about his neighbor, Brandy Burre, a former actor who appeared in the television series, *The Wire* (2002–2008), Greene deftly questions the underpinnings of the documentary form when the actor is asked to portray her life on camera. Is the film a documentary, or has the actor singlehandedly commandeered it into fiction?

Although Shirley Clarke's *Portrait of Jason* and Robert Greene's *Actress* might be considered borderline exceptions, this study mainly looks at fiction films that, through extreme improvisation involving personal material, cross the line into nonfiction. James Solomon's *The Witness* (2015), which deals with impact of Kitty Genovese's murder upon her younger brother, Bill, provides an example of a film that initially started as a scripted film but turned into a documentary. Yet its climax is a restaged dramatic scene that transforms into a psychodrama that becomes frighteningly vivid.

SEEING AND HEARING THE DIFFERENCE

Industrial Hollywood films today continue to be dominated by traditional screenplays and more stylized celebrity acting. Yet, as the following chapters make clear, those filmmakers drawn to creating more personal, independent films often turned to alternative scripting methods that utilize improvisation and psychodrama. The use of improvisation and psychodrama, however, is no guarantee that a film will be more successful than a scripted one. As Kathryn Millard reminds us, "Improvisation can lead to innovative and compelling storytelling. Or not. More traditional compositional techniques can lead to innovative and compelling storytelling. Or not."[41]

Almost by their very nature, improvised films imply an element of risk. And psychodramas can easily fail or lack strong dramatic impact if the protagonist fails to connect with feelings associated with some traumatic event. Most independent filmmakers, however, have turned to improvisation and psychodrama as a way of differentiating their films from mainstream cinema and more conventional Indiewood films. There can be a number of advantages to employing improvisation and psychodrama. Improvisation, especially when utilized in the rehearsal process, can lead to deeper characterization. Or, when ad-libbed, the process can result in something fresh and unexpected. In terms of performance, there is often a noticeable difference between scripted and unscripted lines, especially when first-time actors are involved. As film critic Dave Kehr writes about the performances of the two lead actors, Ray Salyer and Gorman Hendricks, on the occasion of the rerelease of Lionel Rogosin's *On the Bowery*, "The film slips between scripted and unscripted scenes, and it is never hard to tell the difference; Salyer and Hendricks are not professional actors, and they make written lines sound like written lines."[42]

In commenting about the difference between improvised and scripted lines in a film, Sam Fleischner acknowledges, "Yeah, you can hear it." Speaking about improvised performance, he adds, "I think that there is a certain energy that is hard to put your finger on, but it does pull you in."[43] Spontaneous behavior has a sense of immediacy that is compelling. And when it is intimately mixed with deeply personal issues, as in psychodrama, the result can be even more heightened. The goal of both, I would argue, is to come closer to capturing the richness of human behavior in everyday life. The various ways in which independent filmmakers have attempted to achieve this goal is the subject of this study.

1

AND I HATE ACTORS

The New American Cinema

I n conformist postwar America, the newfound emphasis on spontaneity and improvisation represented a radical challenge to tradition.
Nowhere was this more evident than in the arts. In painting, the
free-form gestural application of paint to canvas, as embodied by the
paintings of Jackson Pollock, became the cornerstone of abstract expres-
sionism. Assemblage, which combines disparate materials, became a
new way of making sculpture. In music, Charlie Parker revolutionized
jazz with bebop. The Beat writers, most notably Jack Kerouac and Allen
Ginsberg, altered contemporary literature through their spontaneous
prose and poetry. The Living Theatre incorporated audience participation into their plays, while impromptu theatrical events known as happenings also took the spotlight. The Judson Dance Theater performed
collaborative pieces with artists from other disciplines that pushed the
boundaries of the medium. Robert Frank's snapshot aesthetic in his
photo essay *The Americans* challenged accepted notions of pictorialism
in photography, while a number of independent filmmakers, most notably John Cassavetes, employed improvisation to create an alternative to
classical Hollywood cinema.

Daniel Belgrad has argued that spontaneity represented a distinct and
alternative cultural movement in postwar America, positioning it as a

third strand "opposed to both the mass culture and the established high culture of the postwar period."[1] According to Belgrad:

> Most broadly, spontaneity implied an alternative to the vaunted rational progress of Western civilization, which had succeeded in developing technologies and principles of organization that threatened human life and freedom on an unprecedented scale. In the specific historical context of wartime and postwar America, spontaneity did battle against the culture of corporate liberalism, which was the most recent and local manifestation of these principles.[2]

Within the various arts, spontaneity provided a weapon for artists to challenge the hegemony of corporate liberalism and manifested itself as an assault on established tradition.

Jonas Mekas became the chief proselytizer for spontaneity in cinema. He cited films by Morris Engel, Lionel Rogosin, Alfred Leslie and Robert Frank, and Cassavetes as signs that a revolution was underfoot. In the films of what he termed the "New American Cinema," Mekas describes the defining aesthetic characteristics of this new cinema: "Though made by directors of different ages and temperaments, all these films reveal an open ear and an open eye for timely, contemporary reality. They are similar in other respects: in their use of actual locations and direct lighting; their disrespect for plots and written scripts; their use of improvisation."[3] Mekas attacked Hollywood, the most entrenched film industry in the world, as the enemy of a more radical and alternative filmmaking practice. For Mekas, the notion of spontaneity represented not simply an aesthetic process but a moral imperative: "Spontaneity as liberation, as bliss, as a means of freeing one's self from the moral, social clichés, out-dated mores, the business way of life."[4] Mekas ultimately viewed the filmmakers associated with the New American Cinema as artists who approached reality in a modern way.

Mekas reacted against the professionalism and technical polish of what he perceived to be a lifeless Hollywood cinema. He strongly believed that the professionalism of the industry succeeded in inhibiting creative freedom on every level of the production. Spontaneity would have a liberating effect on filmmakers by freeing them to create a radically new type of cinema. As he explains:

The New American film maker seeks to free himself from the over-professionalism and over-technicality that usually handicaps the inspiration and spontaneity of contemporary cinema, guiding himself more by intuition and improvisation than by discipline; he aims desperately, as his colleague action painter, or poet and dancer, at art in its very flight, at a free, a spontaneous inspiration: art as an action and not as a status quo; art as various states of feeling and not as a series of facts, nature-morts [*sic*], or pastiches.[5]

The use of improvisation became the chief means for filmmakers to create a more spontaneous cinema.

Mekas explicitly blamed screenwriters for keeping cinema so conventional.[6] Not only did he detest the formulaic nature of traditional screenplays, but Mekas held professional actors in contempt as well. In a diary entry dated July 14, 1960, he writes, "Every day a dozen envelopes with photographs, credits on the other side, etc., come in, from actors, sending their pictures. So they think we are making a movie about actors? They can't play anything but actors. They look like actors, they speak like actors, they behave like actors, and they are actors. And I hate actors!"[7] He did not actually hate actors but rather a certain type of actor and controlled style of acting that he considered to be outmoded in which "the director takes an actor, like any other raw piece of material, and begins to build from it a contraption of his own."[8]

Mekas's comments highlight the integral connection that exists between preconceived screenplays and performance. Written dialogue on a page has an impact on the performance of actors because it does not usually allow them to deviate from the lines that appear in the script or to utilize techniques such as improvisation. Mekas was wholeheartedly against "preconceived, worked-out ideas," such as you would find in a written screenplay. In a column in the *Village Voice* on March 2, 1961, he clarifies his own conception of performance: "The young actor of today doesn't trust the will of a director any longer. He doesn't think that the part he is playing is only a part, and he only an actor. He merges with his part entirely, it becomes a moral problem for him, and a problem of existence."[9] For Mekas, the actor in cinema is not directed or controlled but rather is her or his own agent who responds intuitively and spontaneously to what is unfolding in the present moment of the situation.

Improvisation is often connected to naturalism or cinematic realism, as is evident in the arguments that Mekas makes in favor of a new cinema. In his influential article "Notes on the New American Cinema," he charted a revisionist history by citing James Agee, who embraced "works of fiction, played against and into, and in collaboration with unrehearsed and uninvented reality."[10] Mekas traced the realist impulse back to such films as Helen Levitt, Janice Loeb, and James Agee's *In the Street* (1948, 1952); Sidney Meyers's *The Quiet One* (1948); Engel's films, including *Little Fugitive*; and Rogosin's *On the Bowery* and *Come Back, Africa*. He writes: "Formally, one of Rogosin's contributions to the new cinema was an effective dramatization of reality, the use of real life scenes in an organized, planned drama."[11] In discussing *Shadows*, Mekas cites Siegfried Kracauer's notion of "'camera reality'—a film free from literary and theatrical ideas." According to Mekas, the film's formal strength derives from "the people in it, their faces, their movements, their tone of voice, their stammerings, their pauses—their psychological reality as revealed through the most insignificant daily incidents and situations."[12]

MORRIS ENGEL, RUTH ORKIN, AND RAY ASHLEY: *LITTLE FUGITIVE*

The New American Cinema did not blossom all at once but developed in gradual stages. One of the first films to break with the conventions of Hollywood was Morris Engel's *Little Fugitive* (1953), made in collaboration with fellow photographer Ruth Orkin and Ray Ashley (Raymond Abrashkin), who is credited with writing the screenplay. The groundbreaking film, which is built around a specific location rather than story or character, explores the legendary Brooklyn amusement park Coney Island.

Little Fugitive utilizes a simple story frame. Twelve-year-old Lennie Norton (Richard Brewster) resents having to take care of his seven-year-old brother, Joey (Richie Andrusco). When their single mother has to leave to attend to their sick grandmother, the two boys are left to fend for themselves for a couple of days. Lennie and two friends trick Joey into believing he has shot and killed his older brother. Unaware of the ruse, Joey takes the money his mother has left for them and flees to Coney

FIGURE 1.1 Joey explores the boardwalk at Coney Island, *Little Fugitive*

Island roughly nineteen minutes into the film. The narrative, which employs a conventional ticking clock of the mother's eventual return, serves as little more than a pretext to explore the visually exciting world of the enticing amusement park—the rides, arcade games, junk food, and crowded beach—all seen through the eyes of an impressionable young child with an obsession with horses.

Although the acting and story do not quite achieve the naturalism for which Engel was striving, he employs a number of innovative strategies. In using nonprofessional actors in the main roles, the filmmakers even went so far as to consult with child psychologists at the Bank Street School of Education in New York City in order to try to obtain more naturalistic performances from the child actors.[13] They also kept dialogue to a minimum, which no doubt stemmed from the fact that the screenplay from which Engel was shooting consisted of only two pages. As Alain Bergala observes, "The two-page script gave a free hand to Engel, who shot it as a semi-documentary between fiction and reality, part staged, part improvised."[14]

In his review of the film, André Bazin argues that *Little Fugitive* is assisted "by the spontaneity of life," and suggests that it would have been impossible to plan out such a film entirely in advance, even using a short outline. Bazin writes:

> In short, it is the awareness we have of this margin of indetermination that gives the film its charm. Cesare Zavattini has often spoken of the (unrealizable?) film in which the director wouldn't know the ending, a film as free as life itself. In this sense, *The Little Fugitive* [*sic*] is a case study in neorealism, not so much for its socially documentary aspect, which has never really been essential to neorealism, nor for its on-location setting, but for the way in which it approaches that scriptless film ideal wherein the drama arises exclusively from the evolution of the present.[15]

Part of this quality that Bazin so admired had to do with the way the film was shot, which depended on Engel being able to utilize a specially designed camera.

Engel had a friend, Charles Woodruff, make a 35-mm portable movie camera to allow him to shoot Joey unobtrusively as he explored Coney Island, thereby embedding his wide-eyed protagonist in a documentary-like setting where people appear to be unaware of the camera.[16] The sound in the film was postdubbed. Besides the improvised quality that came from not using a traditional script, a big part of the fascination of *Little Fugitive* derives from its lyrical black and white cinematography: the light and shadow patterns under the boardwalk, the oblivious crowds of sunbathers on the beach, the landmark Parachute Jump in operation, a montage of the heads of carousel horses, and an unexpected rain storm that leaves huge puddles of water in the nearby streets.

LIONEL ROGOSIN: *ON THE BOWERY* AND *COME BACK, AFRICA*

Lionel Rogosin's *On the Bowery* (1956), which was made three years after *Little Fugitive*, shares a number of similarities with that film. Unlike Engel and Orkin, however, Rogosin was not an experienced still photographer but rather a disenchanted businessman who decided that he wanted to make socially concerned movies. *On the Bowery* was conceived to be a test run or learning experience for a more ambitious project that he envisioned about apartheid, *Come Back, Africa.*

Rogosin had become fascinated with the Bowery, a former theater and entertainment district in New York City. The construction of the elevated subway known as the Third Avenue El in 1878 had a significant negative impact on the neighborhood, which in the 1890s became a major vice district. According to historian Eric Ferrara, the area continued to decline:

> The Golden Age of the Bowery was fading. By the 1920s and ʼ30s, nearly all of the union halls, theaters and museums were long gone, replaced by manufacturers, warehouses and lodging houses. Population relocation, an economic depression and a concerted local and federal effort to eradicate vice and corruption took their toll on the old entertainment district. All that remained were a few small businesses, greasy spoon diners, shelters and flophouses.[17]

It was during the Depression that the Bowery became associated with Skid Row. After the Second World War, various immigrant groups fled the neighborhood, which was largely taken over by the remaining homeless drunks.

Following the invention of photography in 1839, the Bowery district became the center for many of the city's Daguerrean studios, which succeeded in democratizing photographic portraiture for the average American. In a sense, Rogosin was interested in creating a group "portrait" of the inhabitants of the Bowery, whose haunting faces tell the compelling story of the true ravages of alcoholism. On the advice of Rosalind Kossoff, a distributor of specialized films who served as a kind of mentor to the novice filmmaker, Rogosin approached the film like an ethnographer by immersing himself in the social milieu. For six months, he fastidiously observed what occurred there.[18] Rogosin managed to get to know the men on the Bowery personally, and a number of them became his friends. In order to further understand his subject, he also did extensive research on alcoholism at Yale University and with physicians at Bellevue Hospital.[19]

Rogosin believed that nonprofessional or amateur actors provided a distinct advantage over professional performers when it came to the spontaneity and realism he sought to record on camera. He was critical of traditional screenwriting, "in which the ideas and abstractions are essentially the writer's with professional actors portraying those ideas and abstractions through their personality."[20] In contrast, by casting nonprofessional actors who actually lived on the Bowery, Rogosin was attempting to bridge the divide between actor and role: his performers were essentially portraying themselves rather than someone else's personality on screen. He explains:

> During rehearsals the aim was to induce the actors to add their own experience, poetry and understanding to my bare outline, thus giving flesh and substance to the structure of my brief, intense period of observation of their lives and problems. In this manner, the actor becomes more than a performer by virtue of his contribution of words and expression. This method of dialogue not only adds a quality of realism but also makes use of the intuition and experience which the natural performer possesses.[21]

Writer Mark Sufrin suggested that Rogosin hire Richard Bagley, who had shot Sidney Meyer's *The Quiet One*, to be the film's cinematographer. Bagley, who spent time in Italy where he was strongly influenced by neorealist films of Vittorio De Sica and Roberto Rossellini, initially advised Rogosin that in order to make the film, "You just go and shoot." After a short time of filming, however, he soon realized that they were wasting footage and suggested to Rogosin that he actually needed a script.[22] The director collaborated with Sufrin and Bagley in developing a simple written outline.

Yet, as Rogosin explains, the approach he eventually developed was one that was rooted in visual storytelling:

> This is film—film-making which is visualized, which expresses the place and its people and which in essence is not written. You go with your eyes and see your script on the streets, in the buildings, and you select the images which you describe on paper. You listen to the sounds, the conversations, selecting and outlining them on paper. Then you let these same people give all of this back to the film by their own means of expression.[23]

The wizened faces of the individual drunks turn out to be their most expressive feature. This becomes evident in the scene at the Mission and in the subsequent nightmarish bar scene, which Rogosin considered the centerpiece of the film and compared to a drunken "mad orgy" and Dante's *Inferno*. Parts of the sequence, brilliantly edited by Carl Lerner, were secretly filmed with a hidden camera. Sufrin, who was part of the small crew, describes the process: "Sitting in the midst of the agitated ferment of drunks, we became part of the smell, the gargoyle faces, the wine sores, the sleeping and retching, the whole spasmic disturbance; always imagining that the bartender who glanced over frequently knew that the man with his head down on the bundle was actually a photographer peering through a finder."[24]

On the Bowery takes place over a three-day period. The film tells the story of a handsome trainman named Ray (Ray Salyer) who arrives on the Bowery with only a suitcase. He is befriended by a local, Gorman (Gorman Hendricks), who shows him the ropes. The film's narrative thread becomes scaffolding or a device to show the social milieu of life as it is lived by the men there: the flophouses, the sleeping quarters built

FIGURE 1.2 Ray meets Gorman in a Skid-Row bar, *On the Bowery*

with chicken wire, the regimented alternative of the Mission, the constant harassment by the police, the personal betrayals, as well as the opportunistic thievery. At the Mission's religious service, the Reverend Bolton, himself a product of this environment, refers to the "sadness and the madness" of the Bowery.

Rogosin depicts a dog-eat-dog world where all personal relationships become secondary to the endless quest for the next drink. It is not the story or dialogue that succeeds in holding our interest but the cinematic exploration of this sad and desperate milieu, in which mostly men and a few women drink themselves into oblivion. What truly engages viewers is the distressed look of the Bowery itself, whose history is contained in the buildings, the signage, the texture of the streets, and the dazed and weather-beaten faces we glimpse in the mise-en-scène of nearly every shot. Rogosin captures the endless boasting, passionate arguments about trivia, singing, sentimentality, delusions, and undercurrent of violence that lurks within every drunken encounter. The film utilizes keenly observed street cinematography as the main device to tell the story in more visual terms.

Haunted by memories of the Holocaust, Rogosin went to South Africa with the intention of exposing the social injustices of apartheid. In shooting *Come Back, Africa* (1959), the filmmaker employed many of the same working methods he developed in making *On the Bowery*, such as casting real people and shooting on location. Rogosin and his family spent a year there so that he could observe and understand his subject prior to making the film. He cast a nonprofessional actor, a Zulu tribesman, as his protagonist Zachariah. Emil ("Milek") Knebel, who served as one of the two camerapersons on the film, indicates that Rogosin cast his films in an unorthodox way: "For him the right facial expression of a person and his/her body language were the most important factors."[25]

Rogosin wrote a script in ten days, which was "little more than an outline for shooting."[26] He engaged two South Africans, Lewis Nkosi and William "Bloke" Modisane, to assist him on the script by having them provide the "story," which was conceived in a session that lasted six hours.[27] Rogosin wanted to avoid using written dialogue, so he developed his own alternative method in which the lines were created during rehearsal. As he explains: "I call it 'controlled, spontaneous dialogue' in which no lines are written but general themes for talk are laid down in each scene. On the set, I explain to the cast the situation they find themselves in, and leave the motivation to their own reactions. These, however, are molded in rehearsal until their words convey the themes and demands of the plot."[28] The director then employed two cameras to record the dialogue scenes simultaneously to avoid repeating takes. The African performers, however, proved less adept at improvising on set than the denizens of the Bowery. According to Rogosin, "This was due to the fact that English was not their native tongue, and also to psychological characteristics. The Africans were not as glib, nor as prone to make use of alcohol as an aid to acting."[29]

The opening credit sequence of *Come Back, Africa* indicates that it features the people of Johannesburg, South Africa. The film begins with a panning shot of steel girders and a montage that consists of tall, sterile urban buildings. There are shots of cars and busy sidewalks populated with well-dressed white men and women that are intercut with shots of a large group of black men with suitcases who walk purposefully down the sidewalk. A title then announces: "This is the story of Zachariah . . . one of the hundreds of thousands of Africans forced each year off the land by the regime and into the gold mines." There is a cut to Zachariah looking anxious, then to shots of the gold mine, men being led into it, and Zachariah entering a dormitory where several black men sit on bunk beds. We see images of the immigrant workers being trained how to use shovels, a primitive IQ test being administered, and then hundreds of black workers descending into the mine at night. Zachariah takes jobs as a houseboy, an attendant in a parking garage, and a waiter in a restaurant, but he gets fired from these positions by his white employers.

Rogosin carefully situates the scripted story within a documentary setting: the underground interior of the gold mine, the heavily polluted city of Johannesburg, and a rubble-strewn black township on the city outskirts called Sophiatown, the hub of black culture, which was razed soon after the film was made. Rogosin pretended to be making a film on ethnomusicology in order to obtain a shooting permit. He incorporates shots of the city and street scenes of life in the ghetto into the narrative, embedding the story photographically into the everyday reality of Johannesburg and Sophiatown. For example, in the scene in the parking garage where a white police officer interrogates Zachariah and his friend for going on an unauthorized joy ride in a wealthy white man's car, Rogosin intercuts three shots of the stream of black migrant workers walking through the streets as a temporal transition before returning to a scene where the two of them are let go amidst accusations of Zachariah's friend being a member of the African National Congress.

As Zachariah and his wife, Vinah, head to visit an aunt, the camera gets sidetracked by a street event involving elaborate drumming and dancing, a street band, a small parade, and a wedding that engages the entire neighborhood. Later, after Zachariah and his wife argue, we get more shots of the migrants and a long interlude involving young kids playing music with penny whistles, gumboot dancers, and buskers doing a rendition of Elvis Presley's "Teddy Bear." Following this, young robbers prey on Zachariah's son. Zachariah is also attacked on the way home by a black African named Marumu, who has been identified at the grocery as being a *tsotsi* (gangster).

When Zachariah shows up injured at the *shebeen* (speakeasy), one of the intellectuals tells the backstory of how Marumu came to resort to force, which he extends to racial politics. After a knock on the door, the political discussion is interrupted by a musical interlude as Miriam Makeba enters and sings two songs. As she sings the second one, she stands and dances

FIGURE 1.3 Miriam Makeba sings at a political gathering, *Come Back, Africa*

while the others sing background harmony and sway to the rhythms of her love song. Shortly afterward, Zachariah is arrested with disastrous consequences. As he pounds his fist on the table, Rogosin cuts to shots of African laborers with pickaxes, a busy train platform, workers descending into the bowels of the gold mine, and the myriad lights on the miner's helmets in pitch darkness—all to the sounds of drums.

Both Rogosin's *On the Bowery* and *Come Back, Africa* use tropes involving human bodies. In *On the Bowery*, alcoholism is portrayed as a movement from bodies standing to slumped and eventually prone, as the subjects attempt to blot out the harsh reality of their lives. In *Come Back, Africa*, the spontaneous singing and the rhythmic cadences of the tribal dancing and music of the black Africans contrast starkly with the rigidity of the pass system that appears to constrict the free movement of their bodies within the physical space of a white-controlled society.

ROBERT FRANK AND ALFRED LESLIE: *PULL MY DAISY*

Rogosin's two films were groundbreaking efforts, but the first Beat film, *Pull My Daisy* (1959), generated greater critical attention due to its inclusion of high-profile participants enlisted from the other arts. It was a collaborative effort by noted photographer Robert Frank and multimedia artist Alfred Leslie, and featured the prominent Beat poets Allen Ginsberg, Gregory Corso, and Peter Orlovsky. Jack Kerouac provided the voiceover narration, while jazz musician David Amram created the score. The painters Larry Rivers and Alice Neel played major roles along with Delphine Seyrig, the only professional actor, who worked under a pseudonym.

Frank's photographic essay *The Americans* revolutionized photography when it was published in France in 1958 and in the United States a year later. It consists of eighty-three photographs, which were taken on road trips across the United States over a two-year period and culled from 27,000 photos. Walker Evans, whose *American Photographs* (1938) had given him legendary status within the world of photography, was originally scheduled to write the introduction, but Frank chose Kerouac instead. The choice is not surprising given the fact that *The Americans* could be considered the photographic equivalent of the Beat novelist's *On the Road* (1957). Frank was not really part of the Beat scene, but the two artists shared a similar sensibility. As Ginsberg points out, "I think he [Frank] liked Kerouac, because they both had this spontaneity, an allowance of accidents, and an allowance of accident in mind or accident of space, as part of what was real."[30]

The photographs in Frank's *The Americans* were not artfully composed images but exhibited the grainy, casual look of a quickly taken snapshot. His outsider portrait of America proved controversial. Frank captured America in the Eisenhower era by focusing on the culture of the automobile and the roadside. Jukeboxes and television sets appear in his images like strange objects from outer space. The American flag, which appears in a striking number of photographs, signifies a hollow sense of patriotism. Frank captures the widespread alienation of America's burgeoning consumer society. Even in groups, people don't look at each other but stare in different directions, as if lost in their own private worlds—whether they be religious Jews by the East River, politicians at a rally, kids hanging out in a candy store, African Americans at a funeral, pedestrians on Canal Street in New Orleans, or old folks sitting on benches in St. Petersburg, Florida. The sequencing of the photographs is not linear but associative, like the jazz riffs of Charlie Parker.

Frank and Leslie intended *Pull My Daisy* to be a commercial endeavor that would capitalize on the notoriety of the Beat phenomenon, but the two were soon at odds over how the film should be shot. Leslie was more intent on following the script, but Frank and the poets often subverted those efforts. In discussing the acting, Ginsberg explains, "So what we had to do was invent, following the script in a very general way, not keeping to the actual dialogue and not keeping to the actual scenes. And that's where Robert was good. He didn't make us memorize the script and we didn't have to act, basically."[31] The fact that the film depended on a voiceover narration instead of synchronous sound gave the performers greater liberty. In many ways, *Pull My Daisy* portrays the Beats as a bunch of guys horsing around, ridiculing the strictures of family life and the pretensions of organized religion, as represented by the bishop (gallerist Richard Bellamy) and his entourage.

Pull My Daisy uses Kerouac's poetic narration to provide unity and coherence in telling a very slight story about a group of poets and artists who invade the loft of a railroad brakeman, Milo (Larry Rivers), and his wife (Delphine Seyrig). They sit around drinking beer and wine, smoking weed, and carrying on. When a prim and proper bishop, along with his mother (Alice Neel) and sister, arrive for a visit, Milo's friends interrogate the clergyman about his knowledge of Buddhism and poke fun at him by asking questions, such as whether "baseball is holy." The bishop conducts a religious service in the street below, which is captured in a sequence of stark and grainy shots containing a large American flag that recalls the imagery in *The Americans*. Afterward, Milo's wife becomes upset at the behavior of his friends and slaps him. The camera pans from the wife, past the kitchen to Ginsberg, and finally to the bishop, whose mother plays the organ. Milo and his pal, Mezz (David Amram), however, begin to play their own music, which succeeds in driving away the bishop and his family. After Milo's wife sees the bishop off, she complains bitterly to him about his "beatnik friends," who get up and split. She cries and Milo angrily kicks the chair before joining his pals at the bottom of the stairs. After he does a little jig, they all head out the door.

Pull My Daisy was based on the third act of an unpublished play by Kerouac, entitled *The Beat Generation*, about an incident that occurred when Kerouac visited Neal and Carolyn Cassady in California. Kerouac improvised the narration in three takes while watching the visuals and listening to the music. Frank and Leslie, however, became embroiled in a bitter conflict almost as soon as the film was completed, which has led to differing views of the degree to which the film was actually improvised. Ginsberg, however, considered the film to be largely improvised as well as historically important. He told an interviewer:

> I know I didn't say much about that, but *Pull My Daisy* was one of the first totally improvised films, and in a way it completely changed Hollywood. It affected the entire film world. That and a few other films, like John Cassavetes' *Shadows*, films from the underground, really did have a catalytic effect, altering people's awareness of what you could do: improvise and be open and sexual if necessary.[32]

Largely as a result of tireless promotion by Mekas, *Pull My Daisy* received a great deal of attention upon its release, especially considering the fact that it was a twenty-eight-minute short rather than a feature.

The film's awkward pans and choppy editing fracture the space of its scenes, giving it a seemingly spontaneous home-movie quality that fit the discourse of the time—even if, in reality, it was shot as a professional production with actual investors. *Pull My Daisy* was perceived as embodying the prevailing Beat aesthetic. The film is less reliant on plot and, at least on the surface, appears to be much more free-form than the more overtly narrative *Shadows*. As a result, Frank and Leslie's *Pull My Daisy* became a model for other films, in particular Ron Rice's feature-length *The Flower Thief*, which took the notion of spontaneity in cinema to even greater extremes.

RON RICE: *THE FLOWER THIEF*

The Flower Thief (1960) represents one of the early examples of an independent film that embodied Mekas's notion of plotless cinema.[33] Ron Rice and the poet Taylor Mead combined to make a feature film based on improvised performances rather than a traditional script. Mead, who actually had some professional training in acting, points out, "We knew our daily lifestyle was enough, so we didn't bother to 'act.' Sometimes we made a few expansive gestures and a little extra drama in deference to the Hollywood idea and the fun of pretending we might be stars!"[34] In notes on the film, Rice explained his aesthetic, which harkened back to early cinema. He writes, "In the classic Cinema there is a separation of scenario and image, in short, content and form. We decided to completely throw out content and concentrate only on form."[35] In that sense, Rice was acutely aware of the discrepancy between what can be planned in advance and the images that ultimately appear on the screen.

The Flower Thief was shot in the North Beach area of San Francisco, the epicenter of Beat activity on the West Coast. Both Rice and Mead perceived that the energy of the Beat scene was already starting to wane, and they set about trying to capture the remnants of the subculture before it disappeared entirely. Shot on outdated film stock, *The Flower Thief* is not properly exposed or in focus at times, but that only contributes to its raw and primitive look. The film is looser, more purely improvisational and free-form than *Pull My Daisy*, which nevertheless exerted a strong influence on Rice and Mead, who claimed to be inspired by "just the spontaneity of it. And the picaresque or non-plot thing of Allen [Ginsberg] and Gregory [Corso] and everybody wandering around. And we thought it was wonderful, and that's all you had to do to make a film."[36]

Unlike *Pull My Daisy*, Rice could not afford a professional crew. It was just Rice and Mead (and maybe an assistant) finding interesting locations and improvising as they shot, with many of the other performers being recruited from local bars. It is a prime example of the notion of spontaneous improvisation. Mead observes, "Ron Rice just picked locations and let us do whatever we wanted to, just spontaneous ideas came to us, but it was just various people just discussing what to do at the moment, we didn't plan anything."[37] *The Flower Thief* makes one understand film critic Parker Tyler's rejection of *Pull My Daisy* as steering toward "at times the arty."[38] In many ways, Rice's film epitomizes Manny Farber's notion of "termite art," which the painter and film critic defined as "concentration on nailing down one moment without glamourizing it, but forgetting this accomplishment as soon as it has been passed; the feeling that all is expendable, that it can be chopped up and flung down in a different arrangement without ruin."[39]

The non-diegetic soundtrack of *The Flower Thief* contains snippets of music, poetry, lectures about imprisoning people, human voices recorded backward, and the speech of the Cheshire Cat from *Alice in Wonderland*, which alludes to the fact that "they're all part of a sick society, a sick world." There are references to Ginsberg's *Howl*, to various drugs, and to Wilhelm Reich's orgone accumulator. It includes other social commentary, such as the statement, "The time man has spent in his brothers' prisons can now be measured in light years." It is set in bombed-out looking locations, such as an abandoned power plant, which gives the film a postapocalyptic feel. Sound and image often switch abruptly. The film exhibits the strong influence of Dada—a sense of the absurd—in stringing together incongruous images and sounds. Rice referred to his own approach as "Da Zen Dada."[40]

In narrative terms, the film has a clear protagonist, namely, the flower thief (played by Mead). It also has an antagonist—quite a number of the other characters chase the flower thief around and he is later arrested by two cowboys for urinating in public—which provides some semblance of dramatic conflict. The film even has a romance character in the form of a guy whom the flower thief picks up toward the end. The film consists of a series of episodes involving the protagonist in a number of different locations, but it doesn't have strong narrative coherence until the final section at the seaside carnival (which could even be interpreted as a dream). Instead of causally related events, the film contains a series of incidents, including chases and various comedic situations and skits. It reminds us very strongly of early silent film comedies, especially in its use of slapstick. Mead's actions are those of a highly physical silent film comedian. In effect, he plays an innocent adult who loves to play like a child.

JOHN CASSAVETES: *SHADOWS*

Pull My Daisy and *The Flower Thief*, which were not shot sync-sound, were strongly influenced by the aesthetics of home movies, whereas John Cassavetes's *Shadows* (1958, 1959) more clearly resembles a narrative feature. The initial version grew out of a workshop class "experiment" in improvisation that Cassavetes held for aspiring actors. As he explains:

> The real difference between *Shadows* and any other picture is that *Shadows* emanates from character while in other pictures the characters emanate from the story. I invented, or conceived, the characters of *Shadows* rather than a story-line. The idea of the story fitting the character instead of the character fitting the story is perhaps the main different point about the film.[41]

Characters and a semblance of story were developed through a series of improvisations between Cassavetes and his actors.

Cassavetes valued the collective process over the work emanating from a single individual. He observes, "I cannot help feeling that the stories of many different and potentially inarticulate people are more interesting than a contrived narrative that exists only in one articulate man's imagination."[42] Unlike Lee Strasberg at the Actors Studio, Cassavetes avoided group discussion of characters. He insisted that the improvised character should be the creative work of an individual actor in order to keep the characterization unique and interactions spontaneous between performers.[43]

Improvisation, at least for Cassavetes, was very much a process: "First we improvise to get the feel of the characters; then as the actors become easy in the roles we go back to the text. If it doesn't work out, then we go back and improvise some more; and again return to the text. We keep working like this till we feel complete identification between actor and role."[44] Cassavetes made it a point to withhold information from the actors to prevent them from becoming overly self-conscious. As he put it, "The big thing is not to let the actors know precisely what the ultimate point of what they're doing is; as soon as they know, they try *consciously* to express it instead of letting it emerge as in life, and so they falsify it."[45] Even in the scripted love scene between Lelia and Tony in *Shadows*, we have a strong sense of a slippage between the roles they are playing and their personal lives. To reinforce this connection, the characters share the same first names as the actors.

With *Shadows*, Cassavetes succeeded in creating an actor-centric cinema as opposed to the traditional one governed by the technical aspects of making films, such as the need for actors to hit marks or have their performances restrained by lighting requirements and camera framing. The shots were instead adapted to the actors so that the performers were less restricted spatially in terms of their physical movements within the frame.[46] The most controversial aspect of *Shadows*, however, was the end credit that suggests, "The film you have just seen was an improvisation." As was actually the case, Cassavetes later felt that this emphasis, which he used as a marketing pitch, was misleading. *Shadows* was not completely improvised but derived from a "method" that Cassavetes was exploring to shift the focus from the written page to the performers, whom he felt were what gave "life" to the film. He told Ray Carney, "There was no script, but there was an outline. We stuck to it very carefully. We would work on the idea of each scene before we would shoot it. It was just like revising a script, except that there were no written words—we kept the idea and the script in our minds."[47]

There are actually two versions of *Shadows*. The first was highly praised by Jonas Mekas in his influential movie column in the *Village Voice*: "In any case, 'Shadows' breaks with the official staged cinema, with made-up faces, with written scripts, with plot continuities. Even its inexperience in editing, sound, and camera work becomes a part of its style, the roughness that only life (and Alfred Leslie's paintings) have."[48] The film received the first Independent Film Award from *Film Culture*, the film magazine Mekas founded and edited. Cassavetes, however, was dissatisfied with the completed film. He subsequently worked with a screenwriter, Robert Alan Aurthur, to develop new scenes, reassemble the cast, and reshoot more than 40,000 feet or eighteen hours of new footage, which was then edited together with the old footage. According to Carney, "Cassavetes threw away approximately half of the old scenes (leaving less than twenty-five minutes of the original version remaining) and intercut almost an hour of new scenes into the film."[49] The new version was blown up from the amateur gauge of 16 mm to the professional gauge of 35 mm. It played together with *Pull My Daisy* on a program entitled "The Cinema of Improvisation" at Amos Vogel's Cinema 16 on November 11, 1959.[50]

Shadows deals with the interracial issues involving three siblings. The lighter-skinned, Ben (Ben Carruthers) is an alienated hipster, for whom race is a buried issue. Because he can pass racially, Ben hangs out with his two friends in an essentially white world, but his brooding personality and constant posturing suggest that he suffers from inner turmoil. His dark-skinned older brother, Hugh (Hugh Hurd) is a nightclub singer who self-identifies with the black world and feels that he is continually being discriminated against in the music business due to the color of his skin. The flirtatious Lelia (Lelia Goldoni), on the other hand, initially seems oblivious to the issue of race but later experiences a crisis of identity when she has an affair with a young white man named Tony (Anthony Ray), who has a racial reaction upon meeting Hugh.

At a literary party, Lelia becomes upset when a straight older writer named David (David Pokitillow) criticizes a short story she has written for lacking honesty. In discussing Lelia's story, David does not understand the fact that the woman gets deeply hurt but then acts as if nothing has happened. Lelia answers, "Well, the point is that if you are yourself, you won't get hurt." David tries to convince her that writers today need to be realistic. In Lelia's story, a woman impulsively kisses a stranger on Fifth Avenue. To prove her point, she suddenly stands up and passionately kisses a young man she has just met, Tony. David comments, "It's even more revolting in real life." Tony asks, "Who do you belong to, Lelia?" She answers, "Well, I belong to me." Both David and Tony want to take Lelia home, but she has other plans. Tony asks to accompany Lelia and David to Central Park the next day.

In Central Park, Lelia and Tony quickly ditch David. As the two walk together, Lelia, who indicates that she's twenty, admits her insecurities, while Tony warns her, "You know, I'm not a very nice person. I mean, I have very romantic inclinations. Be forewarned that I'm not one of these storybook characters who's supposed to be all noble and righteous. When I see someone I like, and if she likes me, we accept my romantic inclinations." He invites her up to his apartment. Once inside, he begins to kiss her and tell her he loves her. After a cut, the camera tilts down from a close-up on a mask to a close-up of Lelia's face, as mournful jazz plays on the soundtrack. She and Tony have the following exchange:

Tony: Lelia . . . really. If I had known that this was the first time for you, I wouldn't have touched you.

Lelia: I didn't know it could be so awful.

Tony: Don't be so upset, sweetheart. Baby, it will be much easier next time.

Lelia: There isn't going to be a next time.

Tony: Want a cigarette, huh? Come on, have a cigarette.

Lelia: No.

Tony: I'm sorry if I disappointed you. I guess I did.

Lelia: I was so frightened. I kept saying to myself, you mustn't cry. If you love a man, you shouldn't be so frightened.

Tony: It's only natural. There isn't a girl in the world that wouldn't feel the same way. She's . . . got to.

Lelia: And what happens now?

Tony: What happens? Um . . . what do you mean what happens now?

Lelia: I mean, do I stay with you?

Tony: Lelia, uh. Stay with me? You, you mean live with me?

Lelia: Yes.

Tony: You want to?

Lelia: No. I want to go home.

Tony: Okay. Baby.

Lelia: I thought being with you would be so important, mean so much. And afterwards, two people would be as close as it's possible to get. But instead, we're just two strangers.

Tony: Lelia . . . Lelia.

Lelia: It's over. I know that much about life.

In the aftermath of losing her virginity, Lelia becomes confused and conflicted, which is reflected in the dialogue. There is a sense that Lelia appears to be so disoriented that the viewer wonders whether Goldoni herself might be experiencing a kind of psychic breakdown in the scene, especially at the end, when, in close-up, she insists, "Please don't touch me! Please don't touch me. I want to go home." Given that the two actors have previously had a romantic relationship in real life, we sense that in this traumatic scene, Goldoni has become confused between her own feelings and those of her character.[51] This is an effect, enhanced through editing, that Cassavetes was able to exploit in order to give the scene its raw, off-centered quality.

Following indecision in a cab ride home, Tony accompanies her upstairs. When Hugh and his manager Rupert arrive at the apartment, the camera holds on extended reaction shots of Tony, who suddenly announces he has to leave for an appointment. Nothing is said—the dynamic of the scene is communicated visually through a series of glances among the four characters. Lelia attempts to stop him by saying she loves him, but Hugh

FIGURE 1.4 Lelia becomes upset with Tony after the two have sex, *Shadows*

ends up confronting Tony and asking him to leave. He tells him, "I don't want you around, hurting my sister. I don't want you to hurt anything of mine. Now go!" Tony acts like the wronged party and suddenly shoves Hugh, before Hugh finally pushes him out the door. As Hugh consoles Lelia, she cries, "Oh, I love him so much." Tony later calls Lelia from a phone booth. Cassavetes holds on her reaction shot for fifteen seconds as the phone continues to ring. The second half of the film involves a series of confrontations between and among the other characters, especially once Tony meets Hugh and the racial aspect becomes manifest.

Shadows is more episodic than dramatic. As a result, it is much closer to art cinema than classical Hollywood in terms of its narration. Because the film begins and ends with Ben, the viewer initially assumes that he is the main protagonist, but that proves not to be the case. Ben does not have a dramatic function in the story because his conflict remains internal. In terms of its structure, *Shadows* appears to have been conceived initially as a multiple-plot film. The film establishes the three main characters, but Lelia unexpectedly turns out to be the film's protagonist because her conflict eventually constitutes the main plotline. Lelia, however, is ambivalent rather than goal-directed. Her impulsive sexual escapade with Tony proves to be the dramatic event, or first turning point, that sets everything else in motion, reducing Ben and Hugh's storylines to mere subplots.

The romantic plotline, which gives focus and direction to an otherwise meandering story, ends almost immediately after it begins. Once the two of them have sex, Lelia becomes even more confused about what she feels. The shifts in her dialogue, as we have seen, are abrupt and contradictory. Unlike the character in her short story, Lelia ends up getting deeply hurt by her sexual entanglement with Tony. As a result of her own youthful naiveté, Lelia fails to anticipate Tony's racist reaction upon meeting Hugh. In losing her virginity to Tony, the subject of race seems to be the farthest thing from her mind. The scenes of the aftermath of their lovemaking and the subsequent scene in which Tony meets Hugh form the heart of the film. As Marshall Fine comments, "It was that sequence, principally, that gave *Shadows* its impact. In the space of twenty minutes, Cassavetes presents, examines, and dramatizes the racial questions of his time: racial identity, racial prejudice, interracial romance."[52]

The fact that Cassavetes was an actor strongly influenced his approach to making films. Looking at *Shadows* today, the film clearly represents a different aesthetic approach that privileges acting over the other elements of the film. There are flickers of what Cassavetes was after in *Shadows*, but his reshooting of the film and later reliance on a script stripped away some of its spontaneity. What became his ultimate approach, especially toward the use of improvisation, took time to develop and refine. *Shadows* may be a landmark film in the creation of the New American Cinema, but, as we will see in the next chapter, his later films, such as *Faces* and *Husbands*, actually serve as stronger examples of his approach to alternative scripting and improvisation.

2

LET'S NOT PHONY IT UP ANYMORE

The Films of John Cassavetes

Agreat deal of misunderstanding surrounds the technique of improvisation. As a style of acting, it is often thought to involve an actor's unrehearsed and spontaneous response to a situation, but, as has been suggested, there are a number of distinct variations to the approach. John Cassavetes's use of improvisation represents one version of the technique, but his ideas and films have nevertheless had a profound impact on American indie cinema throughout its subsequent history, including on those filmmakers associated with the recent mumblecore movement, such as Andrew Bujalski, Joe Swanberg, and Aaron Katz. Although Cassavetes's work is most associated with improvisation, scholars recognize that his films, including *Shadows*, were actually scripted. Although this might seem surprising, the relationship between planning and improvisation, especially regarding written scripts, is a complicated issue.

After *Shadows* (1958, 1959), Cassavetes did not collaborate with other screenwriters for a simple reason: his cinema was not based on the written word but instead very much privileged the actor. He noted, "Within the framework of the writing, all that's there is the words. And the rest of it is how it is played. That's where improvisation comes in."[1] For him, the script was not an end in itself but merely the jumping-off point for the actors in a long and difficult process of discovery. According to Cassavetes, "the script doesn't mean a damn thing—rewrite it, do it again, rewrite it. OK, let's improvise it. After improvisation, let's rewrite it again, then let's improvise it. And maybe we won't use anything. Maybe it will be background."[2] In that sense, Cassavetes recognized that scripts had their limitations, especially in terms of having a constricting effect on the final film. Or as he put it: "Scripts lock you in and subject you to your own thinking. They take away freedom and make less out of what could be more."[3]

Cassavetes's use of the word "improvisation" in discussing his own cinematic approach often led to confusion and a number of seeming contradictions. Cassavetes used improvisational techniques in a number of ways. In *Shadows*, he initially used improvisation to generate ideas for the film based on a simple premise: after sleeping with a young woman, a white man discovers that she is mixed race. In subsequent films, Cassavetes used it as an essential part of the rehearsal process, so that the actors had considerable input and helped to shape not only the actual script but the final film.

In addition, Cassavetes employed improvisation during the shooting of the films. His performers, for the most part, did not spontaneously ad-lib on set the way Andy Warhol's or Norman Mailer's performers did. Cassavetes insisted, "There's a difference between ad-libbing and improvising, and there's a difference between not knowing what to do and just saying something. I believe in improvising on the basis of the written work and not on undisciplined creativity. When you have an important scene, you want it written; but there are still times when you want things just to happen."[4] The notion of wanting things to happen on set is precisely what goes against the notion of simply sticking to a written screenplay. Cassavetes's process of improvisation became more complicated beginning with *Faces*, especially in terms of the relationship between the text and improvisation. In *Improvising Cinema*, Gilles Mouëllic writes:

> The system set up in rehearsals and followed up during the shoot makes it possible to re-appropriate the script and breathe life into it; but when improvisation occurs the appropriation becomes different. In acquiring the freedom to invent new proposals and delve beyond the writing, the process exceeds the performance by abolishing the gap between writing and acting: to the improviser, acting is writing.[5]

Or, to put it another way, acting can be another form of scripting or what Steven Maras has referred to as "writing with bodies."[6]

FACES

Cassavetes's *Faces* (1968) best exemplifies the approach to improvisation and performance that he began to develop in *Shadows*. In comparison to *Shadows*, the self-financed film is a mature, nuanced work that breaks new ground through the hyperrealism of the acting. *Faces* grew from a four-page outline into an extremely long screenplay of approximately 320 pages.[7] It was shot, roughly in sequence, over a six-month period in 16 mm and later blown up to 35 mm. The finished film runs 130 minutes and took nearly four years to complete. Although the timeline in the film is a bit unclear, *Faces* takes place over the course of a little more than twenty-four hours. *Faces* deals with white, middle-class characters who are relatively successful but whose jobs and marriages leave them empty and unfulfilled. Heavy bouts of drinking, short bursts of song and dance, extended fits of laughing, a propensity for bad jokes, dirty limericks, tongue twisters, and the lure of a sexual escapade provide the only coping mechanisms for the otherwise empty lives of these characters.

Faces examines the social roles men and women are forced to play, whether in business, marriage, or their everyday lives. The film has very little plot, which can easily be summarized: Richard Forst (John Marley) meets an attractive woman, Jeannie (Gena Rowlands); tells his wife, Maria (Lynn Carlin), that he wants a divorce; and has a one-night fling. In response, Maria ends up having an affair of her own, nearly overdoses, and the married couple confront each other at the end. The structure of the film is equally simple. Starting from the moment Richard announces that he wants a divorce, it can be divided into two halves: his affair and her affair. The section focusing on Maria has a livelier pace than the first section that deals with Richard. Cassavetes indicated that he deliberately structured the first part of the film so that audiences would not be able to anticipate what would happen next. According to the director, "What happens with *Faces*, though, is that the first half of the film really bugs people because it doesn't fit an easy pattern of behavior. Well, I don't know anyone who has an easy pattern of behavior. I know people who are just sensational one minute, and absolute bastards the next. Terribly funny one minute, and morose the next."[8] With its abrupt tonal changes and frenetic, documentary-like style, *Faces* is radically different from conventional narrative films, especially in terms of its acting.

Faces upends traditional notions of what constitutes "film acting" by attempting to present large chunks of unfiltered human behavior. Cassavetes does not attempt to get inside his characters but rather positions the viewer to observe his characters the way we might encounter them in everyday life. Cassavetes did not want the artifice of acting to be obvious. He was not interested in stylistic mannerisms or anything that might seem contrived but rather in somehow capturing the lives of real people. Cassavetes believed that Hollywood movie actors were limited due to an overreliance on scripts. He thought they were incapable of acting like real people, which is the way he felt people were programmed to be in society. Cassavetes believed that people are taught to hide rather than show their feelings, whereas he wanted his actors to express a full range of feelings— no matter how ugly or distasteful they might be.[9] His position is not all that different from that of J. L. Moreno, who believed the only hope for human beings was in being able to respond spontaneously and creatively to any situation that occurred in their lives. Tom Charity writes, "Cassavetes doesn't want you to watch this film; he wants you to experience it, to feel it, to be 'in the moment.' "[10] This happens to be precisely the aim of what Moreno was attempting to achieve in psychodrama. For him, the "moment," in contrast to the "present" contains "dynamic" and "creative" possibilities.[11]

After his experience with the first version of *Shadows*, Cassavetes came to believe in the importance of the writing process, which might explain the excessive length of his screenplay for *Faces*. Writing a script, however, was intricately linked to the rehearsal process, which served as a laboratory for the actors to discover their unique characters. The script was constantly being altered and rewritten as the actors rehearsed the scenes. Cassavetes commented about *Faces*: "The emotion was improvisation. The lines were written. The attitudes were improvised, as they always are, but I think a little more deeply in this case."[12]

Although Cassavetes often gives the impression that he insisted on having his actors deliver the lines as written in the script, this was not always the case. In a film like *Faces*, Cassavetes was focused on the actual performances rather than the script, so he didn't care whether their words were scripted as long as the emotions the actors were expressing seemed honest and real.[13] He is less interested in his actors repeating his written lines of dialogue than in their embodying the characters they are playing, which involves their physical gestures, unconscious reactions, and the movement of their bodies in space as they interact with each other.

The published screenplay for *Faces* provides a unique window into how the original script was transformed through the rehearsal process as well as during filming and editing.[14] The original screenplay is presented on the right side of the page, while what actually appears on the screen is printed on the left side, making for an easy comparison. Most striking is how much of the screenplay was excised at some point in the process. Not only have large chunks of dialogue been altered, but whole sections of the screenplay, including dialogue, have been deleted. This is evident from the large number of blank pages that appear on the left side, which amounts to more than a quarter of the screenplay. In some cases, however, additional dialogue has been added.

Faces was shot with two cameras in a kind of direct cinema style, which gives it a raw quality we associate with the documentary mode. The camera is constantly mobile, seeking to capture the performance of the actors,

FIGURE 2.1 Maria is devastated following her infidelity with Chet, *Faces*

especially the facial expressions of the characters through myriad, often extreme, close-ups. Because it was shot in 16 mm, the image is decidedly grainy. Cassavetes does not use non-diegetic music (until the end) to key us how to respond emotionally to what is occurring onscreen. The film might be shot like a documentary, but it is scripted fiction and the performances are totally unconventional.

How was Cassavetes able to achieve the raw quality of human behavior in his performers, especially with a first-time performer such as Lynn Carlin? Interestingly, Cassavetes claimed that no one in *Faces* is acting.[15] Rather, he equates the quality of a performance on screen with the way the person behaves in everyday life, arguing: "There's no such thing as a 'good actor.' What it is is an extension of life. How you're capable of performing in your life, that's how you're capable of performing on the screen. Everything else is just a failure to accomplish that."[16]

Cassavetes believed that the trick in getting strong performances in film involved setting up the proper conditions, in creating a safe environment for the actors to be open and vulnerable. In a sense, it is analogous to the safe environment of group psychotherapy, such as psychodrama, where people can risk being themselves without the threat of ridicule or judgment. Cassavetes explains, "The simple problem we had in this film was to try to create a situation for people which allowed them to be themselves and to say things without feeling they were going to be electrocuted for saying them. To let them put themselves in a position where they may make asses of themselves, without feeling they're revealing things that will eventually be used against them."[17]

In the scene where Chet (Seymour Cassel) serenades and dances with the four women, Freddie's reticent wife, Louise (Joanne Moore Jordan), finally allows herself to get up and dance. Chet catches a look from Maria that suggests disapproval, which leads to the following exchange:

Chet: I think we're making fools of ourselves.
Louise: What?
Chet: Yeah.
Louise: I'm making a fool of myself?
Chet: Well, we are, yeah.
Louise: Well, who are you to criticize me?
Chet: I'm not criticizing you. I'm just saying . . .

Louise becomes very defensive and upset, slaps him, and heads down the hall. Chet tries to talk to her, but she ends up in tears, comes back, and grabs her coat and leaves. A simple glance from Maria is enough to end the drunken antics, which provides a powerful example of how social inhibitions—the fear of making asses of ourselves—prevent people from acting spontaneously in their lives. This sad and poignant moment, easily overlooked, provides a rich comment on the uninhibited flow of behavior that Cassavetes strove to achieve in his actors, especially in a film like *Faces*.

HUSBANDS

The amateur actors in *Shadows* did not have much time to rehearse and improvise during the reshoot of the film due to budget and time constraints, forcing Cassavetes to rely more heavily on the scripted scenes. In many ways, however, *Shadows* represents something of an anomaly in terms of his working methods. Tom Charity writes, "Save for *Shadows*, a few scenes in *Husbands*, and a few moments elsewhere, all Cassavetes' films were scripted, even if those scripts were sometimes arrived at through close collaboration with the actors."[18] In relation to *Husbands*, Ray Carney attempts to be more precise:

> Beyond a small number of lines of dialogue here and there, only a few moments in *Husbands* were actually "improvised" in the common import of the word—ad-libbed on the set while filming was going on: the singing scene in the bar; parts of Gus and Mary's sex scene; parts of Falk's "take your hand off my hand" scene with the "Countess"; and parts of the men's farewell scene in Harry's hotel room. In general (and including large sections of the above moments), the film was played exactly as it was scripted, from the first page to the last.[19]

Yet, proportionately, the amount of spontaneous improvisation in *Husbands* is substantial, especially because Cassavetes cast a number of nonprofessional performers in the film.

Husbands (1970) begins with a title card that announces that the film is "a comedy about life, death, and freedom," followed by a montage of still photographs of four male friends and their wives and children. The film then cuts to a shot inside a car entering a cemetery for the funeral of one of them following a heart attack. Afterward, the three remaining friends—Gus (played by Cassavetes), Harry (Ben Gazzara), and Archie (Peter Falk)—are left to reflect on their lives, especially their marriages, as they cope with their grief and loss. Instead of going home to their wives and families, they eventually head to a bar to drown their troubles in a lengthy scene lasting roughly twenty-one minutes before fleeing to London.

Biographer Marshall Fine indicates that the initial drinking scene they shot, which involved the three principal actors singing in an empty bar, turned out to be flat and lifeless.[20] The bar scene was subsequently reshot using extras to provide greater realism. But the major transformation occurred when Cassavetes decided to turn the extras into performers by introducing the idea of engaging them in a singing contest. After a number of songs sung mostly off-key as well as two different ones that are sung simultaneously, a former stripper named Leola (Leola Harlow), dressed in a red plaid outfit, attempts a rendition of "It Was Just a Little Love Affair." Harry immediately yells, "Horrible!" The three men proceed to insult, interrupt, and bully her by claiming she has no feeling. Gus shouts, "You are terrible!" They treat her roughly and continue to abuse the woman, who at first appears bewildered and then frightened by their rowdy behavior.

Archie tries to provoke her by suddenly stripping off his clothes. Leola's face registers both surprise and shock. As Archie continues to badger her into mimicking their rendition of the song, Leola tells him, "No, 'cause you scare me." When Leola's turn is finally over after nearly nine torturous minutes, her face turns slightly toward the camera, allowing us to view her sniffle and reddened eyes that betray her true response to the humiliating experience. John "Red" Kullers follows by singing "Brother, Can You Spare a Dime" with such drunken emotion that he easily wins the contest as well as the admiration of the three professional actors. The nonactors, especially Harlow and Kullers, are in many ways far more interesting to watch than the badly behaving movie stars, largely because Harlow and Kullers are not trying to act but are responding as themselves for the camera.

According to Jenny Runacre, who plays Mary—the woman Gus picks up in London and seduces in his hotel room—the two scenes with her are also largely improvised. She told Tom Charity: "That scene in the coffee shop was improvised: when I slapped him it was totally instinctive, from nothing, not even in rehearsals. John was completely taken aback. But he kept it in. And the fight on the bed was improvised."[21] A young South African former model recently out of drama school, Runacre had a different response than Harlow. She fought back against the attempts by Cassavetes to bully her. The two developed an antagonistic relationship during filming, which creates a dynamic tension in Runacre's two scenes: the seven-minute seduction scene in the hotel room and the five-minute breakfast scene the following morning. Their bedroom scene exhibits the same type of radically abrupt tonal changes and unpredictability as the one between Lelia and Tony in *Shadows*. The two appear to have a love/hate relationship. As a consequence, their attempt at foreplay quickly turns into the equivalent of a wrestling match. Gus comes on very aggressively, but Mary, who is quite a bit taller than him, manages to hold her ground. In the next scene, their interaction at breakfast the next morning is again a curious mixture of fleeting moments of affection and outright hostility.

As indicated, Cassavetes cast quite a few nonprofessional performers or first-time actors in *Husbands*, especially in the bar scene and the scenes in London. He told an interviewer: "I really believe almost anyone can act. How well they can act depends on how free they are and whether the circumstances are such that they can reveal what they feel. If I have any special way of working, it's just to set up an atmosphere where what the actors are doing is really important, fun, and nothing takes precedence over it."[22] A number of professional actors felt uncomfortable dealing with the improv approach used by Cassavetes, including Gena Rowlands (who preferred working from a script), Peter Falk (at least in *Husbands*), and Joan Blondell (*Opening Night*). But his methods seemed well-suited to nonactors or inexperienced actors such as Harlow, Kullers, and Runacre.

Part of what makes *Husbands* unusual is the mix among the three professional actors—Cassavetes, Gazzara, and Falk—and the novice performers. Jeremy Kagan, the screenwriter and director, explains the potential benefits of using nonactors:

With non-actors, what happens is you can only get the truth that they can give. Sometimes it will be amazing, because it is what they are, they're not acting it, they are it; other times there will be this awkwardness, and sometimes that might put the other actors off-kilter and bring up a truth for them as well. Because the moment is true: they can't look into the eyes of the non-actor and see another actor, all they can see is the person who is there, which forces them sometimes to be who they are.[23]

Indeed, the most interesting scenes in *Husbands* are the ones that contain the most improvisation, namely the bar scene and the ones involving the three women the men pick up in London.

Although, in various interviews, Cassavetes often liked to play down the amount of control he exerted as director, there are indications that he could be very manipulative in certain situations. In *Husbands*, for instance, he used pitchers of beer to loosen up the extras as performers. John Kullers, in particular, appears to be extremely drunk in the scene, which contributes to the realism of his highly emotional performance. Leola Harlow is desperately trying her best to sing, but she is clearly unprepared for the verbal abuse being heaped upon her by the three male actors. According to the film's director of photography, Victor Kemper, "John [Cassavetes] badgered her until she cried. That wasn't acting. He knew he could get what he needed if he treated her like that."[24] Ray Carney indicates that afterward Harlow was both "genuinely hurt and confused" by the way she was treated in the scene.[25] Runacre acknowledged that she felt "incredibly paranoid" on the set due to the macho behavior of the three principal male actors. She told Tom Charity, "I'm sure that's what John wanted me to feel. He wanted it to be so real that you couldn't act."[26]

Cassavetes often manipulated the actors to elicit more dramatic performances. In *Shadows*, he exploited the fact that Lelia Goldoni and Tony Ray had previously had a romantic relationship by staging an intimate sex scene between them, which confuses the boundary between fiction and actuality. He would give lines to actors and withhold them from others. In the scene prior to the seduction in *Shadows*, for instance, Cassavetes gave Tony Ray lines, but not Goldoni. Ray Carney indicates that Cassavetes deliberately repeated a racist remark to Rupert Crosse, who plays Hugh's manager, in order to get him to be incredibly angry in the scene where he vents at the train station.[27] According to Fine, Cassavetes even resorted to slapping Lynn Carlin, a first-time performer, right before rolling the camera in order to obtain the emotional response he wanted in *Faces*.[28]

In filming *Minnie and Moskowitz*, Cassavetes admitted, "I made Gena [Rowlands] and Seymour [Cassel] hate each other during the picture and kept them off-balance with each other."[29] Carney details the different ploys Cassavetes used during shooting to get his desired effect. In one instance, he deliberately had Cassel awaken Rowlands from a nap on the pretext that her fellow lead actor wanted to rehearse. Cassavetes also didn't tell Rowlands until the last minute that he was playing the role of the husband, Jim. He also played "mind games" in having Val Avery rehearse a scene in *Minnie and Moskowitz* over and over, and then deliberately provoked an argument with Avery to obtain the emotion he was seeking.[30] In response to repeated claims by Cassavetes that he didn't direct actors, Rowlands comments, "He *thinks* he doesn't give directions, but he's constantly telling you what to do."[31]

MINNIE AND MOSKOWITZ

Cassavetes might have written scripts that served as the basis for his films, but certain scenes were altered in intriguing ways. One such scene occurs in *Minnie and Moskowitz* (1971), Cassavetes's loopy screwball comedy about a mismatched couple, Minnie Gordon (Gena Rowlands) and Seymour Moskowitz (Seymour Cassel). It occurs early in the film between Minnie and an older coworker at the museum named Florence (played by Elsie Ames, a

FIGURE 2.2 Minnie accompanies Florence home after the movie, *Minnie and Moskowitz*

nonprofessional performer) as the two women drink together at Florence's house one night after attending a Humphrey Bogart movie.

The brief exchange between the two women does not appear in the original screenplay, published in 1973.[32] At one point, Minnie suddenly asks Florence, who is single, a highly personal question. This is how the scene appears in the shooting script:

> Minnie: Florence, you're . . . are you romantic anymore? I mean I never know if somebody reaches your age if they have any real drive to be loved. I'm sorry if that sounds stupid, but I'd just like to know—does it diminish? Does it go away?
> Florence: Sometimes . . . but there's always frustration. I just don't know if it's the sex thing or the being alone that I'm frustrated about. After a while you don't know.[33]

The scene in the actual film is considerably different. It is more broken up and interactive. The bluntness of Minnie's questioning of her sex life feels more direct, raw, and painful:

> Minnie: Florence . . . Florence, are you still romantic?
> Florence: I sure am.
> Minnie: I mean, I never know when someone reaches your age whether they still have any real need to be loved.
> Florence: I sure do.
> Minnie: Do you still do it?
> Florence: Yes . . .
> Minnie: Yeah? I'm . . . I'm sorry. It's a terrible question. But I . . . I really did want to know. (*pause*) Does it diminish, Florence? Does it go away?
> Florence: Sometimes . . . and I get very frustrated . . . and, a . . . I don't know whether it's the sex thing or whether it's being alone that makes me so frustrated. After a while, I just don't know.

Although the basic idea for the scene is contained in the script, what appears in the film feels much more invasive. Minnie's probing question catches Florence off guard, causing slight embarrassment, which is evident from the flushness in Ames's face. The difference between the scene as written and as performed is that the former focuses on whether Florence still has romantic feelings, whereas the latter has switched the emphasis to her sexuality. In the scripted version, Florence mentions "the sex thing," but the key line in the exchange is when Minnie asks her friend directly, "Do you still do it?" That line comes at Florence with a certain unexpected velocity. It changes everything because it puts her older friend on the spot. Minnie then asks, "Does it diminish, Florence? Does it go away?" In the script, the lines clearly refer to "the drive to be loved," but in the new context, the lines become more ambiguous and could easily be read as referring to Florence's sexual drive.

Once again, the power of the scene derives from improvisation and a certain awkwardness involving an amateur performer. The "acting" or the artifice in the scene has to do with the emphasis of Florence taking a drink of wine and looking away from Minnie before she answers, "Sometimes," and during the pause before she says, "I don't know whether it's the sex thing." Yet Ames cannot hide her actual discomfort at talking about such highly personal matters, especially for a woman her age (nearly seventy), which is what makes the scene so riveting.

LOVE STREAMS

There is a similar scene in Cassavetes's *Love Streams* (1984), which centers on a psychiatric session. Sarah Lawson (Gena Rowlands) has suffered a nervous breakdown, leading her husband, Jack (Seymour Cassel), to seek a divorce. At a second court hearing, her daughter, Debbie, unexpectedly tells the judge that she prefers to live with her father rather than her mother. Sarah visits her psychiatrist (played by Gena's brother, David Rowlands). Sarah insists that love is a continuous stream that never stops, which is the reason she opposes getting divorced. The psychiatrist disagrees with her contention, bluntly explaining that Jack no longer loves her. They have the following exchange:

Psychiatrist: Your love is too strong for your family. (*pause*). I want you to describe your sexual life.
Sarah: (*after a very long pause*) I don't have a sexual life.

Psychiatrist: You do.

Sarah: I don't need a sexual life.

Psychiatrist: What other interests do you have besides your husband? You speak continuously of him, and he doesn't love you.

Sarah: It's . . . that's not true . . . it's, it's, it's uh . . .

Psychiatrist: And of your daughter who chose him over you.

Sarah: No.

There is a marked difference in the impact of the psychiatrist probing the sex life of the mentally unstable Sarah compared to the scene where Minnie questions Florence in *Minnie and Moskowitz*. Although there is no question that Rowlands is a far superior actor to the novice performer, Elsie Ames, the effect of the question is not nearly as strong in this instance. For one thing, psychiatrists routinely probe the sexual lives of their patients, so the question does not seem to surprise or embarrass her in any way. When the psychiatrist asks the question, she is in the process of taking a cigarette from the pack. The question causes her to stop her action. Throughout the shot, her eyes avert his. She breathes out, shakes her head slightly, puts her hand to her face and then leans her arm on the table and rests her head on her hand. She looks at him when she answers emphatically, "I don't have a sexual life." As he says, "You do,"

FIGURE 2.3 Sara Lawson in a session with her psychiatrist, *Love Streams*

off camera, Sarah continues to look at him defiantly as she insists, "I don't need a sexual life." After the psychiatrist suggests that her husband doesn't love her, Rowlands runs one of her hands through her hair. When he mentions her daughter not loving her, she pulls her hair back with both hands.

Cassavetes is directing Rowlands, who, in all likelihood, has rehearsed the scene many times previously. The actions and pauses, especially the duration of them, have been added to make the scene seem more naturalistic. Rowlands clearly knows the question is coming and has worked out her responses to it. In Michael Ventura's *Cassavetes Directs*, his on-set diary of the making of *Love Streams*, he discusses Cassavetes's direction of the above scene. His general direction to Rowlands was "Gotta take it. Gotta take it on the button here. There can't be any defenses."[34] Ventura notes, "John goes to her and whispers so low that even in this small room we hear nothing." Cassavetes then tells Rowlands, "So that, all your behavior is the mannerisms of a real crazy person, but you're not crazy— it's that you don't want to tell him. 'Sex? I don't have any, and the funny thing is I really don't need it.' And it's true, you don't."[35] In addition, Ventura indicates that he interrupted the take of her saying the scripted line, "That's not true," which becomes in the film, "It's . . . that's not true . . . it's, it's, it's uh. . . ." He explains, "John interrupted to get that rhythm." He also directed her to perform a gesture before she responds, "No." Ventura indicates that Cassavetes told her, "Gena, put your hands all the way through your hair, both of them, now throw it in front of your face."[36] In other words, her final gesture is directed rather than unconscious, which is exactly how it reads.

The emphasis of the scene, however, is not on Sarah's sexuality, which she defiantly ignores, but remains focused on her husband and daughter's rejection of her. As a result, this scene turns out to be quite different from the one in *Minnie and Moskowitz*. What we watch and appreciate in that scene are the amateur performer's unconscious responses to the probing question she's asked. Cassavetes believed that the most genuine and authentic response came from an actor discovering something unexpected and interesting in the rehearsal process. Although he was opposed to ad-libbing, spontaneous reactions and responses often came from subtle unconscious moments, which the camera was able to capture during filming.

OPENING NIGHT

In terms of motivation, the characters in Cassavetes's films always appear to be unpredictable. Cassavetes is attuned to the complexity of human behavior found in real life, which shares that same quality and makes his films fascinating to watch. His characters keep viewers perpetually off balance, wondering and guessing what they might say or do next. In *Opening Night* (1977), Myrtle Gordon (Gena Rowlands), an alcoholic actor about to begin the out-of-town run of a new play, witnesses one of her admiring fans get run over and killed by a car as she leaves the theater in her limousine. The death of the young woman deeply troubles Myrtle. It leads her to have a personal crisis not only about the play she is performing, which deals with aging, but also regarding issues in her own life.

Two scenes from *Opening Night* exemplify the complex motivation and seeming unpredictability of scenes and dialogue in Cassavetes's films. The first occurs between Manny (Ben Gazzara), the play's director, and his wife, Dorothy (Zohra Lampert), as they sit in a hotel room in the early morning.

Manny: I need your help, Dorothy. I'm not talking to you as your husband. I don't count. But I'm going to go crazy if you don't tell me what it's like to be alone as a woman. What do you do? Okay, that's it. Will you make me another drink, please?

Dorothy: Sure.

Manny: I'm going to get drunk.

Dorothy: Ah . . .

Manny: Eh, if you want to get hostile, you go ahead. My goddamn life depends on this play. And you should go to all the rehearsals. You should watch everything. You should sit with Myrtle. Fill her in on yourself and be part of it.

Dorothy: Do I get paid for this?

Manny: If you understudy, I'll pay you.

> *Dorothy smiles and briefly acts as if she is considering the offer. The two of them laugh.*

Manny: That's right. 'Cause, I tell you, my life is getting boring. I'm getting somber. My own tricks bore me.

Dorothy: Do you want ice?

Manny: Yeah. There's no humor anymore and all the glamour's dead. You notice that? I can't even stand how they come to rehearsal. They come to rehearsal dressed in terrible clothes.

Dorothy: Manny, I'm dying. I'm dying. I know I'm dying because I'm getting tired. It's always the same. You talk. I sleep. If I'd known what a boring man you were when I married you, I wouldn't have gone through all those emotional crises.

After a cut, Manny pours her a drink, and Dorothy moves closer to him when the telephone suddenly rings, destroying their attempt at physical intimacy.

Manny heads into the bedroom and answers the phone. It is Myrtle, telling him the news about the accident and her problems sleeping. Dorothy has initially responded to the ringing phone with a cold stare. When she comes into the room playfully doing a dance step while holding her robe, Dorothy tells Manny that it's 4:30 a.m., indicating her irritation at the phone call. She continues to try to get her husband's attention by dancing and diving onto the bed and flailing her arms as if pretending to swim. Dorothy wants him to get off the phone and suggests that he call Myrtle back in the morning. As Manny assures Myrtle, "There's no one I love more than you at this moment," he covers the phone and tells Dorothy, "You know I love you."

Dorothy shadowboxes with him and then socks herself, while Myrtle complains to Manny about her issues with being slapped on stage. Dorothy pretends to hit herself again, which knocks her off the bed and onto the floor. She eventually leaves the room, as Manny tries to convince Myrtle that it is not humiliating for her to get slapped as part of her role in the play. He tells her, "Actresses get slapped. It's a tradition . . . Now it's mandatory that you get hit. That's it. Now go to sleep. Right!" The camera holds close on a side view of Dorothy, who turns toward the camera, as Manny comes out of the bedroom and tells her about the accident at the theater, to which she responds, "Let's forget it. Let's not phony it up anymore."

In the above scene, Manny has a vested interest in reassuring Myrtle, who is distraught about the accident and also upset about a scene in the play where she gets slapped, which are contributing to her insomnia. At the same time that he is expressing his love for Myrtle, Manny finds himself in an awkward situation vis-à-vis his wife, who is annoyed by Myrtle's phone call and resents the fact that Manny is doting on his unstable female lead actor. Dorothy is, of course, also jealous, which is why she attempts to distract him during the phone call.

Yet it is the beginning of the scene before Myrtle calls that establishes the rocky relationship between the married couple. After Manny hangs up the phone and brings up the death of the woman in the car accident at the theater, Dorothy shows no empathy. Instead, her line—"Let's forget it. Let's not phony it up anymore"—is ambiguous. Does it refer to his conversation with Myrtle or their relationship? Whatever the case, the dialogue between Manny and Dorothy consists of a series of seeming non sequiturs. Manny complains that he is getting bored and somber. After Dorothy asks him whether he wants ice in his drink, he suddenly tells her, "Yeah. There's no humor anymore and all the glamour's dead. You notice that? I can't even stand how they come to rehearsal. They come to rehearsal dressed in terrible clothes." What is the connection between getting bored and somber and his general contention that there is no humor anymore and that glamour is dead, which he then links to the fact that people come to rehearsal dressed in terrible clothes? It represents a kind of free association, but the last thing one expects is for Dorothy to respond that she is dying and follow it with a pointed reference to the emotional crises that have apparently plagued their marriage.

The subtext of the scene involves the mutual unhappiness of this married couple, as they sit drinking together in a hotel room in the wee hours of the morning. Manny makes it clear to Dorothy that his life depends on the success of the play. He wants her to help Myrtle, but this is a preposterous idea and he knows it. It is also a way of indirectly blaming Dorothy for the situation in which he finds himself. Yet the point is that we have no sense of the direction the scene is taking while it is unfolding, especially Dorothy's use of improvised pantomime to convey her sense of frustration gesturally. According to Gazzara, he had no idea how the scene would be played, so Dorothy's actions caught him totally by surprise.[37]

Lampert has suggested that the lines in the scene were actually scripted and that Cassavetes expected the actors to say the written lines. As she put it, "The actors always spoke the dialogue John wrote. One did not make up one's lines despite the appearance of spontaneity."[38] Although it is generally true that Cassavetes preferred his actors to say the dialogue rather than to ad-lib, the real question is how that sense of spontaneity was achieved. Following what he considered to be a conventional performance by Lampert and Gazzara, Cassavetes had the two actors sit and read the newspaper with the camera rolling until they felt ready to begin, which wasted five minutes of footage. According to Lampert, "Gradually, when our defences had worn away, he signalled us to begin again . . . Thus, in spending waste film, John had bought freedom for the actors."[39]

Not all actors responded to Cassavetes's unorthodox methods. Joan Blondell, a Hollywood star who was used to conventional acting, reportedly became unnerved and intimidated by Cassavetes's approach, which aims to blend actor and role. Carney comments:

> Because of the realism of Cassavetes' dialogue, his toleration of actors' deviations from the script (and his introduction of frequent last-minute changes) and his willingness to keep the camera running with several takes sometimes being done in succession, Blondell said she couldn't tell when the actors were talking privately among themselves and when they were actually saying their lines in a scene. She couldn't tell when a scene started or stopped; what was life and what was film.[40]

According to fellow performers Gazzara and Rowlands, Blondell "was supposed to do nothing, but relax," suggesting a state of being rather than acting.[41] It is understandable why some actors might become confused under such conditions. Yet viewers often have similar problems distinguishing between what is performed and what is real, which is evident in the scene that follows—the rehearsal scene where Myrtle gets slapped.

On stage, Manny begins by demonstrating how they will perform the slap. As her colead, Maurice (Cassavetes), goes to strike Myrtle, she recoils and cries out before taking a number of swings at him in retaliation. Manny tries to comfort the emotionally distraught Myrtle. He reassures her that he loves her, as Dorothy watches from far back in the nearly empty theater. The two actors run through the scene again, in which Maurice makes a series of accusations about Myrtle involving dope, alcohol, other men, and her fear of aging. When he raises his hand to hit her, Myrtle suddenly drops to the floor. The camera pans to Manny and to the playwright and producer sitting up front. Myrtle lies on the stage for thirty seconds. As the camera focuses close on her, she clasps her hands to her chest and yells, "No. No more. No!" David, the producer, at first claps, but when Myrtle continues to vent, he comforts her and suggests calling a doctor. Manny, however, orders him off the stage. He insists that Myrtle is merely tired.

When they attempt the scene again, Maurice impulsively slaps Myrtle, who crumples to the floor and laughs like a crazy person—so hard that tears form in her eyes. When she finally stands up, the playwright, Sarah Goode (Blondell), fails to find the humor in Myrtle's antics. When Goode confronts her about the play, Myrtle confesses that the character she's playing is very alien to her. She tells the older playwright, "I somehow . . . I seem to have lost the reality of the reality." As she says this, the fingers of her left hand fidget noticeably. When Goode suggests that, given her age, it is too late to love, Myrtle criticizes the play for lacking the element of hope.

Part of what makes the scene compelling is its sense of duration. It lasts for eight minutes and Rowlands acts as if she has all the time in the world. The dialogue is more conventional and logical than that of the previous hotel scene, but Myrtle's response to the slap is what confuses the boundary between the performed and the real. When she goes after Cassavetes, it seems to be for real, especially because she tries to hit him back, not once but multiple times. After she lies down on the stage, Rowlands stays there nearly half a minute. Is she actually hurt or in the process of losing it?

FIGURE 2.4 Myrtle collapses on stage during rehearsal, *Opening Night*

Most scenes in dramatic films proceed through a series of beats, with the action rising at predictable points, toward some type of dramatic climax, often where the subtext rises to the surface, but that is not at all the way that Cassavetes structures his scenes. Part of the fascination of what is transpiring is the way it is playing with aspects of the lives of Cassavetes and Rowlands as a married couple, which echoes the marital strife in *Faces*, *A Woman Under the Influence*, and *Love Streams*. In fact, the slap itself was clearly autobiographical, recalling the scene in *Minnie and Moskowitz* where the crew members thought that Cassavetes had actually hurt Rowlands when he struck her multiple times in the role of her abusive married boyfriend. Cassavetes comments, "You know the scene in *Minnie and Moskowitz* when I slap Gena around? The crew thought it was real! They jumped up to restrain me. They gave me the worst looks after that scene! Gena is such a marvelous actress. She didn't get up off the floor after the take. She just lay there."[42] The second time Maurice attempts to slap Myrtle, she falls to the floor, cries out, and also stays there for a long period of screen time, which is what creates a sense of anxiety in the viewer.

A WOMAN UNDER THE INFLUENCE

A Woman Under the Influence (1974) is considered by many critics and scholars to be Cassavetes's best film.[43] In many ways, it embodies everything Cassavetes was striving for in his films. Independently produced against all odds, it proved that everyone in the industry was completely wrong about the kind of movie that audiences wanted to see. Although it was made using his normal working method, very little of it was ad-libbed. According to Cassavetes, "People have such a belief in the 'written' word. When they don't hear a 'written' word, particularly in my movies, they think it's improvised. It's not. Only two lines in *A Woman Under the Influence* were actually improvised. [Falk's 'ba-ba-ba' and Rowlands's driving instructions to her mother]."[44]

A Woman Under the Influence explores the relationship of a couple, Mabel and Nick Longhetti (Gena Rowlands and Peter Falk), with three young kids. As he did for each of his films after *Shadows*, Cassavetes wrote a lengthy script, but it was then up to the actors to give dimension to the characters and the story. According to the director, "Everything was discussed, nothing came from me alone. We write a lot of things that aren't in the movie, as background. So that when we got to the scene, you might rewrite on the spot, but we might have already gone in three, four, five, seven, eight, nineteen different versions of the scene."[45]

Cassavetes indicated that he was often surprised by the responses of both Rowlands and Falk. In discussing Falk's performance, Cassavetes claimed that the actor made a number of "peculiar" decisions in terms of his character. In the scene where the doctor comes to the house, the director suggests that Falk acquiesced and allowed his wife Mabel to go crazy rather than defend her. When Cassavetes asked Falk afterward why he didn't attempt to intervene, the actor claimed that he was reluctant to interfere with Rowlands's performance. Cassavetes notes, "That was a lie. Peter is a tremendously internal man, and I think he *wanted* her to be committed. I think he *wanted* her to go away. I don't think he recognized her worth because to him at that moment she was worthless. She wasn't behaving like he would behave so he didn't want her anymore. That is what *I* saw."[46]

Cassavetes's response is a testament to the unusual way he worked. He was not trying to give the viewer his own vision, but very much depended on the input of the actors because he wanted the film to reflect real life. According to Cassavetes, "Making a film is a mystery. If I knew anything about men and women to begin with, I wouldn't make it, because it would bore me."[47] He lived to be surprised and enlightened by whatever took place in front of the camera. In filming *A Woman Under the Influence*, Cassavetes used two cameras, long lenses, and wound up shooting a large amount of footage. The director estimated that he shot between 600,000 and 700,000 feet of 35 mm film, which amounted to between 110 and 130 hours of footage.[48] This represents an enormous shooting ratio for a typical fiction film. In a sense, Cassavetes shot *A Woman Under the Influence* like a documentary, using extended takes in order to capture the performances. The actors never knew when they were on camera, which helped to keep them focused on set. As the director points out, "Usually the actors don't know what's being shot. Even though we sometimes shoot very tight, they never know when the camera's going to swing on them, so everyone has to play every moment."[49]

In many ways, it is the tour-de-force acting of Rowlands that ultimately defines *A Woman Under the Influence*. As Tom Charity describes her performance, "There's turmoil in every gesture she makes. Under duress, her nervous insecurity fiddles and flinches in involuntary spasms; because she hasn't the language to articulate her desperation it comes out in guttural exclamations, splutters, digital semaphor, airs and affectations, a gurning grimace, or even chop-socky histrionics."[50] Somewhat surprisingly, it is in the pickup scene where she meets Garson that Rowlands's performance seems the most natural, and the scene where she greets her kids after returning home from the mental institution is absolutely gut-wrenching.

There are times, however, when Rowlands adds a stylized element to her overall character: a thumbs-up shrug accompanied by a verbal raspberry. It is a comedic gesture—a patterned use of artifice that gives a sense of tragedy to the character. Her gesture suggests a fragility that contrasts starkly with Nick's violent, even brutal response. Yet, in comparison to naturalism that Cassavetes strove for and often achieved in his early films—most notably in *Faces* and *Husbands*—the acting of Rowlands in *A Woman Under the Influence* is much more traditional and appears far less improvised. Given that, it is not at all surprising that, for her portrayal of Mabel, Rowlands received a nomination for an Academy Award, or that Cassavetes was also nominated for an Oscar for Best Director.

3

PLACE-BASED REALISM

Mackenzie, Loden, and Burnett

J ohn Cassavetes has always been associated with the New American
Cinema movement, even though the director distanced himself
from the New York-based group following the making of *Shadows*.
There were, however, other filmmakers in the period of the 1960s and '70s
whose work was not considered to be part of the discourse surrounding improvisation and alternative forms of scripting. For various reasons,
these filmmakers could be considered outliers. Kent Mackenzie, who was
based on the West Coast, made *The Exiles* in 1961 in relative obscurity,
even though the film shares an obvious connection to the work that Jonas
Mekas was championing in New York.

By the time Barbara Loden made *Wanda* in 1970, the New American
Cinema was more or less over. Charles Burnett's *Killer of Sheep*—which,
like *The Exiles*, was set in Los Angeles—came even later. All three films,
for whatever reason, did not receive the critical attention they deserved
at the time of their release. Yet, in retrospect, Mackenzie, Loden, and
Burnett made innovative films that deserve greater recognition for mining realism by capturing a documentary-like sense of place while dealing
with marginalized groups or individuals.

KENT MACKENZIE: *THE EXILES*

Until *The Exiles* (1961) was finally restored and released by Milestone Films, except for a handful of scholars and cinephiles, who knew that one of the most important Beat films featured American Indians in Los Angeles? Kent Mackenzie's film forces us to rethink the beginning of the modern independent film movement. It bears comparison to Lionel Rogosin's *On the Bowery* and Alfred Leslie and Robert Frank's Beat classic *Pull My Daisy*, especially in terms of its style and content. Its focus on cars, bars, gas stations, juke boxes, neon lights, and advertising recalls Frank's photographic essay, *The Americans*. *The Exiles* doesn't share the same snapshot aesthetic of Frank but rather incongruously harkens back to the pictorialism of Walker Evans's *American Photographs*, giving it the photographic texture of an even earlier time period.[1]

Mackenzie's film presents a similar view of alienation and anomie as the work of Robert Frank by concentrating on a group of American Indians adrift in the urban landscape of the Bunker Hill section of Los Angeles during the Eisenhower era. Jack Kerouac wrote in the introduction of *The Americans* that Frank "sucked a sad poem right out of America onto film, taking rank among the tragic poets of the world."[2] The same could be said for Mackenzie, but the difference is that for nearly fifty years his film languished in relative obscurity, even though, as Thom Andersen points out, "*The Exiles*, like *Killer of Sheep*, was a film that was always hiding in plain sight."[3]

Mackenzie, who went to film school at the University of Southern California, made an earlier documentary short, *Bunker Hill* (1956), about the decaying downtown Los Angeles neighborhood that was about to be razed by urban renewal. A year later, Mackenzie decided to shoot a more ambitious feature film about a group of American Indians who lived in the neighborhood. In 1958, he formally began production on the project, which ended up taking him three-and-a-half years to complete. In terms of his approach, there is an ethnographic quality to *The Exiles*. Mackenzie, an outsider to the American Indian subculture he was obsessively documenting, hung out with the film's main participants over this extended period of time. He involved them creatively in the project, followed them around, and recorded their everyday conversations.

Much of the dialogue in *The Exiles* was not recorded sync-sound but later dubbed in postproduction. It also includes voiceover narration from its three main characters—Yvonne, Homer, and Tommy—as well as a voiceover from outside the film. This latter voiceover occurs over the prologue that contains historical photographs of American Indians by Edward Curtis, who in an earlier era had attempted to document their traditional lifestyle before it disappeared. The prologue provides an historical context for the displacement we see in the film. It was partially the result of a voluntary government plan, the Urban Indian Relocation Program, which paid American Indians to relocate from the reservations to large cities, such as Los Angeles.

The dubbed dialogue, voiceover narration, and deliberate restaging of events for the camera could be criticized as heavy-handed techniques that detract from the authenticity of *The Exiles*. There are several scenes—the card game, for instance—in which the camera seems to be on the wrong person, but these potential flaws are minor when compared to Mackenzie's otherwise brilliant use of improvisational techniques. Although the credits on the film indicate that it was "written, produced, and directed by Mackenzie," at least according to John Morrill, one of the film's three cinematographers, "There was never any script."[4] Instead, Mackenzie wrote various outlines and even created a list of shots. These outlines did not contain any written dialogue but were intended to be observed case studies involving real people. Although Mackenzie thought of *The Exiles* as a "restaged" documentary in the poetic tradition of Robert Flaherty, the film, in fact, seems more like a "plotless" narrative rooted in realism. In many ways, it is exactly the type of cinema that Mekas was actively promoting during this period through his lavish praise of the first version of *Shadows*, *Pull My Daisy*, and *The Flower Thief* in his movie columns for the *Village Voice*.

Mackenzie was critical of both the social documentary and Hollywood narrative feature. He was not interested in creating a social documentary because he did not think that there was a simple solution to the plight of the American Indians hanging out on Main Street in Bunker Hill.

Mackenzie also believed that Hollywood theatrical films were inherently phony and did not bear any resemblance to real life. He wrote:

> In many types of films we saw events conspiring in a way that we had never seen in real life. People spoke to each other in a dramatic and philosophical manner that was alien to our experience. Men and women appeared more perfect and glamorous than any we had ever known. Actors used gestures and mannerisms that we had never observed on the street. Homes looked more sparkling and orderly than any we had ever lived in. We saw glossy lighting effects that we had never seen away from the screen and heard the swelling strains of orchestral music playing behind actions in a way that it never did in our own lives.[5]

In response, Mackenzie became determined to make a more realistic type of fictional film.

Mackenzie wanted to avoid the dramatic conflict/resolution structure that lies at the heart of Hollywood narrative features. In contrast, his film would be largely impressionistic and contain a series of observed situations rather than dramatically charged incidents. His cast would improvise their own dialogue during rehearsals. Their costumes would be the clothes they wore. The locations would be determined by the places his characters inhabited, and each location would be respected for its specific sound quality. The film would be shot in sequence, making it easier for his inexperienced cast.[6]

Mackenzie eschewed writing a conventional screenplay in favor of improvisation. He believed that what resulted from improvised rehearsals with his nonprofessional cast was far better than anything that he might have written in advance, mainly because it yielded a certain specificity—gestures, physical movements, and visual details—that he could not have anticipated otherwise. As he put it, "Every detail of their existence was important, and the way a beer bottle looked under a particular kind of bar light or the manner in which someone opened a pack of cigarettes seemed fully as significant as any other more conventional dramatic event or detail."[7] Mackenzie came to understand that his role as director was less about controlling the action and elements of the production than in creating a relaxed environment for his actors simply to be themselves. As he put it, "Essentially, the whole process of 'directing' the non-professional players in *The Exiles* was a painstaking and detailed process of building the environment they were used to in front of the camera."[8]

Due to Mackenzie's unorthodox approach, the film's naturalistic dialogue reflects the way his American Indian performers spoke. It doesn't sound like scripted movie dialogue, which is more to the point and direct, as well as more purposeful and expository in nature. Mackenzie is again drawing upon his own observations about everyday human conversations:

> Rather than spouting their philosophies of life in meaningful speech at every opportunity, most people that I had observed usually seemed to express themselves in an indirect manner and apparently without conscious thought. They seldom spoke of important matters directly; they seldom spoke clearly and coherently when they did speak; and their everyday language was full of overlaps, interruptions, and communications through looks, gestures, and shrugs. Many sentences were not completed because the opening statement made the end understood. What a person said seemed less important than how he said it.[9]

Like Cassavetes, Mackenzie blocked his scenes according to what would be more natural and comfortable for the actors.[10] Although Mackenzie used an improvisational approach, he did not shoot random footage of the film's participants. He wrote: "I think we felt from the beginning that expressing an inner reality was not merely a matter of more and more naturalistic recording of outer reality, but a question of careful selection and emphasis. As a result, there are only two sequences in *The Exiles* which were not rehearsed and staged."[11] One is the drunken scene and fight at the Columbine bar; the other depicts the police making an arrest at bar time, which was filmed with a hidden camera.

Mackenzie was very careful about casting. He made it a point to get to know his performers before selecting them. The exception was Claudine, whom he had only met twenty minutes prior to shooting the exteriors of the scene at the Ritz bar. According to Mackenzie:

> I had been turning down girl after girl that Tommy had been bringing in when he finally found Claudine that evening. She was completely natural from the beginning, did three long dialog scenes in the bar the second night, and was always ready and relaxed. I think she was just this way

under any circumstances—a sort of female Tommy. In general, of course, all the cast seemed much more relaxed and less inhibited than someone from the middle class.[12]

Despite the fact that Mackenzie was scrupulous about the individuals he cast, he nevertheless experienced numerous problems during the lengthy production of the film. A number of his performers wound up in jail during the shooting, which caused continuity problems or forced him to recast certain parts. In addition, according to the director, "Characters had their features changed in fights, or the costumes they were supposed to wear in the film ripped from their limbs in brawls, or stolen while they lay drunk. Involvement in the filming became so intense for some cast members that staged fights erupted into real brawls."[13] Homer Nish also quit the production for ten months following the fight scene at the Columbine bar, because, as Mackenzie speculates, "it was getting too close to his own life."[14] Mackenzie was at a loss for how to restructure the film without one of his three main characters. By sheer luck and a change of heart, Nish unexpectedly returned while the director and crew were shooting retakes of the scene at Hill X, and he was able to be incorporated into that important scene.

The resulting final film is a visually stunning twelve-hour portrait of down-and-out American Indians, who seem not so different from the Beat characters that populate *Pull My Daisy*. The Beats celebrated the social outcasts or underdogs of society, and no one could be more marginal than the likes of Yvonne Williams, Homer Nish, and Tommy Reynolds—the three principal characters Mackenzie follows in *The Exiles*. Ironically, the men seem to share the same sexist values as their fellow white hipsters, especially in their concern with being free from responsibility and predilection for male camaraderie. The women, much like Milo's wife in *Pull My Daisy*, are merely there to administer to the needs of their husbands and children, to suffer physical abuse, or to dole out cash, while the guys get to carouse with friends, pick up women, and engage in all-night drinking binges.

As much a city portrait of downtown Los Angeles as one of an American Indian subculture trying to survive within it, the film introduces us to the pensive and pregnant Yvonne as she shops at a public market. Yvonne is happy that she'll at least get to have a child she wants even if the rest of her life, especially her marriage to Homer, is already imbued with a sense of resignation and disappointment. Yvonne's arrival home with the groceries is met with utter silence by Homer and his friend, who sit reading comic books and listening to rock music, while another guy sleeps on the bed. As she makes dinner for the men, Yvonne conjectures, "If I hadn't met him, I probably would have been all right now maybe. I would have had what I wanted." Williams was not actually married to Nish in real life—she was actually in a relationship with Clifford Ray Sam, who plays Cliff—but when viewers assumed the former in test screenings, Mackenzie decided to accept this discrepancy from reality, so that Nish plays her husband in the film.

Homer provides his own narration by explaining, "When I want [to] go into a bar, I don't like to just sit around, you know. I like to . . . have some kind of excitement . . . get in a fight or something." He discusses being a high school dropout, coinciding with his starting to drink, which accelerates after he gets discharged from the military. As Homer reads a letter from home, the film cuts from a snapshot of his folks to his actual family

FIGURE 3.1 Homer and friends get drunk at the Columbine bar, *The Exiles*

in Arizona, providing a striking contrast to his current life in Los Angeles as he waits in front of a liquor store for his friend Rico to buy more booze. Homer later claims, "Truthfully, man, I think . . . white people got more troubles than the Indians do, you know. They usually have . . . something on their mind all the time. My people mostly roamed all over the place two, three hundred years ago, before the white man came in. I'd rather be in that time than I would, you know, in this time now."

Homer and his buddies still roam like their ancestors, but it is to each other's houses to get cash and gamble at cards, as well as to the bars. Although Yvonne remains on the straight path, her disillusionment makes her more vulnerable, even as she reaffirms her resolve not to become like the others. She confesses, "Well, I stopped going to church and all that already, but I haven't started drinking or hanging around Main Street yet. No, that will never come for me." Yvonne hopes that Homer will change once she has the baby, but we sense that she already knows in her heart that this is unlikely. Instead of going home, Yvonne visits her friend Marilyn and sleeps over there to forget her loneliness. After the bars close, both Homer and Tommy end up on Hill X, a haunt where American Indians go to drum, sing traditional songs, and drink to excess. At dawn, Yvonne wakes up and watches out the window as Homer and the other drunken revelers stumble along and finally disappear down the street on the way to her house.

Despite being screened at the prestigious Venice Film Festival and other major festivals, The Exiles was unable to gain a theatrical release in the United States. This is hardly surprising given the fact that Hollywood was a closed system. It was virtually impossible for independents to get their work shown in commercial theaters at the time, especially a film as unconventional and challenging as The Exiles. Mackenzie made only two major features in a brief career before passing away in 1980 at the age of fifty. His other feature, Saturday Morning (1970), a documentary about a teenage encounter group, also had difficulty being commercially released, but it did eventually receive very limited theatrical exhibition the following year.

The arduous nature of making The Exiles and its failure to find a theatrical release apparently took its toll on Mackenzie, who grew disillusioned with the approach he had developed in the film. In his subsequent MA thesis about the production, he ends by repudiating precisely the aspects of The Exiles that make it such a groundbreaking film. Mackenzie attributes many of the problems he encountered to his own lack of experience and lack of control over the production. In considering future film work, he writes: "I would like to see much more adequate research and preparation than we had on *The Exiles*, including a script, storyboarding with stills, careful production pre-planning, and possibly an intensive period of rehearsals with the cast and camera crew prior to shooting."[15] At the same time, he questions the degree to which conventional techniques and even professional actors might be able to be incorporated into the production in order to make a better film. Mackenzie also speculates that attempting to deal authentically with the lives of real people might ultimately be the biggest liability because "It may limit the depth to which a subject can be probed or the control which can be exercised over the selection of the images."[16]

On the positive side, Mackenzie believed that recent changes in technology—faster film stocks and lenses, better sound and lighting equipment, and more portable, lightweight cameras—would have a positive impact on future filmmaking efforts rooted in realism. He also cites the example of other international filmmakers, such as those associated with the French New Wave and the work of John Cassavetes, as having a revolutionary effect on the art of cinema. Mackenzie concludes:

> Although financing for independent projects is still very difficult to obtain, and it continues to be hard for young people to work their way into any position of freedom in the film business, all of these developments in films and equipment seem to be making it much easier for someone to consider experimenting today in the direction which we felt impelled to explore with *The Exiles*.[17]

Unfortunately, Mackenzie did not live long enough to see his first feature recognized as one of the major early works of American indie cinema.

Despite the fact that this sobering portrait of American Indians is based on a painful stereotype involving alcoholism, Mackenzie's empathy for his characters manages to supersede political correctness. Sherman Alexie has defended the film as an important document of a neglected aspect of American Indian urban culture. He told Dennis Lim, "It's a little problematic in that it's a white guy's movie about us. But in learning how the film was made, I think people will discover it was truly collaborative.

The filmmakers ended up in the position of witness as much as creator.[18] Seeing *The Exiles* makes us view other indie films, such as Charles Burnett's restored masterpiece *Killer of Sheep* (1977)—a work that also documents a minority neighborhood in Los Angeles by utilizing poetic realism, nonprofessional actors, and visual storytelling—in an entirely new light. The unfortunate neglect of Mackenzie's *The Exiles* had consequences. Burnett explains in an interview: "[Mackenzie] was ten years ahead of me. I started in the late sixties and he started in the late fifties. He had already worked out his aesthetics, but I have only heard about him recently. It's too bad he wasn't known. I think it would have saved all of us a lot of experimenting."[19]

With the passing of time, Mackenzie's *The Exiles* has become a memory piece—an ode to a place that no longer exists. There is an irony in the fact that the government first encouraged the American Indians to relocate from reservations to poor urban neighborhoods such as Bunker Hill only to bulldoze them under the guise of urban renewal, adding another layer of exile to those already exiled in their own country. Shot on 35 mm, running a mere seventy-two minutes, and completed the same year as the infamous First Statement of the New American Cinema Group in New York, *The Exiles* now takes its place among the seminal films of the independent film movement, alongside works by Morris Engel, John Cassavetes, Alfred Leslie and Robert Frank, Shirley Clarke, Ron Rice, Lionel Rogosin, and Jonas Mekas.

BARBARA LODEN: *WANDA*

Cassavetes's rehearsed approach represents an important strain of improvisation in American indie cinema. Kent Mackenzie's ethnographic engagement with his subjects provides another. Like Cassavetes, Barbara Loden was also an actor, but she used a different strategy in her first and only film, *Wanda* (1970), in which she plays the lead role. *Wanda* won the Critics' Prize at the Venice Film Festival, had a limited theatrical run in New York City, but failed to gain wider distribution. The film was made for $115,000, shot on 16 mm and later blown up to 35 mm, which accounts for its gritty look.[20]

Loden teamed with documentary filmmaker Nick Proferes, who had previously worked with D. A. Pennebaker (and as a cinematographer on Norman Mailer's *Beyond the Law* and *Maidstone*), and used only a skeletal crew. With the exception of Michael Higgins, the actor who plays Mr. Dennis, she otherwise used a cast of mostly nonprofessional performers. Loden explained, "Actors would have made the parts more interesting perhaps, but they would not have been real. You are always conscious that you're watching an actor, especially in character parts. So the people I used in the film—the factory boss, the traveling salesman, almost everybody that Wanda meets—all of these people are real."[21] Necessity mandated that there was no time for storyboards or for the performers to rehearse, resulting in a more spontaneous form of improvisation.[22]

Wanda was shot in a documentary style by Proferes, taking advantage of public locations where the "extras" in the background seem totally unaware of the camera. Although *Wanda* contains much less dialogue than a traditional feature-length narrative, Loden nevertheless wrote a screenplay, even though the film turned out to be largely improvised. Some of the reasons for this were the result of the film's low budget, her use of nonprofessional actors, and the DIY approach she was forced to adopt during production, especially regarding the performers and locations. As Loden indicates, "The movie itself started growing and becoming a separate entity—quite different from the script that I had planned out. It was improvised in the sense that I didn't know exactly what I was going to do, what I would be able to do, or even what I was supposed to do."[23]

In many improvised films, the director takes one of the main acting roles. Examples include John Cassavetes, Norman Mailer, William Greaves, Joe Swanberg, and Nathan Silver. In many ways, Loden's approach in *Wanda* is exactly the opposite of Gilles Mouëllic's concept of "directing from the inside," in which the director controls the dynamic of improvisation from a position within the film.[24] Her character is so lacking in agency that her responses to situations are entirely reactive. Wanda rarely initiates anything but instead gets swept along by situations and events that happen to her. Loden indicated that there was a strong autobiographical element in this: "I had no identity of my own. I just became whatever I thought people wanted me to become. Like Wanda I had no focal point in my life."[25] Loden responds to other characters—her husband, her employer, the traveling salesman with whom she has a one-night stand, Mr. Dennis, or the soldier at the end—with such an indelible sense of self-loathing and blank identity that she almost single-handedly carries the film through her understated performance.

Set in the depressed anthracite coal-mining area around the city of Scranton in Northeastern Pennsylvania, *Wanda* presents a character study of a downtrodden woman named Wanda Goronski whose desperate life manages to plummet into even greater freefall. In one of the early scenes, we view Wanda in an extreme wide shot as she trudges slowly across a vast expanse of coalfields on her way to collect her paycheck. The shot zooms slowly closer, and then pans for nearly two minutes. The sustained image of Wanda—a small white figure moving through an environmentally ravaged landscape reminiscent of an Edward Burtynsky photograph—becomes a trope for her life.

Wanda is married to a coal miner and has two kids, but her estranged husband has already taken up with another woman and wants a divorce. Her hair in curlers and smoking a cigarette, she turns up late for court and offers no rebuttal to her husband's myriad complaints about her inadequacies as both a wife and parent. In fact, to the judge's surprise, she readily agrees that her husband and kids would be better off without her. Wanda subsequently gets involved with a petty thief, Norman Dennis. After Wanda learns that he is wanted for the robbery, she becomes a willing captive to Dennis, a cruel and abusive psychopath who is addicted to painkillers as a result of constant headaches. Wanda refers to him as "Mr. Dennis," reflecting misplaced deference as well as his emotional distance from her. Mr. Dennis is not so much the romantic lead but rather the antithesis of one, undercutting similarities to Arthur Penn's highly romanticized *Bonnie and Clyde* (1967). Loden bristled at any comparison to the earlier film, insisting "*Wanda* is an anti-*Bonnie and Clyde* movie."[26]

Barbara Loden came from a poor rural family in North Carolina and was raised by her grandparents. In an effort to escape her dead-end roots, she arrived in New York City at age seventeen and set about attempting to transform her life. She worked as a pin-up model and danced at the famed Copacabana nightclub. She studied Method acting with Paul Mann and eventually found parts in plays, television, and films—most notably, *Wild River* (1960) and *Splendor in the Grass* (1961)—and married the much older and established producer and director Elia Kazan in 1967.

The genesis of the idea for *Wanda* derived from a newspaper account of a woman named Alma Malone who thanked the judge for sending her to prison.[27] According to Loden, "I got the idea from a newspaper item some years ago. In the *Sunday Daily News* they used to have a feature called, 'Did Justice Triumph?' They had true stories about murders and criminals, and this was the story of a girl who was an accomplice to a bank robber."[28] What fascinated Loden about the story was trying to fathom the motivation of such a person: "I was intrigued by this girl's psychology, how she'd arrived at that state. I thought, 'What kind of person would welcome being sent to prison for twenty years?' "[29] Although the basic plot elements of the bank robbery gone awry derived from the newspaper account, Loden based the character of Wanda on herself. As she explains, "I made up the girl's character based on this statement that she made, and also from myself really, ways that I had felt in my life. It was all from my imagination or my feelings."[30]

In his autobiography, Kazan writes, "One day years ago, [Loden] gave me a newspaper clipping, said it would make a good movie. I thought it skimpy, but when she asked me to help her turn it into a screenplay, I roughed out something in three days. It was called 'The Gray World.' Then she went to work on it, and it became *Wanda*, in all essentials her screenplay."[31] Despite taking claim for writing an initial draft of the screenplay, Kazan nevertheless credits the eventual script for *Wanda* as being entirely Loden's work. Other than certain elements of the plot, however, the screenplay is of little consequence to the final film because Loden ended up substantially deviating from it during production.

According to Kazan, "Nick Proferes and Barbara were well matched. He supplied everything she lacked, and vice versa. They made the film in a way that fascinated me, largely improvisational, departing at every turn from the script."[32] Loden had no experience as a film director, but she understood that the French New Wave and American "underground"— works by the Mekas brothers, Shirley Clarke, and Andy Warhol—had already created a model for what was possible. It eventually dawned on her: "Just take a camera and film it: Why couldn't I do that?"[33] Even so, Loden secretly hoped to find someone else to direct her script. She told Kevin Thomas: "I just wanted to play the part as an actress. But I never met anybody who understood it as well as I did. It came down to being a necessity: if I wanted to get it done I'd have to do it myself."[34]

Kazan, who cast Loden in Arthur Miller's stage play *After the Fall* (1964), was critical of her range as a performer, while indirectly praising her considerable acting abilities:

> But in the arts, versatility is an overvalued asset. Barbara could range from A to B, but within that range she went deep. Every value the great British academies of acting value—and correctly value—she lacked. Her voice was squeaky, her body without notable grace, she had very little variety and less brains than cunning. What she did have was passion, and in the right role, there was no one like her.[35]

Kazan is discussing Loden's acting skills in a traditional play, for which she received a Tony Award. Yet the acting values of great British academies have no bearing on Loden's abilities to play a character with which she so obviously identified.

Kazan emphasizes Loden's unique ability to improvise a character. In conversation with the French writer and filmmaker Marguerite Duras, Kazan discusses the fact that, for Loden, scripts were never fixed but fluid, providing an opportunity for her to breathe life into parts through improvisation: "Her acting career showed her that no script was permanent. For her, there was always an element of improvisation . . . a surprise, in what she was doing. The only one, as far as I know, who was like that is Brando when he was young. He never knew exactly what he was going to say, therefore everything would come out of his mouth very alive."[36]

Duras, who did not know Loden personally, hints at another aspect of *Wanda* that she found intriguing when she comments, "She's even more real in the movie than in life; it's completely miraculous."[37] Duras suggests this quality did not have to do with Loden's acting, an odd claim, which is disputed by Cristina Álvarez López and Adrian Martin who argue that "it is indeed through a superb conjunction of body, behaviour and space that Loden the actor and Loden the director achieve this heightened quality, this revelatory laying-bare of Wanda's presence on screen."[38] The authors also comment about the difference between Loden's acting style and the improv approach of Cassavetes, of which she was critical. The authors write: "Where the force of Cassavetes' cinema is externalised, melodramatic, explosive, often (in both the psychoanalytic and everyday senses) *hysterical*, Barbara Loden chose to explore a more mysterious and *implosive* energy.[39] In psychodramatic terms, the heightened internalized quality in her performance could be explained as stemming from Loden's intense self-identification with the character.

In the film, Wanda and Mr. Dennis provide a stark contrast. He is completely motivated by a desire for money, whereas she is totally passive in comparison. As Loden explained, "This apathy is her defense, her way of surviving."[40] In the scene in the open field where Mr. Dennis drapes his coat over her shoulders and suggests her hair looks terrible and she should get a hat, she questions where she would get the money:

Wanda: I don't have anything. Never did have anything. Never will have anything.
Mr. Dennis: You're stupid.
Wanda: I'm stupid?
Mr. Dennis: You don't want anything, you'll never have anything. You're nothing. You may as well be dead. You're not even a citizen of the United States.
Wanda: I guess I'm dead then.
Mr. Dennis: What do you mean? Is that what you want to be? Dead?

Their conversation, reflecting their radically opposed views of life, is suddenly interrupted by a remote-controlled toy plane flying overhead.

The scene of the toy plane was improvised during shooting and represents a serendipitous event that Loden and Proferes were able to incorporate into the film. As the plane flies away, Mr. Dennis, now holding a bottle of liquor in his hand, chases after it. He waves his hands at the plane and yells, "Come here! Come back here!" He then runs back and stands on top of his car, shouting and frantically waving at the model plane that glides and dives overhead. He yells again, "Hey, come here!" Mr. Dennis turns to Wanda, who sits on the car, and suddenly exclaims with a sense of frustration in his voice, "Why didn't you get a hat?"

In discussing the scene, Loden commented in an interview: "Actually, the airplane sequence just happened that way and we thought, 'Well, maybe we can use it. Maybe somebody will think it's symbolic.' I think it's a Don Quixote image where Mr. Dennis is flailing at imaginary things against him or reaching for something unattainable. The unattainable object just happens to be a toy airplane buzzing over his head."[41] Symbolic

FIGURE 3.2 Mr. Dennis (*offscreen*) criticizes Wanda's hair, *Wanda*

or not, it is the one scene where Mr. Dennis lets loose in an unhinged sort of way—as if his inner demons are suddenly being released—even though there is a sense of implicit blame in his voice when he unexpectedly returns to the issue of Wanda's need for a hat.

Loden admitted that the lack of dialogue, especially for her character, was intentional: "I tried not to explain things too much in the film, not to be too explicit, not to be too verbal. My subject matter is of people who are not too verbal and not aware of their condition."[42] In the scenes in court and at the dress factory, when confronted with decisions that negatively impact Wanda's life, Loden's response is to create long awkward pauses, blink repeatedly, swallow her sentences, stammer slightly, avert her eyes, give looks of bemusement, or stare straight ahead nervously, as if she's not quite comprehending the gist of what is being said to her. In terms of body language, when put on the spot, she has a tendency to fidget. Her natural expression is one of apology. In her interactions with others, one has the sense that she would prefer to become invisible.

Mr. Dennis behaves like a bully. In the restaurant shortly after they meet, he remains taciturn, except to tell Wanda to wipe spaghetti sauce from her mouth. As the two lie in bed, he turns his body away from her.

Mr. Dennis does not even care to know her name. Noticing that he is wearing a wedding ring, Wanda asks, "Are you married?" He responds, "I don't like nosy people!" She reaches over and touches him, but he recoils and snaps, "Look, don't touch my head!" When she explains that she's only trying to be friendly, he barks, "I don't like friendly people." He then orders her to get him something to eat. His gruff demeanor toward Wanda becomes the weapon he uses to control someone he perceives as weak and dependent.

Despite his abusive behavior, Wanda latches on to him because she has no other options. After reading the account of the bar robbery as they are driving in a car Mr. Dennis has just stolen, she asks, "Hey, what are you trying to get me into? . . . Huh?" He pulls over, opens the car door, and shouts, "Get out!" Wanda stares at him, then at the open car door, and back at him before she says in a very childlike way, "I didn't do anything." Once she closes the car door, her fate is sealed. Unfortunately, Wanda's escapade with Mr. Dennis turns out to be short-lived. After he is unceremoniously gunned down robbing the bank, Wanda is back on her own once again so that, by the film's end, her life has managed to come full circle.

CHARLES BURNETT: *KILLER OF SHEEP*

The highly verbal films of Cassavetes privilege performance over more aesthetic concerns. Yet other indie films that employ improvisation, such as *Little Fugitive, On the Bowery, The Flower Thief, The Exiles,* and *Wanda,* also focus on the cinematic aspects of the moving image. While Cassavetes continued to explore his actor-centric cinema in the 1970s, Charles Burnett made a remarkable debut film that epitomized the tendency to mine the visual aspects of cinema by using a spare script and turning the camera on his own neighborhood. Born in Vicksburg, Mississippi, Burnett grew up in South Central Los Angeles, the scene of the 1965 Watts riots in which thirty-four people were killed and over a thousand people were injured. Burnett was part of a group of African American filmmakers—Haile Gerima, Julie Dash, and Billy Woodberry, among them—who came out of the UCLA film program during the blaxploitation years of the 1970s, and became associated with a movement that became known as the L.A. Rebellion. While completing his MFA, Burnett received the Louis B. Mayer grant for the most promising thesis film, which became *Killer of Sheep*, a film which remained largely unseen by the general public for several years.

Burnett considers *Killer of Sheep* to be "practically an ethnographic film" in a similar manner to Kent Mackenzie's *The Exiles*, adding, "And at the same time, I didn't want to reduce the complexity of the real to a simple plot."[43] Burnett shot the film using a highly unorthodox method. He cast friends and people from his neighborhood to be in the film, with the exception of Henry G. Sanders. Sanders, however, was not the director's first choice; necessity forced Burnett to cast a professional actor in the lead role. He explains, "At the beginning I wanted to use only non-professionals, people from the community. But the man I wanted to play the role of Stan was in prison, so I had to use an actor, Henry Sanders. The other characters are interpreted by people from the community, which forced us to film on the weekends."[44]

Burnett experienced problems with his actors similar to what Mackenzie encountered in making *The Exiles*, especially because his non-professional performers were working on the film in their spare time and often failed to show up for scheduled shoots. This, in turn, caused problems with Burnett's professional crew members, who were recruited from UCLA. They became impatient at having to wait around for the actors, forcing Burnett to replace them: "So I used other people for the technical team: myself, the actors and the children. They were very young, but they did the sound, helped with the lighting . . . 90 percent of the movie was made with children. But this way of working, on weekends, over a long period of time with non-professionals, affected the structure of the movie, more than I would have wanted it to."[45] Although Burnett's aim was for the film's "texture to be rough," the final result wound up being far more primitive than he imagined. This worked for his purposes, however, which was to document his community at a particular moment in time. Burnett comments, "This movie was also made to preserve, to write down in the memory. In music, in the thirties and forties, we had blues; what I tried to do here is to preserve a certain form of life, to record it."[46]

The protagonist of Burnett's *Killer of Sheep*, Stan (Sanders), who works in a slaughterhouse, closely resembles Loden's passive main character, Wanda Goronski, in terms of agency. As a result of being subjected to the everyday horrors of his environment, Stan suffers from insomnia, impotence, and a growing sense of depression about the futility of his life. He is so beaten down by life's daily grind and by the dehumanizing effects of his job that he suffers from inertia. Given the social milieu that Burnett portrays, it is certainly not hard to understand why. *Killer of Sheep* depicts the physical violence and the sense of despair and hopelessness that pervades life in the ghetto. It provides a glimpse of a world many viewers do not know anything about, especially because, for the most part, they are never given an opportunity to see this type of representation of the black experience in mainstream Hollywood cinema, which, as Burnett laments, only perpetuates stereotypes.[47]

When Stan complains to a friend named Oscar early in the film that he's working himself into his own hell—he cannot sleep at night and does not have peace of mind—Oscar responds, "Why don't you kill yourself; you'll be a lot happier. Go out like Johnny Ace." When Stan presses a warm cup of coffee to his cheek and suggests that it reminds him of making love to a woman, another friend, Bracy, answers: "Myself, I don't go for women who got malaria." Various threats surface as Stan struggles against the travails of his day-to-day existence. Although Burnett relied upon a script and storyboards, when he was asked about the use of improvisation in *Killer of Sheep*, he indicates, "there were moments of improvisation, like Kaycee yelling at those guys on the porch. And in the car, I just kind of gave a general direction and let them say whatever they wanted . . . It's supposed to be a naturalistic sort of thing. The idea was supposed to be just fit in, do what you do normally. It's a story of people living, each moment counts."[48]

In the scene on the porch, two acquaintances, Scooter and Smoke, attempt to get Stan to join them in some type of criminal activity that involves murder. When Stan's wife (Kaycee Moore) overhears them, she confronts the two men:

Stan's Wife: Why you always want to hurt somebody?
> *Scooter looks around to see if she might be talking with someone else.*
Scooter: Who me? That's the way nature is. I mean, an animal has his teeth and a man has his fists. That's the way I was brought up, god damn me.
Smoke: Right on.

Scooter: I mean, when a man's got scars on his mug from dealing with son of a bitches every day for his natural life. Ain't nobody going over this nigger, just dry long so. Now me and Smoke here, we're taking our issue. You be a man if you can, Stan.

Stan's Wife: Wait! You wait just one minute! You talk about being a man and standing up. Don't you know there's more to it than with your fists, the scars on your mug, you talking about an animal? Or what? You think you're still in the bush or some damn where? You're here. You use your brain; that's what you use. Both of you nothing ass niggers got a lot of nerve coming over here doing some shit like that.[49]

Burnett explains how the scene came to be improvised: "We tried to do this thing on the porch with Kaycee. We had it written and then it was rather not as effective, not as exciting. And Kaycee is very good at challenging people and creating this tension and so . . . just let her be herself, let her be Kaycee Moore. She's very good at that."[50] The resulting scene has an intensity that derived from Moore's volatile response and moral

FIGURE 3.3 Stan's wife (Kaycee Moore) berates Scooter and Smoke, *Killer of Sheep*

indignation at Scooter and Smoke's attempt to implicate her fictional husband, Stan, in a crime.

Scooter's equation of masculinity with violence takes on bitterly ironic overtones because Stan's job and depression cause him to lose his sexual drive, driving an emotional wedge between him and his wife. Stan's wife thwarts Scooter and Smoke's attempt to involve Stan in their murder plans, but the scene underscores the constant temptations for someone like Stan, who later denies his own poverty. He claims that he gives things to the Salvation Army and compares himself to other neighbors less fortunate than him. Stan tells Bracy, "You want to see somebody that's poor, now you go around and look at Walter's. Now they be sitting over an oven with nothing but a coat on, and sitting around rubbing their knees, all day eating nothing but wild greens picked out of a vacant lot. No, that ain't me and damn sure won't be."

This discussion of poverty causes Stan to make one attempt to take action, which provides the only semblance of a plot thread in an otherwise impressionistic film consisting of a series of vignettes. Right after this, he tells another friend, Gene, who wants to better himself by getting a car, "Tomorrow after I cash my check, let's go over to Silbo's and buy that motor and put it in." True to his word, Stan cashes his check at the liquor store, and he and Gene show up at Silbo's to dicker over the price of the motor. While there, Silbo's nephew lies on the floor with a large white bandage wrapped around his head. When Gene asks what happened, it turns out that two men beat him up, and one kicked him in the face. After Stan asks why, the man answers, "He didn't have nothing else to do with his hands and feet, nigger." The nephew later makes crass sexual remarks to a woman named Delores, whose later response—"You about as tasteless as a carrot"—turns out to be one of the best lines in the film. Delores follows this by also kicking the injured man in his head. In the midst of the ensuing ruckus, Silbo agrees to take fifteen dollars for the motor.

Stan and Gene eventually place the heavy motor in back of the pickup truck, but it falls off when they fail to secure it properly. The camera pulls away from the motor, which remains where it has landed in the street. This sudden flattening of a dramatic arc is mirrored again toward the end of the film, when Gene finally gets his car running and they all set off for the racetrack. Their expectations, however, quickly get deflated when the car develops a flat tire and Gene doesn't have a spare. Bracy raps, "Man,

I'm out here singing the blues, got my money on a horse can't lose, and you're out here on a flat. I always told you to keep a spare, but you's a square. That's why you can't keep no spare. Now how are we going to get there, huh?" All of them get back into the car.

A number of critics have discussed *Killer of Sheep* in terms of Italian neorealism, but films such as Roberto Rossellini's *Open City* (1945) or Vittorio De Sica's *Bicycle Thieves* (1948)—two films often cited as influences—have strong dramatic arcs, whereas Burnett either ignores or undercuts narrative progression. Like many independent filmmakers, such as Jim Jarmusch in *Stranger Than Paradise* (1984), Gus Van Sant in *Mala Noche* (1985), or Allison Anders in *Gas Food Lodging* (1992), Burnett is less interested in creating dramatic tension than in characterization. Burnett's real focus is on creating a portrait of Stan's life within this particular social milieu. As Burnett explains:

> This was made as a demonstration to show the working class who they were. There were a lot of student films about the working class and the poor that had no connection. A lot of people were making films where they said if you do ABC, then D will happen; there will be some sort of resolution. But life just isn't like that. [*Killer of Sheep*] was an attempt to make a film about the people I grew up with and their concerns.[51]

Nothing at all changes over the course of the film for Stan, so that his character lacks an arc as well. Burnett insists that the problem of black people is too pervasive to be solved by "superficial" films that focus on a single individual's success. He told James Ponsoldt, "The problem is systematic, it's systemic, it's in the culture, it's in the school system itself, it's in the political system, it's in this country. It's inherent in this country's policies on education. And these films don't address this."[52]

Throughout *Killer of Sheep*, Burnett continually draws a comparison between the fate of the neighborhood children and the slaughter of sheep. At the beginning of the film, Stan Jr. and his friends engage in a full-fledged rock fight. One of them appears to get hurt, but after a brief pause, the fighting erupts again. The next shot is from a moving train as the kids hurl rocks at it. Burnett depicts a barren landscape of dust and dirt and almost no vegetation except for occasional palm trees. The kids play on a train, pretending to push one of the cars on top of a child lying on the tracks. In the neighborhood of South Central, even play has become a constant battleground.

When we first meet his father, Stan, he's busy doing home repair work. In this scene, his daughter, Angela, wears a huge dog mask, which seems to reference Levitt, Loeb, and Agee's classic documentary, *In the Street*. When the friend asks him when he last went to church, Stan answers not since "back home." This suggests the effects of dislocation that African Americans have experienced as a result of the migration from the rural, agrarian South to urban centers such as Los Angeles—a subject that Burnett would explore in his later film *To Sleep With Anger* (1990). In a mean gesture, Stan Jr. scrunches his sister's dog mask before running off. Stan's two other friends also poke at the little girl's mask as they walk by. Angela goes outside and hangs on the fence with her hand in her mouth while a little boy stands nearby. Such a scene is thematically evocative, but it does not serve to advance the narrative in any conventional way.

In the overall structure of *Killer of Sheep*, poetic details, such as Angela wearing the dog mask, are given equal weight in the narrative. The script for the eighty-one-minute film is considerably shorter—roughly thirty-one pages—suggesting that *Killer of Sheep* relies primarily on visual storytelling and contains very little dialogue.[53] When we think of the *Killer of Sheep*, we remember its striking images, including documentary-like ones at the factory, where the Judas goat leads the sheep to slaughter. For instance, there is the scene in which Angela sings off-key to a song by Earth, Wind & Fire, while she plays with a white doll. Others include: the kids trying to spin tops in the rubble; the scene where the older girls are dancing and the boy on the bike tries to act like a tough guy and they beat him up and he goes away crying; the dangerous shots from below of the kids jumping across the tops of buildings; the scene toward the end when Stan comes home from the factory and knocks over the two kids who are doing handstands and headstands. There is also the scene where a man in a soldier uniform wants his clothes back, while a woman upstairs brandishes a gun and her two young children sit on the couch nearby. This tense situation provides entertainment for the entire neighborhood, including Stan, who witnesses the incident while passing by.

There are scenes between Stan and his wife that show her sexual frustration. In one, Stan and his wife dance to music of Dinah Washington's "This Bitter Earth." For his wife, the dancing has an erotic charge, but

Stan, who is shirtless, appears to be merely going through the motions. After the record ends, she attempts to engage in foreplay, but Stan extricates himself and leaves his wife standing alone against the sunlit window. In voiceover, we hear what sounds like a poem: "Memories that just don't seem mine, like half-eaten cake, rabbit skins stretched on the backyard fences. My grandma, mot dear, mot dear, mot dear, dragging her shadows across the porch. Standing bareheaded under the sun, cleaning red catfish with white rum." Stan's wife picks up a pair of white baby shoes and presses them against her bosom, then exits the frame. The scene lasts nearly four minutes and represents the growing physical and emotional gulf between Stan and his wife, which is communicated visually. As Paula J. Massood points out, "The difference in this scene is that both Stan's alienation from his wife and her frustration with him are nonverbally communicated through her facial expressions and body language which register desire first, then desperation, and finally frustration and anger."[54]

After he returns from work later on, Stan, his wife, and daughter are all together in the kitchen. His wife suggests to Stan that they go to bed, but Stan sits silently at the table while she clears the dishes. Angela comes over to her father. She puts her arms around his neck. He looks at her lovingly, while Angela stares at her mother, who sits there despondently. Burnett ends the sequence by framing the shot from behind Stan's wife, so that we watch Angela playfully touch her father's face and then look over for her mother's reaction. The above scene is appropriately followed by the one of the little girl in the dress, who carefully places freshly laundered clothes on the line. Burnett cuts to a shot of a hole in a garage door. A boy crawls out, walks over, and spies on the girl. He returns to the hole, and four more kids of varying sizes climb out. Burnett cuts back to the girl, whose back is turned, and the boys throw dirt all over the clothes hanging on the clothesline. As she turns and stares, the camera holds on her haunting look, which parallels the one of both Stan's wife and daughter in the previous scene. Burnett cuts from the young girl in the dress to shots of the Judas goats at the slaughterhouse.

Burnett usually composes a shot and then doesn't cut unless it is absolutely necessary, which results in a film that manages to take its sweet time. Besides the leisurely pace and episodic rather than dramatic structure, *Killer of Sheep* maintains the overall feel and texture of an independent film in other ways than its minuscule original $10,000 budget. Its narration is much closer to international art cinema than classical Hollywood. *Killer of Sheep* employs symbolism and ambiguity—two characteristics of art cinema. Plot is also minimized in favor of the film's powerful visual imagery. The central metaphor, reinforced by the title, would no doubt seem too obvious were the film not made by one of America's greatest film poets.

4

EXPERIMENTS IN PSYCHODRAMA

Mekas, Warhol, Clarke, and Mailer

Due to the fact that J. L. Moreno conceived of psychodrama not only as therapy but also as theater, he wanted his psychodramas to be performed in public before an audience. According to John Nolte, Moreno first instituted weekly public sessions in 1942 at the Psychodrama Institute's Park Avenue location in Manhattan. He writes:

> Anybody could attend, although the groups were mostly made up of students and mental health professionals. The Psychodrama Institute [renamed the Moreno Institute in 1951] eventually moved to 236 W. 78th Street and, beginning in 1961, public sessions were conducted every night from 'Monday to Saturday at 8:30.' Open to everyone, the attendees paid a small fee.[1]

J. L. and Zerka Moreno, his wife, usually led the Friday night sessions. According to their son, Jonathan Moreno, "Groups ranged from ten or twelve to over a hundred, even two hundred, people."[2]

Zerka Moreno notes, "From the time we opened our doors in 1942, actors and student actors had appeared, and as we were more accessible at West 78th Street, their attendance increased." Actors were attracted to Moreno's theater of real life in attempting to discover how psychodrama might be adapted to create more authentic performances on the stage and screen. Although this was actually not Moreno's own vision of psychodrama, as was evident from his earlier experience with spontaneous theater in the 1920s, a number of playwrights, directors, actors, and filmmakers, including Alan Alda, Dustin Hoffman, Arthur Miller, and William Greaves, nevertheless saw the potential of psychodrama to tap into the deep recesses of the human psyche for dramatic effect.[3] Zerka Moreno recalls that Woody Allen once did what seemed like a character sketch, which did not go over very well with the audience.[4] He was using the psychodrama session as a kind of public test run rather than to explore his own personal growth. The audience at the Moreno Institute sensed the difference, which is why they reacted negatively. They did not come to be entertained but rather to experience an actual group psychotherapy session in which the protagonist would grapple with his or her own personal demons in real life rather than via some type of performance.

According to the psychodramatist Marcia Karp, the playwright Arthur Miller claimed "he came to psychodrama to see raw drama. In other words, rather than writing about an alcoholic, he saw in the raw flesh what an alcoholic was feeling and thinking."[5] Moreno's public sessions of psychodrama were intended to be therapeutic experiences, which is what drew this particular audience to attend his sessions. In a true psychodrama, Karp explains, "Closure follows the warm-up and enactment, enabling people in the group to share experiences similar to those experienced by the protagonist. It normalizes a brave journey and shifts their perceptions of their own relationships."[6]

Other theater groups at the time had similar goals to those of J. L. Moreno. The theatre critic Eric Bentley, for instance, noted that the major theatrical event of the 1968–1969 season was the visit of Julian Beck and Judith Malina's The Living Theatre to New York City. As Bentley clearly understood, The Living Theatre was attempting to change the nature of theater by engaging the audience directly in their productions through active participation. He observes, "They wanted to exercise a therapeutic influence. On the audience, of course; but also, as they proclaimed, on themselves: the audience was to help cure *them*."[7] The critic's realization that the ultimate goal of The Living Theatre was a form of group therapy caused Bentley to connect it to Moreno's pioneering work in this area.

Bentley notes a major difference between psychodrama and traditional theater, namely, that the protagonist in a psychodrama plays himself or herself, whereas a traditional play is based on a script where the performer plays a fictional character. Real life replaces the written text, which by its very nature inhibits spontaneity. Bentley writes:

> Here there is nothing but advantage in improvisation. The protagonist is a patient, and only his life matters. I have remarked that even the audience in psychodrama exists for the sake of the protagonist, not vice versa, as in drama. The dialogue, a fortiori, is all his. Even the director is not an author but at best a sort of film editor. Nor are there any prescribed forms of dialogue or character, as with the *commedia dell'arte*, which the psychodramatic "actor" must follow.[8]

Bentley subsequently began to attend Moreno's public psychodramas, which he considered to be as absorbing as anything occurring in avant-garde theater at the time.[9]

JONAS MEKAS: *THE BRIG*

A number of American indie filmmakers during the late 1950s and 1960s attempted to move away from written scripts and embraced spontaneity, improvisation, and what could be described as psychodrama. An early example of psychodrama was Jonas Mekas's *The Brig* (1964), which, not ironically, was a filmed version of a production by The Living Theatre. *The Brig* documented an autobiographical play by Kenneth Brown that was based on his experiences as a marine in Japan. He had been put in the brig for thirty days as punishment for returning to base four hours late and being declared AWOL.[10] Brown's prison experience amounted to a full-fledged nightmare. Mekas shot *The Brig* in one night, which was necessitated by the fact that the police were about to confiscate the building that housed The Living Theatre due to the radical theater group not paying taxes. Mekas chose to shoot the play as if it were a documentary event, using a handheld, probing camera and very long takes. The breaks, indicated by intertitles, correspond to the time it took for him to reload the camera. The camerawork suggests that Mekas himself was not always sure what would happen next.

The cast reportedly participated in seven-hour rehearsals in which they were subjected to intense physical and psychological torture.[11] They engaged in "role reversal," which was an important technique that was used in Moreno's psychodrama. The performers took turns switching between playing the guards and imprisoned soldiers in order to understand the mentalities and perspectives of both sets of characters. Through the camera, viewers are made to feel and experience that intense mental abuse as well. Like the performers in the play, there are moments when we, as viewers, start to lose our own grip on reality in the ensuing chaos and loud racket—the play, in effect, creates a total madhouse. This aspect of the production showed the profound influence of Antonin Artaud's Theatre of Cruelty. *The Brig* aimed to assault the audience mentally, especially with loud sounds.

ANDY WARHOL: *DRUNK* AKA *DRINK*

Andy Warhol also experimented with elements of psychodrama in the period that he made films (1963–1968). Warhol achieved the effect in various ways. One was by recording subjects for extremely long periods of time, so that temporal duration caused the film to become a battle between the subject and the camera. In Warhol's ninety-nine-minute silent portrait, *Henry Geldzahler* (1964), the curator sits on a couch, which suggests that the film is a psychiatric session. The film begins with its subject full of confidence and swagger and ends with him reduced to an infantile state through the sixty-six minutes of actual recording time (Warhol recorded his silent films at 24 fps, but screened them at 16 fps).

Once Warhol teamed with the playwright Ronald Tavel, he began using various strategies to extract psychologically revealing performances from the people who participated in his films. In *Screen Test #1* (1965), Tavel stages an inquisition on Warhol's unsuspecting lover at the time, Philip Fagan. Fagan becomes so uptight when he realizes that he has been set up and is being victimized that he shuts down emotionally. Although it was deemed a failure by Warhol at the time, from a psychological perspective, *Screen Test #1* is just as fascinating as *Screen Test #2* (1965), which brutally exposes and plays upon Mario Montez's insecurities about being a transvestite.

Warhol's *Drunk* aka *Drink* (1965) was restored and premiered at the Museum of Modern Art in November 2016. The film had been suppressed for a number of years due to the refusal of the subject—well-known documentary filmmaker Emile de Antonio—to allow it to be shown. Shot on the staircase of the Factory from a high angle, the film consists of two thirty-three-minute reels in which de Antonio proceeds to drink a quart of J & B Scotch in the first twenty minutes. De Antonio initially acts a bit haughty, as he consumes the scotch mixed with club soda and ice. He speaks very little, but gradually begins to slur his words. There is a time gap between the two reels, but by the second one, de Antonio begins to mutter incoherently and eventually is unable to move his body, so that he appears to be stuck in the frame like an insect pinned to flypaper.

Like Henry Geldzahler in his portrait, de Antonio also begins to regress as time goes on. He turns his body from the camera's fixed stare and claws the wall and slowly bangs his head against it, like a frustrated infant, before he eventually collapses on the floor, so that his body lies prone on the right side of the frame. Warhol's film is terrifying to watch because there is a real possibility that de Antonio might die. *Drunk* is nothing short of a game of Russian roulette, played for the camera. Even in Warhol's cinema, which often veered into psychodrama, the film involves risk—not just psychic risk but physical risk—that creates enormous discomfort in the viewer. Watching the film, we feel that we should immediately call 911, despite the fact that we know it is a film shot in 1965 and that de Antonio did not actually die. Yet it nevertheless induces a sense of palpable anxiety and utter helplessness in the viewer.

I have already written in great depth about Warhol's use of a form of psychodrama in my book on Warhol's cinema.[12] In *I, A Man* (1967), Tom Baker attempts to seduce Valerie Solanas, a militant lesbian and the author of the feminist tract *Scum Manifesto*, in a dark hallway. The manipulated setup was created to elicit an intense emotional reaction from Solanas, who later shot and severely wounded Warhol in 1968. *Bike Boy* (1967–1968) punctures the bravado of a motorcycle rider, Joe Spencer, whose macho posturing is tested by Viva with devastating results. Viva herself is subjected to intense scrutiny in *Blue Movie* (1968) when she is asked to perform an act of sexual intercourse on camera with Louis

Waldon—something that proved far more difficult than either performer ever imagined.

Alcohol, drugs, and mental instability often served as a catalyst to extract highly revealing performances, as evidenced by the drunken rebellion of Marie Menken as Fidel Castro's sister in *The Life of Juanita Castro* (1965). Due to his perceived vulnerability and fragile mental state, Eric Emerson's LSD trip in *The Chelsea Girls* (1966) is terrifying to watch. Equally disturbing is the performance by Patrick Tilden-Close, who is high on drugs throughout the filming of *Imitation of Christ* (1967–1969) and appears to be downright fearful and paranoid about the unstable Andrea Feldman's attempts to have sex with him. But the most extreme example of psychodrama in Warhol's films occurs when Ondine physically assaults an unsuspecting Ronna Page in *The Chelsea Girls*. Not only is the violence real rather than simulated, but Ondine's angry outburst continues for a good time afterward. Ondine is not the least bit repentant but instead tries to rationalize his behavior by expressing moral indignation and insisting that he is the victim of what has transpired rather than the other way around.

SHIRLEY CLARKE: *PORTRAIT OF JASON*

Shirley Clarke, who made *The Connection* (1961) and *The Cool World* (1963), was one of the early leading figures of the New American Cinema. In making *The Connection*, Clarke claimed, "I used, on purpose, a documentary style in the shooting and in the acting to create a greater sense of reality. All the camera movements were basically improvised by me as we went along (we shot in sequence) to create the kind of 'spontaneity' inherent in the documentary. The actors were encouraged to improvise 'on camera.'"[13] Although Clarke had an aesthetic interest in realism, as indicated by her two prior independent features, *Portrait of Jason* (1967) represented a major shift in direction.

Clarke was influenced not only by cinéma vérité but even more so by the work of Andy Warhol, who had made unedited film portraits or *Screen Tests*, especially *Screen Test #2*, and an extended series of fictionalized portraits of Edie Sedgwick, most notably *Beauty #2* (1965) and *Poor*

Little Rich Girl (1965), the first half of which was deliberately shot out of focus. There is some indication that Warhol had considered filming Jason Holliday (i.e., Aaron Payne), but apparently nothing ever came of it.[14] Yet Clarke's *Portrait of Jason* added another dimension to Warhol's filmmaking, as J. Hoberman notes, "both by introducing a racial component and upping the existential ante, as Clarke compelled her subject to perform for 12 hours."[15]

Clarke met Jason Holliday through her collaborator and long-time companion, Carl Lee, the son of the famous boxer and actor, Canada Lee. Clarke even employed Holliday as a house cleaner at some point, but they appear to have had a falling out. She considered him funny but also untrustworthy and even "dangerous." She cites an incident in which he placed "poppers" (amyl nitrate) under her nose, causing her to fear that she was about to have a heart attack. Clarke indicates that she had not spoken to him for a couple of years when she happened to bump into Holliday and told him about a new idea she had for a film and that he would be the perfect subject.[16]

In an interview with Jonas Mekas in the *Village Voice*, she considered the new film to be an experiment: "Cinéma vérité has called to our attention that people are the most interesting subject. Yet, we have rarely allowed anyone to really speak for himself for more than a few minutes at a time. Just imagine what might happen if someone was given his head and allowed to let go for many consecutive hours. I was curious, and WOW did I find out."[17] Given the precedent of Warhol's films, this is an odd claim, given the fact that Warhol's whole notion of "superstars" was founded on this very premise.

Clarke indicated that she would have been too self-conscious to be the subject herself. She notes, "I would have both over-censored or over-directed myself, and I knew that a valid film could only be made if you were free enough to reveal the truth."[18] Clarke claims that it was a difficult balance: she had to know the subject well enough—but not too well—in order to avoid what she terms "dual-self-consciousness." She believed Jason would not be savvy enough to "control" his own image during filmmaking, which she felt Robert Frost had done in her Academy Award-winning documentary, *Robert Frost, A Lover's Quarrel with the World* (1963), by "always playing a mirror image of himself."[19] Clarke also indicates that in making the film she was able to surrender control over it and respond to what was occurring in front of the camera. She told Mekas, "I finally became part of the situation myself, not the deus ex machina but ONE with Jason and the camera. At last I found the ability to swing along with what was happening spontaneously, with no preconceived judgments."[20]

When asked by Mekas about the uncontrolled elements in the film, Clarke notes, "One thing I never expected was the highly charged emotional evening that took place. I discovered the antagonisms I'd been suppressing about Jason."[21] She adds, "We had a tiny crew, plus two old friends of Jason who knew all his bits and had suffered from his endless machinations as well as enjoyed his fun and games."[22] Clarke elsewhere provides information about the two other people she specifically arranged to be present during the shooting: Carl Lee and someone named Richard. According to Clarke, "One of them was a fellow he's been in love with for a long time, fairly unsuccessfully, and the other is a fellow he's had an eye out for. I had them there for a particular reason."[23]

The two people appear off camera throughout the filming and are never seen, but Carl Lee—the first person mentioned—can be heard speaking throughout, prompting Holliday to tell various stories. Clarke can be heard as well, especially asking probing questions about Jason's mother. Yet it is Carl Lee who becomes excessively hostile and belligerent toward Jason at the end of the film. In the interview with Mekas, Clarke suggests, "How the people behind the camera reacted that night is a very important part of what the film is about. Little did I expect how much of ourselves we would reveal as the night progressed."[24]

What the people behind the camera reveal about themselves does end up reflecting on them. Contrary to her initial claims, Clarke, in a 1983 interview with Lauren Rabinovitz, admits that she planned to confront Jason at the end. She explains, "I had every intention of having a climax of something taking place. I knew that I would have to get Jason to face the truth at some point. But I wasn't positive how. In other words, I was going to let Jason do whatever he wanted for as long as I could, and then I was going to challenge him to come clean, tell the truth."[25] Clarke apparently harbored a certain degree of animosity toward her subject. She acknowledges to Rabinovitz, "An interesting and important fact is that I started that evening with hatred, and there was a part of me that was out to do him in, get back at him, kill him. But as the evening progressed, I went through a change of not wanting to kill him but wanting him to be wonderful."[26]

Robert Fiore, who was a production assistant on the film, confirms that Clarke "had some kind of animus, I guess you would call it, toward Jason for something that he had done that she wanted to get him to admit to."[27] In fact, a direct confrontation between Clarke and Jason took place in one of the later rolls, but the filmmaker decided not to include it in the final film because she felt it wasn't believable.[28]

Clarke was well aware of the ethical implications involved in such a project. In discussing the subjects—an eccentric mother and daughter living in a dilapidated mansion in the Hamptons—featured in the Maysles brothers' documentary *Grey Gardens* (1975), Clarke comments, "Of course they are willing victims. They want to be stars! Everybody does. People want to be in the movies. They don't care. They will totally exploit themselves. The moral issue for the filmmaker, therefore, becomes an interesting one."[29] Jason Holliday was a willing victim as well. For one thing, there was a monetary inducement. Clarke paid him $500 to be in the film, as well as 10 percent of future profits.[30] Nevertheless, Jason had mental health issues. There were additional factors that fed into the dynamic: he was black, gay, and barely scraping by at the time. When James Baldwin—to whom Jason bears some physical resemblance—was asked by a white interviewer, "When you were starting out as a writer, you were black, impoverished, homosexual. You must have said to yourself, 'Gee, how disadvantaged can I get?' " Baldwin responded, "No, I thought I hit the jackpot. It was so outrageous, you could not go any further, you know. So you had to find a way to use it."[31] The same could be said of Jason Holliday, who used his race, sexuality, and poverty as part of his hustle in order to survive.

Jason drinks liquor and smokes joints throughout the long night. He experiences wild mood swings throughout the process of being filmed over a twelve-hour period to the point that the viewer begins to wonder whether the reels are being shown in chronological order. Clarke, however, maintains that she did not alter the film's chronology, and she attributes the radical difference between takes to Jason being high on marijuana.[32] The shooting began at 9 p.m. on December 3, 1966, and ended the next morning. It took place in the living room of Clarke's penthouse apartment at the Chelsea Hotel. The set is minimal: a mantelpiece on which sits a vase of flowers, two jugs in front of it, a couch on the left, and a chair with a feather boa on the right side of the frame. A small human skull sits on top of books behind the chair. Jason was told to stay within the defined area. Contrary to what has sometimes been asserted, the film was not filmed continuously for twelve hours.[33] Film magazines had to be loaded and unloaded, resulting in sections of black that contain only sound. The first camera stopped working, and another camera had to be rented. There appear to be gaps in the filming. According to Clarke, "The only editing I did was to cut the film from four hours to less than two hours."[34] The filmmaker employs "focus" as a formal element in the film. It is used for transitions, but also provides a kind of improvisatory commentary on what is occurring in front of the camera.

Portrait of Jason begins with the image out of focus. As the crew indicates that the camera and sound are rolling, we hear Clarke say, "Okay, Jason, go." In stark close-up, an African American man, wearing black horn-rim glasses and smoking, speaks directly to the camera: "My name is Jason Holliday." He repeats: "My name is Jason Holliday." After a pause, he laughs and says, "My name is Aaron Payne." Clarke asks, "What do

FIGURE 4.1 Jason Holliday (Aaron Payne) addresses the camera, *Portrait of Jason*

you mean, 'Aaron Payne?' " He responds, "That was my given name." He then goes on to tell the story of how "Jason Holliday" was created in San Francisco. Thus, the film's opening sets up the dynamic of the film—the performed versus the real—as Jason begins to explain why he decided to adopt a new name.

After nearly four minutes, Clarke asks, "What do you do for a living, Jason?" Standing in a medium shot, he looks at the camera and sheepishly answers, "I hustle." As he and the others off-camera laugh, he adds, "I'm a stone whore." He begins to tell stories about hustling and suggests that he'll do anything "to avoid punching the clock." He seems drunker than in the first take, and, as he continues to talk about his life, it starts to become evident that Jason is performing for the camera. If fact, he flat out tells us, "What I'd really like to do is what I'm doing now—perform." As Jason talks, he becomes very animated, especially when he starts discussing sex, exclaiming, "I've been balling from Maine to Mexico, and haven't got a dollar to show for it." He describes himself as a "male bitch" and suggests, "I go out of my way to unglue people, you know."

Jason discusses various topics, such as being a houseboy, in which he talks candidly about social class and the racism he has experienced. He remarks, "They think you're just a dumb, stupid little colored boy and you're trying to get a few dollars, and they're gonna use you as a joke. And it gets to be a joke sometime as to who's using who, you know." After discussing being called racist names by his employers, he collapses on the couch. Jason also talks about his frustrated aspirations to become a night-club entertainer. He hopes to provide sex, comedy, and tragedy in his act, and adds, "People love to see you suffer, believe me."

Jason sings a song from *Funny Girl*, and afterward discusses his repeated failures to follow through on his plans for a nightclub act, which he has been using to con people into giving him money. Although he claims to feel guilty about it, he relishes recounting how people keep falling for the same scam time and again. Jason talks about missing an appointment with a psychiatrist and getting six phone calls as a result. As he smokes a joint, he laughs hysterically and again collapses on the couch, forcing Clarke to cut the scene. Jason reveals that the two psychiatrists he sees are always probing him about his sexuality, asking him about the size of his penis or whether he pleases the other person sexually. He talks about being busted for hustling, which led to his being incarcerated. Jason claims he caused such a ruckus that he wound up in the psych ward at Bellevue Hospital.

At around forty minutes, Lee asks Jason to do one of his night club routines. Jason gets a bag of props and proceeds to do impersonations of Mae West, and of Katharine Hepburn from *Stage Door* (1937). In a camp manner, he performs scenes from *Gone with the Wind* (1939) and *Carmen Jones* (1954). With prodding, Jason talks about his performance in Clarke's film, emphasizing that "Oh, this is my chance to really feel myself, and say, 'Yeah, I'm the bitch!'" At forty-eight minutes, Lee calls Jason a "big con artist." Jason talks about love, performs imitations of black queens, tells a story about an old man in San Francisco and a white lover he picked up at the bus station in Los Angeles.

Lee asks Jason to talk about "Big Tough," who turns out to be Jason's father. "Brother Tough," as Jason actually calls him, is a macho guy with big muscles. A "bootlegger" and a "gambler," he was upset that he had an effeminate son who was "out in the street skipping rope." Jason laughs and asks, "What can he do? I'm his." Jason discusses his traumatic childhood, especially the fact that his father often beat him with a razor strap. He acts out a scene where he stood up to his father one time. "Oh, Lord, what a childhood," Jason laments. "But I'll never tell," he continues, and snaps his fingers.

Clarke also asks pointed questions about Jason's mother. He refers to her as "a nice colored lady . . . who stayed in her place." Clarke asks Jason whether he loves his mother. He describes his family as having "black souls but white attitudes," and insists, "That don't make it at all." After rambling a bit, he calls his mother a "cunt" and suggests he would like to call her that just once. Like a psychiatrist, Clarke inquires, "Jason, did you hate your mother?" Lee later asks, "Did your mother ever talk to you about being a faggot?" Clarke asks Jason whether he ever "made it with a chick?"

The questions keep getting more personal, but it turns into an interrogation in the film's last twenty minutes once Lee broaches the subject of Jason's life on the Bowery. The focus of the image also shifts more radically in this final section. After Jason finishes a monologue about Dinah Washington, whom he claims to love, the image goes out of focus. Jason suddenly whispers seductively to one of the people offscreen, "I love you, Richard. I do, you'll see. Don't trust me, Richard. Don't trust me, 'cause

I'm out to get you. I'm out to hang you, baby. I wanna fuck you up. I really wanna fuck you up, so you'll be mine." Clarke tries to exhort everyone by announcing that they have only one roll of film left.

Lee goes on the attack, accusing Jason of writing "dirty rotten" letters about him. He asks, "Why did you do that to me? Rotten queen!" As Jason lies back on the chair, in a close-up shot, he says, "Oh, Carl . . . without you, I wouldn't know anything about anything. And if you don't know that I love you, then, man, you don't know anything . . . about anything." The ensuing exchange results in Jason being reduced to tears. As tears stream down his cheeks, Jason asks, "Do you know how much that hurts? It only hurts when you think of it. And if you're real, you'll think of it a long, long time. That's for sure. Those are the dues." The image has gone out of focus, but when the focus sharpens, Jason quickly snaps out of it. Carl and Jason continue to spar until the end of the film, with Carl demanding of Jason, "Be honest, motherfucker! Stop that acting!" He suggests that Jason is blowing his big opportunity and that he won't get another chance. Jason says, "Oh, all I need now is to have an orgasm." Carl responds, "Let's see you. Let's see you have an orgasm," to which Jason lets out a huge guffaw. As Clarke calls a "wrap," Jason tells her, "Oh that was beautiful. I'm happy about the whole thing." Clarke responds, "Oh, that's nice," as she announces, "The end!"

Portrait of Jason is a controversial film, especially because it raises the issue of the exploitation of its subject. Like what occurs in Warhol's *Screen Test #1, Screen Test #2,* or *Beauty #2*—in which Chuck Wein betrays Sedgwick for the sake of the film—*Portrait of Jason* was intended to become an elaborate trap for the performer, Jason Holliday. Clarke has created a psychodramatic situation in which Jason will eventually be put on the spot for something terrible he had done in the past. What he did— the issue of sending the dirty rotten letters—is never made very clear. The film becomes an attempt to use the power of the camera as a weapon against him by literally serving as his "screen test." As becomes obvious in the film, Jason has always aspired to be a performer, but he never had the determination to pursue it as a career. Instead, it is another of his many hustles to con people out of money. As Carl Lee keeps reminding him toward the end, this film is Jason's one and only chance.

Jason clearly understood what was at stake for him. He reportedly cried at the film's screening at the New York Film Festival and expected that his career would take off soon after. Clarke remarked, "I think he expected to be a star the next day, and I had to explain to him this isn't MGM."[35] Although Holliday became widely known in certain New York social circles as a result of the film, he never achieved the kind of success he craved. Intentionally or not, *Portrait of Jason* is ultimately a critique of direct cinema filmmaking. Instead of using an observational approach to the subject, Clarke orchestrated a full-fledged battle with Jason in order to ascertain the truth. Clarke suggested in interviews that, contrary to some of the critical attacks made against her for staging this, Jason actually came out the victor. As she indicates, "I picked somebody who was going to win. Jason ends up winning in that film."[36] This is certainly true, on some level. Yet a psychodrama, such as the one that Clarke concocted for Jason, can only be successful provided the subject is open and vulnerable. That was not the case with Jason—and how could it be otherwise?

In his portrait, Jason proves to be a charming chameleon who wears a series of masks that he has been forced to adopt as a means of survival. Whether as a gay child in a black family headed by a macho father, a houseboy for rich white people, or in compromised relationships with more prosperous white men, Jason has learned to hide his true feelings—to play a series of roles—so it is hardly surprising that his personality has become so fractured. He appears to get lost in the labyrinth of the various lies and deceits that he mines throughout the night, including the roles, impersonations, songs, and skits he tirelessly performs for us. Jason proves to be his own best audience, as he frequently laughs hysterically and self-deprecatingly at his own material, which no doubt was exacerbated by alcohol and drugs. A true psychodrama is not possible with a dedicated con artist because the goals are at odds with each other. The aim of psychodrama is to respond spontaneously; whereas Jason performs versions of himself that he has repeated so often they are seemingly rehearsed. If Clarke had hoped for some type of catharsis at the end, Jason is actually able to muster tears when placed under extreme duress, but the viewer quickly realizes that these tears are also part of his act.

Jason can't stop acting because his entire life is nothing short of a giant masquerade. He is not going to reveal anything else about himself other than the persona he has painstakingly crafted over the years as a much-needed defense mechanism. As a psychodrama, *Portrait of Jason* ultimately fails to unmask its protagonist. Yet Jason's performance nonetheless ends

FIGURE 4.2 Jason Holliday with boa, *Portrait of Jason*

up being an utterly fascinating portrait, precisely for what it reveals about the inherent power dynamic of the situation, which brings up thorny issues involving race, class, and gay sexuality in the late 1960s.

THE FILMS OF NORMAN MAILER:
WILD 90, *BEYOND THE LAW*, AND *MAIDSTONE*

There are scenes in the films of John Cassavetes, such as the love scene in *Shadows*, where the line between acting and real life blurs, creating confusion in the minds of viewers as to whether what is happening is fiction or nonfiction. Marshall Fine recounts an acting exercise between Cassavetes and Lelia Goldoni that turned into an actual fight, "with Goldoni and Cassavetes wrestling onstage, pulling hair, squealing and grunting with effort and pain in what seemed like a genuine struggle."[37] The exercise represented an effort by Cassavetes to get Goldoni in touch with her anger. Yet there is a fundamental difference between Cassavetes's techniques and those of Norman Mailer. Cassavetes was trying to deepen scripted performances through the rehearsal process, whereas Mailer—like Warhol and Clarke before him—wanted to probe the psyches of his performers for the sake of the camera.

Although he was strongly influenced by the work of Cassavetes and Warhol, Mailer was highly critical of the two filmmakers, whose films were most closely aligned with improvisation in the 1960s. He claimed to hate all of Warhol's films other than *Kitchen* (1965) and was dismissive of the work of Cassavetes for not being truly improvised. In discussing Cassavetes, Mailer tells an interviewer: "I always thought it was false improvisation. It was semi-improvisation. They knew where the scene was going. My whole feeling was that the one thing you didn't want—the lock I wanted to get out of—is the knowledge of when a scene is coming to an end. Primarily because when a scene comes to an end a skilled actor puts the book down."[38]

Mailer did not believe in either a script or much preplanning but in having his untrained performers improvise spontaneously once the camera was running. Mailer recognized that improvisational filmmaking was largely dependent on luck as well as the lived experience the performers brought to their roles.[39]

Mailer developed his theories of cinema from his own practice in making three low-budget narrative experiments in the late 1960s. He articulated these theories in two articles. The first of these, "Some Dirt in the Talk: A Candid History of an Existential Movie called *Wild 90*," was published in the December 1967 issue of *Esquire*.[40] The second, "A Course in Filmmaking," Mailer published in *New American Review* in 1971 and included as an accompanying essay to his after-the-fact transcribed script to *Maidstone*.[41] His ideas synthesize many of those expounded by Jonas Mekas concerning the screenplay, acting, and cinematic realism.

Even though he was a writer, Mailer had little regard for the conventional screenplay. Like Mekas and Warhol, Mailer felt that the studio films produced by Hollywood paled in comparison to events that occurred in actual life. He claims, "The moment you know what you're going to do, you make a preparation. The moment you make a preparation, you're a step removed from the *moment* in life. You see, I'm an existentialist, through and through and through. And I have a certain amount of respect for the moment, because I think the moment is a mystery."[42] Mailer's criticism also rests on the fact that ideas for Hollywood scripts usually derive not from the screenwriters, but from other sources, such as books, magazine articles, plays, or even other films. For Mailer, "The moment a writer moves away from his basic connection to that unconscious which gives original words to the pencil in his fingers, art in its turn has given up a half-life."[43]

Mailer was also critical of the fact that the industrial practice of the Hollywood studios conspired to crush "every surface of cinematic reality" in order to produce "cinematic works of the most predictable encapsulation."[44] He writes:

> It was assumed that movies were there to tell a story. The story might derive from the stage, or from the pages of a book, or even from an idea for a story, but the film was asked to issue from a detailed plan which would have lines of dialogue. The making of the movie would be a fulfill-ment of that script, that literary plan; so, each scene would be shaped like a construction unit to build the architecture of the story.[45]

Mailer's reaction against what Kathryn Millard has termed "the gospel of story," was to defy the rules of conventional cinema by choosing to forgo a script, employing nonprofessional actors and improvisation, and shoot-ing his fictional films in a direct cinema or documentary-like style.[46] In the case of *Beyond the Law*, he used three different cameras to record the action occurring in separate spaces of the police station, while in *Maidstone* he had five different crews covering the action as it was occurring in different locations. Mailer also believed that the Hollywood apparatus was inimical to capturing contemporary reality.

Like Erving Goffman, Mailer viewed all human interaction as a social performance. Yet, for Mailer, everyday life also held the possibility for some type of transformation. He observes, "We are always looking for real stories to ensue which never exactly enact themselves as we expect, yet we still work at such times as actors in the real story of our life, pursuing roles which can become our life at any instant the psychological can become the real—as occasionally it will."[47] This is precisely the reason why Andy Warhol wanted to keep the camera running continuously. Like Warhol,

Mailer was fascinated by the intersection between fiction and nonfiction and sought to create and capture those transformative moments and situations where the behavior of the performer ceases to be a role and suddenly becomes real.

Mailer's first film, *Wild 90* (1968), demonstrates the difficulty of trying to improvise a film without much preplanning. It derived from Mailer and friends pretending to be Italian gangsters in a Greenwich Village bar after performances of his play *The Deer Park* in 1967. In deciding to film the improvisation, Mailer saw his Mafioso gangsters as a macho reaction to Warhol's *The Chelsea Girls*. In *Wild 90*, Prince (Norman Mailer) and two other friends, Cameo (Buzz Farbar) and Twenty Years (Mickey Knox) sit around a warehouse apartment in Brooklyn, drinking and insulting one another. Mailer at various times attempts to instigate something dramatic by challenging the masculinity of the other two men. The three men flaunt actual weapons to add tension to their interactions. At one point Twenty Years suggests robbing a Korean grocery store in the neighborhood, but Cameo mocks the plan as being incredibly stupid, and the three of them get into a brief scuffle.

Other characters make appearances, including Twenty Years's younger brother, the police, Prince's wife, and José Torres, a professional boxer and light heavyweight title-holder. Mailer attempts to outbark Torres's ferocious German shepherd and even shadowboxes with the prizefighter for a round. Like what often occurs in a bar full of drunks—as we witness in both Rogosin's *On the Bowery* and Mackenzie's *The Exiles*—the various scenes contain an undercurrent of impending violence. Mailer, in a highly stylized performance, continually taunts the other performers, but nothing significant ever develops. A final credit indicates that what we have just witnessed derived "from a script that did not necessarily ever exist."

Mailer's next film *Beyond the Law* (1968) turned out to be far more successful than his initial effort. He recruited a number of his friends to create another improvised film about the symbiotic relationship between cops and suspected criminals set in a police station. Like Warhol, Mailer was not interested in the contrivances of plot, which he considered detrimental to cinematic realism. In his book *The Spooky Art*, Mailer devotes an entire chapter to the differences between "real life versus plot life." According to Mailer, our lives have elements of plot, but they appear to us as discontinuous. He speculates, "One could make the case that our love of plot—until it gets very cheap indeed—comes out of our need to find the chain of cause and effect that so often is missing in our own existence."[48] For Mailer, plot does not come first but grows from the development of character. If there is a semblance of story, it is found in the process of making the film. Instead of resorting to plot, Mailer used a situation—a police lineup during the course of an evening. According to Mailer, "What I was trying to do in *Beyond the Law* was to create the reality, if you will, below the reality, beneath the reality, within the reality of an evening in the police station."[49]

In *Beyond the Law*, Mailer plays an Irish police lieutenant named Francis X. Pope, as various criminals are interrogated about their crimes. Pope accuses one man of being a pedophile, which elicits a strong reaction from the person who pushes the lieutenant away from him when he gets too close, nearly starting a fight. He accuses a black man of molesting an eight-year-old girl, before he is informed that it is a trumped-up charge. This appears not to matter to the lieutenant. Another man (Edward Bonetti) confesses to killing his wife with an axe. A belligerent long-haired biker, played by the poet Michael McClure, gets dragged in and questioned, but he quickly starts a fierce brawl with the cops, which escalates when his motorcycle pal (Rip Torn) also joins in. Pope barks at him, "God and asshole are the essence of criminality. You mix the two and it is the beginning of all evil." When he gets together with his wife (Mailer's actual wife, Beverly Bentley), she complains about the fact that he is too consumed with his job and is never home. She demands a divorce and confesses that she's been having an affair with Rocco Gibraltar (Buzz Farbar), who at the moment is attempting to pick up two attractive women with his pal Mickey Berk (Mickey Knox). Pope finds Rocco at the restaurant, pulls him into the bathroom, and bluntly asks, "Are you tooling my wife?" He then winds up coming on to an attractive college-age woman, but his wife shows up and throws a drink in the woman's face before she and her husband order the woman to leave.

Mailer's self-financed third film, *Maidstone* (1970), made on a much larger budget of roughly $200,000, managed to push his ideas about cinema to the limit. He recruited a large cast of actors and friends for a five-day shoot, in which he plays Norman T. Kingsley, a porno film director who is also running for president of the United States. In the film, Mailer, feeling the megalomania of a politician, continually insults people, especially women, while possibly being set up as the target of an assassination plot. Divided into twelve chapters, the film is like a large political rally held at country estates in the Hamptons, intermixed with a free-love orgy and scenes involving political power brokers and black power militants.

Mailer planted a number of rumors among his cast, including that someone was packing a gun, to give the participants in his film an appropriate sense of unease and paranoia. He wanted them to believe that anything might happen during the course of making the film. To add to the tense atmosphere of possible violence, Mailer actually punched and broke the jaw of one of his actors, Lane Smith, when he criticized the director.[50] The film builds to a climactic scene of a party, where we fully expect the assassination to occur, but it fizzles out. The scene cuts to an argument with his wife, Beverly Bentley, over the fact that he truncated her scene the night before, which leads to bitter animosity and actual tears. The next day, Mailer lectures the gathered cast about the true nature of what he was attempting to achieve in the picture, which he compares to a military operation that leads to an attack on the nature of reality. He explains, "You can't say that this is real now, what we're doing, you can't say what we were doing last night is real."

The twelfth chapter is entitled "The Silences of an Afternoon." There are shots of cast members walking through a rural setting on Gardiners Island. We see shots of Rip Torn, who plays Rey in the film. He reaches into a backpack on the ground and takes out a hammer. He walks toward the camera and discards his sunglasses. As the camera frames him in a profile close-up, a guy, referring to Mailer, says, "He sort of likes this role of a patriarch going out with everybody, showing them a good time and lording it over the family." After a wide shot of Mailer's wife and kids by a windmill, Mailer can be seen standing under a tree. The man asks Torn, "So where does that leave us now?" Torn answers, "Well, we just have to search."

From a shot of Mailer's wife and kids walking toward us and a young boy calling to his father, the film cuts to a close-up of Torn's face. The camera holds on him, while the other man remarks, "Kinda nice out here." Torn's eyes flicker slightly; his contemplative look slowly turns to a menacing smile. In wide shot, Torn approaches Mailer under the tree and strikes him twice in the head with the hammer. Mailer shouts,

"You crazy fool," as the camera zooms in closer while the men circle each other. Torn insists, "I don't want to kill Mailer, but I must kill Kingsley in this picture." As Torn makes another move toward him, Mailer grabs Torn and viciously bites his ear, as they wrestle to the ground, with Torn on top. They negotiate a break but quickly go after each other again. This time Torn has a stranglehold on Mailer, who finally manages to break loose, but Torn gets him in a headlock. Bentley screams, "Oh shit! What is this? What is this? What have you done?" She smacks Torn in the head and pulls his hair, and attacks him, yelling hysterically, "What have you done? You motherfucker!" A man enters the frame and tries to separate them. Bentley keeps screaming, "What have you done? What have you done?" As another man intervenes, Bentley pulls Torn's hair and whacks him hard in the face with her hand as kids cry loudly in the background. When Torn lets go, Mailer instinctively grabs him from behind. Now Bentley begs him to stop. Mailer claims not to be hurt and that Torn is the one more injured, but this is clearly not the case.

FIGURE 4.3 Rip Torn choking Norman Mailer, *Maidstone*

When Mailer announces that Torn hit him with a hammer, Bentley becomes even more hysterical. As the kids continue to wail in the background, Mailer becomes irate. Pointing at his children, he shouts at Torn, "Look what you did to my kids." Bentley shouts, "Oh, what the fuck have you done!" In one of the most telling lines, Mailer comments, "That's an actor for you." Still bleeding from his head wound, Mailer consoles his crying children. Torn tries to explain himself, but Mailer raises his fist and snarls, "Get away from me. Or I'm gonna cold-cock you!" Bentley moves in to separate them. As Torn persists, and the cries of the kids grow louder, Bentley screams maniacally, "You go home. The kids are here and there ain't gonna be no fuckin' fight. I'll kill you! I'll kill you!" Torn insists that he did it for the sake of the movie. As the camera zooms in over Mailer's shoulder to Torn's face, Mailer tells the actor, "You did it in front of my kids. That's what I can't forgive you for. Cocksucker!" Torn answers, "When is assassination ever planned?" The two exchange insults. Torn calls Mailer a fraud; he responds by calling Torn a cocksucker. The two men are in a standoff. Mailer finally comments to the crew offscreen, "You might as well turn off this tape because he's a very dull talker, and he never stops as long as anything is run."

This sequence, which lasts for over eight tortuous minutes, epitomizes everything Mailer was striving for in his films. Warhol understood early on that the camera had the power to alter events that occurred in front of it, but he soon recognized that he needed to set up the right circumstances for dramatically interesting things to happen. It became standard practice at the Factory to interview performers in order to locate vulnerabilities that could be exploited in the films. If Warhol's superstars had a narcissistic urge to perform themselves for the sake of the camera, Mailer attempted to be his own onscreen catalyst by making himself the central character in his three films. As he put it, "The way I make the film, I have to act in it. It's the only way I can direct it. Because there's no script, something has to be going on in scenes. And so there has to be somebody in the scene who really has some conception of what he's driving toward."[51]

In the case of *Maidstone*, it seems clear that Mailer had attempted to set up various subplots among his cast members, including the threat of assassination to a presidential candidate—a possibility that resonated after Robert F. Kennedy recently had been shot. Rip Torn has indicated in interviews that it was Mailer's idea for one of the cast members to take him out. It was not a coincidence that a camera crew was ready to record the event as it occurred, despite the fact that the film was supposedly over. But two aspects of Torn's hammer attack on Mailer were not fully anticipated by the director. Mailer apparently had wanted it to occur at the Grand Assassination Ball. There are shots of Torn, who is sweating profusely, but the much-anticipated assassination attempt—for whatever reason—failed to occur, except for a minor scuffle in which a black man is forcibly dragged out. In the film, Mailer appears annoyed that Torn's eventual assault drew blood. But his real objection and what causes the scene to continue for eight minutes is the fact that Torn chose to do it in front of Mailer's children, which, as might be expected, proved to be a traumatic experience for them. His wife, Beverly Bentley, manages to escalate the fight through her own volatile reaction to what is occurring. Mailer's crying children serve as additional testimony to the scene's authenticity.

FIGURE 4.4 Torn shouts at Mailer offscreen, as a distraught Beverly Bentley looks on, *Maidstone*

In Warhol's *Afternoon* (1965), the Pop artist tried to use insults to create dramatic conflict between Ondine and several of Edie Sedgwick's society friends, such as Arthur Loeb, but it failed to work. The same might be said of Mailer's attempt to create a combustible situation in *Wild 90*. If insults failed to create the necessary dramatic conflict in which the psychological reality of characters becomes truly manifest, then physical fighting seemed to hold that allure for Mailer. Such activity occurs briefly in *Wild 90* and serves as a subtext throughout the film. Rip Torn and Michael McClure start a ruckus with the police in *Beyond the Law*, but this pales in comparison to the physical assault and aftermath that occur in *Maidstone*. Torn and Mailer are not acting but are truly engaged in a full-blown, ugly fight in front of Mailer's family.

Torn is literally trying to strangle Mailer, which is what causes an offscreen cast member and Daniel Kramer—a still photographer for *Look* magazine who happened to be on set that day—to intervene. Kramer felt it necessary in order to prevent Torn from suffocating Mailer. He observes, "In reviewing my contact sheets (like the photographer in *Blow Up*), I have come to believe that Norman and Rip had planned a moment of confrontation for the camera, but Norman never expected the hammer— certainly not the hammer blows to his head with his children nearby. It just all got out of hand."[52] Like Ondine's vicious assault on Ronna Page in Warhol's *The Chelsea Girls* or Shannon Baker and Audrey Henningham's vehement shouting match in *Symbiopsychotaxiplasm Take 2½*, this scene from *Maidstone* serves as one of the strongest cinematic examples of an improvisation that pushes into the realm of psychodrama.

Mailer often referred to his films as a form of psychoanalysis.[53] Like Warhol, he was experimenting with his own version of psychodrama. As Torn indicates, Mailer was deliberately provoking the participants in *Maidstone*: "Tremendous hostility built up, like a thundercloud. He did that deliberately. He did things out there to people that were cruel. He wanted to see how much they could take."[54] The violent scene between Torn and Mailer was, in many ways, the logical outcome of Mailer's process, including how his strategy backfired on him. Mailer would later suggest that if he really wanted to explore improvisation more successfully, he needed to have a company of actors and develop scripts to push deeper into the technique. As he put it, "I recognized that to make movies the way I wanted to make them you had to be totally devoted to improvisation all of your life."[55]

5

HUMAN LIFE ISN'T NECESSARILY
WELL-WRITTEN

William Greaves's *Symbiopsychotaxiplasm:*
Take One and *Take 2½*

ailer clearly intended to turn the making of *Maidstone* into his own form of psychodrama. Two years earlier, William Greaves also created a film where the cast and crew, unbeknownst to them, unwittingly became engaged in a sociodrama as well. Greaves went even further than Mailer, however, by utilizing a Moreno-trained psychodramatist, Marcia Karp, in the production. In *Symbiopsychotaxiplasm: Take One* (1968–1971), Greaves creates a fictional scene between two characters—Freddie and Alice—played by five different pairs of actors and directed by a seemingly incompetent director (the filmmaker himself) in the middle of Central Park.[1] All aspects of the production, including crew members, are recorded by multiple cameras in the manner of a reflexive documentary, thus creating a film-within-a film.

Born and raised in Harlem, Greaves had an extensive background as an actor, appearing briefly on Broadway and in black-cast films in the late 1940s. Disenchanted with the type of stereotypical "Uncle Tom" roles available to African American actors at the time, Greaves moved to Canada in 1952 and eventually worked for the National Film Board of Canada, where he was involved in the production of over eighty films in various capacities, before returning to America in 1963 to work for the film division of the United States Information Agency (USIA).[2] In 1968, Greaves became the cohost and—following a successful coup by the African American members on the staff—the executive producer of the prestigious television program *Black Journal*, a position he held until 1971.

SYMBIOPSYCHOTAXIPLASM: TAKE ONE

Greaves conceived of *Symbiopsychotaxiplasm* as a series of five movies. For the first, *Take One*, in the spring of 1968, he assembled a cast of performers, including some drawn from the famed Actors Studio, where he taught acting. The cast had varying degrees of experience. Two of the actors—Shannon Baker and Audrey Henningham—had a background in psychodrama, which no doubt explains why Greaves arranged to have Karp work with them during production (even though this is not shown in *Take One*). Greaves also chose an eclectic group of crew members. The two main cinematographers, Terry Filgate, whom Greaves knew from the National Film Board of Canada, and Stevan Larner, who shot films for the USIA, were both highly skilled professional camerapersons. The two most vocal crew members, Jonathan Gordon, the sound person, and Bob Rosen, the production manager, did freelance film work for Amram Nowak Associates, a New York-based production house. Nowak produced a documentary, entitled *King, Murray* (1969), which Gordon codirected with David Hoffman, who also had a minor crew position on *Take One*.

King, Murray combines staged scenes with real scenes, blurring the divide between fiction and documentary in creating a portrait of an insurance agent from Long Island named Murray—a sad, money-obsessed braggart.[3] Although Gordon was not a seasoned professional like Filgate and Larner, he had seen a number of independent and avant-garde films which fell under the rubric of New American Cinema, including work by John Cassavetes, Shirley Clarke, George and Mike Kuchar, Jack Smith, and Ron Rice. He was also a huge fan of The Living Theatre and attended their production of *Paradise Now* at the Brooklyn Academy of Music multiple times.[4]

For *Take One*, Greaves shot 130,000 feet of 16 mm film or fifty-five hours of footage, employing four cameras to record a melodramatic scene using multiple pairs of actors, while self-reflexively recording the process of making the film itself.[5] Greaves wanted the film not only to be politically revolutionary but also intended it to be a radical attack on conventional cinema. In notes prior to and during production, he wrote, "The film is <u>rebellion</u>! Rebellion against traditional cinema form. The hippies on the crew are for love and rebellion, in contradistinction to the

<u>screen test</u> characters, Alice and Freddy [Freddie], who are suburbanites, caught in a life of conformity."[6]

Greaves deliberately kept both his cast and crew in the dark by keeping "explanation" to a minimum. According to Greaves, "To give more will kill the truth and spontaneity of everyone."[7] He compared the film to jazz and emphasized its improvisatory nature. Greaves wanted the film to mimic life in being unfathomable in its unfolding. He told Scott MacDonald, "At the end you say, 'Wait a minute, what was *that* about, and why was I so transfixed by it?' Well, life is like that, life keeps you totally absorbed from moment to moment to moment and yet oftentimes you can't tell what it's about. I like that paradox."[8]

Commercial moviemaking involves a military-like, hierarchical structure. On the set, the director is in a position of control through being responsible for shot selection and performance. In *Take One*, Greaves proves to be an atypical director, which soon becomes evident to the crew and cast as the production veers into chaos almost from the very start. Greaves very subtly plays the part of an inscrutable director, as he good-naturedly fails to give the production any semblance of the type of direction that everyone expects of him on the set. Through his feigned ineptitude, Greaves attempts to provoke rebellion among his cast and crew. As MacDonald points out, "For Greaves, in other words, the *Symbiopsychotaxiplasm* project was to be a metaphor for the sociopolitical experience of the sixties, a paean to rebellion against oppression—in this case, the oppression of the conventional, hierarchical power structure of director/actors/crew that had developed during the history of commercial cinema."[9] Greaves wanted those involved in his sociodrama to respond spontaneously and creatively to the oppressive situation of the film production as it developed in the middle of busy Central Park.

J. L. Moreno had coined the term "sociodrama" to refer to a psychodrama that deals with the social organization of the group and its various prescribed roles. In *The Theatre of Spontaneity*, Moreno explains:

> The difference between psychodrama and sociodrama is one of structure and objective. Psychodrama deals with a problem in which a single individual or a group of individuals are *privately* involved. Whereas sociodrama deals with problems in which the collective aspect of the problem is put in the foreground, the individual's private relation is put in the background. The two cannot, of course, be neatly separated.[10]

In this instance, Greaves has created an experimental work that interrogates the group structure of a professional film shoot.

In the opening of *Symbiopsychotaxiplasm: Take One*, a character named Freddie (Leslie Redford) chases after his wife, Alice (Louise Archambault), as she tries to elude him. Once Freddie catches up to her, Alice tells him, "Why don't you just go away? Why don't you just get out of my life permanently?" Freddie responds, "Stop acting, Alice, will you?" As she moves away, Alice tells him, "Don't touch me!" Freddie insists, "Come on, Alice, stop acting." The image of Freddie turns into a split screen. But a different Alice—Susan Anspach rather than Archambault—responds, "No, I said, don't touch me, please. Don't ever touch me ever again, ever." As they argue, Freddie, played by another actor, finally says, "Listen, I don't have to stay here and listen to all these hysterics." This is followed by a third couple, Patricia Ree Gilbert and Don Fellows, as they continue to enact the scene between Alice and Freddie. She complains about having

FIGURE 5.1 William Greaves directs Don Fellows, as Jonathan Gordon records sound, *Symbiopsychotaxiplasm: Take One*

abortion after abortion. He claims to want a child when "things are right between us." She counters, "All right, then, why don't we have a baby?" In split screen, the two continue to argue, as Alice accuses Freddie of being a "faggot."

In *Take One*, Greaves creates his own "screen test"—a scene involving an unhappy married couple named Alice and Freddie, which is supposedly part of a fictional feature he has humorously titled *Over the Cliff*. Although the genesis of the scripted text remains a mystery, Greaves indicated that he often used a scripted scene as an exercise when he taught acting classes. In program notes for the film, he admits the script itself is "banal," but can become exciting through inspired performance: "In this sense, the text, like the film, is a kind of tour-de-force—a paradox, which is what I wanted to achieve. In the classes where I train actors, I have the actors regularly perform what I call 'neutral' dialogue with changing sets of motivations. The text of the screen test is partly based on this acting exercise."[11] Greaves explains how neutral dialogue can change as a result of different circumstances and motivation. He told MacDonald: "For example: 'Hello. How are you? What's new? Nothing too much. Have you seen so and so? No, I haven't' means almost nothing. But if one person is a killer and the person he's talking to is a potential victim, the same dialogue is entirely different."[12]

The dialogue in the text—accusations of forced abortions and closeted homosexuality—is not exactly neutral in the same sense as the lines above, but Greaves provides additional complexity to the situation. By employing multiple cameras, he records everything surrounding the production, including the cast and crew members, as well as the onlookers at the locations in Central Park. Whatever occurs becomes part of the film, whether it is a woman with bouncing breasts on a horse, a police officer on horseback checking permits, school children wanting to become movie stars, a shirtless young man rowing a boat on the pond, or a homeless drunk who stumbles upon the production shoot. Greaves runs the "screen test" numerous times, mostly with two actors, Fellows and Gilbert, but also with several others, including a couple who sing their lines as in a French musical and an interracial couple (Baker and Henningham) at the film's end. Despite their misgivings about the production, the cast and crew members play their professional parts on the set. There is no overt rebellion against the director, except for Gilbert who becomes visibly angry and storms off during one of the takes, which, ironically, the crew fails to record because they have run out of film.

Four days into the production, as a joint gets passed around after the shoot, the crew decides to gather together in a recorded session to discuss the film they are making. Jonathan Gordon, the sound person, articulates many of the concerns and complaints of the rest of the crew: "We realized that here is an open-ended film, with no plot that we can see, with no end that we can see, with an action we can't follow." Bob Rosen, the production manager, complains that Greaves "is so far into making the film that he has no perspective and if you ask him what the film is about, you know, he just gives you some answer that is vaguer than the question."

As a result of an optical effect, the medium shot of Rosen recedes into the frame as two other scenes from the film are revealed on either side and grow larger than the one containing Rosen. The image of Rosen eventually expands and fills the frame. An African American production assistant, Phil Parker, is even blunter in his assessment of the perceived incompetence of Greaves: "He doesn't know how to direct. He's into blocking. That's what he does. He sits around; he gives movement. After reading about something about what this film is based on, he's not doing anything which he has put down on paper. There's no communication between him and the actors." Gordon, on the other hand, wonders whether it might be more productive to discuss the significance of Greaves's "non-direction."

In a later section of the film, Rosen criticizes what he considers the bad writing of the script. Someone offscreen interjects, "Human life isn't necessarily well-written, you know." They all seem to agree that this is the point. Rosen's insightful attempt to clarify what Greaves is striving for provides a telling example. In discussing cinematographer Terry Filgate's point that Greaves is also playing a part in the film and "acting" any time the camera is on him, Rosen claims:

Somewhere the director is hiding, you know. I think he's making this film . . . to get it out into the open. That he has in some way some kind of need, you know, to find out where the line of his acting and everybody else's acting . . . where that drops off, where it stops being [a performance] . . . where you pass that line of manipulation to where you're just being yourself.

Rosen is absolutely right in his assessment: the fine line between acting and nonacting and between the performed and the real indeed proves to be one of the film's central concerns.

Greaves begins with a written script, but he gradually employs improvisation as a technique to bring the material much closer to the actors. In one take on a bridge, Gilbert responds to Fellows's denial of being gay by exclaiming, "Yesterday you were a fag, today you're not, tomorrow you're just going to fuck the little robins or chipmunks here in the park. How about that, huh? Why don't you try a mosquito next?" As Gilbert starts to become emotional, Greaves abruptly ends the take, which causes her to become even more upset. The director and actor have the following exchange:

Greaves: Take it easy.
Gilbert: Why should I take it easy? Why?
Greaves: It's going very well.
Gilbert: It's not! And you know it!

We hear Fellows explain that Gilbert is upset because she was building toward the big climax of the scene, which Greaves has deliberately short-circuited. We hear a cameraperson's voice indicate that Gilbert has just "flipped out," but unfortunately two of the film magazines have run out. We watch as Bill chases after the distraught actor, but there is no accompanying sound.

This last shot is overlapped with a recorded critique session with the crew. Maria Zeheri, an assistant cameraperson, claims that the film is really an "experiment," and, according to the brief synopsis she previously read, Greaves "is experimenting with the different ways of directing the same dialogue." Gordon, however, asks, "But why film it?" Filgate criticizes the fact that everything they are shooting is the "same" regardless of the performers, who are actually stage actors rather than film actors. He suggests that what they are doing is more appropriate for videotape than for film and concludes that he doesn't see that "there is any build in the film at all." Stevan Larner, who is offscreen, chimes in, "Now you're getting down to the nitty gritty . . . Not really much is happening, if you ask me." The female crew member recording the sound, Nicky Kaplan, responds, "Not having read Bill's concept, it seems to me that there's some exploration of the levels of reality, and the supra-levels of reality. Okay, so this is even another level of reality that we are establishing here. And it may be the biggest put-on of all time." Rosen interjects, "Recognizing the reality or nonreality, trying to establish that, is useless. For all anybody knows, Bill is standing right outside the door, and he's directing this whole scene. All right, it could be. Nobody knows. Maybe we're all acting, all right?"

Following another run-through of the scene in which Fellows this time kisses Gilbert roughly on the lips, which elicits a stunned reaction from her, Gordon talks with the cast, crew, and the director during a break. He comments, "You haven't been here for eight days and listened to this sordid, horrible conversation over and over and over again, with black faces, white faces, tall ones, old ones, young ones, skinny ones . . . You know, convincing ones, unconvincing ones . . . It does funny things to you." Greaves responds by saying that he would like to see Gordon surface with a better script. Gordon complains about the language, which he does not

FIGURE 5.2 Freddie (Don Fellows) kisses Alice (Patricia Ree Gilbert) roughly in one of the scenes, *Symbiopsychotaxiplasm: Take One*

find realistic. Greaves defends himself by invoking the original concept of the film, which Gordon admits he hasn't read. He tells everyone assembled: "The point is this: the screen test proves to be unsatisfactory from the standpoint of the actors and the director. And then what happens is that the director and the actors undertake to improvise something better than that which has been written in the screen test." He compares the palace revolt to "the revolution that is taking place in America today" and places the onus for coming up with creative suggestions on them. After Rosen claims not to understand, Greaves then insists that what really matters is being able to come up with a more "exciting and creative" film as a result of their "collective efforts."

Right after this, Greaves again tests the patience of both crew and cast by having a couple sing the lines in a similar vein to Jacques Demy's *The Umbrellas of Cherbourg* (1964)—a reference that is underscored by having the actors walk through Central Park in the rain while carrying a large black umbrella. Failing to grasp the humor of the allusion, Gordon asks Greaves why he is now having them sing the dialogue while sitting on a park bench, but the director is evasive.

The female actor, Susan Anspach, recognizes singing as a valuable exercise tool in releasing other imaginative elements in a performance, but she also questions the value of their trying to do the scene as a duet. Greaves suggests that it can add an "interesting texture to the film." The assistant cameraperson, Clive Davidson, however, claims that there is no sense of reality to the scene because people don't behave this way in actual life. We hear the voice of a homeless drunk named Victor, who turns up to supply that missing element of realism: "What is this thing? I spoke with you, yes, you're from Canada, right? Oh, it's a movie. So, who's moving whom?" The scene with Victor lasts eight minutes. The film ends with an interracial couple, Shannon Baker and Audrey Henningham, being filmed in another screen test involving Freddie and Alice.

Symbiopsychotaxiplasm: Take One was shot in 1968, but took three years to complete, largely due to having so much footage to edit, the need for optical effects, and the financial costs of blowing the film up to 35 mm for distribution. Once the film was finally completed, Greaves thought he had created a masterpiece, but his hopes were dashed when he personally took the film to Cannes, where it was rejected by the festival. Greaves told MacDonald: "I thought I could get it into the Cannes Film Festival, and I flew over to France. The problem was that Louis Marcorelles, the influential critic, went to a pre-screening of the film and the projectionist got the reels all fouled up. *Take One* is already chaotic. It's so fragile that if you mix it up even a little, you lose the film."[13] The film remained in obscurity until 1991, when it was screened at the opening of a retrospective of Greaves's work, curated by Dara Meyers-Kingsley, at the Brooklyn Museum and then at the Flaherty Film Seminar, where, it is fair to say, it was recognized by attending filmmakers, curators, and scholars as a neglected masterpiece of reflexive filmmaking.

What impact did it have on American indie cinema that *Symbiopsychotaxiplasm: Take One* remained unknown for twenty years? Richard Brody, the film critic for the *New Yorker*, notes, "For starters, it would have exalted the very notion of an independent filmmaker as a process-oriented filmmaker, of a political filmmaker as a personal filmmaker—and of a black filmmaker as a sophisticated aesthete and a master of complexity, as an intellectual artist of the first rank." He observes that Greaves deserves a place alongside two of the major figures of indie cinema in the 1960s: "Greaves was up there with John Cassavetes and Shirley Clarke in the blend of sophisticated modernism and emotional fury, of self-implication and formal innovation, of self-revelation and revelation of the heart of the times."[14] In some ways, Greaves, however, shares more in common with Warhol and Mailer in the sense that he created a filmic structure that allows for the unplanned, the unexpected, and the unforeseen—one that was open to spontaneity and serendipity. This is obvious from his stated influences, such as jazz, Heisenberg's Uncertainty Principle, Arthur Bentley's *Inquiry into Inquiries*, the Second Law of Thermodynamics, and J. L Moreno's psychodrama.[15]

Although there is no way that Greaves could have known in advance that his crew members would secretly film their own blistering critique of *Take One*, he created a reflexive film structure that could incorporate such events, including random occurrences such as when Victor wanders into the production and inadvertently provides a trenchant critique of social and political inequalities. Victor, whom Brody describes as a character right out of a Céline novel, vents about everything that's wrong in America in the late 1960s. By the same token, the secret critique by the crew members might not have been anticipated, but Greaves was nevertheless open enough to incorporate this material into the final film.

Discussing Paul Morrissey's derisive criticism of Warhol's similar lack of direction in his films, the actor Joe Dallesandro commented, "Paul was always there when Andy shot his films. He was always on the sidelines giving everybody direction while Andy sat behind the camera. But when a person sits behind the camera and is controlling the editing by turning the camera on and off, it doesn't matter what you're told to do in front of the camera if it's not on."[16] In a similar manner, Greaves had the power to edit the crew's critique into the film or to leave it on the cutting room floor. Although the crew was frustrated by the events occurring on set, Jonathan Gordon maintains that it was not their aim to insert themselves into the final film. He claims, "What our intention was: slip it [the footage] in the dailies and Bill's going to see it and can do whatever he wants. He can freak out. He can enjoy it. He can whatever. He made the decision to put it in—an incredibly bold and wonderful decision."[17]

SYMBIOPSYCHOTAXIPLASM: TAKE 2½

The actor and director Steve Buscemi saw *Symbiopsychotaxiplasm: Take One* at the 1992 Sundance Film Festival, where it screened out of competition. Buscemi, and later Steven Soderbergh—who learned of the film from his sound person—became fans and were instrumental in eventually getting the film restored and released. Soderbergh also provided additional financing for Greaves to produce a follow-up version, which became *Symbiopsychotaxiplasm: Take 2½* (2005). He once again chose to shoot the film in Central Park, but this time during the annual New York City Marathon.

Take 2½ begins with footage from 1968 in which Greaves introduces the crew and explains the importance of numbering the different rolls for synching purposes. Throughout both films Greaves, however, shows a complete disregard for their technical advice. In *Take One*, the camera operators constantly worry about proper exposure, but Greaves seems not to care at all. At one point in *Take 2½*, one of the cinematographers, Philip Parmet, attempts to explain a continuity problem with Greaves's blocking of a scene, but he proves to be wasting his breath. Greaves insists on doing it his way and suggests that in the editing room he can simply cut away to a shot of row boat or the foliage to cover the continuity mistake, which is something he actually does in the editing of the film. As Dallesandro said of Warhol, "It doesn't matter if someone's telling him, 'We should shoot this.' It was his way of making his films. I mean, I'm sure he understood what Paul [Morrissey] was saying, but he had his way of doing things and he wasn't gonna change."[18] Likewise, Greaves was not going to change because he believed that his method, which entailed a wholehearted embrace of spontaneity, would somehow result in an interesting film.

Take 2½ focuses on the interracial couple (Shannon Baker and Audrey Henningham). We watch their various rehearsals of the same Freddie and Alice scene that was shot during the production of *Take One*. Henningham has initially been given an action—she applies makeup—presumably to take her mind off acting. The two actors give an entirely different reading than Fellows and Gilbert. It is much less theatrical and so naturalistic that it borders on being flat. As he discusses the scene with the two actors, Greaves tells Shannon Baker:

> In the last time that we worked on this, it seemed to me that not enough of your aggression, not enough of your virility, you know, was coming through. That is to say . . . it was very moving. You were very emotionally involved, you know, with her, but it seemed that we could use other colors as well as that particular color of your warm feelings toward her. Let's also have the areas where you're aggressively, you know, related toward her.

Greaves's direction appears to be contradictory. He suggests that Baker is not being virile enough but then claims that what he's doing is actually very moving.

His remarks are perhaps explained by his compliment that Baker appears to be emotionally engaged in the scene. Yet Greaves's suggestion that he would like to see a different "color" to the scene could easily be read as a parody of true direction, similar to having the actors sing lines in *Take One*. In such instances, we have the sense that Greaves is not actually directing, as the crew contends, but performing the role of director in a fairly obvious manner. Meanwhile, the crew members continue to discuss the issue of acting. Stevan Larner, one of the camerapersons, poses an important question: What is the difference between an actor playing an imposed role and a nonactor "playing a role which he thinks is imposed on him from whatever psychological need he might have at this moment?"

Right after this, Greaves huddles with the actors and the psychodramatist Marcia Karp. He tells them, "What we're doing now. We're going to do another psychodrama." Karp explains that they are going to do "Freddie confronting Freddie—the strong Freddie confronting the weak Freddie." She asks Freddie if he wants to fight. While Baker easily manages to overpower her, Karp insists that she will always win regardless. Baker gets on top of Karp and covers her mouth, momentarily preventing her from being able to speak. She, however, taunts Baker, "Look how strong I am. You just play with me. You don't fight. You never kill me. You think you do, but you don't. You think you've won, right? Don't you?" Greaves cuts the scene.

Baker admits afterward that Karp was on target. Greaves is curious to see what has been added to their characterizations through the removal of certain emotional blockages and the actors' newfound empathy, and whether their conflict will now become more manifest. He tells the performers, "So what we're doing now is going from improvisation to the scene. Well, we're going to start on the scene and we're going to go from psychodrama, from reality to the reality of the scene, you see. And see how and if they can in fact feed each other." We then watch the scene between Alice and Freddie, which shows marked improvement. In the session with the crew, Gordon talks about the fact that the film "will take its final form precisely because an indeterminate action took place in it and altered it and changed it, and made it something." Right after this, almost on cue, a rain storm interrupts the shooting.

The film then cuts to a film festival, where *Take One* has just been screened to an audience that includes Gordon and Baker. Afterward, they join Buscemi and Greaves on stage for the question-and-answer session. Buscemi talks about the fact that the film has never been released, as well as the irony that they are now planning to do a sequel. When Gordon asks Greaves to explain what he has in mind for the new version, the director, in a manner similar to how he behaved in *Take One*, sidesteps the question.

Take 2½, most of which was filmed in 2003, picks up the lives of Freddie and Alice thirty-five years after the initial scene. Freddie (Baker) has asked Alice (Henningham) to return to New York from Germany, where she's become a successful singer. He indicates to her on the phone that he is ill, but his real intention is to ask Alice to take care of the daughter of one of his girlfriends, who has recently passed away. He is now HIV positive and dying and worries about the fate of his "adopted" daughter, who is also a singer and reminds him very much of Alice. After she discovers the reason that Freddie has brought her there, Alice is stunned. She values her independence and cannot believe that he is asking her to care for the young woman. Alice resents that Freddie is responsible for the fact that she does not have children. As a result, her initial warmth turns to anger and bitterness.

Greaves has made it clear at the film festival screening that the conflict between the crew members and the director over his competence fueled *Take One*. He indicates that he worried at the time that conflict had been missing during the production until he saw the additional footage that had been shot by the crew in the editing room. In an interview on the Criterion DVD, Greaves explains the importance of creating some type of conflict in a film:

> I studied dramatic writing with Lajos Egri, in which he talks about any drama that you would go to see you're dealing with the problem of conflict. Protagonists, antagonists, a rising conflict, a crisis period. And in *Symbio*—it has all of these elements in it. There is a protagonist—that's me. There are antagonists—that's Bob Rosen and Jonathan Gordon. There is a rising conflict, where people are becoming progressively unhappy about what's going on and the thing is reaching a boiling point. The operating question is: What do you do in a situation like that? When does a revolt against authority take place? With this group of people, can you get an interesting movie out of it?[19]

On the set on *Take 2½*, Gordon acknowledges the different contexts of the two films. They have all seen *Take One* and now understand the thrust of Greaves's particular agenda, but another crew member wonders aloud what could possibly provide the conflict in the new version.

Whereas *Take One* could more aptly be described as a sociodrama that explores the hierarchical social organization of a film production, *Take 2½* is a psychodrama that deals with the process of acting. In *Take One*, the focus appears to be on the screen test, but, through its reflexivity, it shifts from the actors to the dynamic between the director and the crew members. *Take 2½* overtly uses the crew as a kind of chorus for what is occurring. Gordon, for instance, has been brought back not as a crew member—he had left the filmmaking profession by then—but, along with Buscemi, as a commentator on the film.

The sessions with the crew members are no longer clandestine but have been incorporated as part of the film. Parmet has issues with Greaves's blocking of a particular scene for continuity purposes, but there is nothing he can do about it because Greaves is both the producer and director of the film. He also acknowledges that he might not fully understand Greaves's motives, so he decides "to go with the flow." Although the crew is given their say this time, it is actually the screen test itself—the actors and the process of acting—that turns out to be the true subject of the film. *Take One* wound up interrogating the social roles involved in a film shoot (sociodrama), but *Take 2½* explores the boundary between the fictional characters and the real lives of the performers (psychodrama).

Greaves was highly critical of traditional Hollywood acting: "One of the things that kept bothering me about a lot [of] Hollywood movies was that the acting was very stiff and lacking in spontaneity."[20] As a member of the Actors Studio, which he joined in 1948, Greaves was impressed by the more spontaneous acting of fellow performers, such as Marlon Brando and Julie Harris.[21] Greaves's own interest in a more spontaneous and realistic form of acting was reinforced by his exposure to and engagement with J. L. Moreno's psychodrama, which he discovered at some point before he moved to Canada and which he continued to be involved in after his return to New York City.[22]

In an interview with Scott MacDonald in *A Critical Cinema 3*, which was published in 1998, Greaves discusses his ideas for making a second version of *Symbiopsychotaxiplasm*. Having been to Germany where *Take One* was popular, he wanted to cast Henningham, who was living there, along with the same actor who played Freddie, Baker, who still resided in New York City. Greaves told MacDonald: "So they would interact on several different levels: on the level of the basic screen test (the argument between them), *and* on a psychodramatic level (they did have a relationship with each other in real life); *and* on a third level, in terms of their here-and-now professional and personal realities and whatever has happened to them in the interim."[23]

Greaves indicated in the same interview that he was interested in the element of time and how that would affect the relationship between Freddie and Alice. In many ways, *Take 2½* perfectly illustrates the relationship among text, improvisation, and psychodrama. Psychodrama is not necessarily intended as the endpoint of the process because Greaves ostensibly wants to use it as another tool to get deeper into the characterization of the script. Henningham had been living in Germany for many years. She was not a well-known singer—that part is fictional—and arrived back in New York City just prior to production. Because there was no scheduled rehearsal time, Henningham was unable to prepare for the role before being thrown into the highly charged situation of Freddie and Alice and what has become of their lives many years later.

Before Freddie has a chance to make his proposition, Alice has offered to pay for him to take a trip back with her to a spa in Germany. But once Freddie springs the request about his friend's daughter, Jamilla, her response turns decidedly negative. The situation evokes a gendered response from bystanders. In the mobile trailer on set, a young African American female crew member wants Henningham, playing the role of Alice, to break through her defensive shield and let Freddie have it. Gordon has a different take, which he delivers with an almost religious inflection. He suggests to Buscemi that although he understands the wound, there is no sense of forgiveness on Audrey's part almost from the start. Buscemi wonders, "Why did she come?" Gordon wants Alice to show more warmth toward Freddie. Immediately afterward, Greaves tellingly observes, "What I love about making films is that everybody wants to be a director, everybody wants to be a producer. This is what *Symbio* is all about—that wonderful thing in the crew room where everyone expresses their need to control the creation of reality, you know, the cosmos."

Greaves tells Buscemi that he wants the performers to begin the scene on a higher emotional pitch. He suggests that Freddie and Alice have been pretending to be happy in being reunited only to discover their unresolved issues. Once the film cuts to the scene of Freddie and Alice, the viewer might ask: What is it that so upsets Alice about Freddie's request? Alice believes that he has lured her from Germany to America under false pretenses. She has come because Freddie indicated that he was sick, and presumably because she still has feelings for him. Freddie, however, makes certain revelations, such as his casual admission that he's been taking drugs. Alice is caught off guard by this but also by the real reason he has contacted her. It angers her that Freddie did not tell her in advance. Had he told her his true motives on the phone, Alice makes it clear that she would not have ventured all this way to see him. She could have had her own child, which he prevented her from having years earlier. And now he wants Alice to become a surrogate mother to someone else's grown child? Her bitterness over what happened in the past resurfaces.

In a discussion among Greaves, Buscemi, and Gordon, Buscemi suggests that Alice came because she thinks Freddie wants to be involved with her again, which he then shares with Henningham. Gordon raises the issue of self-control: "You have a coming together here that is so weighted with old emotions, and how these old emotions trigger things. And the self-control of these people is sometimes a little disconcerting to me because this self-control is so overwhelming." As Henningham defends the fact that she was trying to play the scene with more subtlety, the screen suddenly begins to shrink and then divides into three different images—an optical effect Greaves created in editing. In discussing the situation with Henningham, Greaves suggests that given her background she might be more apt to explode, but he postpones shooting the scene until the next day.

Early in *Take 2½*, in footage that was shot in 1968, Larner suggests that "life is role playing," and alludes to the fact that this is "the whole big bag the Moreno folks can explain more knowledgeably than any of us." The reference to the "Moreno folks" is a bit puzzling. To whom is he referring? Of the members of the cast and crew, it appears that only Greaves, Baker, Henningham, and Karp had any knowledge about psychodrama. Yet, in *Take 2½*, it turns out to be the technique that Greaves ultimately deployed to bring out the latent conflict between the actors/characters in his screen test involving Freddie and Alice. It is difficult to analyze what transpires in the scene involving Karp this time, but her very presence proves to be one of the trigger points. In the psychodrama involving Baker, Henningham, and Karp in 1968, Baker seems to be antagonistic toward her as the psychodramatist, or perhaps he is merely using her in order to generate the anger and aggression necessary within the scene.

In *Take 2½*, everything builds dramatically to the scene involving Karp. As Baker and Henningham walk toward her, Karp announces, "I've been waiting for you for thirty-five years." She kisses them and informs them cheerfully, "I'm going to work with you again. We're going to do psychodrama." Henningham seems genuinely confused and caught off guard, while Baker clearly remembers their earlier session years before. After they walk together, which is intercut with shots of marathon runners in the streets surrounding Central Park, the three of them sit on a large tree branch. Karp explains:

> We're going to talk about psychodrama as a tool for the actor in enhancing the characterization. For example, the line you had just this morning, saying "no, no, no" . . . and we wanted you to get enraged. And it was very slowly creeping into your voice. It's just that in psychodrama we can get to that jewel quicker by having perhaps a "double," somebody, be you, with you, to go to the unspeakable feelings.

Baker quickly responds, "Let's do it."

As they walk around, Karp analyzes the subtext of the scene, or what Freddie is not saying in the situation. Henningham indicates that she is confused at the new direction the scene is taking, but Karp insists, "Just follow it!" Karp will employ an important technique of psychodrama called "doubling." In the enactment, the double operates as a surrogate for the protagonist by mimicking his or her physical gestures while verbalizing what cannot be spoken by the protagonist for whatever reason. Karp begins doubling for Freddie but then switches and doubles for Alice. When Alice says, "I know this man from before," Karp interjects, "And I wanted a child with you." Freddie, however, immediately tells Karp to "shut up" as she imitates Alice's behavior through doubling. When Karp tells Freddie, "Don't tell me to shut up," he becomes more hostile. As their exchange turns more heated, Henningham asks, "Are you Freddie now, or what?" When he answers, "No," she indicates she has a problem.

Henningham contends that she has been interacting with Freddie the whole time, but it now becomes clear to her that it has actually been with Baker, who insists, "I'm dealing with the reality of the moment." Baker argues that he has changed in thirty-five years, but Henningham complains that his method is still the same—he could have told her his intentions on the phone. When Karp, copying her gestures and speaking for Henningham as the double, says, "I feel scared in my soul. I feel scared,"

Baker becomes very irritated. As Audrey, Karp is essentially telling Freddie that she finds him to be a very scary person.[24] He points at Karp, "Now just a minute, this asshole . . ." Henningham interrupts and insists that she came over because she thought he was dying. He counters, "You did not think that. Come on. . . ." When Karp, as Audrey, insists she came because of him, Baker suddenly stops and tells Karp, "You've got such a mouth. Someone should smack your mouth!" Henningham asks Baker if he's Freddie in this moment, thirty-five years later. When he agrees, Karp interjects, "I came because you were ill." Freddie snaps, "Shut the fuck up!" The following exchange occurs:

> Alice: I came here because you needed me.
> Freddie: Right.
> Karp: You!
> Freddie: Shut the fuck up!
> Karp: No! I came because of you.
> Alice: Hey, I can't take this type of bullshit.

Henningham starts to walk away. Karp speaks for Henningham, while also imitating her gestures and announces, "I'm going to sit down here and sulk."

The scene cuts. Alice makes it clear that she wanted a child, and expresses regrets about having an abortion. Freddie is dismissive of her feelings. A discussion among the three of them reaches a boiling point:

> Freddie (*shouting loudly*): Hold it a minute! Hold it a minute! I thought
>   I was wrong!
> Alice: Don't you shout at me!
> Freddie (*shouting over Alice*): Yes I will! Because you have blamed me for
>   thirty-five years! Yes, you have!
> Alice (*shouting*): Asshole!
> Freddie (*shouting*): You blame me. And listen . . . you, you . . .
>   *Alice points her finger at him.*
> Alice (*shouting*): And there are women everywhere. They have their
>   babies and they still have their professions! And don't you talk to
>   me . . . you stupid . . .
> Freddie (*shouting*): Oh, yeah! . . .

FIGURE 5.3 Freddie (Shannon Baker) explodes in anger at Alice (Audrey Henningham) during psychodrama with Marcia Karp, *Symbiopsychotaxiplasm: Take 2 ½*

Greaves steps in and yells, "Cut! Bullshit. Cut . . . Cut . . . Cut!" As he comes forward and reaches his hands out toward the two actors, he says, "Now then. I think at this point . . . I think we'd better go back to the script."

Karp suggests that Freddie is trying to give Alice something by offering her Jamilla. Alice reacts by saying, "This is too much pressure. This is not helping me at all because Alice is not a crybaby." Henningham insists that Alice is a very independent woman and wants to do it on her own terms. Greaves suggests they go back to the text. As they begin to rehearse, the two soften toward each other, Greaves tells them, "Wonderful! Shit, that's wonderful. Beautiful . . . keep going." Alice apologizes to Freddie and comments, "You're asking a lot." He tells her, "Give [Jamilla] a chance." He kisses her hand and the two appear to reconcile. After a very long pause, Alice asks Freddie, "What if she doesn't like me?"

As the two of them hug, the scene cuts to Jonathan Gordon in the trailer. He comments, "When people have asked me what the film is about, I say it's a study of the film acting craft as it intersects with real life." Gordon also talks about it intersecting with something much larger and real, which is the massive marathon event that surrounds the personal drama between Freddie and Alice. The scene cuts to Alice meeting Jamilla. She asks the young woman, "What's your name?" The actor (Ndeye Ade Sokhna) answers, "Ade." Greaves yells, "Cut, cut, cut, cut, cut. . . . It's Jamilla." The brief exchange, even though it represents a mistake by the performer, brilliantly reinforces the boundary that Gordon references between acting and real life.

The scene involving the employment of psychodrama is worth analyzing in detail. How did psychodrama result in the explosion between the two actors? The dynamic is quite complicated. As Greaves indicated, we know that Baker and Henningham previously had a relationship in real life. In *Take 2½*, the unresolved issues within their personal relationship become confused with the text involving Freddie and Alice, which ends in an explosion. Interestingly, it seems that Greaves and the others had hoped that Henningham would become enraged in the situation, but instead it turns out to be Baker, whose sudden and unexpected tantrum is what unleashes the pent-up anger in Henningham.

Looking back on what transpired in the film, Karp remarks, "I think that Shannon and Audrey were each trying to find a way to their own truth, which was very different from the truth of the other, both in their professional and personal lives . . . and I think that's what has created that explosion."[25] Although Greaves could not possibly have anticipated or predicted what would happen, he deliberately chose to incorporate psychodrama into the film by bringing Karp back to work with the same actors again. Karp has indicated that her role in the production was not as a clinician.[26] She was, however, employing one of the main techniques of psychodrama by playing the role of the double; a technique, which, according to Peter Felix Kellermann, "may be the most effective instrument in understanding resistances."[27]

In footage shot for *Take One*, but only included in *Take 2½*, Baker seems to harbor animosity toward Karp, who at the time was a young and well-respected psychodramatist in the field. Almost from the start of her taking on the role of the double in *Take 2½*, Baker becomes outwardly hostile toward Karp by telling her to shut up, calling her an asshole, and even going as far as suggesting that "someone should smack your mouth." This is quite unusual. Because psychodrama is a form of group psychotherapy, the double is often someone chosen from the group who takes on

FIGURE 5.4 Marcia Karp playing the role of the double, *Symbiopsychotaxiplasm: Take 2 ½*

the supportive role in order to assist the protagonist. The double is, therefore, considered to be an ally. As psychodramatist Tian Dayton suggests, "The double speaks the inner life of the protagonist, bringing the material that is lodged in the background toward the foreground. The double gives voice to the interior reality of the protagonist."[28]

In this case, we have dual protagonists, Baker and Henningham, who have not chosen the double but rather have had the double imposed upon them by the film's director. During the exchange involving Karp as the double, Baker appears to resent Karp and accuses her of not understanding the situation between Henningham and him when he complains, "You have no idea what you're talking about. She [Henningham] knows what we're talking about." Karp actually did not know the two actors well. She had worked with them on *Take One*, and now once again thirty-five years later in *Take 2½*. Henningham also suggests that what is transpiring in the psychodramatic encounter is "too much pressure" and claims it is not helping her. According to Dayton, "If the protagonist experiences the double as out of touch with her inner world, she should be allowed to correct or even ask the double to leave."[29]

Because this situation is occurring in a film rather than in a clinical setting, this is not an option. Rather than viewing Karp as a supportive ally, Baker, for whatever reason, has turned the double into an antagonist. It appears obvious that Henningham feels uncomfortable with the direction the scene is taking, but she is nevertheless encouraged to follow along anyway. She does not seem at ease with the resulting conflict, which Baker is escalating through his outright contempt for the double. When Henningham walks away in disgust, claiming, "Hey, I can't take this type of bullshit," she is genuinely upset. Henningham is no longer responding as Alice but as herself. Karp, however, doubles her sulking state. Because of their personal relationship, both actors choose to view the double as an interloper. Yet this additional conflict is exactly what results in the scene having the raw energy it was previously lacking. In the course of the psychodrama, the actors confuse the boundaries between themselves and the roles they are playing, which is what flips the scene from the fictional conflict between Alice and Freddie to the unresolved tensions within their personal relationship.

Karp offers an intriguing perspective on what occurred between the two actors in this pivotal scene:

Well, you see, spontaneity comes from "sua sponte," which means from within one's self. What I think got released between the two of them was they were shouting from within themselves, both in the character and personally. Both. Now if you stripped away the character—cause, let's understand, they're consummate actors—but if you stripped away the character and said, "Okay, you two go at it," I don't think there would have been as much furor. Or, if you stripped away their personality and just said, "Let these characters go at it," I don't think there would have been much furor. I think what we saw was a parallel lack of resolution and an enormous frustration of: "You're at fault! You fucking think I'm at fault, you're at fault. You fucking think I'm at fault?"[30]

Karp is suggesting that the volatility of the scene stems from the two of them blaming each other in the situation, but psychodrama nevertheless allowed certain unresolved emotions in their relationship to surface. She argues that the power of what occurred derived from the intersection of their own lives with those of the characters.

Greaves shared Moreno's interest in the therapeutic aspect of acting. According to Louise Archambault, who was married to the director and also served as a producer on *Take 2½*:

> For [Greaves] I think, acting was definitely therapeutic. In fact, his teaching, which he was wonderful at, really focused on the individual's psyche and its expression. I think that he was more interested in that person's evolution and realizations than the character's, but he didn't separate the two. For him, they brought their life into that character and into the words, but it was coming from a deep—unconscious, to some degree—part of themselves. If they can tap into it, that for him was so exciting. It was really exciting. And he was very encouraging and supportive of people revealing who they were. I mean, I think he was in search of his own self and thought that . . . [psychodrama] could help the actors break through whatever barriers or defenses they had built up.[31]

Even though the process proved to be a struggle for the two actors, Henningham and Baker ultimately managed to express genuine anger in the scene with Karp. They are no longer acting the parts of Freddie and Alice but actually shouting at each other.

According to the actors, the pressures of filming the psychodrama scene with Karp in *Take 2½* forced the tensions inherent in the scene to develop more quickly than they anticipated.[32] Both Baker and Henningham felt that they were taking a shortcut in the psychodramatic process, which Karp readily admits. In her defense, this was not a true therapeutic situation but rather a scene involving two actors in a feature film. Yet Karp, in the role of the double, managed to touch a nerve in both performers. As a tool for getting the actors in touch with their feelings in the scene, the use of psychodrama resulted in an incredibly raw and highly volatile dramatic situation, one that even Greaves later admitted "scared the shit out of me."[33]

Archambault insists that Greaves was always careful about not pushing situations too far when it came to acting. A more realistic performance was his goal in the case of Baker and Henningham, but he respected the boundaries of his performers:

But, on the other hand, he recognized that it may just be going beyond where they would be willing to go. He was very sensitive to respecting the actors' privacy. Even when he wanted them to feel and reveal, there was a limit to what he felt they could handle emotionally and that they would regret perhaps later on. He didn't believe in pushing you beyond. He said, "I'm not a psychiatrist." He distinguished between his role as a teacher, a director, an actor, and a psychiatrist—which he was not.[34]

Not every film director respects those distinctions.

The raw dramatic display of emotions as Baker and Henningham shout angrily at each other provides a powerful climax to the scene of Freddie and Alice in *Take 2½*, but Greaves intervenes and attempts to calm the actors by gently nudging them back to the safety of the written text. They might not have completely resolved the issues in their own relationship, but, in terms of the film, the viewer sees the Freddie and Alice scene in a new light, as inhabited by two actors who—through psychodrama and the use of the double—have left the realm of performance. They are finally able to "stop acting," as Freddie requests of Alice early in *Take One*, and instead are finally able to interact with each other as themselves.

6

BEYOND THE METHOD

Abel Ferrara and Harvey Keitel

I
n addition to J. L. Moreno, William Greaves cites both Stanislavsky
on theatre and acting and Strasberg on acting among the "influences,
concepts and aesthetics" for *Symbiopsychotaxiplasm: Take One*.[1] In
discussing Stanislavsky's *An Actor Prepares*, Moreno, however, was critical because, like the work of Freud, his techniques are rooted in the past
rather than the present moment.[2] After moving to America, Moreno continued his theatrical work, which came to be known as "impromptu theatre." According to René Marineau, "The work at the Impromptu Theatre
had started informally in 1929 [and] continued to take place at Carnegie
Hall for some time and focused mainly on spontaneity training, the 'living newspaper' technique, and impromptu theatre performances based
on conflicts presented by members of the audience."[3]

Moreno also became involved with the Group Theatre, a collective
based on the principles of Stanislavsky, which lasted from 1931 until it dis-
solved in 1941. Although he was not a prominent member himself, Moreno's impromptu approach nevertheless had a significant influence on the
group, which counted among its members Harold Clurman, Stella Adler,
Clifford Odets, Sanford Meisner, and Elia Kazan, who later cofounded the
Actors Studio. According to Jonathan Moreno, Kazan used the techniques
of psychodrama in rehearsals for plays, as well as *On the Waterfront* (1954).
He also indicated that J. L. Moreno demonstrated psychodrama at a theater in Connecticut, in which Clurman and Adler were in attendance.[4]

Greaves was a longstanding member of the Actors Studio and also taught acting classes at the Lee Strasberg Theatre Institute for a number of years following the shooting of *Symbiopsychotaxiplasm: Take One*. Although Greaves embraced Strasberg's approach to Method acting, Strasberg's idiosyncratic interpretation of Stanislavsky has always been controversial within acting circles. As Cynthia Baron and Sharon Marie Carnicke point out, Strasberg emphasized only one small aspect of Stanislavsky's larger system, which the Russian director had actually abandoned. They note, "Indeed, Strasberg's emphasis on losing oneself in the part and on affective memory is distinctly at odds with Stanislavsky's focus on the actor's duality of consciousness and on playable actions."[5] In contrast to Adler, for instance, Strasberg emphasized the psychological rather than the physical aspects of acting. Adler was focused on the script as the basis for developing the character, whereas Strasberg was more concerned with the inner life of the actor, including an emphasis on releasing emotional blockages, which were explored in a series of exercises he developed that Anthony Frost and Ralph Yarrow describe as "personal psychodrama."[6]

Critics of Strasberg's version of Method acting, such as Richard Hornby, argue that it is actually "more ideology than theory."[7] According to Hornby:

The tenets of this ideology can be summed up as follows: Theatre imitates life, the more closely and directly the better. The good actor therefore repeats on stage what he does in everyday life, drawing on his personal experiences, but, more important, reliving his emotional traumas. Strasberg specifically maintained that an actor, through an interesting process called affective memory, should learn to stimulate in himself a dozen or so real-life emotions, which he could then call up singly or in combination for all possible acting situations. The actor plays himself, not somebody else; acting is basically a form of emotional release. Acting training is primarily a process of coming to know yourself, and of removing emotional inhibitions.[8]

Early in *Symbiopsychotaxiplasm: Take One*, Greaves seems to incorporate such criticisms of Method acting into the film. Not only does Freddie admonish Alice to "stop acting," but he also complains, "Listen, I don't have to stay here and listen to all these hysterics." In her book on Method acting, Shonni Enelow makes explicit the connection between Method acting and hysteria:

> That Method acting entails a form of hysteria is one of its most enduring critiques, alongside the criticism that Strasberg's techniques "resemble psychoanalysis itself—or a parody of it." Both the techniques and the aesthetics of Method acting were linked to the look and feel of hysteria, neuroses, and psychic excess, and not only in representations of Strasberg's teachings but also in his sometime colleague's directing: in 1963, film critic Andrew Sarris wrote of Actors Studio cofounder Elia Kazan, "Kazan's violence has always been more excessive than expressive, more mannered than meaningful. There is an edge of hysteria even to his pauses and silences, and the thin line between passion and neurosis has been crossed time and again."[9]

In *Symbiopsychotaxiplasm: Take One* and *Take 2½*, Greaves deliberately mixed Method acting with techniques drawn from Moreno's psychodrama. Individual actors and directors have sometimes taken Method acting itself to such extremes that the resulting performances themselves become a form of psychodrama.

As might be expected, psychodrama hit its peak in terms of popularity in the period of the 1960s, when it also gained prominence in film. For the next two decades, improvisation and psychodrama were overshadowed by a return to an emphasis on the screenplay in independent film circles, largely due to issues having to do with film financing, exhibition, and distribution. Institutions such as the Sundance Lab and American Playhouse emphasized the importance of professional acting and the screenplay as key elements for independent film projects to become commercially viable. Yet improvisation and psychodrama did not die out entirely. Like Norman Mailer and William Greaves, Abel Ferrara saw making films as a form of personal therapy, or, as he put it, "my journey towards some sort of fucking understanding. To be somebody better."[10]

The actor Harvey Keitel, who studied with Strasberg and Adler at the Actors Studio and served as copresident of the training lab, also conceives of performance in therapeutic terms. In an interview with the painter and filmmaker Julian Schnabel and Zöe Lund about his role in the *Bad Lieutenant*, Keitel commented:

> Zöe was saying that without owning pain and rage, it's difficult to trust someone's sense of what is good. And it seems to me that a person has the *right* to own that pain and to scream as a result of it. And we have to teach that to ourselves, our friends, and, most importantly, our children. When I was a kid, I wish someone had said, "You have the right to break any fucking thing around you because of the suffering you are going through"—instead of "Shut up!"[11]

Ferrara cast Keitel in two films during the early 1990s, in which the Brooklyn-born actor, due to a personal crisis in his marriage, pushed himself to such extremes of personal emotion that both *Bad Lieutenant* and *Dangerous Game* transformed into what can easily be viewed as psychodramas.

BAD LIEUTENANT

Ferrara's cult classic *Bad Lieutenant* (1992) might be the most demented independent film of the 1990s. The story of a New York cop, who descends into a nightmarish hell of compulsive gambling, sex, and nonstop drug abuse, *Bad Lieutenant* is most notable for Ferrara's abject subject matter, religious symbolism, and stylistic excess. The script was cowritten by Ferrara and Lund, a heroin addict at the time, who also appears in the film and died seven years later, reportedly from a drug-related heart attack. Added into the mix is the film's obsession with baseball player Darryl Strawberry, who would later wage his own public battles with substance abuse. The bravura lead performance of Keitel, however, turns out to be the defining factor in *Bad Lieutenant*.

Ferrara had originally cast Christopher Walken to play the role of the Lieutenant, but the actor bowed out of the production several weeks before shooting was scheduled to begin.[12] When Keitel was then offered the lead role, he at first turned it down. The chance to play the lead character in a feature film, however, finally became a strong enough inducement for him to take the part.[13] Keitel was experiencing the greatest personal crisis of his life at the time. He had recently found out that his partner of twelve years, fellow actor Lorraine Bracco (later known for her role as Dr. Melfi in the hit television series *The Sopranos*), had been cheating on him. Bracco ended up leaving him for Edward James Olmos, causing Keitel to feel betrayed, despondent, and at the breaking point. Enelow has emphasized the connection between Method acting and trauma:

> The Freudian conception of trauma as an unsurpassable, cataclysmic event around which the psyche organizes was the implicit referent for Method acting: Strasberg's actors, in the emotional memory exercise, the controversial core of his technique, practiced recalling and reliving "once-in-a-lifetime joyful or traumatic experiences" in order to produce the emotions of their characters—and thus actors influenced by the Method imbued their characters with the kinds of feelings produced by once-in-a-lifetime (more often traumatic than joyful) events.[14]

Keitel somehow managed to incorporate the pain and anger of the traumatic experience into his own acting. As biographer Marshall Fine indicates, "Suddenly, he no longer had to try and imagine the kind of unhappiness and torment his characters were going through, because he was living with it. It was eating him alive—and he was channeling that torture directly into his performances."[15] For Keitel, as he himself acknowledged, playing the part of the Lieutenant became a form of therapy—an opportunity for him to confront and purge his own frightening inner demons. As Fine suggests, "Here was a chance to actually go crazy, in a way that wouldn't land him in jail."[16]

Bad Lieutenant begins with a scene of the Lieutenant taking his two sons to school after they apparently missed the bus because their aunt monopolized the bathroom. Their father berates them, "I'm the boss, not Aunt Wendy. When it's your turn to use the bathroom, you tell Aunt Wendy to get the fuck out of the bathroom. What are you: men or mice? She's hogging the bathroom. Call me—I'll throw her the fuck out!" As soon as the police officer drops the kids off at school, he immediately snorts coke in his car. A visit to a crime scene becomes an occasion to gamble on the major league baseball playoffs. He then buys and smokes crack, becomes involved in a sexual threesome, shakes down two African American hoods who have robbed a Korean grocery, and visits a girlfriend (Lund), with whom he freebases. Lund claims in an interview that rather than use a retractable needle, the two actors insisted on injecting themselves with saline solution. She notes, "We were holding some shots longer than one normally would in sort of a Warholesque fashion and it disturbs people. These moments are very conscious, a sort of transgression where things become too real."[17]

Bad Lieutenant is technically a crime film, but it sidesteps genre by being highly episodic. Other than a series of incidents in which the Lieutenant indulges in numerous vices and abuses his power, the thin plot centers on his escalating gambling debts and a heinous crime involving the rape of a nun in Spanish Harlem by two young thugs. Ferrara intercuts the rape with an image of Christ on the cross as he cries out in agony. When the Lieutenant learns that the Catholic Church is putting up a $50,000 reward, he responds cynically, "Leave it to the Catholic Church. Girls get raped every day. Now they're gonna put up 50 Gs just because these chicks wear penguin suits." As the Lieutenant investigates the crime, he peers at the naked body of the nun from a crack in the door of her hospital room and learns that she was sexually violated with a crucifix. The saintly nun, however, confounds the Lieutenant by forgiving the perpetrators and refusing to identify them.

If the graphic rape of the nun—we see her underwear and habit being ripped off—is not shocking enough, as rain falls, the Lieutenant pulls over a car containing two young women who have just visited a nightclub. When they cannot produce their license and registration for the vehicle, he forces one to expose her bare buttocks and gets the driver to simulate oral sex as he masturbates. The disturbing scene lasts for eight agonizing minutes. As Roger Ebert observes, "no scene of sexual harassment in movie history has ever shown more effectively how frightening and damaging it is than the scene in *Bad Lieutenant* where Keitel stops two girls who are driving without a license, and forces them to participate in what can only be described as a verbal rape."[18] According to Ferrara, the scene involving the two teenage sisters from New Jersey was something that Keitel improvised during filming, which was luckily captured in a single take.[19]

One of the female actors, Bianca Hunter [Bakija], who had studied Method acting at the Lee Strasberg Theatre Institute as a teenager but had not actively pursued an acting career, turned out to be a close family friend

FIGURE 6.1 Harvey Keitel as cop who pulls over two Jersey girls, *Bad Lieutenant*

of Harvey Keitel. Unbeknownst to the lead actor, Hunter had accompanied an actor friend to the casting session and wound up auditioning for a different part in *Bad Lieutenant* but ended up being cast in the scene involving the two young sisters from New Jersey. Hunter, who plays the driver, and Eddie Daniels, who plays the passenger, were not given "sides" for the scene and had no idea what to expect once they arrived on set. Things took a decidedly dark turn, however, when Lund, who was high on drugs, informed them prior to shooting that they were to do whatever Keitel told them in the scene, no matter how demeaning it might seem. According to Hunter, this managed to terrify the two first-time actors.[20]

In the sketch of the scene as it appeared in the original script, Keitel was supposed to force the driver to bare her breasts so that he could lick them. When Keitel discovered that Hunter was one of the actors just prior to filming, he became very upset and refused to perform it as conceived. Because Keitel felt he could not play the scene due to the overt sexual contact with Hunter, he managed to come up with a new scene, which he then proceeded to improvise on camera. Ferrara has indicated in an interview that the scene was shot in a single take, but, according to Hunter, it was actually shot in three takes, with Keitel coaching both her and Daniels between each of them.[21]

FIGURE 6.2 Bianca Hunter (driver) and Eddie Daniels (passenger) as the two Jersey girls, *Bad Lieutenant*

Although the performances of the young women were captured in three separate takes, there are actually two different angles—one camera angle shows the Lieutenant walking up to the car in the rain and then focuses on the teens inside, while the other camera angle frames Keitel as he stands outside the car, as rain continues to fall.[22] There is a sense in watching the scene that the young women have no idea what will happen next, which was essentially true due to its improvised nature. As a result, Hunter and Daniels play the scene with a sense of uncertainty, fear, embarrassment, and moments of nervous amusement—as if the two actors are not sure whether to laugh or cry at the situation in which they find themselves. When the Lieutenant asks for their license and registration and they do not have either, the women laugh inappropriately. Of course, Keitel's timing in the scene is impeccable. Once he mentions certain suggestive words or phrases, such as their being "bad girls," you can feel the wheels turning inside his brain, and the two women can as well.

When the Lieutenant asks the women where they were, there are long pauses. Offscreen, one of them, her voice trailing off, finally responds, "Yeah, we were at the Cat Club . . . big deal." The Lieutenant threatens to call their father. Daniels hesitates, draws her hand toward her face, shakes her head sideways, and tells him with a sense of urgency, "Don't . . . don't do that." Distraught, Hunter starts to lean her head on the steering wheel but instantly pulls it back and runs her hand through her hair. The Lieutenant asks them if they got stoned, to which Daniels responds, "We smoked a little grass." He threatens to tell their father again, and adds that they are "a couple of very beautiful girls." Daniels asks, "Couldn't you just give us a warning?" The Lieutenant once again raises the idea of some type of exchange. He asks whether they have boyfriends. Hunter looks over at Daniels, who answers, "No." The Lieutenant again threatens to tell their father. Daniels insists, "You can't do that." The Lieutenant counters, "What will you do for me if I don't do that?" Daniels answers, "Whatever you say. You can't call our father."

After a long pause, in which the film cuts from the apprehensive expressions of the women to the Lieutenant outside the car, he indicates he will give them a "warning," and suddenly asks, "You ever suck a guy's cock?" The women initially cover their faces and Daniels suddenly laughs at the absurdity of the situation. Hunter asks, "Are you serious?" The Lieutenant presses Daniels, "Did you?" She answers defiantly, "Yeah . . . so?" Her eyes averted, Hunter stifles a laugh and shakes her head in disbelief as the Lieutenant berates them. Daniels asks the Lieutenant to let them go, but he suddenly asks to see her ass. Hunter's eyebrows instinctively furrow; her head turns quickly to her sister. As Daniels strips and partially exposes her buttocks, Hunter's eyes dart over to Daniels.

The Lieutenant, however, demands that Hunter show him "how she sucks a guy's cock." Hunter appears bewildered and unsure what to do. She hesitates. The focus of her eyes shifts between his face and groin, and, at one point, she inadvertently stares directly into the camera. As Hunter simulates oral sex—her tongue moving tentatively inside her mouth—the Lieutenant fantasizes about her sexually while he masturbates. As he does so, his facial features gradually grow more contorted from exertion and his body stiffens as he approaches orgasm. He groans slightly as he climaxes, breathes deeply, quickly zips up his fly, then turns and walks away. The camera pans to frame the two women in the car. Hunter says something inaudible to Daniels who fixes her clothes as Hunter stares over at her. Hunter crooks her neck to look back at the Lieutenant, then moves her hand to her hair. As Hunter leans against the steering wheel and stares ahead, Daniels says, "Let's go."

Keitel's improvised performance is excessive, pushing the scene into territory that makes most viewers feel extremely uncomfortable. Not only is the Lieutenant blatantly abusing his power, but he is doing so with two teenage women. The Lieutenant's behavior is degrading and humiliating to them. He is exploiting both their youthful naiveté as well as their vulnerability. Lawrence Cohn in *Variety* writes of Keitel: "His tour de force, seemingly improvised method acting is matched against their unaffected, nervous naturalism. Sexual content of this scene is suggested rather than explicit but proves quite startling."[23] This quality no doubt stems from the fact that because the Lieutenant is forcing the women to enact his sexual fantasy, the spotlight is really focused on them.

When the Lieutenant asks to look at Daniels's ass as part of the bargain of letting them go, the quick exchange of glances between the two sisters is what alerts the viewer to the women's palpable sense of embarrassment. Each of the women is now a witness to the other's humiliation. The scene is not played through dialogue—their few tentative and fractured verbal responses to the Lieutenant's verbal manipulation and abuse—but through the interplay of their physical gestures, particularly their fleeting exchange of glances. When Hunter turns her head away from the Lieutenant toward Daniels, she seems to be smiling nervously, as if the two are privy to some absurd joke, especially at the moment he orders Hunter to engage in simulated oral sex.

Keitel controls the scene with the Jersey girls. Relying on an exaggerated form of Method acting, he's improvising the scene of a cop losing his sense of power through his mounting gambling debts. His verbal rape of the young women is an ugly and brutal attempt to regain his loss of personal power by terrorizing the two young women and turning them into his unwitting victims. There is a sense that they have no idea what to expect next. As a result, Hunter and Daniels are not trying to act—to play two teenage sisters stopped by a cop who turns out to be a maniac—but are forced to react to the utterly demeaning situation in which they find themselves. No matter what they might have been told beforehand, their scene, as a result of Keitel's improvisation, has suddenly taken an unexpected psychodramatic turn. The two women consequently are forced to respond in the only way possible, which is as themselves. Gavin Smith's comments about the performances of Hunter and Daniels seem completely on the mark when he writes: "Subjected to harrowing sexual degradation by Harvey Keitel, their reactions and responses are instinctive and totally spontaneous, all trace of performance or playing a part stripped away along with their dignity."[24]

Afterward, as he drives though the city and snorts more cocaine, the Lieutenant listens to the playoff game. After the Mets once again best the Dodgers, he becomes so enraged at losing another wager that he shoots out his car radio, puts on his siren, and screams expletives as he races through city traffic. His bookie warns the Lieutenant at his daughter's First Communion that the mob will blow up his house for not paying his debts, but the desperate cop continues to double his bets in hopes of getting even. After the Mets win another game, the bookie tells him, "You think maybe because you're a cop, he [the mobster] won't kill you. You're this close already to death." His face bathed in red bar light, the Lieutenant acts as if baptism has immunized him against harm. He boasts, "I've been dodging bullets since I was fucking fourteen. No one could kill me. I'm blessed. I'm a fucking Catholic." After placing a bet on the final playoff game, the Lieutenant visits his junkie girlfriend who helps him to shoot up. As he nods off, she tells him, "Vampires are lucky. They can feed on others. We gotta eat away at ourselves . . . We gotta suck ourselves off. We gotta eat away at ourselves till there's nothing left, but appetite." Ferrara presents a William Burroughs-like view of the world, in which human beings are the sum total of their addictions.

The Lieutenant later confronts the nun in the church as she is praying. He offers to avenge what has been done to her, but she questions his religious faith. After she gives him her rosary and leaves, the Lieutenant groans as he falls on his knees and continues to moan and cry out like a wounded animal. In a drug-induced hallucination, the Lieutenant imagines a statue-like Christ in the center aisle. He screams out, "What? You got something that you want to say to me? You fuck! You rat fucker! You rat fuck!" He throws the rosary and shouts. As he sobs, he apologizes profusely, "I'm sorry, I'm sorry, I'm sorry . . . I did so many bad things." He rants about trying to do the right things, but laments the fact that he is weak. The Lieutenant crawls down the aisle, begging for forgiveness, and kisses the bloodied feet of Christ. A Latina woman from the neighborhood, holding a gold chalice, leads him to the two hoodlums afterward. He smokes crack with them in an abandoned building and threatens to shoot them, thus putting his religious faith to the ultimate test. As the

Lieutenant pulls up in front of Penn Station, he is assassinated by the mobsters in a drive-by shooting.

Harvey Keitel dominates virtually every frame of *Bad Lieutenant* through his virtuoso performance, such as the hallucinatory scene in the church where he manages to express his character's inner torture and grovels and kisses the bloodied feet of Christ. Ferrara explains how he worked with the actor in this film: "My shooting isn't separate from what he's doing—in other words, he does what he does and we film it."[25] Donald Lyons writes about Keitel's performance:

> It is a performance totally in the key of Method improv: the running fau-
> cet of profanity can seem barely scripted, and you wince and you cringe
> and you cry for an editor, but in the big picture the Method indulgence
> for once beautifully justifies itself. For the numbing verbal repetitiveness
> and the shameless, wild exposure of the full body and the full soul are
> finally like Jackson Pollock squiggles that mysteriously add up. Here they
> give us a soul in hell.[26]

As Kent Jones suggests, "In a sense Ferrara is an actor's dream, because his work is so rooted in concrete action. But he is also extraordinarily demanding of actors, because they are required to go so far."[27] Not sur-prisingly, in Ferrara's next film, *Dangerous Game*, Keitel plays a director, who, in a scene of similar degradation, demands of his actor, Frank Burns, played by James Russo, "I need you to dig down into fucking hell."

DANGEROUS GAME

Following the success of *Bad Lieutenant*, which grossed $2 million at the box office, Ferrara conceived of another project, *Dangerous Game* (1993), written by frequent collaborator Nicholas St. John, which deals with sub-ject matter that also clearly derives from elements based on Keitel's own personal crisis involving his breakup with Bracco. If *Bad Lieutenant* is a fictional film that turns into a form of psychodrama through Keitel's extreme performance, *Dangerous Game* is less a fictional film than a series of psychodramatic encounters involving Keitel and the three other major performers, namely Madonna, Russo, and Nancy Ferrara (Abel Ferrara's wife at the time).

On many levels, Ferrara is a very misunderstood director, especially regarding his work with actors, such as Keitel and Madonna. As Jake Cole writes in *Slant*:

> Ferrara often gets lumped together with John Cassavetes for his extensive use of improvisation and his predilection toward actorly madness over intimate drama, but Cassavetes at least used improv to get to a fixed point, reminding viewers that it was the journey, not the destination, that revealed most. Ferrara doesn't even have the destination in mind; his actors stumble in total darkness, using their explosive outbursts like echolocation, the searching quality in their halting improv an indication of how both they and their characters gradually define their context and being.[28]

Intended as a criticism of Ferrara, Cole's remarks actually point to a critical difference between Cassavetes's use of improvisation and Ferrara's deployment of psychodrama in films such as *Bad Lieutenant* and *Dangerous Game*.

Psychodrama, by its very nature, does not have an endpoint. As we saw with Greaves in *Symbiopsychotaxiplasm: Take One* and *Take 2 ½*, he could not predict what would ultimately transpire in either of those two films. His steadfast belief in spontaneity as a method or process, however, represented a high-wire act that entailed a great deal of risk and uncertainty about the eventual outcome. Just as Greaves interrogated the notion of what constitutes "performance," Brad Stevens sees Ferrara, in films such as *Dangerous Game*, as "investigating that narrow line separating 'acting' from 'being,' assembling films on an improvisational basis in which impulses are privileged and narratives become deformed as actors express their free wills."[29]

Largely because of this psychodramatic process, *Dangerous Game* proved highly controversial. Funded by Madonna's production company, Maverick Films, as a star vehicle for the noted pop singer, Madonna bitterly denounced the film before it was released, claiming that Ferrara had used his "director's cut" to alter what she considered to be the feminist bent of the film's initial script as well as her performance.

Ferrara countered that Madonna was "being paranoid and scared, and that's the reason she can't act, because she hasn't got confidence. Because if you don't have confidence, the camera sees that and comes barreling through."[30] To grasp the controversy between Madonna and Ferrara over *Dangerous Game*, it is important to understand what transpired during the shooting of the film.

Madonna had been impressed by Ferrara's *Bad Lieutenant* and was interested in making a film with him. This project became *Dangerous Game*, but, as the subsequent title suggests, she had no idea what was in store for her. Given Ferrara's background in exploitation films, it was a serious miscalculation on the pop singer's part. According to Madonna biographer, Andrew Morton:

> Within minutes of the start of shooting, however, Madonna suffered a rude awakening. First of all Ferrara threw away most of the script and insisted on improvisation, urging the actors to explore not just the characters they were to play, but themselves. They spent hours discussing motivation, filming their discussions, filming themselves in the process of breaking themselves down.[31]

Ferrara's tactics undermined Madonna, who spent her entire career carefully crafting her public image in order to achieve celebrity status.

As was the case with *Bad Lieutenant*, Ferrara was not at all interested in personas but in deeply probing the inner psyches of his actors. Morton explains, "The whole process was raw, uncompromising and dark, as much an exercise in group therapy as in shooting a film. A large part of the reason for this was because the movie, exploring themes of personal breakdown, was being shot as the marriages of Abel and Nancy Ferrara and Harvey Keitel and his wife Lorraine were in trouble in real life."[32] Janet Maslin, reviewing the film in the *New York Times*, writes that *Dangerous Game* "is angry and painful, and the pain feels real."[33] That is because, in making the film, the boundary between fiction and the actual lives of Ferrara and his cast was constantly being confused and crossed. This gives the film a discomforting power, even if viewers at the time were not quite ready for such a visceral and psychic assault, especially with Madonna being cast as the sacrificial lamb in the psychodrama that Ferrara deliberately fostered on set.

Dangerous Game, originally titled *Snake Eyes*, is a virtual hall of mirrors. Ferrara and St. John conceived a film based on Keitel's own personal crisis involving the end of his long relationship with Bracco, which resulted in a bitter custody battle and court case involving child support. Because Keitel had been instrumental in developing her acting career, he felt victimized by Bracco. She countered in court documents that he was abusive to her throughout their relationship.[34] Issues of betrayal, abandonment, and abuse certainly come up in the film over and over again.

There are multiple layers to Ferrara's psychodrama. Keitel is playing a film director named Eddie Israel, who is shooting a fictional film entitled *Mother of Mirrors*. Ferrara's own wife, Nancy Ferrara, has been cast as Eddie's wife, Madlyn. The film Eddie is making turns out to be a psychodrama about the breakup of a marriage involving a couple named Russell and Claire. They are played by two fictional actors named Sarah Jennings and Frank Burns, who are played by Madonna and James Russo. In his book, *Impromptu Man*, Jonathan Moreno provides a quick summary of some of the various concepts developed by his father to facilitate psychodrama:

> To describe his techniques J. L. invented a new vocabulary. "Auxiliary egos" can take the role of one's parents, children, spouses, lovers, friends, coworkers, or anyone at all, including those who were dead or who never lived. One could "reverse roles" with those with whom one was in conflict, or "double" for someone who was unable to articulate how they truly felt, or "mirror" the behavior of another.[35]

Dangerous Game employs familiar techniques from Moreno's psychodrama, all of which have been set in motion by the film's unseen director, Abel Ferrara.

While Eddie clearly identifies with the male character, Russell, he nevertheless encourages Claire to retaliate against Russell for his brutality. Eddie is the one having the affairs rather than his wife, which is a reversal from Keitel's own life situation at the time. Throughout the filming, however, he clearly derives sexual pleasure from watching Russell's abuse of Claire. Eddie encourages Frank to build his character and, when they argue in the trailer, he accuses Frank of constructing a barrier between "you and the desperation." He then yells, "I stuck up for you. Now don't you abandon me! Don't you abandon me! I need you to dig down into fucking hell." In the scene that follows, Russell rants against Claire's religious conversion and insists that he desperately needs drugs, alcohol, and sex. From the sidelines, Eddie encourages Russell to direct his tirade to God. In a manner reminiscent of Keitel's scene in the church in *Bad Lieutenant*, Russell shouts, "I need these things," as he falls to his knees and grovels, as Eddie looks on. Russell cries in a low voice, "She's not there." Eddie responds, "That's right. She's not there."

Sarah and Frank later get stoned together. She discusses what she needs from him in order to make the scene better, which leads to a discussion about the nature of acting and the role that emotions play in terms of performance. Sarah asks, "How can he act if he doesn't feel it?" She poses the question, "What is the difference between acting and feeling?" She concludes that Frank has to love her to play the part effectively. This verbalizes what is at the heart of *Dangerous Game*, which, as in psychodrama, is an effort to obliterate the boundaries between the true feelings of the performers and their actual roles in the film. In his psychoanalytic analysis of *Dangerous Game*, Xavier Mendik discusses the performances of Keitel and Dennis Hopper's portrayal of Frank Booth in David Lynch's *Blue Velvet* (1986). He argues, "Both actors rely on excessive physical movements and manic gestures whose impact leaves an audience questioning if they have witnessed an excessive 'fictional' performance or a *genuine* display of mental aberration."[36]

Mendik suggests that our reception of these performances is often informed by extra-cinematic factors dealing with the celebrity status of the actors. He writes, "Equally, the fragmentation of identity that these roles provide is furnished by the fact that they clearly draw on an established set of extra-cinematic factors relating to the real life, unconventional (and well publicised) backgrounds of both actors."[37] Of course, Madonna adds her own extratextual readings to bear on the film. The whole religious conversion of Claire makes little sense given the character we see in the film, but it brilliantly plays off Madonna's stage name and highly publicized career, especially regarding her use of sexual imagery to advance her career.

The key to *Dangerous Game*, however, is the rape scene in which Sarah accuses Frank of crossing the line between simulating sex and the real thing. There is something about Sarah's reaction to what occurs in the scene that suggests that Frank and the film have somehow gone too far. There is an odd delay in her emotional response. After the scene cuts, she is not immediately angry, but her outburst comes almost as an afterthought. Once she sees Frank among the crew members in the back of the frame, she suddenly swings at him and shouts, "You fucking piece of shit!" As Frank moves away from her, she asks, "What are you smiling about?" Eddie insists, "The scene is over." "No, it's not," she responds with irritation.

> Eddie: What's the matter?
> Sarah: You know what the matter is.
> Frank: What?
> Sarah: Fuck you, Burn[s].
> Frank: Aw, come on, eh. Jeez.
> Sarah (to Eddie): He can't fucking act, man. He has to do everything for real.
> Frank: What are you talking about?
> Sarah: You know what I'm talking about.
> Frank: What are you doing . . . tell me?
> Eddie (to Sarah): Listen. Go tell him.
> Frank (to Sarah): Don't cry to him.
> Eddie (to Sarah): Go ahead. Go ahead. What is it?
> Sarah: Fuck, he has to drink to play a drunk. He has to fucking . . . he doesn't have to have . . .

As Frank storms off with Eddie following after him, he punches the mirror on the way outside. A crew member, who has been standing just outside, instinctively checks the mirror. We hear what sounds like the angry voice of Frank say, "Fuck her. Fuck this shit . . . Look at her."

In discussing the above scene, Brad Stevens comments, "The difficulty of determining where life leaves off and fiction begins, of saying how far is too far, of deciding at precisely what point a rape scene filmed with raw and uncompromising reality becomes a genuine rape, is directly confronted when Sarah attacks Frank after shooting Russell's rape of Claire. What happened during the filming?"[38] Stevens suggests that although we have watched the scene, it is impossible to say for sure, but he claims that it partially confuses the separation between performance and actuality.

FIGURE 6.3 Harvey Keitel as director comforting an upset Sarah (Madonna) after intense scene, *Dangerous Game*

What is it about the scene that makes us think that Madonna might not be acting, but is actually upset with Russo? For one thing, her response is delayed rather than immediate. It is triggered by seeing Russo, whose presence provokes her to lash out at him rather than after the scene itself. In addition, Madonna's confrontation with him takes place away from the camera. Like an event occurring in everyday life, it feels chaotic rather than something intentionally framed by a camera. We do not actually see Russo's smile, but we can assume that Madonna does, which raises her level of anger because she feels that he is mocking her. Stevens suggests that for Ferrara, character is revealed when confronted with the unexpected.[39] This is, of course, another way of saying that Ferrara is interested in characters who are able to respond spontaneously to a new situation, which, for Moreno, was the ultimate goal of psychodrama.

Moving away from a written script toward improvisation would create characters that begin to behave in unpredictable ways. Yet psychodrama moves beyond unpredictability by having characters respond to each other in the moment. Eddie asks Sarah, "What's the matter?" Her response, with its awkward syntax—"You know what the matter is"—suggests anger rather than any sort of scripted reaction. She also calls Frank "Burn" rather than his fictional name "Burns," which again would seem to attest to her anger. Sarah complains that Frank has to do everything for real, but she lapses into inarticulateness by saying, "Fuck, he has to drink to play a drunk. He has to fucking . . . he doesn't have to have. . . ." Sarah's stammering gets cut off, but Madonna's performance seems to reflect that she is flustered by something that happened in the scene.

In the case of Joe Swanberg's *Nights and Weekends*, an erection—whether intentional or not—becomes an indicator of a transgression. We do not have that as a barometer here, but Madonna's angry reaction conveys her unhappiness at being exploited in *Dangerous Game*. Her acting is much more realistic than Russo's. As Russell, he has been playing scenes with exaggerated machismo, occasionally punching mirrors for dramatic emphasis. His acting style might be described as Method acting gone bonkers, while Madonna displays an uncharacteristic vulnerability. Nancy Ferrara acknowledged as much by suggesting that the scenes where Madonna is not in control were the most revealing of her personality: "It is one of her best films, fascinating because it says so much about her. That's why she wouldn't endorse it. It was too close to the bone. She hit on all that emotion and couldn't face it."[40]

Madonna, however, had other reasons for not endorsing the film. Her reaction to seeing the cut of the film was a series of embittered faxes to Ferrara, accusing him of ruining her career. To this day, Madonna has not forgiven him for turning her from what she thought was a strong protagonist into a pathetic and abused victim. Many of the lines of dialogue in the film can be read as overt critiques of Madonna as a person. As Morton points out, "More than that, the movie morphed into a commentary of Madonna herself, becoming a crude, if compelling, biography. 'It's a film about her as much as a film about what we were making because I forced her to confront many of the issues in her life,' Abel Ferrara admits."[41] If that is indeed true, it is understandable why Madonna would be upset. According to her, "When I saw the cut film I was weeping. It was like someone punched me in the stomach. [Ferrara] turned it into *The Bad Director*. If I'd have known that was the movie I was making, I'd never have done it. He really fucked me over."[42]

In pushing the actors to extreme psychological states that mirrored their personal lives, Ferrara's two films, *Bad Lieutenant* and *Dangerous Game*, which exploited his own version of psychodrama, were an anomaly as far as indie cinema of the 1990s. The use of improvisation also continued to wane during this period. Although *Bad Lieutenant* was successful at the box office, Quentin Tarantino's *Reservoir Dogs*, made the same year, overshadowed it in terms of impact. When Tarantino followed the success of *Reservoir Dogs* with *Pulp Fiction* grossing an astonishing $100 million, the screenplay once again exerted its dominance. During the decade, those filmmakers who could write screenplays became prominent, such as Quentin Tarantino, Hal Hartley, Ang Lee, Todd Haynes, Todd Solondz, Richard Linklater, and Kevin Smith.

7

TIED TO A MACHINE

The Films of Gus Van Sant

ndie cinema experienced a crisis as the 1990s came to an end. Yet, as the new century began, there were hopeful signs of change. One major development was that Gus Van Sant, whose career spanned both independent and successful studio films, felt a need to rebel against the constrictions of industrial production. Inspired by international art cinema, he decided to abandon the screenplay in favor of more rigorous formal experimentation. The second major change resulted from the impact of digital technology, which greatly cheapened the costs of production. As a result, a group of younger filmmakers, who came to be associated with the movement known as "mumblecore," began to cast their friends as performers and experiment with a new type of naturalism. Their strategy, epitomized by the work of Joe Swanberg, was to harken back to the early days of the New American Cinema by making films that were more improvised and less dependent on written screenplays.

Originally shot for a mere $25,000 and using a cast of nonprofessional locals, Van Sant's first feature, *Mala Noche* (1985) more closely resembles a cinematic prose poem than a plot-driven narrative. In making the film, he relied heavily on storyboards. Once he embarked on making larger-budget productions, such as his next film, *Drugstore Cowboy* (1989), Van Sant found that creating storyboards became too cumbersome, and he "started doing something completely different, which was covering the scene with long tracking shots, intending to cut out the tracking parts."[1] His penchant for tracking shots is noteworthy given his unusual career. Van Sant made a number of major Hollywood films—*To Die For* (1995), *Good Will Hunting* (1997), and *Finding Forrester* (2000)—before returning to lower budget, more independent films that granted him the stylistic freedom he did not have on industrial projects. As Van Sant notes, commercial filmmaking "was tied to a machine that made a story that resembled other stories in a way to fit into the audience's expectations. Sort of like television."[2]

Part of breaking out of what he considered to be a rigid style of industrial narrative filmmaking grew from what he came to believe was an overreliance on a traditional written screenplay. Van Sant explains:

> Scriptwriting used to be notes jotted down by the director, and then all of a sudden it became a classification. People became scriptwriters when in fact, maybe before that, there wasn't a scriptwriter. Then there might have been a playwright, and [filmmaking] sort of followed the stage model. But after reaching its pinnacle, with maybe *Citizen Kane* as the ultimate, it has worked its way down the slope to today, where people are questioning that model.[3]

As he saw it, filmmakers have a choice: "Either you perfect the model, or you just try and figure out ways to work outside the model, to subvert it or change it or deconstruct it, maybe in the same way that James Joyce was trying to in his novels."[4] It occurred to Van Sant that some of the international film directors he most admired—Béla Tarr, Chantal Akerman, and Abbas Kiarostami, among others—had successfully discarded the old model and were attempting to create new ones in its place.

GERRY

Gerry (2002) represents Van Sant's most radical experiment with image and sound. Working on a smaller scale in desert locations and without a conventional script gave Van Sant a newfound sense of freedom. Instead of being based on dialogue, the film was shaped by locations, which largely determined shooting. These locations were a composite of Death Valley, Argentina, and the salt flats of Utah, but where to film within them also turned out to be a critical factor. According to the director, "We just had a selection of locations, and we chose at that moment, or maybe the day before, where to shoot."[5] *Gerry* did not have a traditional script. Van Sant originally wrote an outline and then created what he terms a "fake script," which was written very quickly in order to register ownership of the film.[6]

The two actors, Matt Damon and Casey Affleck, share writing credit on the film with Van Sant. He describes the unorthodox scripting process:

> So when we made *Gerry* first, I was still interested in not going through that screenplay stage. [Casey, Matt, and I] had meetings—"scriptwriting" sessions—for a number of months using outlines. Those were pretty undisciplined. We were just writing ideas down. Then out of those ideas, we made an outline. A week before we shot, Casey and Matt did more traditional dialogue writing. [When we started shooting, we] knew the progression to the end, but it changed as we reacted to things as we went. We threw away ideas, which you wouldn't ordinarily do if you were shooting a script.[7]

The script sessions involved a lot of free association by the actors, which Van Sant would write down, but the process was very fluid and would change from session to session. Like many improvisers, Van Sant has a tendency to trust his initial instincts. As he puts it, "I'm like, the first thing is the best."[8] But the actors kept reworking and changing the material for the scenes, even though the final result appears to be a kind of improvised exchange between the two principal actors, Damon and Affleck.

The dialogue, however, is not the driving force behind the film in any conventional sense. In fact, Van Sant wanted the conversations between Damon and Affleck to have an ordinary, random quality. As he explains, "That randomness is an element in real life [that] I'm trying to introduce because it makes the film life-like. So it doesn't really matter what the actors are talking about, they're just talking."[9] Dialogue in *Gerry* does not necessarily propel the plot forward, reveal character, or create any sort of dramatic tension between the characters. In fact, Van Sant actually considers the dialogue in *Gerry* to be a form of "nondialogue," and compares it to the type of dialogue found in Chantal Akerman's *Jeanne Dielman, 23 Quai du Commerce, 1080 Bruxelles* (1975), which he refers to as being "similar to pieces of furniture."[10] In other words, dialogue functions as simply one of the many elements in the film, but it is not dominant or privileged, which is often the case in narrative features.

In terms of the dialogue, the two Gerry characters riff on an expression like "Fuck the thing," which alludes to the endpoint of their journey. They also appear to discuss a character on *Wheel of Fortune* who screws up an obvious puzzle phrase "barreling down the road." It is almost as if the viewer is eavesdropping on a conversation without necessarily understanding the context for what is being said. The scene at the campfire appears to reference the exchange in *My Own Private Idaho* (1991) in which Mike (River Phoenix) confesses to his fellow hustler, Scott (Keanu Reeves), that he loves him. The scene in *Gerry* begins with Damon's Gerry telling Affleck's Gerry, who wears a large yellow star on the front of his shirt, "I hate you." Affleck responds, "Not really, though, right?" About a half hour into the film, Affleck gets stranded on a monumental rock. In the roughly twelve-minute scene, the two actors appear to improvise their exchange of dialogue, as Damon uses a "shirt basket" (literally his shirt as a basket) to transport dirt in order to soften Affleck's fall when he finally jumps. The scene includes back-and-forth banter in which the two of them say very little of substance given their dire predicament, and even manage to step on each other's lines.

The lengthy scene of Affleck stuck on the gigantic rock was something that appeared in the original script, but, once again, the relationship between what was written and what was filmed turned out to be

FIGURE 7.1 Casey Affleck atop a large rock in desert; Matt Damon below, *Gerry*

very much in flux during production. In discussing the scene, Van Sant explains, "That was a scene that was written in the *real* script. But the real script was actually thrown away, mostly out of indifference to it, but then remembered for a lot of the scenes. In a lot of the scenes we were remembering the script as written, and the rock was always something we were looking for, but (a lot of the dialogue) was basically improvised."[11] Nearly an hour into the film, when they are lost, the camera follows Affleck who suddenly stops walking. The camera then tracks in the opposite direction, picks up Damon and follows him to the point where the two characters meet up and say "Fuck you" to each other before exiting the frame.

The film creates a subtext between the two characters, even though the dialogue, which is delivered in a serious tone, at times amounts to gibberish. Affleck, for instance, says, "There's a lot of dinosaurs near here." He also talks about a *Civilization*-like video game involving a fantastic mythical story that ends with his being "one horse shy of saving the city." At other times, the two invent their own personal form of communication—a kind of secret-coded language—as they discuss how they have managed to get lost based on the position of the sun on their previous "scout-abouts." Even the word "gerry" is used in a number of different ways to suggest different meanings.

Late in the film, the two characters, completely dehydrated from the scorching sun, lie in the sand. Barely able to speak, Affleck asks Damon with great irony, "How do you think the hike is going?" After a long pause, Damon responds, "Very good." After Affleck tells Damon, "I'm leaving," he then slowly reaches over to Damon who turns his body toward his younger companion. Damon then climbs on top of Affleck and slowly strangles him to death—not out of malice, but to put his dying friend out of his misery.

Although *Gerry* operates on a narrative level in telling the story of these two men who end up getting hopelessly lost in the desert, the plot seems considerably less important than Van Sant's exploration of image and sound involving two figures in a landscape. Van Sant's approach is rigorously formal, akin to that of a painter in the sense that the landscape is given equal—if not more—weight than the human figures. In paying homage to Béla Tarr, Van Sant uses a number of long takes and tracking shots throughout the film. In one memorable scene reminiscent of *Werckmeister Harmonies* (2000), the two Gerry characters walk in unison in a close two-shot for nearly three-and-a-half minutes. At another point, starting from behind Affleck's head, the camera slowly rotates 360 degrees around him, revealing tears slowly falling from his eyes as he sits alone in the desert landscape. The spectacular shot lasts roughly three-and-a-half minutes as well. *Gerry* is concerned with formal cinematic elements: light, time, and space. There is an existential element to the plight of the two characters, a sense of futility in the face of high temperatures and the vast desert expanse once they become lost. Nature overwhelms the two Gerry characters, rendering their hapless efforts to find their bearings almost comical in a Samuel Beckett-like way, were it not for Affleck's ultimate fate.

ELEPHANT

Gerry was based on a little-known incident, but Van Sant used the high-profile massacre at Columbine as source material to create his follow-up feature, *Elephant* (2003). The school shootings, which occurred at Columbine High School on April 20, 1999, resulted in the deaths of twelve students and one teacher, and injured over twenty additional people. The two student perpetrators, Eric Harris and Dylan Klebold, initially planned their deadly rampage not as a shooting but as a bombing, with the intention of killing hundreds of people. Fortunately, the bombs did not detonate as planned, but the two students then turned their assault weapons on their classmates. Harris, who concocted the plan, turned out to be a dangerous psychopath, while Klebold was more of a follower. At the time, the media rushed to interpret the horrendous event in a number of facile ways: the perpetrators were raised by negligent parents or rendered insensitive by video games; they were Goths, closeted gays, or part of a trench coat mafia. In *Elephant*, Van Sant embraces all the media clichés about Harris and Klebold to show that, on some fundamental level, the real motivation behind the shootings remains an unfathomable mystery.

Van Sant originally wanted Harmony Korine to write the screenplay for *Elephant*, but, for whatever reason, Korine was unable to deliver. The director then turned to JT LeRoy, the "teenage" author of the novel, *Sarah* (2000)—Van Sant was then unaware that the author's persona was a literary hoax. LeRoy wrote something that Van Sant considered "a beginner's script," which did not impress either the director or HBO.[12] The director wanted to do something along the lines of *Gerry*, but he doubted that the executives at HBO would be willing to fund a project without a script. This proved not to be the case.

Van Sant did eventually write a short script that he consulted during production. As he explains, "The script was actually twenty-three pages, and that's what we used on the set. And nine of those pages were just the girls talking, but it was me thinking about what they were talking about. It wasn't what they actually talked about, because I asked them to talk about real stuff."[13] Van Sant cast amateur teenagers actors based on a series of improvs with a casting director.[14] By casting nonprofessionals to play the students, Van Sant was able to use their improvised dialogue to create a greater sense of realism, especially because their own words help to create vivid snapshots of the characters. According to the film's producer, Dany Wolf, "Making *Elephant* without a traditional screenplay and with real high school students enabled Gus to bring us even closer to reality."[15]

The first draft of the script for *Elephant*, dated July 24, 2002, is actually twenty-six pages in length.[16] It contains all the main characters from the film, even though many of them are unnamed. What is unusual about the short script is that Van Sant includes the number of minutes in the film's running time at various intervals, suggesting that he was thinking of the script in terms of using long tracking shots that would determine the length of various sequences. In line with the rigorous formal camera movements found in *Gerry*, Van Sant uses the architecture of the school to structure his story, which focuses less on the perpetrators, who are unnamed, but pays more attention to the victims. The screenplay is more of a sketch or a detailed outline. We get a sense of the characters and a few scenes, such as John and his father driving to school and when Acadia finds John crying and gives him a peck on the cheek. There are other details: Michelle's inhibitions about changing into gym clothes; Carrie's possible pregnancy; the eating disorders of Brittany, Jordan and Nicole; and Benny's heroism.

The screenplay also provides basic information about Alex and Eric, who are not yet developed as characters. Alex is picked on by the other students who hit him with spitballs in class. He and Eric order weapons on the internet and make out in the shower. There is a hint of a repetition in the scenes of Benny leading Acadia out the window to safety. The film, however, reorders the various scenes and fills in a number of important details, while forging stronger links between the characters through Van Sant's complicated tracking shots. What the short screenplay clearly indicates is how much of the film the director improvised during production.

The resulting film is essentially a network narrative, presenting brief snapshots of the various characters. John becomes a connecting link between Eli and Acadia, Mr. Luce, and Brittany, Jordan, and Nicole, as well as Michelle. He is also the one who first sees the two shooters, Alex and Eric, as they enter the school building dressed in paramilitary outfits. Part of the brilliance of *Elephant* is how Van Sant links characters through his long-take camera movements, presenting the same event from multiple perspectives, such as the scene where Eli and John meet and do their elaborate handshake and Eli complains about his parents as Michelle runs past them. The camera follows John as he goes outside and gets a friendly dog to jump in the air. The same scene is later presented, but from the perspective of two other characters, an effect reminiscent of cubism.

The sequence of Nathan walking down the hall is first presented with the camera following him past Brittany, Jordan, and Nicole, as the young women swoon over his good looks (rather than John, as appears in the screenplay), and later from their perspective, which ends in a spectacular six-minute extended tracking shot in which they enter the school cafeteria. As they get their food, the camera veers off to show workers in the kitchen before picking up the young women who eat lunch and spy John outside as the dog jumps in the air. The shot ends with them vomiting in the bathroom stalls. Through repeating scenes from different perspectives, Van Sant creates a sense of temporal simultaneity, but he breaks the linear pattern by jumping back in time to the day before after Alex is hit with spitballs in class.

Elephant contains less than a hundred shots. The film builds slowly, establishing its characters through the first two acts, then accelerates the cutting and pace in the short, eighteen-minute final act, which includes the prelude and then the actual shootings after the bombs fail to detonate. Whereas *Gerry* never builds dramatically, *Elephant* creates a very slow fuse that results in an inevitable dramatic explosion. Because the viewer is already familiar with the Columbine massacre, the outcome is virtually guaranteed. The final twelve minutes of the film depict the two shooters gunning down their fellow students, which commences with the killing of Michelle in the library. Van Sant carefully avoids depicting some of the murders as spectacle—such as the deaths of Brittany, Jordan, and Nicole, as well as Nathan and Carrie at the end—but instead leaves them to the viewer's imagination.

One of the great achievements of *Elephant* is the fact that Van Sant is able to tell an engaging story through a more structural approach to narrative, which eschews conventional notions of plot and character in favor of a more experimental style that explores such basic cinematic elements as space and time. The film's success largely depends on its imaginative temporal structure by turning extended tracking shots into a highly complex and engaging account of a mass killing that otherwise might have struck contemporary viewers as something that has become all too familiar.

LAST DAYS

Gerry, Elephant, and *Last Days* comprise Van Sant's "Death Trilogy." *Last Days* (2005) is a fictional account depicting the final days of the rock musician Kurt Cobain, the lead singer and songwriter of Nirvana, who died of self-inflicted gunshot wounds in 1994 at the age of twenty-seven. Van Sant is not interested in presenting a factual biographical account—a traditional biopic—but in rendering a poetic sketch of the missing last three days of the rock star, renamed Blake (Michael Pitt) in the film, who has reached a state of deep personal crisis. The film begins with a wide shot of Blake, muttering to himself, as he walks through the woods, presumably after escaping from rehab. He undresses and takes a swim, wearing only his undershorts and black sneakers. While standing on a rock, he urinates into the water. At night, Blake sits by a bonfire and quietly sings "Home on the Range" before singing it very loudly and discordantly. The next morning, after walking through more woods, he arrives at a large mansion, wanders around it, and enters the greenhouse to get a shovel, while Hildegard Westerkamp's "Türen der Wahrnehmungen" plays on the soundtrack. The music fades as Blake uses the shovel to dig up a cigar box containing drugs he previously buried on the property.

Attempting to avoid a music world that has turned into a personal prison, Blake has become a recluse. He avoids contact with others as he ambles around his mansion and property, often muttering to himself incoherently. Blake nevertheless cannot help the fact that he has become a planet around which other characters want to orbit, including his own entourage of two young couples who hang out at the large run-down mansion without heat: Scott (Scott Patrick Green), Luke (Lukas Haas), Asia (Asia Argento), and Nicole (Nicole Vicius). Other characters also turn up unexpectedly: a yellow pages salesman, twin Mormon missionaries who seek new members for their church, a record executive (Kim Gordon), Blake's friend Donavan (Ryan Orion) along with a private detective (Ricky Jay) obsessed with a famous Chinese magician who died through a strange mishap. Blake tries his best to hide from everyone, but he is in such a desperate state that the film ends up focusing more on the peripheral characters than on him.

Van Sant wrote a fifty-two-page screenplay for *Last Days*, which is dated June 8, 2002.[17] Certain elements from the film are evident in the script, but, even though the screenplay is far more detailed than the shorter one for *Elephant*, the final film is even less recognizable. Van Sant has indicated that "*Elephant* was cast before the script was written, but *Last Days* was written before we cast."[18] The director's comments suggest that casting radically altered the film, which is often the case when the scripting process remains open and fluid. In the DVD commentary to the film, Haas twice comments that they were working without a script.[19] As a result, he used personal material as the basis for his character.

In seeking to make his music more personal, Luke tells Blake a story about having the best sex of his life with a woman in Japan. She kept contacting him afterward, but he never answered and now wants to write a song as a form of apology. Luke also has a sex scene with Scott, which the actor indicates was something he had never done before and that the scene was performed quite differently in two separate takes. Green also reinforces the idea that the actors were asked to draw on their own personal experiences. As an example, he points to the scene where his character implores Blake to buy the kind of jet heater used at football games to warm the mansion and indicates that the lines, in a similar manner to Luke's, were improvised rather than scripted.

In the same commentary, Pitt discusses the scene with the yellow pages salesman (Thadeus A. Thomas) who turns up at the door asking Blake to renew an ad, which was improvised by the two performers. Thomas, in fact, worked for the yellow pages and showed up in the costume area of the production office and tried to sell them an ad. Van Sant recounts, "And then he introduced himself, and he wouldn't stop. No matter what, he was just selling you yellow pages. And I said, 'Wow, we could just put him into our set and he would just sell.' Which is what we did."[20] As Blake stalks around the house wearing a dress, coat, and hat and carrying a rifle, someone rings the bell at the front door. When Blake comes down the stairs and answers, he is greeted by an African American man, Thadeus, who is selling ads for the yellow pages.

Once inside, Thadeus asks Blake, "So, how's your day so far? As Blake slowly takes his seat, he simply mumbles, "Another day." Thadeus informs Blake that he ran an ad last year for a locomotive shop that sells parts. As they discuss the ad in an utterly deadpan, serious manner, Blake removes his coat, revealing he is wearing a black dress. As Blake moves forward,

FIGURE 7.2 Thadeus selling Blake a yellow pages ad, *Last Days*

Thadeus instinctively recoils and repositions himself on the chair where he is sitting. During their conversation, Blake suddenly slaps his neck and tells Thadeus, "Bugs." Blake begins to nod off. In response, Thadeus sets up another appointment. Since the scene was improvised, neither performer could predict what would happen next, which creates a sense of palpable tension in their interaction.

Another improvised scene occurs shortly afterward and involves two very tall twin Mormon missionaries (Adam and Andy Friberg) who also show up at the door. This time, it is Scott who invites them inside. He offers them a drink, which they refuse. Scott asks them, "Don't you . . . the blood of Christ thing?" They tell him, "We don't drink anything that's bad for our bodies." He asks the missionaries if they encounter freaky things going door-to-door, but one answers, "Not normally." The two brothers hold their bodies very rigidly, as one of them explains that they are there "to give him background information of their religion in hopes that you come to one of our services." Fidgeting nervously and pausing as if losing their train of thought, the two give a very convoluted explanation about their religion involving the need for sacrifice and purity, but then suddenly become nervous when others congregate and abruptly announce they have to go.

The scene of the Mormon missionaries is interrupted by a cut to Blake in an empty room. Right after the scene with them ends, Blake slowly collapses. He crawls and positions his body against a door. When Asia opens the door, Blake sprawls on the floor. In a similar vein to what also occurs in *Elephant*, Van Sant shows the same event from the opposing perspective, creating a sense of temporal simultaneity. The viewer suddenly realizes that she or he has seen this same scene earlier. In this case, Asia had opened the door previously, causing Blake's body to slump to the floor just prior to the arrival of the Mormon missionaries.

The scene disrupts a sense of what the viewer had assumed was linear time. Yet the effect of this approach in *Last Days* is somehow different than in *Elephant*. Mario Falsetto discusses the implications of Van Sant's strategy in *Last Days* by suggesting that a disjointed timeline is used to create a subjective sense of the protagonist's mental disorientation in the viewer: "The spatial and temporal repetitions formally represent Blake's dislocation in the world. As we watch the film, our sense of space and time becomes as disconnected as the main character's. The spatial dislocation and nonlinear temporality in the film induce a dislocation in the viewer."[21] The ultimate effect, he argues, "helps create the feeling of dream logic."[22]

The sequence that most embodies this is the lengthy tracking shot involving Scott singing to the Velvet Underground's "Venus in Furs." As Scott, Luke, Asia, and Nicole arrive at the house, Scott puts on the record, takes a seat, and begins singing the lyrics to the song. A minute-and-a-half into the song, Scott puts on a knit cap with a skull and crossbones emblem and starts to walk left. The camera follows and settles on Luke who trails after Scott and watches from a distance as he urinates in the bathroom. The camera stays on Scott as he resumes his seat by the turntable. Scott wanders into another room where Luke is talking to Blake about wanting his music to be more personal. He speaks to Luke and the camera follows the two of them out of the room. Scott warns Luke that they need to split because of the arrival of the private detective. The two enter the bedroom, disrobe, and begin kissing each other. Part of the scene of Scott singing to "Venus in Furs" is repeated later on, but the chronology appears to defy temporal logic.

One of the most memorable scenes occurs when Blake plays music, but the scene, which we see from multiple perspectives, is shown from outside the windows of his studio. We see him pick up his guitar and begin to play music as the camera begins to track out very slowly. At his most personal—playing his music—the camera remains distant during the five-minute sequence. Blake's death is another pivotal scene. After visiting a music club where he runs into a friend (played by Harmony Korine), Blake returns to the greenhouse. He is found dead the next morning by the gardener.

As the gardener stares at his clothed dead body, a naked figure of Blake, representing his soul, leaves his physical body by climbing up a ladder and escaping out of the frame. Scott, Luke and Nicole, who have already left the mansion, learn about Blake's death on the news. Fearing they will be implicated, the three decide to head to Los Angeles. The camera holds on Luke and Nicole, as he strums his guitar inside the car. The camera stays on an exterior shot of their car as it drives along the highway. Van Sant cuts back to the greenhouse where the police deal with the corpse, while the music of Clément Janequin's "La Guerre" plays on the soundtrack.

MILK AND *PARANOID PARK*

During the six-year period 2002–2008, Gus Van Sant moved away from the traditional written screenplay by relying on alternative forms of scripting in such films as *Gerry*, *Elephant*, and *Last Days*. Yet in making *Milk* (2008), a $20 million film for Focus Features, Van Sant worked from a highly detailed screenplay by Dustin Lance Black. Almost as a knockoff project before he headed into production on *Milk*, Van Sant filmed *Paranoid Park* (2007), which he adapted from a teen novel by Blake Nelson about a guilt-ridden teenage skateboarder who is inadvertently responsible for causing someone's death.

The script for *Paranoid Park* was only thirty pages in length. Van Sant lifted the prose directly from the novel and adapted it to screenplay form in a process he referred to as "almost like Xeroxing the story."[23] *Milk* certainly made substantially more money at the box office, but *Paranoid Park* turned out to be just as critically acclaimed. Is it merely that some critics prefer art-cinema narration to classical narration, or can an overwritten script present constraints that an outline or sketch do not? Using Van Sant's *Paranoid Park* and *Milk* as examples for comparison, it appears that when it comes to cinematic storytelling, sometimes a more streamlined or minimal screenplay can offer a number of benefits.

Using an outline or short script would seem to go against the grain of conventional thinking, because a well-developed screenplay is often the key to obtaining financing as well as attracting cast and crew on a larger budget, industrial film. In this particular case, Dustin Lance Black's screenplay for *Milk* has been widely acclaimed, winning the Academy Award for Best Original Screenplay over Courtney Hunt's *Frozen River*, Mike Leigh's *Happy-Go-Lucky*, Martin McDonagh's *In Bruges*, and Andrew Stanton and Jim Reardon's animated film *WALL-E* (all 2008). Dennis Lim has outlined some of the pitfalls of the biopic, which he calls "surely the most reductive of movie genres."[24] He notes, "All biographers face the task of wrangling the unruly particulars and generally undramatic shape of a life and a career into a coherent narrative. Writers working on doorstop-size volumes find this hard enough; a two-hour movie wrestles with the same challenges more acutely—and is much more likely to fail."[25]

Among the challenges facing the biopic, Lim lists an eye toward Oscar nominations for actors, character composites and making the story fit the constraints of three-act structure, becoming overwhelmed by sheer data, hagiography, viewers already knowing the ending in advance, and creating a one-note psychology for the protagonist.[26] In terms of having too much data, Black admits that "Gus sometimes says I'm long-winded. . . ."[27] His script for *Milk* was initially 110 pages, whereas Van Sant wanted it to be 89 pages. The shooting script for the film, which has a final running time of 128 minutes, turns out to be 104 pages.[28] Black's comments about having to trim the script are revealing. He complains, "I could only use about one-tenth of the people who were really in Harvey's life. If that. Those were really difficult decisions."[29] These decisions involve historical accuracy, but they point to another problem of writing biopics. Screenwriters often face the sensitive issue of having to rely on living sources to advise and provide personal information about the subject. In the case of *Milk*, the political activist's inner circle and contemporaries "were script advisors and appear as extras" in the film.[30] Black later notes of Harvey's inner group of misfits: "Meeting most in person, I grew to truly love them all, so every cut was a tough one."[31]

Whenever Van Sant wanted Black to cut something out, he met resistance. Van Sant paraphrases the screenwriter's response: "Well, I just feel guilty—there's so much that we are already leaving out, I can't throw away dialogue talking about somebody's relationship, for instance, or something that happened that day, or just the weather, you know."[32] In addition, which adviser ends up becoming a character can influence who and what appears in the film. One of the driving forces behind *Milk*, for instance, was Cleve Jones, who worked as an intern in Harvey Milk's office while he was a student in the 1970s. A friend of Van Sant, he actually brought Black's script to him and became instrumental in getting the film made. It should not be surprising that Jones (Emile Hirsch) plays both a major and heroic role in the screenplay and film. Moreover, this was a project that, according to *Milk*'s cinematographer, Harris Savides, Van Sant had wanted "to do for at least ten years."[33]

Issues of historical accuracy can affect a film in other ways. Because Milk was such a prominent figure, the first openly gay politician to get elected to public office, Van Sant considered it important to portray the time period in which the film was set accurately—San Francisco in the 1970s. Thus, the art direction became crucial in creating a believable setting, which included recreating Milk's camera store on Castro Street in the exact original location. In addition, the film's visual look had to match the archival footage that would be cut into the film. David Geffner writes, "In fact, capturing the period look of San Francisco is such a major part of Harvey Milk's story, Savides muted his color palette to more accurately reflect film stocks from that era."[34]

Milk begins with historical footage of gay men being arrested in bars in various cities—an addition to the script. After an intertitle that announces it is 1978, Harvey (Sean Penn) sits in his kitchen and dictates into a tape recorder, indicating that this "recorded will" should only be played in case of his assassination. Harvey's recorded will serves as a frame for the film, allowing him to narrate his own story. We move from the kitchen, to Harvey's political activism, to news footage of Dianne Feinstein announcing his death, which serves as a kind of prelude to the film. We then meet Harvey in 1970 in New York City, where he is a closeted insurance agent who picks up a young hippie (James Franco) on the subway stairs on his fortieth birthday. When the two decide "to run away" together, the film jumps to 1972 and San Francisco, where Milk opens a camera store on Castro Street in an Irish-Catholic neighborhood, experiences hostility to gays by other local merchants, becomes a community organizer, and runs for city supervisor. Black uses Milk's voiceover to introduce characters, such as Jim Rivaldo and Dick Pabich, and to show police violence against gays. Harvey meets an eighteen-year-old sometime street hustler, Cleve Jones, whom he tries to radicalize, but the kid is not interested.

In seeking their political endorsement, Harvey becomes frustrated with the gay establishment, as represented by Rick Stokes and David Goodstein, who own the major gay newspaper *The Advocate*, but insist on playing it safe. Harvey runs again in 1975 with a new straighter or less hippie-like look, and in 1976 for State Assembly. On the eve of the election (page 31 of the shooting script), Harvey remeets Cleve who has lost his swagger and now becomes one of Milk's recruits even though he loses the political election. We don't meet Harvey's antagonist, the ex-cop Dan White (Josh Brolin) until page 40.

This brief summary should make it obvious that Black's script contains a great deal of backstory, exactly the kind that Van Sant was careful to excise from Cobain's biography in *Last Days*. *Milk* attempts to set up a host of characters. But why is any of this important other than to adhere to historical accuracy? The first act goes to great lengths to establish discrimination against gays in the 1970s, even in a city like San Francisco. It concentrates on how Harvey Milk became "Mayor of Castro Street." The script contains many political speeches by Milk, covers his three losing races for public office, and establishes the ragtag group that gravitated around him. One of the difficulties of the first act is that it attempts to collapse too large a time frame, as we move from 1970 in New York City to San Francisco in 1972, to the three separate political races. As is typical of a biopic, Milk's personal life is depicted as entailing a sacrifice to a larger cause, in this case, the gay liberation movement.

Dramatically, however, the story has yet to get going, especially because the antagonist, Dan White, does not appear until the second act. There are far too many characters. The dialogue is long-winded and expository. Harvey's tape-recorded voiceover narration, which Black explains as an attempt to personalize the story, tells us what we already know.[35] Even the archival footage of Dianne Feinstein informing us of the assassination of Mayor Moscone and Supervisor Harvey Milk would be familiar to most viewers, so it is questionable why Black feels compelled to include it. Yet, in his notes on the script, Black explains, "My hope in having this at the head of the film was to put the audience in the same headspace as Harvey: sure he would be killed, but never sure when or how."[36]

In some circles, *Paranoid Park* was better critically received than *Milk*. In the *IndieWIRE* annual critics' poll, for instance, *Paranoid Park* ranked number 6, while *Milk* was number 15.[37] In the *Film Comment* poll, *Paranoid Park* came in number 7, while *Milk* placed number 10.[38] Typical of this critical response to the two films was Manohla Dargis of the *New York Times*, who, in 2008, called *Paranoid Park* "the one great film from Gus Van Sant to come out this year."[39] She writes:

> Mr. Van Sant's other film, of course, is "Milk," a touching if aesthetically unremarkable biography of Harvey Milk, the assassinated gay rights pioneer. I like "Milk," which has a strong, showy, often moving performance from Sean Penn as Milk and one gorgeously directed and choreographed sequence—shot by the great cinematographer Harris Savides—in which Josh Brolin, oiled in flop sweat and hair grease as Milk's killer, Dan White, walks alone through a series of grim institutional

corridors that put the killer's existential isolation and desperate journey into bold visual terms. "Milk" is undeniably moving, but it earns most of its power from its historical resonance and because it holds up a mirror to another charismatic community organizer who rose from the streets on a message of hope.[40]

Dargis suggests that *Milk*, while successful as a biopic, is not as aesthetically interesting as *Paranoid Park*.

Van Sant cast the nonprofessional teenagers in *Paranoid Park* using an open call on the social media website Myspace in an attempt to create a greater sense of authenticity. The film begins with a shot of the massive steel bridge straddling the river in the city of Portland, as cars in fast motion traverse the expanse, with the city in the background and gray clouds in the sky. Alex (Gabe Nevins) writes the words "Paranoid Park" in a lined notebook. We see him walking in a field with a dog. As he does so often in *Elephant*, Van Sant follows his subject from behind as Alex strides toward the beach, where he sits on a bench with his notebook and reflects. In voiceover, he describes Jared (Jake Miller) and the skateboard haven known as Paranoid Park. Alex doesn't believe he's ready to go there, but Jared convinces him otherwise.

About a month later, Alex gets called out of class at school. Once inside the main office, Detective Richard Lu (Daniel Liu) questions Alex about his whereabouts on a particular September evening. Alex is more articulate in describing the contents of his Subway sandwich than in providing details about the night in question. Lu's line of questioning tries to establish a rapport with the teenager, when, in fact, there is an enormous chasm between them. In a subsequent scene, Lu calls in various skateboarders. He suggests that they can call him "Rich," and discusses his desire to make contact with this particular "community"—a concept that completely eludes these kids. After Alex later wonders about Lu's suspicions, one of his friends remarks that cops are paid "the same as a janitor."

In the first scene with Lu, we learn certain background information about Alex, namely that his parents are in the process of getting a divorce, as well as the fact that he has a younger brother and girlfriend. When Lu indicates that a skateboarder from Paranoid Park was most likely at the scene of a horrific crime, the camera slowly moves in closer

FIGURE 7.3 Alex at his school locker, *Paranoid Park*

toward Alex, eventually framing the blank reaction on his face, as we hear the sound of a loud scream offscreen. After Alex returns to class in a slow-motion tracking shot down the school hallway, Van Sant shows documentary shots of skateboarders and other people, whose faces have been blackened out.

Jared announces his desire to go to Paranoid Park the next day. Alex also explains the issues with his cheerleader girlfriend. He claims that Jennifer (Taylor Momsen) is nice, but she is still a virgin. Alex knows that sooner or later they will have sex and things will get a lot more complicated. Alex borrows his mother's car and heads to Paranoid Park where he meets a hardcore skateboarder named Scratch (Scott Patrick Green). Alex thinks the park is great, but he also worries about his parents and the stress their impending divorce is having on his younger brother. He also wishes that he and Jennifer had more in common, but he really wants to ride the freight trains with the other train hoppers from Paranoid Park.

We learn from a female friend named Macy (Lauren McKinney) that Alex has broken up with Jennifer. Macy also suspects that he harbors a dark secret. She flat out asks him, "Did something happen to you?" Alex does end up acknowledging that something has happened. It is only at the end of the film, however, that we realize that Macy is the one who has convinced Alex to write down the events that he narrates as a way of purging himself of what is weighing on his mind. She tells him, "Write it to me." He does but burns the evidence. The weight of the crime causes Alex to lie on a number of occasions—to Detective Lu, his mother, Jared, and even to Macy, who seems to know when he is being untruthful. There is a scene where Alex's mother asks him about a phone call to his Uncle Tommy, with whom his father is staying. When it turns out that the call was made at 4:35 a.m., Alex suggests that he was "half-asleep" or "maybe even sleepwalking." His mother does not call him on it, which makes its own sad statement.

Although adaptations create a different set of issues, especially if a fictional book is well-known, Van Sant took a great deal of license in adapting Nelson's *Paranoid Park* in a mere two days. He freely transposed certain sections, including the dialogue, and shuffled events around. As one might imagine, the novel provides a great deal more exposition, especially about the interior panic of its unnamed protagonist once he accidentally kills the train guard. In Nelson's novel, the teenager, who is a lot more articulate about his feelings, has a revelation about himself while lying in bed one night: "*I was a bad person. I was. I realized it all at once. That explained everything. Character is fate. My English teacher had written it on the board at the beginning of school. I had a bad character, I was a bad person, and now my fate had caught up to me.*"[41]

Unlike Black's screenplay for *Milk*, however, Van Sant doesn't transpose this expository material into the film. Instead, Van Sant creates a boldly free-form, impressionistic look at this introverted kid's world—his relationships with his estranged parents, friends, and his jealous and demanding girlfriend, Jennifer. Van Sant speeds up and slows down time, giving equal weight to long lyrical passages of kids skateboarding, aided by Leslie Shatz's brilliant sound design. Sounds of birds suggest the inner turmoil of Alex, connecting him to the troubled shooter of the same name in *Elephant*.

Alex says of the crime, "I tried to put that part out of my mind," but Detective Lu's pictures of the victim's severed body bring it vividly back. We see Scratch and Alex hopping the freight train and the security guard running after them. After the gruesome accident occurs, Van Sant cuts from the victim's face as he crawls toward them, to two different shots of Alex, to Detective Lu, then back to the security guard and Alex's startled reaction. As Alex flees the train yard afterward, we hear his confused internal monologue—the rationalizations and jumble of thoughts flooding his mind.

In the film's most spectacular visual sequence, Alex showers in an attempt to wash away the guilt of the crime. We see his lowered face as water spills over his hair. As a result of Van Sant changing the camera speed, narrowing the shutter angle, and moving a handheld 2K light, the scene fades to black and then turns lighter as Alex puts his hand to his face before the image darkens again.[42] Images of birds decorate the wallpaper in the background as Alex slowly slides down in the shower and the sounds of birds keep getting louder, which creates an eerie effect. After ice skating one afternoon, Jennifer seduces Alex. He lies there impassively in a lovemaking scene that is rendered as light reflected off her blond hair and the deadpan expression on his face. Alex later breaks up with Jennifer in a scene in which the diegetic sound of their argument has been replaced by music.

With *Milk*, Van Sant sticks closely to the screenplay instead of doing what he did so successfully in his previous four films, which was to improvise from a sketch, outline, or minimal script, using them as a springboard for films that emphasize the cinematic aspects of the narrative. Reacting against the existing industrial split between the screenplay and production, Kathryn Millard insists that screenwriting should be conceived of as a process rather than an end in itself, and the screenplay needs to be a "flexible document" rather than a rigid blueprint for a production.[43]

Although it is clear that Van Sant wanted a much shorter script for *Milk*, he allowed Black to deliver an overwritten screenplay. Whether due to the larger budget, the inclusion of star actors, the pressure of dealing with an iconic gay figure, or his personal friendship with Cleve Jones, Van Sant essentially "translated" the existing script to the screen, which gave him little room to add his own visual interpretation. In *Paranoid Park*, which had a final running time of seventy-eight minutes, the thirty pages of script Van Sant transposed from the novel gave him a great deal more flexibility to interpret the story cinematically.

Andrew Bujalski observes, "As a screenwriter, you try to tell the story in a fairly streamlined fashion. You have to be careful about making characters' motivations too complex on the page, because then the script becomes gobblety-gook."[44] In *Milk*, Harvey constantly explains his own motivations. He tells us early on, "I wish I had time to explain everything I did. Almost everything that was done was done with an eye on the gay movement."[45] In the screenplay and in the film, Harvey identifies with Dan White, whom he somehow thinks is in the closet. He tells his advisers, "I know what it's like to live that life. That lie. You can see it in Dan's eyes . . . The fear, the pressure . . ."[46]

The film critic J. Hoberman observes, "It's a truism that the best movies are made from the worst material, and vice versa."[47] One explanation for this is the fact that conventional dramatic films tend to be plot-oriented, whereas great literature is more character-centered. As a medium, film appears to be less able to convey psychological points of view and moods, whereas film's strength lies in depicting images and sounds. Like the work of Dreyer, Van Sant's elliptical rendering of the novel benefits from subtraction—less somehow ends up being more. Alex becomes more inscrutable as a result of Van Sant choosing to remove exposition as well as certain suspenseful and dramatic scenes, while sticking to the surface. The book's epigraph comes from Dostoevsky's *Crime and Punishment*: " 'Young man,' he went on, raising his head again, 'in your face I seem to read some trouble of mind.' "[48]

Instead of exposition and character motivation, Van Sant focuses on his teen protagonist's face. Because Nevins's face is not transparent, the director's scrutiny of it, and its lack of disclosure, only serves to imbue the character with an even greater sense of complexity and mystery. Cinematographers Christopher Doyle and Rain Kathy Li's camera focuses more heavily on the light that illuminates Nevins's angelic face, which, as Amy Taubin points out, "bears a striking resemblance to the subject of Correggio's *Portrait of a Young Man*, the similarity emphasized by the way Nevins wears his turned-around black baseball cap with the back pulled down over his forehead and his light brown shoulder-length hair fluffed out beneath."[49]

As it becomes clearer that the screenplay is undergoing a transformation in this digital age, the form will no doubt vary greatly depending on the project. Kathryn Millard suggests that the development process in her experience leads to screenplays that are overdeveloped rather than underdeveloped as they attempt to conform to industrial norms.[50] She also asks whether "it is more appropriate to consider the screenplay as an open text that sketches out possibilities and remains fluid through the film-making process?"[51] Van Sant clearly treated *Milk* as a closed text in the industrial tradition, whereas he approached *Paranoid Park* as an open one, which suggests that sometimes an underwritten script can have advantages.

8

I LIKE HOW YOU TALK

The Films of Joe Swanberg

J oe Swanberg is considered a leading member of the so-called
mumblecore movement, an eclectic group of young, media-savvy
filmmakers who came into prominence at the SXSW Film Festival
in 2005 by making lo-fi, naturalistic films that dealt with the problems of
their own generation, namely people in their twenties.[1] Besides Swanberg
and Andrew Bujalski, other filmmakers initially associated with the group
included Aaron Katz, Mark and Jay Duplass, Frank V. Ross, Susan Buice
and Arin Crumley, and Ronald Bronstein.

Within the realm of indie cinema, mumblecore films often rely on nonprofessional actors, which has changed the standards of cinematic performance. There are several factors that might account for this. This is
a generation that has grown up constantly being video-recorded. Many
events are now recorded and played back instantaneously. It is therefore
hardly surprising that professional acting, which is highly dependent
upon artifice, is no longer the benchmark for mumblecore filmmakers,
especially when the comparison is to reality and the goal has switched
to naturalism. Performance in mumblecore films tries to avoid histrionics and even attempts to negate our awareness of the gap between actor
and role. Instead, the viewer has the sense that the character bears some
resemblance to the performer. This is not an accident.

At the 2016 SXSW Film Festival, Swanberg gave a keynote address that provides one of the clearest explanations of his own conception of improvisation:

> What I'm really encouraging people to do, via the improv, is just not act. If I give you the lines ahead of time, you're going to figure out a performance, and I don't want you to do that. I want you to be forced to just exist in the moment that we're filming, and I'm casting you because I want you to be you. I like you, I like how you talk, I like the kinds of jokes you make, do those in my movie; don't go create a character that's something else. In a way, the lack of a script is a forced presence, ideally.[2]

Swanberg's view of acting amounts to the equivalent of nonacting. He does not want his performers—even the well-known professional actors he has cast more recently in his larger budget films—to act, but to be themselves, which tends to be the cornerstone of naturalism.

Instead of writing his films like a more traditional indie director, Swanberg simply casts people to play parts that would reflect their own vison of the characters rather than his. He explains, "When I started making my own work, I'd ask myself, 'What do I know about being a 22-year-old woman who is just out of college and doesn't have a boyfriend? Why would I sit down and write that dialogue? Why not just cast somebody who's going through all that and let her say those things?'"[3] Cassavetes was likewise intent on capturing the behavior of real people in his films, which is why he often cast his friends and family and sometimes people who did not have acting experience. Swanberg claims, "I am more inspired by the aesthetics of YouTube and reality TV than I am by the history of cinema."[4]

KISSING ON THE MOUTH

Swanberg's first feature film, *Kissing on the Mouth* (2005), deals with the lives of three roommates living in Chicago. One of them, a young woman named Ellen (Kate Winterich), begins having sex again with her ex-boyfriend Chris Bucket (Kevin Pittman), mostly out of boredom but also due to a lack of direction in her life. Her roommate, Patrick (Joe Swanberg), who is working on a secret project that involves interviewing young people about their lives, has a crush on her and becomes jealous. In *Kissing on the Mouth*, Swanberg focuses on people in their twenties, often shooting the types of scenes that would be elided from most films, such as personal grooming and masturbation.

As part of the bonus features on the DVD for the film, Swanberg includes an interview with Winterich prior to shooting, which helped to generate ideas for the film.[5] At one point, she interprets the naturalistic project they are doing as "People for Dummies." Swanberg also includes three "scripted" rehearsal scenes, so that we are able to judge how they were altered for the final film. One segment includes a secretly filmed session where he and the two female actors, Winterich and Kris Williams, discuss how a scene—in which Ellen comes out of the shower and puts on deodorant—should be shot. All the scenes give insight into Swanberg's working method, demonstrating that he is essentially improvising the film with his actors as he goes along. He explains, "It's a good illustration of how the making of the movie went, where, basically, we showed up on set not knowing what we were going to do, and then talked it through, and then did it."[6]

HANNAH TAKES THE STAIRS

Swanberg's working methods continued to be similar in subsequent films, such as *Hannah Takes the Stairs* (2007), which represents a big leap forward in his filmmaking, mostly due to the believable performances he was able to generate from his actors, especially Greta Gerwig. In terms of the improvised performances, the film is also more effective than *Kissing on the Mouth*, largely because it maintains the temporal and spatial unity of shots instead of being constructed through editing, which allows viewers to read the gestures of the actors as an intrinsic part of their acting. Swanberg again did not use a script or even some type of detailed outline but allowed his actors to help create the film during the process of making it. Swanberg indicates that he had two written pages of ideas, which he shared with the producer, but not the actors. He explains:

> Early in my career I wasn't even working from outlines the way I am now. I was working from a hunch, or a theme, or some sort of notion. With *Hannah Takes the Stairs* I probably wrote two pages that Anish [Savjani], my co-producer and I could use to talk about what we wanted. And it never got looked at again. It was never on set. It wasn't emailed to any of the actors. It was just a way to think about the movie.[7]

In the press kit to *Hannah Takes the Stairs*, there is a slightly different account:

> Once filming began on the feature in mid-July, random scenes were shot from a basic outline and later pieced together. As the shoot progressed, the theme of chronic dissatisfaction emerged, and Joe and Greta wrote a one-page synopsis for the remainder of production. The overall structure of the film was developed during Joe's nightly editing sessions, and the cast would check out the footage each night before discussing the next day's scenes.[8]

In Swanberg's *Hannah Takes the Stairs* and *Nights and Weekends*, which he cowrote and codirected with Greta Gerwig, she plays characters who reflect her personality. *Hannah Takes the Stairs* is about a young woman, Hannah (Gerwig), who gets involved in three different love affairs over the course of a summer in Chicago. As viewers, we are not sure why Hannah begins these relationships, nor is she, other than the fact that she is young and attractive and confused about her life.

The scene where Hannah gets together with her coworker, Matt (Kent Osborne), exemplifies the power of improvisation in creating a sense of realism. When Hannah sees bottles of vitamins and drugs at Matt's apartment, she questions him about the different prescription drugs he is taking. The main drugs turn out to be Lexapro and Wellbutrin—two different antidepressants. She asks him why he is on them. He explains that he started taking the drugs two years earlier due to depression following a breakup. As Matt discusses the effects of depression, he becomes

FIGURE 8.1 Matt (Kent Osborne) and Hannah (Greta Gerwig) reveal themselves, *Hannah Takes the Stairs*

very animated. Osborne appears to be speaking from his own experience, which the viewer gleans from his speech patterns, rapid eye movements, and unconscious gestures, such as when he suddenly scratches the side of his head. He describes depression like being in a gigantic hole and uses hand gestures to explain how impossible it is to get out. He indicates that antidepressants provide a floor to begin to climb out of the hole and again uses his hands to suggest the enormous effort that it takes.

The fact that Matt reveals his vulnerability has a strong impact on Hannah, especially given the circumstances that caused his depression. Hannah suddenly realizes, "I can't treat you with carelessness." After a cut, she tells Matt, "I tend to leave destruction in my wake." When Matt asks her how things are going with her boyfriend, Paul, she stares out the window rather than at him and responds, "I don't know." As the camera moves in close on Gerwig's face, she tears up behind her large red-rimmed glasses. Matt asks, "Is everything okay?" After a pause, she answers, "Ah . . . no. It's like . . . otherwise, why would I be here?" She tries to laugh and suddenly begins to sob, as the camera stays very close on her. The fact that such raw emotions are coming from inexperienced performers makes it seem as if the two actors are dredging up deeply personal feelings.

SWANBERG AND GERWIG: *NIGHTS AND WEEKENDS*

Swanberg and Gerwig collaborated on the film that followed, *Night and Weekends* (2008), sharing writing and directing credits. The two did not have a complete sense of the overall film before production began. As a result, shooting the film remained in a state of flux, which reflected the vicissitudes of their relationship over the course of making the film. According to Swanberg, "On *Nights and Weekends*, Greta and I exchanged emails, but there was never anything written down, or anything on set, that resembled any kind of structure. We were just attacking it scene by scene."[9]

In *Nights and Weekends*, Mattie (Gerwig), a nursing student, and James (Swanberg), who works in the video game industry, are struggling to maintain a long-distance relationship. A year later, Mattie and James are no longer a couple. On a visit to Manhattan to do an interview and photo shoot, James, now a successful video game designer, gets together with Mattie. The distance between them is obvious, and Mattie is clearly insecure as she sits in on his interview. She eventually participates in his

FIGURE 8.2 Mattie is mistaken for James's girlfriend at a photoshoot, *Nights and Weekends*

photo shoot when the photographer assumes she is James's girlfriend and thinks they make a cute couple.

After the two go back to his hotel, Mattie changes into a bathrobe. She pretends it's a joke, but then asks to have sex. In the middle of their love-making, they get into a disagreement over sexual position, which creates an intensely disturbing scene. In both the initial sex scene and this one, Swanberg's erection indicates that he is aroused. That he plays the lead character rather than casting a different actor confuses the boundaries between fiction and actuality even further. It creates an undeniable sub-text to the film, namely that he and Gerwig are enacting some type of psychodrama for the camera, which is precisely what gives the film its raw power. The final unconsummated sex scene only serves to up the ante.

It is Gerwig's performance that rivets our attention, especially in the second half of the film. She is the vulnerable character, which is evident in a painful scene where Mattie summons the courage to ask James for help with her career. The scene has the awkwardness we find in interactions between characters in Bujalski's films, but this exchange feels as if Swanberg has managed to burrow even deeper. As filmmaker and critic Dan Sallitt suggests:

> Perhaps the clear emotional vectors of the second half are a setup for the movie's startling climax, which uses sex as a pathway back into the conflicts and contradictions of the unconscious mind. The discomfort of this messy but authentic sexual encounter hangs in the air, casting its shadow on the couple's stark farewell scene (which gives a final, unexpected flip to the romantic balance of power), and following us out of the theater.[10]

Gerwig admitted in interviews that the film was a difficult experience for her.

Gerwig indicates that she and Swanberg got into a number of quarrels over the film and did not speak to each other for three months. In fact, during production, the entire tone of the film shifted from the original plan of making a "happy" film to something much more complicated. In terms of the seemingly authentic sex scenes, Gerwig comments: "But having someone touch you on camera is really . . . [long pause] It's really kind of an awful experience. Because half of your brain is like, "Okay, I wanna make this look real, because I want it to feel real for the audience," but then you're also fighting to say, 'But it's not real.' But it is actually real, because somebody is actually touching you."[11]

What Gerwig is suggesting here involves the blur between fiction and actuality that is implicit in the kinds of intimate sexual scenes depicted in *Nights and Weekends*. Josephine Decker, presumably as herself rather than the character, makes a similar comment to Swanberg when he asks her how she felt about the just completed explicit sex scene of the film-within-a-film early in *Art History*. She tells him, "Yeah, I felt business-like, but it's not businesslike what we're doing." It is hardly surprising that his next film after *Nights and Weekends, Alexander the Last* (2009), deals with the subject of a married female actor, Alex (Jess Weixler), who develops romantic feelings for the male lead, Jamie (Barlow Jacobs). At one point, the director of the play (Jane Adams) attempts to stage a sex scene between Alex and Jamie. She asks, "But how do you fake sex?" The director continues, "If he backs up, like, if he doesn't have, like, his underwear down and a full erection, where are we?"

UNCLE KENT

Kent Osborne first appeared in Swanberg's *Hannah Takes the Stairs* and improbably wound up playing the role of the romantic lead, a part he again played in *Art History*. A consummate nerd, Osborne would seem an unlikely candidate to become the subject of an entire film, but that is exactly what occurs when Swanberg makes him the focus of *Uncle Kent* (2011), a film he made prior to *Art History*. While Osborne has some notable credits to his name—mainly as a writer and storyboard artist for *SpongeBob SquarePants*—he is, in reality, a forty-year-old single guy living in Los Angeles with his cat.

Uncle Kent revolves around a situation rather a plot. When Swanberg visits, Kent defends his bachelor status while they chat together in the swimming pool. Swanberg tells his friend, "You have a bleak view of marriage. It's a lot more fun than that." Kent explains, "I think I just missed the boat." His feels his life would be different if he had met the love of his life twenty years earlier and they got married.

Kent meets an attractive twenty-nine-year-old woman, Kate (Jennifer Prediger), on the chat website, Chatroulette. Kate comes to spend the weekend with him, but it turns out that she actually has a boyfriend. Kate is extremely flirtatious, gets Kent to disclose very personal things about himself, including his masturbation habits and sexual fantasies, but she refuses to have sex with him. At Kate's suggestion, the two of them respond to a sex ad on Craigslist involving a female librarian named Josephine (Josephine Decker) who wants to explore lesbian fantasies. When they get together, it ends in a threesome, but Kent ends up being the odd man out. What Swanberg seems to be suggesting is that Kent's lack of interest in settling down and having children has become less a badge of freedom than a liability.

Intentionally or not, Kate tours Kent's life and then simply leaves. As she toys with him after the embarrassing threesome by pretending to be a cat, she is oblivious to his wounded feelings. He wants to work, but she wants attention. Kate is basically playing a mind game with him, as she has been doing the entire time. In *Marriage Material*, it is the woman, Emily, who shows vulnerability and ends up getting hurt, whereas in *Uncle Kent*, it is Kent who shows a vulnerable side, only to wind up a voyeur rather than a participant in his weekend with Kate. Like Swanberg's *LOL* (2006), identity and even sexuality are defined by social media rather than interpersonal interaction.

ART HISTORY

Making *Uncle Kent* proved liberating to Swanberg after he wound up getting creatively blocked trying to make *Silver Bullets*. Following *Uncle Kent*, Swanberg quickly shot *Art History* (2011) and *The Zone* (2011) and also finally completed *Silver Bullets* (2011), the three films that constitute the *Full Moon Trilogy*. *Art History* returns to the same issue raised in *Alexander the Last* of simulated versus actual sex. As is typical of his working method of improvising on set, Swanberg began with a single page of "notes for myself." He explains, "For *Art History* I had a one-page outline that just said, 'Day 1, Day 2, Day 3, Day 4, etc.' and had a few scene ideas. These would be broad descriptions like, 'They shoot second sex scene.

Director leaves to look at footage. Actor and actress talk, start kissing, have sex. Director sees them having sex. Director gets jealous.'"[12]

In this film-within-a-film, a director, Sam (Swanberg), who has romantic feelings for his lead female actor, Juliette (Josephine Decker), becomes jealous when her performed sex scenes with her male lead, Eric (Kent Osborne), cross the line into actual sex. In a scene with Swanberg early on, Osborne discusses getting a stiff erection during a sex scene with Juliette, which he describes as being like that of a seventeen year old. He is grateful to Swanberg for casting him in the film but wonders how his attraction to Decker will ultimately affect the film positively or negatively. Swanberg responds, "I don't know. We'll find out." That question is eventually answered when, during the final sex scene, Sam storms out, and the film ends with a clash between Juliette and him in the swimming pool.

Although *Art History* is a fictional exploration of the attendant problems and emotional fallout of shooting sex scenes, Swanberg is acting the role of director and staging the kinds of situations that can occur on an intimate set during production. As he explains, "And hopefully the movies do get into those complicated relationships of being sexually attracted to the bodies you're filming, so feeling conflicted and guilty, but also the fact that those are your collaborators. *The Zone* gets the most into this issue, but *Art History* starts this conversation about responsibility."[13] That his pregnant wife is also present on the set and she discusses their relationship is an indicator of how much is being contrived, even if there is always the issue of slippage, as Swanberg openly admits, that can occur as a result of naked bodies and simulating sexual acts on screen.

On this subject, Swanberg explains, "Early on, I was really cavalier about filming sex scenes. I just assumed that everything was okay because we were friends and because these weren't high-pressure business situations. If people weren't comfortable, I thought it would be easy for them to tell me that. I would then realize that they had been uncomfortable but hadn't said anything."[14] That Swanberg has been mining seemingly autobiographical material is evident in his confessional director's statement, in which he writes, "This film is an apology to anyone I have hurt because of the way I work or because of my own emotional recklessness. As the title suggests, I hope all of these instances are in the past."[15]

SILVER BULLETS

Despite its preoccupation with some of the same issues dealt with in previous films, *Silver Bullets* (2011) represents a different type of film for Swanberg. It deals with genre, for one thing, and is also heavily stylized rather than naturalistic, relying on colored gels to create mood and atmosphere. The cutting, especially the continual use of crosscutting, is more pronounced. The use of a soundtrack by Orange Mighty Trio creates a sense of frenetic anxiety, amplifying the emotional tenor of various scenes. As Swanberg observes, "*Silver Bullets* was definitely a response to what started to feel like a trap for me—realism or mumblecore or whatever. I had this feeling that I was only walking down a straight line, along one path of something like documentary realism. I was like, 'Shit. I'm going to really fuck myself if I start doing this over and over again.' I started noticing myself getting into ruts."[16]

In creating a personal challenge for himself, Swanberg proved that he could expand the range of his work beyond naturalism. Yet he continues to use his own life as fodder for his films. *Silver Bullets* deals with personal issues—a crisis, actually—having to do his own disillusionment with filmmaking itself. It continues to explore the intersection between making films and his own life, including questions about artistic integrity and how early success can become a detriment, as the inclusion of snippets from an interview with David Foster Wallace makes clear.

Bookended by a scene involving a middle-aged couple (Jane Adams and Larry Fessenden) and an epilogue between the main characters that occurs two years later, *Silver Bullets* focuses on an independent director named Ethan (Swanberg) and his actor girlfriend, Claire (Kate Lyn Sheil) who has been cast in the lead role of a new werewolf film by a hot young director of horror movies named Ben (indie horror director Ti West). Ethan becomes immediately jealous about the situation, especially because Claire is making a commercial genre picture, which Ethan frowns upon for being frivolous entertainment. In response, Ethan decides to cast Claire's friend, Charlie (Amy Seimetz) to play his girlfriend in his own movie, which Claire knows will involve intimate sex scenes with Ethan.

When the two discuss the situation that night, which is shot in a continuous take, Ethan is framed in the foreground of the shot, while Claire sits on the bed with a beer bottle on the night stand next to her. As they talk, Claire continues to question how Ethan could be so insensitive to her feelings about the issue. After a pause lasting eight seconds, he responds, "It's also for a finite period of time, right?" The couple finally reaches a painful stalemate in their discussion, as the music becomes more frantic, while the two say nothing for forty seconds, which is an incredibly long pause in a film conversation. Claire suddenly asks, "What are you not saying?" The improvised scene is noteworthy for how it uses the gaps in their conversation to represent all the things that are being left unsaid between the two of them. Of course, Ethan's insistence on casting Charlie will drive Claire closer to Ben, and ultimately to the dissolution of their relationship, as we learn in the film's epilogue.

Silver Bullets raises questions about sexually intimate scenes that preoccupied Swanberg in films since *Nights and Weekends*. It is not a totally fictional question, as we subsequently watch Swanberg enact explicit sexual scenes with Seimetz. The fact that it is time-bound and occurring within a film does not necessarily mean that it is not going to impact personal relationships outside the film. Dan Sallitt discusses the fact that by being part of the film, Swanberg can have some control over the direction of improvised scenes, such as the one described above, where through his refusal to answer Claire, he won't concede anything about the fears and insecurities that she is bringing up. Sallitt argues that this places the burden of the improvisations on Sheil, relying less on her acting skills than "her intelligence and her emotional balance." He adds, "Like all Swanberg's films, *Silver Bullets* requires a level of creativity from its performers beyond what any scripted film can elicit."[17]

THE ZONE

Made right after *Art History* and during a period when Swanberg appeared to experience a crisis regarding his own filmmaking, *The Zone* (2011) explores issues of directorial control versus spontaneous, improvised acting by foregrounding them within the very process of filmmaking itself. The film is loosely based on Pier Paolo Pasolini's *Teorema* (1968), in which a mysterious visitor has sex with the various members of an Italian middle-class family, thereby altering their lives. In Swanberg's film, the Italian family is replaced by three roommates: Larry (Lawrence Michael Levine) and Sophia (Sophia Takal)—indie filmmakers and actors and a real-life engaged couple—and their housemate, actor Kate Lyn Sheil. To add to the authenticity, *The Zone* is filmed in their cluttered Greenpoint, Brooklyn apartment, which the housemates referred to as "The Zone."

The interloper turns out to be filmmaker and actor Kentucker Audley, who uses his cellphone to record his ensuing sexual encounters with the three residents. After this thirty-minute section of the film, the screen goes black, and we hear Swanberg's voice say, "All right, that's it. That's the end of the cut." A curtain is pulled back revealing the director sitting at a computer, surrounded by Larry, Sophia, Kate, the cinematographer Adam Wingard, and filmmaker Dustin Guy Defa. Thus, we now have a film within a film, as the actors discuss their responses to the footage.

Larry is critical. He feels the footage is grossly imbalanced and worries that viewers will be struck by its heterosexual bias. Swanberg has spent more time depicting naked women by concentrating mostly on Kate and then Sophia, whereas Larry has been given limited screen time. Although the cell phone footage depicts the naked bodies of the three actors, the sex acts themselves remain unconvincing, echoing Jane Adams's remarks in *Alexander the Last* that you need to view the entire act itself, and, if a male

FIGURE 8.3 Joe Swanberg discussing the footage they shot, *The Zone*

is involved, it is imperative to see an erect penis to be convinced that the participants are genuinely aroused.

After kissing Kentucker, Larry does not have an erection when he removes his bath towel. Kentucker is also filmed in wide shot from behind and the film cuts abruptly before he engages in oral sex. The big issue in terms of authenticity centers on the fact that there is neither any frontal nudity of Kentucker in any of the sex scenes nor clear shots that depict the various sex acts. The viewer watches Sophia from behind as her naked body moves up and down on Kentucker, who is obscured beneath her. In another shot, we only see Kentucker's buttocks as he makes pumping motions on top of Sophia, but such shots appear to be workaround strategies for being unable to film the sex act itself. This might be acceptable in a conventional Hollywood movie, but Swanberg has always been interested in breaking those taboos.

Throughout his career, Swanberg has been attacked by some feminist critics for his voyeuristic depictions of female bodies. He has also appeared naked in his own films, even engaging in a sexual scene on camera with Gerwig in *Nights and Weekends*. He filmed a sex scene in his very first film, *Kissing on the Mouth*, and, as previously indicated, also masturbated onscreen. In a sense, he is not asking his performers to do something that he hasn't been willing to do himself. In fact, naturalistic depictions of ordinary bodies and sex have become a trademark of Swanberg's films. He told an interviewer:

> My first movie, *Kissing on the Mouth*, really came from that. I had a couple of questions I was asking. Why aren't we seeing realistic sex in movies? What is it that's scaring people? And additionally, there was a more political attitude of the importance of putting real bodies on camera, not just these made-up, perfectly groomed, beautifully lit sex scenes and bodies. So that we can see stuff in the media that reflects our actual lives. It can drive you crazy if you're not seeing yourself in the stuff you're watching.[18]

His question—what is scaring people?—lies at the heart of *The Zone*. From the start, Larry expresses anxiety about Kentucker and the idea of another male engaging in sexual activity with his fiancé, even if it is for the sake of a film. This is understandable because actors are extremely vulnerable in such situations, which involve both safety and trust.

The first thirty minutes of the film, however, are deemed a failure by the other participants, as well as the director. The absence of Audley causes a dilemma for the production. In giving Larry more screen time in *The Zone*, there are limited choices now that one of the principal actors is no longer there. Joe suggests that they can use the iPhone option to film the sex scene between Larry and Kentucker, which means it will now have to be filmed from a subjective point of view. The film cuts iPhone footage of Larry sitting naked on a chair. Larry indicates that he would feel more comfortable and the scene would be much more erotic for him if Sophia filmed him rather than Joe. Once Sophia takes over the operation of the camera, she acts surprised when Larry quickly gets an erection as he begins to masturbate for the camera, but she also appears befuddled at having to simulate Kentucker's point of view. The masturbation scene lasts for roughly three minutes.

The other scene the participants believe is still needed for the film involves a threesome with Larry, Sophia, and Kate. Larry adds an ominous note when he indicates that his mother, who he claims has psychic powers, warned that engaging in such an act might damage their relationship. The filming is interrupted by Sophia, who indicates that it is okay for Larry to kiss Kate as well. Larry alludes to the "script," but Joe tells them to forget about the outline and try to respond naturally to whatever is occurring in the scene. Larry would prefer to receive directions from Joe, because he would find that less risky in terms of preserving his relationship with Sophia. The three of them begin kissing and fondling each other. The scene cuts to Sophia interviewing Larry afterward. She is curious if watching Kate and her kiss was a turn-on for Larry and whether he got a "boner" as a result. He suggests that she is slowly ensnaring him in a trap. As Sophia strokes Larry's stiff penis, she describes an erotic fantasy involving the two of them and Kate, which then cuts to a shot of Joe watching a scene from the film on a monitor.

As Sophia shoots Joe with the iPhone, she discusses the threesome. She wants him to take more control of the scene, but Joe expresses misgivings. He doesn't want to put their relationship in jeopardy. When Sophia downplays his power, Joe responds that he never thought he had such power until people got hurt and blamed him for exploiting them. He tells her, "I mean, I improvise. I don't . . . it's not like I made anyone ever do anything or say anything, but that doesn't change the fact that they got hurt." When Sophia suggests that people were being "babies," Joe insists that he now realizes "how loaded and complex that situation is." In terms of the scene, however, Joe admits that the footage of the threesome they shot doesn't work. He tells her, "The stuff doesn't work, and it's because it's too controlled, it's too safe." He questions whether it's worth pursuing and gives her the option not to do it. Sophia answers, "I'd rather make a good movie." Joe cannot guarantee that the scene will make it a good movie, but he believes that reshooting it would at least make it a better scene.

Joe films the three of them as they redo the initial scene of the group prayer. He then cuts to the bedroom where they again attempt to have a threesome. When Larry and Kate begin to kiss more passionately and he sucks on the nipple of Kate's breast, Sophia, who has been temporarily excluded, begins to slap Larry repeatedly, as Joe and Kate attempt to get her to stop. Sophia then bolts from the bedroom, as Joe checks to make sure the other two performers are okay, and then heads after her. Larry quickly puts on his clothes and follows, leaving Kate alone on the bed. When Joe reappears from offscreen, she comments with some irony, "I guess we're not doing the threesome." After a pause, she adds, "I just don't want to be in the middle of this bullshit." Sophia returns and gets back into bed, apologizes, and is ready to attempt the scene again, but neither Joe nor the other two actors are willing to proceed.

In the next scene, a weary Joe sits in the foreground, while Kate slumps in a chair in the background of the shot. Sophia, who is filming Joe with the iPhone, complains about all the time that she put into the movie and accuses him of not wanting to finish it. Joe claims to be "tired of this shit," even though he admits that he created it. He tells her emphatically, "I can't do it anymore. I can't feel responsible for this stuff . . . and I do." As Joe and Adam put away the equipment, Larry comes in and moons the viewer and laughs. The scene fades and cuts to a shot in Swanberg's living room as he sits holding his baby (Jude). His wife, filmmaker Kris Swanberg, offers her own critique, adding still another layer to the concept of a film-within-a-film. She tells him, "It just becomes another movie about you complaining about making movies." Kris also criticizes it as feeling "thrown together." In her most telling criticism, she remarks: "I'm not sure if I believe it when Sophia hits him during the threesome." Kris also thinks the film repeats what he did in *Art History*. Joe admits he ran out of steam, which is why the film is unfinished, but Kris doesn't fully buy this explanation.

Did Sophia actually become jealous and explode during the threesome, or was that something decided upon beforehand? That is one of the central questions, not only in terms of what we see on screen (which does not seem spontaneous), but also in light of Kris's criticism regarding the believability of what occurs. Earlier Larry, Sophia, and Joe have alluded to the outline. One reading of the film is that Swanberg has deliberately created a loaded situation in order to raise questions about a filmmaker's ethical responsibility in using improvisation, even though the film could be judged a failure on those terms. It is not a question of performance on Sophia Takal's part but has more to do with Swanberg's personal decision not to follow through on a psychologically charged situation, especially following his experience on such films as *Nights and Weekends*, which *The Zone* appears to be addressing.

In many ways, *The Zone* is a transition film, which came during a period when Swanberg was making films very quickly. It was shot in roughly five days, with Swanberg shooting and editing the film at the same time, which, as Levine suggests, "creates a blurry line between hanging out and making a movie."[19] Such an environment contributes to the blend Swanberg manages to create between fiction and real life. Takal and Levine had met Audley previously, so he was not a total stranger to them as the film suggests. Like Takal and Levine, Audley is also a filmmaker, whose first feature *Team Picture* (2007), set in Memphis, was strongly influenced by the early mumblecore films, especially those of Swanberg.

Although there was a rough outline of what was to happen in the film, all of the dialogue was improvised or ad-libbed by the actors.[20] Sophia's blow-up during the threesome appears to be fictional, allowing her and Joe to have a scene where he discusses his decision not to finish the film. It becomes a means for Swanberg to dramatize the fact that his improvisational approach can lead to dangerous psychological territory, and he no longer wants to deal with the emotional fallout that can result from taking the approach to its logical extreme. *The Zone* presents Swanberg's strongest auto-critique of his own filmmaking to date, framed by additional criticism from his wife, whose life was also indirectly affected by it.

Given its limited shooting schedule and the use of a single interior set of a Brooklyn apartment, *The Zone* might be considered a kind of knock-off film for Swanberg. As a consequence, it did not receive much festival play or critical attention compared to his other films. Yet the ideas and questions Swanberg raises in *The Zone* are extremely important, especially in terms of improvisation. What is the boundary between acting and real life? What is the difference between sex on the screen and real-life sex? Is it simply a matter of intention? Actors who perform intimate scenes on camera have to create a sense of believable passion, but what happens when that line—intentionally or not—gets crossed?

Swanberg was asked by an interviewer about the sexual tension between his lead actors in *Drinking Buddies* (2013), Jake Johnson and Olivia Wilde. He responded:

> I could never have created it. It was there and we were all feeling it, and it was very exciting. I didn't feel it off set. I talked to Jake about it, and he also said he didn't feel it off set. Which leads me to believe that it was Olivia who could turn it on and off when the camera was rolling. They were just great together. I don't know what to say about it. I attempted to analyze it myself, but Jake said it was the damnedest thing for him. As soon as the day was over, they would go their separate ways, and not see or speak to each other until the next day and then it was just really there, and you could feel it.[21]

Swanberg suggests here the ability of a professional actor to turn on and off sexually for the camera without the feelings spilling over. That kind of compartmentalization might be required of actors, but, as the question suggests, it is undoubtedly a slippery slope for both performers and directors.

Many directors—Cassavetes, Warhol, Clarke, Mailer, and Ferrara, to cite the most obvious examples—have created situations that raise ethical issues about directorial power and control. Swanberg has at times pushed his performers to extremes, raising similar questions about exploitation. *The Zone* foregrounds the ethical problems involved in doing that. The film serves as a form of confession, an acknowledgement of mistakes Swanberg has made in the past. In doing so, it set the stage for the next phase of his career, which is exemplified by the film's concluding scenes, especially the final one of Swanberg putting his baby son to bed in his crib. As a filmmaker, Swanberg has always drawn from his own personal experiences. It is therefore hardly surprising then that his subsequent films deal with a set of problems connected to the next stage of his life, namely, issues involving marriage and family.

MARRIAGE MATERIAL

In many ways, *Uncle Kent*, which was made just prior to the *Full Moon Trilogy*, can be viewed as a complementary work to Swanberg's *Marriage Material* (2012). The fifty-five-minute featurette, which was distributed for free on Vimeo, is also built around a simple situation rather than much of a plot. Joe and Kris Swanberg visit two friends in Memphis, Andrew (Kentucker Audley) and his live-in partner, Emily (Caroline White), and leave their seven-month-old son, Huckleberry (Jude Swanberg), with them overnight in order to have some time to themselves. The film quickly establishes a striking contrast between a married couple with a baby and two people who have been living together for some time without making an actual commitment.

Cassavetes, of course, was opposed to this more spontaneous, unscripted form of improvisation. Yet *Marriage Material* demonstrates that if you create a strong dramatic situation and choose the right performers, the results can be quite engaging. Swanberg's strategy here involves choosing two people whose real-life situation mirrors the fictional one that he wishes to explore in the film. Swanberg uses his own recent decision to become a parent to generate a discussion about the issue between two friends, Audley and White, whose long-term personal relationship turns out to be far more tentative than his own. Emily says numerous times that now that she's seeing other friends have kids, it suddenly seems within the realm of possibility. The key sequence occurs when they lie in bed together, which could be described as a sort of mini-psychodrama that lasts for fifteen minutes.

The baby becomes a catalyst for Emily to discuss her relationship with Andrew, which leads to a series of revelations that appear to cross the boundary between fiction and actuality. It is almost as if Swanberg has set up a surveillance camera inside their bedroom, as we observe a very intimate domestic dispute that develops between these two people who do not portray characters so much as perform their own personal lives for the camera. Watching this couple interact in extended takes proves fascinating for what viewers can glean about their relationship, including how they physically occupy the same spaces. In the bedroom scene, so much of the information derives from the long pauses in their conversation, the stammering, the nervous gestures in their body language, and the sudden and unexpected shifts in the emotions that arise, especially from Andrew's attempt to blame Emily for her feelings of wanting something more substantive from their relationship.

It is instructive to discuss briefly the differences between *Uncle Kent* and *Marriage Material*. Although both deal with the issue of marriage and use the technique of improvisation, *Uncle Kent* creates a far more contrived situation. Kent's weekend date with Kate and their subsequent threesome with Josephine is clearly a fictional situation, even though Kent is more or less playing himself in the film by responding to events that are occurring. The dynamic between Audley and White, on the other hand, cuts much closer to the bone. They are not playing a couple discussing marriage, but the two are an actual couple grappling with deep personal issues. In many ways, both *Uncle Kent* and *Marriage Material* serve as transition pieces. They represent a move away from Swanberg's self-absorption in the *Full Moon Trilogy* toward a greater a kind of maturity, especially in terms of subject matter, which becomes even more evident in his subsequent films, including the film he made next, *All the Light in the Sky*.

ALL THE LIGHT IN THE SKY

Considering the sheer number of feature films that Swanberg has made in his career, *All the Light in the Sky* (2012) might be easy to overlook, especially following the success of his commercial breakthrough, *Drinking Buddies*. Inspired by and starring Jane Adams, who will forever be identified with Joy, the family loser in Todd Solondz's *Happiness* (1998), *All the Light in the Sky* tells the story of a middle-aged actor, Marie, who finds herself moderately successful but also very much isolated and alone. The genesis of the film began on *Alexander the Last* and can be seen in the short precredit sequence of *Silver Bullets*, in which a woman named June (Adams) complains to her friend Sam (Larry Fessenden) that she is getting "old and fat." *All the Light in the Sky* picks up that same theme, but with different character names. The arrival of her twenty-five-year-old niece from New York, Faye (Sophia Takal), an aspiring actor, causes Marie to experience a minor mid-life crisis when it leads to

FIGURE 8.4 Marie (Jane Adams) in *All the Light in the Sky*

the sudden realization that the trajectory of her life is now on a downward slope.

There is something so casual about *All the Light in the Sky* that it seems
invented on the spot. Much of the film's strength derives from the performance of Adams, who, though her character attempts to remain upbeat,
allows occasional flickers of sadness to appear in her eyes. Adams, who
shares writing credit, describes the process of making the film in an interview in *Entertainment Weekly*: "We sent emails back and forth for a long
time with ideas—and text messages even. Joe wrote an outline and sent it
to me and we made a few adjustments and then he showed up with two
actresses, Lindsay and Sophia, and we just started improvising and shooting. It was an exciting process."[22]

As Adams explains elsewhere, there is no approval or rejection of ideas
per se in their exchange: "There is no 'official' sense to anything. I think one
day I mentioned how I was going to make a carrot cake when my character's niece arrives so I wondered if we would shoot that on the first day. Joe
listens and then sends an outline with the carrot cake included in it. There
really is no reason for me to know everything that will happen because I
trust him."[23] Adams describes Swanberg's unique approach to improvising
a film. Adams claims that she had much more input on *All the Light in the*

Sky than on previous Swanberg films: "This time was little bit different. He worked with an outline but this time he and I both had a lot to say about the scenes we were shooting. Each day I was coming up with scenes that I felt needed to be shot that weren't in the outline. When I had worked with Joe before, I was just saying, 'What do you want me to do next?' "[24]

All the Light in the Sky is easily Swanberg's most thematically integrated film, yet it also appears to be his most effortless. The flow of conversations seems as natural as the tide we watch going in and out or the subtle changes in the bright California sunlight that illuminates so many scenes. Swanberg's film seems to go beyond simple naturalism by confusing the boundaries between the artifice of performance and real life. Although it might be tempting to interpret the film as based on Adams's own life, she disavows such a reading: "It's like that thing where you steal from your friends' experiences and you throw it in, but it wasn't mine."[25]

Improvised films, such as *All the Light in the Sky*, depend on a close rapport between the actors because they need to play off each other and take risks. This is why directors who improvise, such as Cassavetes and Swanberg, often like to work with the same actors over a series of films. Although Swanberg has constructed certain films through editing early in his career, Adams describes what she considers to be unique about his approach to improvisation:

> When people think of improv people think of rambling dialogue which is cut down in editing but with Joe he has already written the scenes in his head. He will then get a couple of actors who know what he wants said. I think this is why he works with people who also like to direct because they know what it takes to make a scene. Joe is very aware of this. He shoots 1 or 2 takes.[26]

Takal, who had worked with Swanberg previously, did not know Adams, but quit another film in order to work with the seasoned actor. According to Takal, "One of the many reasons I think Joe is able to get great performances out of people is because there's a rapport developed with people over and over again, as opposed to you showing up to set one day and having to do a scene with a person you've never met before."[27] In addition, Swanberg shot the film himself, which no doubt also contributed to the intimate dynamics of the production.

DRINKING BUDDIES

Drinking Buddies represents both a continuation and departure for Swanberg, since he was working with well-known professional actors and a larger budget. That certainly changed the equation and raised expectations. In some interviews, Swanberg has emphasized the continuity:

> "Drinking Buddies," definitely career-wise and commercial-wise has different expectations, but weirdly, I worked in a pretty identical way to how I've always made movies. There was a 40-person crew and a lot more money and infrastructure, but it was still improvised and I wrote it in the same way that I've written the other ones. I worked with the actors in the same way. So it's the start of a new chapter, but then in a way, it is just a continuation.[28]

Yet the larger budget did seem to force a change in his working methods. Despite the fact that the dialogue was still improvised by the actors, the narrative, for instance, was more carefully planned than the earlier micro-budget films. According to Swanberg, "It's the most 'written' thing that I've ever done in terms of the story being laid out ahead of time. It was really heavily plotted. We went into production with a 45-page script. The actors never saw that. They got a two-page, bullet-pointed outline

FIGURE 8.5 Kate (Olivia Wilde) and Luke (Jake Johnson), flirtatious coworkers at the craft brewery, *Drinking Buddies*

that walked them through the story with one-sentence descriptions of each scene. They're generating the dialogue."[29]

Some of changes in his working methods in *Drinking Buddies* had to do with Swanberg wanting to exert greater control over the film. It also resulted from a growing confidence in his abilities as a director as well as becoming more at ease with the narrative form itself. As Swanberg explains, "I still don't write dialogue. I still let my actors speak for themselves, but I've definitely gotten more interested in shaping the structure of the films and turning them into the stories that I'm interested in telling at that time."[30]

There is a similarity between the working methods of Cassavetes and Swanberg, especially in how they work with actors. For both, making a film is a process of discovery—a collaboration with the actors. Cassavetes, however, strongly believed in writing scripts, endless rehearsals, shooting large amounts of footage, and filming numerous takes. In contrast, Swanberg works from outlines, doesn't rehearse, and develops the film largely during the process of production, even if he tends not to shoot a lot of takes of the action.

9

IMPROVISATION AND PLACE

Putty Hill, Stand Clear of the Closing Doors,
and the Films of Sean Baker

T he highly formal films of Gus Van Sant and the improvised films
of Joe Swanberg helped to define the radical change that took
place in indie cinema in the new century. Van Sant and Swanberg,
as well as his mumblecore cohort, however, were not the only filmmakers
to challenge the hegemony of the screenplay. Other indie filmmakers, like
Matthew Porterfield, Sam Fleischner, and Sean Baker, utilized a combination of improvisation and place as an alternative form of scripting. Their
more ethnographic approach reflected strategies employed by earlier
indie filmmakers, such as Morris Engel, Lionel Rogosin, Kent Mackenzie,
Barbara Loden, and Charles Burnett.

In making *Putty Hill*, Porterfield used only a short outline, improvising
a film that was shot in his Baltimore neighborhood. Fleischner set his film
in the New York subway system and his hometown of Far Rockaway, but
Hurricane Sandy ultimately forced him to adapt his script and rely more
on improvisation. Baker's films also depend heavily on their settings,
which range from a busy Chinese takeout restaurant in upper Manhattan
to Donut Time, a site of transgender prostitution in Los Angeles.

The use of place can be an important element in alternative scripting. Nicole Elmer has argued that traditional written screenplays usually
involve a level of fabrication that increases costs for budget-conscious
indie filmmakers. She writes, "However, stories as they exist around us,
with the people we know, in the places we live . . . or films integrating

these elements, become more approachable financially because they are happening already without our manipulation. We don't have to pay for life to roll out its strange course."[1]

MATTHEW PORTERFIELD: *PUTTY HILL*

Porterfield originally wrote a feature-length screenplay about teen-age metal heads in Baltimore entitled *Metal Gods*. After financing fell through, however, he put together a five-page treatment, which he indi-cated was "based on the specific people and places I found in the process of developing it."[2] The resulting film, shot guerrilla-style over twelve days on a budget of $20,000 raised on Kickstarter, turned out to be *Putty Hill* (2010). Comparing Porterfield's treatment to the final film provides a tell-ing example of how not having a traditional script allowed the filmmaker to engage more imaginatively with every aspect of production.

Porterfield's five-page outline for *Putty Hill* consists of roughly nine-teen scenes (or perhaps half the number found in a conventional feature script of the same eighty-seven-minute length) that contain only minimal description of the action.[3] Set in Porterfield's own working-class neigh-borhood in northeastern Baltimore, the fictional scenes are punctuated by mostly documentary-like interviews with the friends and family of a young guy named Cory, who has died from a drug overdose. Following the credits, a group of young people, wearing protective face masks, play a spirited game of paintball in the woods. After one of the players, James, gets hit in the face with a pellet of yellow paint, he is interviewed by the offscreen voice of the filmmaker. James reveals expository information, namely that his older brother, Cory, died a week earlier, and that the funeral is scheduled for the next day.

In the next scene, Cory's uncle, Spike, an ex-con with long blonde hair, gives a tattoo to a client and discusses prison (he's done time for murder), his nephew's sudden death, and his estranged daughter, who has come from Santa Monica for the funeral. The various characters who appear in *Putty Hill*, such as Spike, were discovered in casting the previous scripted film. Porterfield explains, "But during that process, we'd also seen many people who didn't fit many of the roles we'd written, but who were so

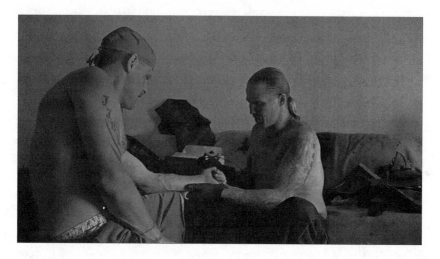

FIGURE 9.1 Spike giving a tattoo, *Putty Hill*

interesting that when I shaped the scenario for *Putty Hill*, I just used them as the basis for this story about a community that comes together to commemorate the loss of one of their own."[4]

In the outline for the film, Porterfield describes the next scene as three teenage girls walk through Double Rock Park. He writes, "Morning light shines down through a canopy of trees. There's a slight breeze. Though it's late summer, the forest remains lush and bright green."[5] His description suggests an interest almost solely in the visual texture of the location. In the actual film, there are four rather than three young women and he does indeed focus on the sunlight shining through the heavy growth—patterns of light and shadow, a shot of an insect in a pool of water, and the sound of a helicopter overhead. Porterfield also adds an important incident to the scene that is not contained in the outline. As the teens emerge from the forest, two men holding rifles question them about seeing a white guy with a beard who has robbed a nearby bank and shot two people. The girls' response is to ridicule the seriousness of the situation. They claim that they saw a black man with a long white beard, but he was young, "like on the order of four," and one of them also suggests that he was "eating birds and might be insane." As the two men with rifles chase them off, the teens giggle mockingly.

The next scene occurs outside a Greyhound Bus Station, where Cory's sister, Zoe, arrives from Delaware. In an interview, she claims not to miss Baltimore but looks forward to having a good time at the funeral with her friends. Cody and Dustin arrive home from the game of paintball. Their mother sits at the kitchen table and strums a guitar as Cody's African American girlfriend holds their baby. The mother sings a catchy tune about "looking for your brain." There is no mention of the song in the outline, so it represents an intriguing addition, especially due to Cody's reaction. As he listens, Cody stirs his coffee loudly and rudely leaves in the middle of the song to go to the bathroom. Afterward, his older brother Dustin is interviewed in his bedroom upstairs. He claims to have spent time in prison with Cory. In discussing his own life, he talks about being "unsuccessful" and is now stuck at home, trying to get his life in order. While Dustin indicates a desire to change his ways, he does not inspire confidence that he will actually be able to stay out of prison. He also elaborates on Cory's drug use, indicating that his friend was shooting heroin at the time of his death.

Meanwhile Jenny (musician Sky Ferreira, the only member of the cast with performing experience) sits with friends in an apartment. She turns out to be Spike's daughter from California. Although *Putty Hill* is a family portrait, as well as a group portrait of a neighborhood community—hence, the title—Jenny turns out to function as the closest thing we have to a protagonist. She helps to link the other characters together, along with the device of Cory's fictional overdose from drugs. According to Porterfield:

> The nice thing about the project, and what was really satisfying about the process of making this film, was that we had this chronology from a five-page scenario that laid out how these characters—these nonprofessionals who were playing themselves—would appear. And the sort of binding and glue that held everything together was this narrative construct. So, within that, that was the rule—that was the sort of fiction they all had to play into.[6]

Conventional films generally establish the protagonist early, yet, interestingly, Jenny does not appear until approximately twenty-seven minutes into *Putty Hill*.

For another scene, Porterfield's outline gives the location as Hemlock Gorge. He simply writes, "Zoe swims off some rocks with a bunch of friends." Zoe and friends get high, drink beer, splash in the water, and hang out together. The scene contains no dialogue per se, other than the snippets of natural dialogue that were recorded while filming the scene, which lasts for over three minutes. Some scenes—the one of Tyrell driving with Dustin—were shot but deleted in the final cut, while others are edited in a different order, such as when James picks up his younger sister, Marina, at the library. The librarian reads from the children's book William Steig's *Sylvester and the Magic Pebble* (a detail not included in the treatment), which concludes: "They were miserable. Life had no meaning for them anymore. Night followed day and day followed night over and over again." The scene of Jenny visiting her grandmother, Virginia, at the Harford Care Nursing Home differs considerably from the scene in the outline. It is the specific details—the three elderly women we view in exercise class, Virginia smoking a cigarette, and her habit of asking and answering her own questions—that bring the scene to life.

An extremely long scene in Carroll Skate Park features skateboarders and BMXers, interspersed with a long interview with Cody and shots of him and a friend stopping at a small grocery store nearby. A skateboarder spray-paints "Rest in Peace: Cory" on the wall of a red building at the park. The scene is only seven lines in the outline but lasts roughly nine minutes, and, other than the interview with Cody, serves as one of the strongest examples of visual storytelling in the film. Following this sequence, Jenny leaves the nursing home, takes a cab back to Spike's house, and gives an extended interview. She worries about not being able to cry at the funeral and reveals sad details about her conflicted feelings about her dad. Later that night, Jenny breaks down after watching Spike tattoo someone in subdued light while he and three black men do drugs. As Jenny weeps uncontrollably on the back porch, Spike claims not to understand her behavior. He asks, "What is your problem? You're not telling me anything." Jenny responds tearfully, "What the fuck do you think it is? I know what you're doing." He comes back out a second time. She tells him, "I can't even look at you. You disgust me."

The intense crying scene, which does not appear in the outline, is the most dramatic material in the film. In a sense, Spike's bewilderment epitomizes the detachment from everyday life that these characters appear to experience. None of them can fathom Cory's death. They know it is a tragedy but are incapable of mustering any semblance of emotional expression. As human beings, they have become deadened by alcohol and drugs or distracted by paintball skirmishes, tattoos, BMX bikes, and skateboard parks. All of them seem to live with their mothers—their fathers are conspicuously absent from their lives.

The next scene is described in two sentences in the outline: "[Virginia] sits in the recreation room, watching television. Cathy enters and sits down beside her."[7] Yet the dialogue between the two women captures a sense of numbed emotion that characterizes Cory's friends and other family members.

> Virginia: And I guess you're ready for tomorrow.
> Cathy: Are you going?
> Virginia: No. I just cannot do that. I just cannot. I want to remember
>   things like they were. . . . Heavy heart!

Virginia then discusses Reba McEntire and her love of country music. As the two sit there in awkward silence in front of the TV, the elderly woman concludes, "But this too will pass."

The memorial service, which is the final scene in the treatment, turns into a bizarre event. It is held in a karaoke bar, where folks drink pitchers of beer. Someone does an off-key version of "Amazing Grace" (a last-minute replacement for the Rolling Stones's song "Wild Horses" that created copyright problems), but it soon lapses into empty testimonials and spirited dancing that seem more suited to a wedding. Jenny sings the Dolly Parton song, "I Will Always Love You," as the camera frames a picture of Cory.

Porterfield's poetic sensibility is reflected in the film's stunning shot compositions. His scenes unfold at a languid pace, but each is a feast for the eye as well as the ear. In *Putty Hill*, cinematographer Jeremy Saulnier uses a dark muted palette and plays with low light, sometimes using as little as possible. The final scene where Cory's sister, Zoe, and a friend visit his deserted house contains so little light—the two walk through the rooms carrying a flashlight—that we struggle to make out the identities of the two young women. The scene, however, provides a fitting bookend to the film's opening shots of Cory's cluttered bedroom and empty apartment, in which exterior light creates warm patterned reflections on the wall that slowly fade during the opening credits.

The director's staging of scenes is extremely imaginative in terms of the interplay between image and sound. In an early scene in which Spike gives a muscular white guy a tattoo, the buzz of the tattoo gun nearly drowns out the dialogue, so that Porterfield includes subtitles. In another early scene, four teenage girls hang out together on a couch. Two of them get up to have a cigarette. The camera follows and frames them, but the two who remain offscreen are miked instead, causing a disjunction between what we are hearing and seeing. When Zoe arrives in town for the funeral, she is interviewed in front of a busy highway. In the night scene of the tattoo at Spike's place, music drowns out the dialogue.

The director's decision to use the documentary technique of interviewing the fictional characters is perhaps one of the more intriguing aspects of *Putty Hill*. Who is the person asking the questions, and what is his relation to the narrative that is unfolding? With nonprofessional actors, who are not all that emotive to begin with, the interview technique has a practical advantage: it tends to draw out the subjects, confusing the divide between performer and role in fascinating ways. Porterfield explains his use of the strategy: "I guess I think about it as a disembodied voice—a voice coming from the camera—asking questions in the voice of the filmmaker, maybe the voice of the camera, but also the voice of the audience; but not as a physical body needing any reason to be there."[8]

The biggest advantage of Porterfield's use of an outline is that it allows him to tell his story through more formal means—through composition and blocking. He chose interesting characters and locations and built a bare-bones story around them. According to Porterfield:

> I put a lot of emphasis on composition and like to rely on wide masters. There's a certain economy in that too. I also like to see what kind of breadth can be captured in respect to both time and place. For example, you have people in their own homes—most of the scenes in *Putty Hill* feature people in their own environments—who are moving across the spaces they're familiar with because they're theirs. In a way, these master shots are borrowed just as much from documentary techniques as the interviews are. It's a way to respect time and think about time, duration, and space in way that I care about.[9]

Because his story is not dialogue-driven, Porterfield focuses instead on scenes that employ visual storytelling. He carefully chooses places and situations that resonate visually: the opening montage of Cory's deserted house, the paintball battle in the woods, outdoor scenes of the teenage girls walking in Double Rock Park, the night scene of Spike giving a tattoo, and the final scene of Zoe and a friend visiting Cory's house, including driving scenes that transform car lights into colorful abstract patterns.

Porterfield's short treatment provided him with characters and specific locations, so that he could improvise while filming by taking both into account. At the 2012 SXSW Film Festival panel entitled "Shooting and Editing the Non-Scripted Feature," Amy Seimetz, who wrote and directed her own indie feature, *Sun Don't Shine* (2012), comments, "There's a freedom in your brain when you're improvising that it's okay to screw up because you can just do it again. . . . unlike a scripted film, where you're thinking, 'It has to be this way. Why isn't this working?' "[10]

Interestingly, the only line of written dialogue in Porterfield's treatment didn't make it into the film. It belonged to Spike: "I shot a guy in the face on Putty Hill. Then I got lunch and waited for the cops to come. . . ."[11] The spare outline forced Porterfield into a more collaborative and open-ended process during filming, especially in terms of working with nonprofessional actors, such as Spike, a heroin addict, whose story of doing prison time for a vengeful murder is based on his actual life. Porterfield observes, "Working with someone like that is as much about letting go as it is about maintaining control."[12] Porterfield believes that giving up control made *Putty Hill* a better film than his earlier scripted film *Hamilton* (2006). He notes, "It's a much more open film; it contains more magic than my first film does because we were open to the possibility of magic."[13]

SAM FLEISCHNER:
STAND CLEAR OF THE CLOSING DOORS

In a *New Yorker* profile on the career of Kenneth Lonergan, the author recounts a scene from his first feature *You Can Count on Me* (2000), in which the estranged brother, Terry (Mark Ruffalo) and his sister, Sammy (Laura Linney), smoke a joint together outside the house as she discusses a possible marriage proposal. A moth flutters around Sammy and heads toward Terry who guides it to land on his hand before it flies off and disappears out of the frame. Ruffalo observes, "But in this film we continue the scene, because we know that we are living, moment to moment, with the kind of openness that Kenny [Lonergan] wants us to have with each other, listening and responding."[14] The actor adds, "It was probably one of the most profound moments I have had as an actor—where the world collided with the work, and it was seamless."[15]

Lonergan, who served on the jury of the Tribeca Film Festival, was one of the very first supporters of Sam Fleischner's *Stand Clear of the Closing Doors* (2013), which premiered at Tribeca and received a Special Jury Mention. The connection, however, goes deeper. Ruffalo's anecdote about the moth and being in the moment epitomizes Fleischner's open approach to filmmaking. According to Fleischner, "For a while, I've defined filmmaking for myself as being an exercise in awareness. The more that you are aware of your surroundings, the sharper you can be about how to incorporate all of the elements that are everywhere."[16] Based on an actual 2009 event that Fleischner read about in the *New York Times*, the film tells the story of a thirteen-year-old autistic boy named Ricky Garcia (Jesus Sanchez-Velez) who gets lost in the New York subways in the period leading up to Hurricane Sandy.[17] In order to increase awareness and understand his subject's ordeal, the director attended a retreat prior to filming. As he explains, "I did a ten-day silent meditation retreat in advance of making this film as a way to experience what the duration of ten days was, because that's what Ricky's journey was. What it meant to sit and not talk for ten days, in terms of a chunk of time. I mean, I wanted to do it for personal reasons as well, but I liked to think of it in relation to what Ricky's going through."[18]

Although the film employs a dramatic framework—a family's search for a lost child with a disability—the film is notable for Fleischner's impressive use of improvisation and visual storytelling. *Stand Clear of the Closing Doors* recalls one of the very early American independent films, *Little Fugitive*. Like Engel, Orkin, and Ashley's film, which explores the legendary Coney Island amusement park, *Stand Clear of the Closing Doors* is built around two locations: Far Rockaway in Queens and the New York subway system. Fleischner turns his film into a political statement couched in a poem. It deals with the enormous stress placed on an undocumented

Mexican immigrant family struggling to cope with a disabled child within an institutional system that views them as an unwanted burden.

Fleischner started with a screenplay, written by Rose Lichter-Marck and Micah Bloomberg, even though it was created in a somewhat unorthodox manner. As the director explains, "There was a lot of back and forth during this writing experience. I outlined the story; Rose fleshed it out into prose. I put it into script format, and then it was continually passed between us and crafted for almost two years. Finally, we brought on Micah Bloomberg to help with the dialogue to fully form our characters on the page."[19] Yet from the very start the film was dependent on a number of unpredictable factors, especially because a great deal of the film takes place within the subway. No matter how much could be planned in advance, shooting on a public subway—even more so than in the open-for-business Chinese restaurant in Sean Baker's *Take Out*—is impossible to control, no matter how many extras could be deployed. Fleischner notes, "You actually don't need permits to shoot on the subway, as long as you are 'handheld.' There were a lot of happy accidents that came from the chaos, but overall it is a very unforgiving environment for shooting a narrative film."[20]

This sort of unpredictability and chaos forced the filmmaker to rely heavily on improvisation, but his interest and background in documentary predisposed Fleischner to take this approach: "But philosophically, I generally like the idea that things are more interesting if they evolve naturally rather than if they are predestined. That's a big part of documentary filmmaking, just being as observant and aware as possible, and I try to apply that to everything I do."[21] The subway itself provided a constantly changing environment that created logistical problems for filming due to the sheer flow of people getting on and off the train at various stops. As Fleischner explains, "You know you're pulling into stations so quickly and the passengers are changing physically. You can't have any control really, and you have to let go of a lot of ideas. I'm into that sort of thing, just kind of letting go and being open to things that are not planned. There's a lot of nice accidents in there and characters who you really would meet in the trains."[22] Instead of trying to control shooting, the director decided to take advantage of serendipitous events. He used two different crews: one specifically for filming on the subway, and another larger one for the rest of the film. Shooting on the subway demanded a more condensed unit that could blend in more unobtrusively with the commuters. According to the director, "So we had a stripped down crew. At times it was just myself. Or just me and one of the DPs."[23]

Fleischner could also not possibly predict that Hurricane Sandy would strike while he was still in the process of shooting the film. The natural disaster profoundly affected production, which was set in Far Rockaway, one of the areas in New York City that was hardest hit by the powerful storm. Although it greatly impacted the film—even causing production to stop completely—the director was ultimately able to turn a catastrophe into an advantage, mainly because his ability to adapt to shifting circumstances had become such an integral part of his process of making the film. Fleischner observes:

> Sometimes there is mimesis between what you create and the process of creating it. In this case we were in the middle/end of our production when the storm came. Living right next to the ocean, I had a natural inclination to record what I could. We had to break from shooting for a few weeks while we recovered, and during that time I realized how the storm fit into the story.[24]

As a result of the damage from the hurricane to the Rockaway Beach landscape, the director was forced to rethink the ending of the film.

Despite having a script, Fleischner also resorted to improvisation with his lead actor, Jesus Sanchez-Velez, who was found through an Asperger's blog by the film's casting director, Eleonore Hendricks.[25] Because Sanchez-Velez has a disability and no previous acting experience, he presented something of a challenge for the director. Fleischner, for example, encouraged the young first-time actor to free-associate about shoes, which resulted in his inventive monologue that is heard in voiceover on the soundtrack. According to Fleischner, "I would give him starting points and end points. I felt like I was interviewing him, and encouraging him to riff. That scene went like that, straight from him, and I really love it."[26] The young performer was also not asked or required to say any scripted dialogue. As the director indicates, "For pretty much all the dialogue, I would let him put it into his words. He has a really cool way of speaking, so I didn't want to interfere with that."[27] To help create a sense of a bond between the actors that play the mother, daughter, and son, they lived as a family in the apartment during production. In order to make the actors feel more comfortable, Fleischner also tried to shoot the film in chronological order as much as possible, which helped to create a greater sense of naturalism.[28]

Stand Clear of the Closing Doors begins with the sound of bagpipes and a shot of its protagonist, Ricky Garcia (Jesus Sanchez-Velez). Ricky has skipped school to hang out at the beach, which, along with a local sneaker store, is one of his favorite haunts. He returns to the school steps, where his older sister, Carla (Azul Zorrilla), walks him home. Ricky, who is somewhere on the autistic spectrum, excels at computers and drawing, especially dragons, but struggles with everyday tasks. He urinates on the top of the toilet seat, often forgets to eat, and resists taking his meds. After his mother, Mariana (Andrea Suarez Paz), chastises him for his truancy and his sister fails to pick him up at school, Ricky attempts to walk home alone. Fourteen minutes into the film, he follows a guy wearing sneakers and a jacket with an emblem of an Ouroboros (a symbol of a serpent or dragon eating its tail) sewn on the back into the subway, where Ricky proceeds to ride the trains for days.

Fleischner utilizes a parallel structure—Ricky's personal odyssey in the subway and his mother's search for him. Mariana is a beleaguered

FIGURE 9.2 Ricky Garcia lost in the crowded subway station, *Stand Clear of the Closing Doors*

mom. She cleans house for a wealthy white guy (Kevin Bewersdorf), while her husband works somewhere upstate and her rebellious teenage daughter would rather be anywhere else. Ricky's disappearance causes the family unit to fracture even more. Mariana, who lives in isolation from her neighbors due to her undocumented status, turns up at the neighborhood sneaker store and gets help from the African American saleswoman, Carmen (Marsha Stephanie Blake), who encourages her to take action. Together they design and put up "missing person" posters, while the police turn out to be virtually no help at all. It is a great touch that one of the gruff detectives who visits them breathes with the aid of an oxygen tank.

Meanwhile, Ricky rides various subway trains, getting weaker and weaker from lack of food and water. For the most part, the other riders appear indifferent to him. A homeless black man gives him a banana, but one teenager becomes disgusted and abusive when he realizes that Ricky has wet his pants (because the public bathrooms inside the subway are, of course, all locked) and dumps a drink on his head. Although viewers might expect that the search for a missing autistic child would elicit heightened suspense, especially once we learn that Hurricane Sandy is imminent, this proves not to be the case.

Fleischner chooses not to exploit the inherent drama of the dire situation, even though we watch Ricky's plight with great concern. Instead, one of the main strengths of *Stand Clear of the Closing Doors* is that it allows viewers to experience the underground world of the New York subways through his eyes. We see it not only as a microcosm of diversity—the interaction of people of all ages, races, and ethnic groups—but as a wondrous kaleidoscope of abstract patterns of color, light, and sound. Fleischner mixes staged scenes and documentary footage so skillfully that it is sometimes hard to tell the difference between the two. The staged scenes include the fight on the subway (featuring filmmaker Josh Safdie), the scene where a drink is poured on Ricky's head, the African American man who offers Ricky a banana, and the gray-haired man who tells a young child in a stroller an anecdote about "Louie the Tailor."

An example of a scene that was not staged is the kid who becomes very angry at his parent, which was a situation that Fleischner captured on the subway. We overhear snippets of conversation—a crazy woman makes an anti-Semitic remark about the mayor and expresses plans to vote for

Mitt Romney, two arrogant guys grossly underestimate the power of the approaching storm—and watch teenage break dancers perform intricate dance movements for the benefit of the riders. On Halloween, people in scary costumes populate the subway, transforming it into a surreal carnival, before the trains finally shut down due to the hurricane. Yet, through all of this, Ricky's detachment at being lost becomes our own detachment, so that the family drama involving his disappearance feels as if it is occurring in an alternate universe.

Shot by Adam Jandrup and Ethan Palmer, *Stand Clear of the Closing Doors* manages to capture the kinetic energy of the subway, and, in the process, the character of New York City. The film's power derives largely from its subjective point of view and carefully observed details. Fleischner joins a group of American indie filmmakers—Tim Sutton, Eliza Hittman, Jeremy Saulnier, Josephine Decker, and Chloé Zhao, among others—who appear to be moving away from mumblecore's overreliance on dialogue in favor of a new emphasis on filmic style and visual storytelling. *Stand Clear of the Closing Doors* harkens back to the early days of the New American Cinema, to filmmakers, such as Engel and Rogosin, who, in the name of realism, reluctantly used scripts but allowed everyday life and reality to seep into their films in an attempt to blend it together with fiction.

THE FILMS OF SEAN BAKER:
TAKE OUT AND *PRINCE OF BROADWAY*

After beginning his career with *Four Letter Words* (2000), Sean Baker reinvented himself with two stellar microbudget features released at the same time, *Take Out* (2004), which took years to screen theatrically, and *Prince of Broadway* (2008). Both films vied for the John Cassavetes Award (films made under $500,000) at the 2008 Independent Spirit Awards. The double nomination brought the director a great deal of critical attention within the realm of indie cinema.

Baker and Shih-Ching Tsou's *Take Out*, a documentary-like look at the life of an undocumented Asian delivery person, was shot in an actual Upper West Side Manhattan restaurant during business hours, featured lots of B-roll camera shots and interspersed actual orders with Baker and Tsou's fictional story. Baker explains, "Because we had no budget, we couldn't ask the owner to shut down for our production even for a minute, so we had to shoot while the business was open, working around the customers and real cooks (all of whom were illegal immigrants themselves)."[29]

Although it made shooting there extremely difficult, the cowriter and codirector make it clear that such a strategy had its advantages. According to Baker, "Realism was our number one goal with this film and I don't think we would have been able to catch the energy of a bustling NYC take-out without shooting in one during operating hours."[30] Tsou adds, "If we had to rent that location out for 30 days or build a set, it would have cost us thousands of dollars. So a free and central location was the biggest savings on the budget."[31] An additional bonus involved the candid responses of the nearly thirty customers (solicited via Craigslist) to the home delivery person, Ming Ding (Charles Jang), who, despite his desperate need to pay off pressing debts to loan sharks, is much too shy and proud to ingratiate himself with customers in order to get bigger tips.

Prince of Broadway shares the same gritty realism as *Take Out* in telling the story of immigrants who sell counterfeit goods on the streets of New York City. One is a fast-talking West African hustler named Lucky (Prince Adu). The other is his boss, Levon (Karren Karagulian), a middle-aged Armenian from Lebanon whose bare clothing store serves as a front for a secret back room full of luxury-brand knockoffs—from Gucci to Louis Vuitton. Levon has married an attractive young woman in order to get a green card. Although he yearns for his marriage to be more than a matter of expediency, their relationship is already on the skids.

The catalyst occurs roughly twelve minutes into the film, when Lucky's Latina ex-girlfriend, Linda (Kat Sanchez), dumps off a baby (Aiden Noesi), claiming that he's the father. She tells him, "Be a man for once." Linda indicates the situation will only be temporary, but it soon becomes clear that the baby is interfering with a relationship she has developed with a new boyfriend—a muscle-bound, jealous thug, who beats up Lucky when he chases after Linda. "I have no papers," Lucky later pleads to her mother, "what can I do with this baby, please?"

Like *Take Out*, *Prince of Broadway* utilizes a ticking clock—in this case, a DNA test to prove paternity—but Baker is careful not to use it in a heavy-handed way. The film focuses on the bond that slowly develops between Lucky and the baby, whom he calls Prince. It also centers on Lucky's relationship with Levon, who serves as a father figure even though he is hardly the ideal role model. Levon asks him, "Do you know what you're getting yourself into?" He gives Lucky money and instructions on how to hold the baby properly. He puts the baby's hat on and tells Lucky, "Hold the kid, man. You're going to drop the kid!" When Lucky doesn't listen, he shouts, "Are you fucking kidding me? Hold the kid!"

Baker likes to blend and confuse documentary and fiction. His films have a raw power that makes it seem as if he has stuck his camera into real-life situations. The script for *Prince of Broadway* is credited to Baker and his producer Darren Dean, but, as a final credit indicates, "The characters' dialogue was realized through improvisation and a collaborative process with all actors." Although many independent filmmakers have forsaken the traditional screenplay in favor of alternative forms of scripting, such as structured improvisation, Baker admits there is often a stigma attached to working this way. He told an interviewer, "But [with *Prince of Broadway*] the improvised is simply the dialogue. Every scene had a beginning, middle, and end . . . it was just

FIGURE 9.3 Lucky pushes Prince's stroller through the snow, *Prince of Broadway*

the dialogue. Some people think you are not doing your work if you don't have the full fleshed out script."[32] As Baker explains, "You're dealing with a business, you're dealing with Hollywood, in which, if you're being financed in any way, people simply can't trust an artist to be making things up as they go along, or to be writing in the different stages of production."[33] As a consequence, having a written script, he contends, generally functions as a form of "insurance."

Baker prefers a more flexible and open approach to making films, especially one that includes incorporating found elements. He uses a hybrid form of a script and a treatment, which he refers to as a "scriptment." As he explains:

> These scriptments, for me what they allow is that room to find, to have those happy accidents and, especially in this style of filmmaking, to allow the outside forces to dictate certain things, but hopefully in a positive way . . . And, also, when you're shooting on the street, and you're trying to capture a certain realism, part of that scripting is allowing whatever is going to happen that day, that particular day—the events of that day—to become part of this, and to accept it.[34]

Although *Take Out* is a fictional film, it has the look and feel of a documentary, especially in how it was shot. Baker openly acknowledges his influences, which run the gamut—from Dogme 95 and John Cassavetes to the Dardenne brothers, Ken Loach, and Mike Leigh. The indie director, however, insists that he has created his own unique style of shooting, which he sees "as a combination of security cam, voyeur cam and hidden camera."[35]

In *Take Out*, Baker spends a great deal of attention focusing on the preparation of food in the kitchen. Using a functioning, open business, such as a Chinese takeout restaurant, meant that actual customers who showed up there would sometimes become part of the film. The same was true of the customers Ming delivered orders to at home, who were not professional actors but everyday people the filmmakers found through advertising on social media. According to Baker, "That's a special case, because we were meeting those people for the first time as we got to their door. So, we had to quickly size them up, see what sort of character they could possibly play, and this was based purely on physicality, persona, and first impressions."[36] In one instance, Ming makes a delivery to an African American woman in a housing project. While paying for her order, her young child unexpectedly escapes down the hall, only to be dragged back by her mother. Another person, who we never see, fails to give Ming a tip. Karren Karagulian, who plays Levon in *Prince of Broadway*, turns up as one of the customers and refuses to accept his order because he wanted beef rather than chicken. Back at the restaurant this mistake causes Ming to get into a shoving match with one of the cooks, as the tension mounts in his attempt to raise enough money before the short deadline given to him by the loan sharks.

If the use of improvisation has become common in microbudget indie features, the editing in Baker's films is unusual. In *The Way Hollywood Tells It*, David Bordwell explores the concept of "intensified continuity" and why the cutting of Hollywood films keeps getting faster and faster.[37] Indie films, especially naturalistic ones, have generally shared with art cinema a contrarian impulse—the story often unfolds in long, leisurely takes, as is evident in the films of Gus Van Sant, such as *Gerry*, *Last Days*, and *Elephant*. Yet Baker fractures the space and time of his film through the employment of manic cutting. An editor by profession, Baker's impulse is to cut often, which gives his film a kinetic energy. As a result, *Take Out* and *Prince of Broadway* never feel boring. In exploring the subcultures of those engaged in the underground economy, Baker provides an exciting glimpse into the lives of largely invisible characters who live on the margins.

TANGERINE

Baker's *Take Out* and *Prince of Broadway* take an ethnographic approach toward their subjects. *Starlet* (2012) and *Tangerine* (2015), which also deal with characters living on the margins, are set on the West Coast rather than New York City, following the filmmaker's move to Los Angeles. Shot with an adapted iPhone 5s and propelled by blaring bursts of trap music on the soundtrack, *Tangerine*, which premiered at the Sundance Film Festival— where it was picked up for distribution by Magnolia Pictures—represented his biggest critical and commercial success to date. Like previous Baker films, *Tangerine* revolves around a location, in this case, Donut Time, a doughnut shop in the transgender red-light district of West Hollywood. Baker again turned to first-time actors, in this case, Mya Taylor and Kitana Kiki Rodriguez. Baker met Taylor at an LGBT center, and she, in turn, introduced him to Rodriguez.[38] The bond of friendship between the two main characters, Alexandra (Taylor) and Sin-Dee Rella (Rodriguez), who are transgender prostitutes, provides the emotional core of the movie. Yet it is the highly volatile Sin-Dee, who sets the plot in motion.

Following her release from spending twenty-eight days in jail, Sin-Dee meets Alexandra at Donut Time to celebrate Christmas Eve. When Sin-Dee brings up a secret involving her drug-dealing pimp boyfriend, Chester (James Ransone), Alexandra inadvertently mentions that he's been fooling around with another woman—a straight, white "fish" named Dinah. Alexandra tells her, "All men cheat. That's why they're called 'trade.' Do them just as dirty as they do us. Out here it is all about our hustle. And that's it." But Sin-Dee is not buying it, and she immediately storms off to find Dinah. This becomes the main plotline, but Baker creates two other parallel lines of action—one involves Alexandra's desire to be a singer, while the second deals with an Armenian cab driver named Razmik (Karren Karagulian). Razmik picks up a number of passengers in the neighborhood: a bereaved elderly woman with an empty dog carrier, a young Asian woman who takes selfies wearing a Santa hat, an elderly Cherokee Indian from Oklahoma (veteran actor Clu Gulager) who is upset at having a female name and appears on the verge of a heart attack, and two drunken guys who vomit all over his taxi.

FIGURE 9.4 Alexandra celebrates Sin-Dee's release from prison at Donut Time, *Tangerine*

Baker cuts back and forth between the three narrative strands at a frenetic pace. As Alexandra watches, Sin-Dee consults a drug dealer named Nash regarding the whereabouts of Chester. Averse to the kind of "drama" that Sin-Dee creates wherever she goes, Alexandra walks out. Sin-Dee eventually turns up at a sleazy motel, kicks in the door, and finds Dinah (Mickey O'Hagan) among the prostitutes working there. She takes Dinah captive, dragging her roughly through the streets. After Razmik arrives too late at the club where Alexandra performed, he heads to Donut Time, but so does his mother-in-law, Ashken (Alla Tumanian), who has grown suspicious of him and manages to convince an Armenian cab driver named Karo (Arsen Grigoryan) to take her there. This causes the three plot threads to come together in a highly charged and extended comedic climax that also includes Razmik's wife, Yeva (Luiza Nersisyan), and their young child. A final dramatic twist occurs when Sin-Dee learns that Alexandra has also betrayed her with Chester, but the film ends with a touching scene of reconciliation that takes place in a laundromat.

Baker attributes the massive consumption of media today with novices suddenly being able to act in films: "I think that a lot of nonprofessionals or first-timers are exposed to so much media and content that anybody can almost have aspirations to act these days."[39] As with a filmmaker like Joe Swanberg, one of the keys is having the performers play versions of themselves. Of course, not everyone has the ability to act, but considerably more people than ever before seem capable of convincing performances

FIGURE 9.5 Sin-Dee with her hostage, Dinah, on the bus, *Tangerine*

when the bar has been set at realism. Speaking of first-time actors, Baker observes, "When they cut their teeth, they are basically presenting themselves and delivering themselves in a realistic fashion. I think that it does take talent, though. I have to say that, in the case of *Tangerine* with Mya and Kiki, they do have the skill, and they are wonderful at comedic improvisations because they're simply just funny people and they're witty and fast." Yet Baker nevertheless finds that it takes a certain type of personality to be able to do it successfully.

Baker laments the fact that there is such an overemphasis on three-act structure in industrial cinema when it comes to scripts, and insists he is much more interested in character. He observes, "Even though I think we've been brainwashed into thinking that we all need a story, that we need a beginning, middle, and end, and everything that goes along with that—protagonist, antagonist, etc.—I think, when it really comes down to it, we identify more and we connect more with character and we appreciate character." *Tangerine* is definitely a study of its two main characters, Sin-Dee and Alexandra, who manage to keep viewers engaged the entire time through their intense and manic repartee. Baker witnessed their chemistry when he first met the two actors and wanted to capture it in the film. The first scene establishes that unique dynamic between Sin-Dee and Alexandra. In approaching that scene, he told his performers, "So, we have to keep the audience engaged with your personas, with your dialogue, and with just your energy." Both Taylor and Rodriguez managed to deliver those qualities, even if Baker—as the shifting backgrounds outside the windows of Donut Time indicate—enhanced and constructed the opening through fast-paced editing.

According to Baker, he and his cowriter Chris Bergoch developed the scriptment of the film in three or four stages. It was actually Bergoch who pushed to set the film on Christmas Eve and came up with the third-act twist that Alexandra also cheated with Chester while Sin-Dee was locked away. Baker notes, "This is a very good example of how things are, to a certain degree, left open for being found. When we shot, we did not have that third-act twist of having Alexandra also have been with Chester. That came from something that we witnessed over the course of shooting." The initial treatment was seven pages, which was sufficient to get approval from the two lead actors, Taylor and Rodriguez. Baker explains, "Everything was there minus that third-act twist, but everything was written out in terms of the plot. Perhaps, one or two places, we had a line of dialogue, just as an example to show the colorful dialogue."

After workshopping scenes, the two writers created a scriptment of about forty pages. One problem was that the dialogue for the Armenian family had to be written and then translated for the actors, two of whom— the ones who play Yeva and Karo—came from Armenia to play the roles. These sections had to be very tightly scripted. The line, which is said by Ashken, to the cab driver—"Los Angeles is a beautifully wrapped lie"—is one that seems most obviously written, but it was in fact suggested by the two Armenian actors, Karagulian and Grigoryan. By the time of filming, the scriptment for *Tangerine* had grown to roughly sixty or seventy pages.

Like Cassavetes, Baker believes very strongly in the rehearsal process. According to the director, "*Take Out, Prince of Broadway, Starlet,* and *Tangerine,* I think, have had pretty much the same amount of designated days, full days, in a rehearsal room, a rehearsal space, just playing through the scenes." He believes it is important to rent a professional space to rehearse in, which professionalizes the acting process. As Baker explains, "There is a level of casualness that I want to keep on set, but . . . it's a fine line. It's, like, getting people prepared in a professional way but then hopefully losing that professionalism around set." Gulager came with three different prepared monologues, and Baker chose the one he felt was most appropriate for the film. Like Cassavetes, Baker also prefers to keep ad-libbing to a minimum, though on occasion he will let the actors freely improvise, such as the scene toward the end where Chester and Dinah smoke meth outside Donut Time. According to Baker, "That was just us out there, saying, 'Let's just roll the camera for ten minutes and see what we get.'"

In some of the minor supporting roles, the director also tried to create short character sketches in order "to establish them as living, breathing human beings." In order to accomplish this, he allowed the actors to work from their own experience during the rehearsal process. For example, in the scene where the two cops are sitting in their patrol car before the scuffle breaks out between Alexandra and her nonpaying john, Baker had the male police officer tell a story to his female partner about an experience of going on a date and being offended that the woman ate off his plate. Baker comments, "And it really contradicted sort of the macho cop image that is usually represented in film. So, I thought that would be actually very interesting and I just allowed him to do that. So we rehearsed it a few times, and then we did it on set a few times. That's how that worked." In the case of the madam at the motel, Baker asked the actor, Chelcie Lynn, if she could come up with a personal story about growing up. He recalls, "And then, she gave me several examples and one of them happened to be this skating rink that was a date night, and so I just thought there was something sweet about the fact that this madam couldn't get a date and had to go with her sister every time."

Baker believes in the benefit of having workshop sessions with the actors. In the scenes of Sin-Dee and Dinah prior to the club scene, the director suggests that the session entailed "just riffing and being vulgar, and us throwing in lines and seeing what we could come up with." Baker also recorded the workshop sessions of Sin-Dee and Dinah with his iPhone and indicates, "And then later, I would transcribe the best of the lines, so the script for that scene came from our workshop sessions." A film like *Prince of Broadway* was much more improvised than *Tangerine*. As Baker explains, "In *Tangerine*, we actually did script out a tremendous amount of dialogue, but I just encouraged improvisation based on that dialogue." Shooting the film with an adapted iPhone gave Baker another major advantage, both in shooting on the streets, as well as with his first-time lead actors. The smaller camera gave the director greater mobility and flexibility. Given the prevalence of the iPhone, no one felt intimidated by the simple technology that Baker cleverly employed in shooting his low-budget film.

Baker has honed his process since making *Take Out* and *Prince of Broadway*. In many ways, the director employed various types of improvisation in *Tangerine*. While his method of scripting is unorthodox, especially in using a scriptment in various stages rather than a traditional written screenplay, he might fall into the rehearsed category of improvisation favored by Cassavetes. Yet Baker remains open to found elements or serendipity once the production process begins by blending the different forms of improvisation—the rehearsed, the planned, and even, to some extent, the spontaneous.

10

REDISCOVERING PSYCHODRAMA

Frownland, Heaven Knows What, and *Stinking Heaven*

Psychodrama hit its peak during the 1960s with the films of Andy Warhol, Norman Mailer, Shirley Clarke, and William Greaves. In a manner similar to John Cassavetes, Joe Swanberg discovered something equivalent to a minor form of psychodrama in improvising films based on his own life. On the other hand, Ronald Bronstein was familiar with J. L. Moreno's psychodrama. He inadvertently arrived at the technique while employing what he imagined to be the rehearsal methods of Mike Leigh, whose unique approach bears resemblance to the therapeutic techniques used by Moreno. Just as directors and actors from theater and film were fascinated by Moreno's real-life dramas in the 1960s during the peak of his popularity, filmmakers—such as Bronstein, Josh and Benny Safdie, and Nathan Silver—also became intrigued by the power of psychodrama, as is evident in such films as *Frownland, Heaven Knows What,* and *Stinking Heaven*.

RONALD BRONSTEIN: *FROWNLAND*

Ronald Bronstein's debut feature *Frownland* (2007)—the title comes from a Captain Beefheart song—is easily one of the most idiosyncratic and distinctive works to be initially dubbed mumblecore. The film is a character study of a highly dysfunctional, mentally challenged young man named Keith Sontag (Dore Mann) who happens to resemble David Berkowitz, the notorious Son of Sam. Unlike the serial killer, Keith is more or less harmless, but, with his baggy clothes, grimacing facial tics, and obsessive-compulsive gestures, he seems to be a walking time bomb, incredibly frustrated by his inability to connect with those around him. Bronstein originally wrote a script for the film—an experience he calls "a pinheaded endeavor"—but, because *Frownland* is more character-based than plotted, things changed once he cast the actors. In an interview, Bronstein explains:

> All the immediacy and emotionality gets lost. Like a dubbed voice. Maybe this approach can work if you're making something grounded in heavy plotting, where the characters and the dialogue exist chiefly to move the narrative from A to B. But I want to work in the reverse. I want the progression of the story to form organically out of the characters themselves.[1]

After Bronstein cast the actors, he worked with them over a six-month period to develop their characters through a process that delved deeply into their personal and emotional lives through lengthy rehearsals. Bronstein would later transcribe the rehearsal sessions. He notes, "I ended up with hundreds and hundreds of pages, which I would then pare down, so it was like writing with somebody's brain instead of writing with a pen."[2]

In rehearsals, Bronstein developed a workshop approach inspired by the performances in the early films of Leigh, which he describes as having "a heightened, grotesque quality, but it's so loaded with nuance that it feels real. It's actually hyper-real." Bronstein adds, "But [Leigh is] very tight lipped about his process. You hear he works for several months with actors doing character building, then he networks them, and there's not much more that we know."[3] It is true that the British director has often been reticent to reveal the specific details of his process. Leigh explains, "If you want to know why I am generally reluctant to talk about what I do, it's because you can't really describe it, you can't really do it justice, any more than Van Gogh could explain the sunflowers, other than by describing technically how he applied the paint."[4]

Leigh attempted at times to minimize or be evasive about his working process and specific techniques, referring to them as "a trade secret."[5] Various interviews with him and his actors, however, give us some insight into his idiosyncratic methods. As Howie Movshovitz notes in his edited volume *Mike Leigh Interviews*, "The more Leigh talks about the unconventional way he grows his films through lengthy improvisations and rehearsals with his actors, the more it becomes clear that Leigh has obviously refined his approach, and that with each film the process works somewhat differently from the others."[6] Although the process has evolved over the course of his career, some aspects remain the same.

Leigh does not actually begin with a script, but he might start with a very short written outline. At this stage, the actors are not given anything that has been written down. As a number of them have emphasized, there is no actual script. In a sense, Leigh works backwards from the traditional approach because the script is not written beforehand but rather is generated after the extensive rehearsal period. That is at odds with a director like Cassavetes, who, with the exception of the first version of *Shadows*, believed in the writing process and began his films with a detailed screenplay, even though he further developed the film during the painstaking rehearsal process with the actors. Leigh was initially influenced by Cassavetes, but he managed to take improvisation to a more radical level. Yet there are similarities in their ultimate objectives. Like Cassavetes, Leigh was also disappointed with the characters in Hollywood movies because he believed they did not act like real people. According to Leigh, "And of course what we're dealing with is making people like people really are, behaviorally."[7] The behavioral aspect of the film is developed as a result of working directly with the actors. During a grueling rehearsal process, characters are built from scratch so that both the story and the film are allowed to grow organically.

Leigh often begins his project with an idea or vague notions about something he is interested in exploring. Choosing the actors for a film is a crucial step in the process for him. Once the actors are cast, they begin to develop their characters based on a person or a composite of people they know or have known in their lives. Through continual questioning and discussions with Leigh, as well as extensive improvisations, various possibilities and directions for the character are explored in depth. The lives of the characters are explored from infancy to the present, with various details being filled in. The demanding process can cause both mental and physical strain on the actors, especially in creating a psychological blur between the character and themselves.

For *Frownland*, Bronstein developed a process similar to that used by Leigh in rehearsals with his actors: "We talked about their job histories, personal histories, emotional histories, how they speak, how they think about the world, taking certain traits that are in the actual performer in real life and exaggerating them and bleaching away other ones that didn't suit the movie's needs."[8] He also built contrasting characters separately, in a manner that resembles Leigh's method, in order to create dramatic tension once the characters would interact during rehearsals. A case in point is the very different attitudes that the film's protagonist, Keith, and his roommate have toward paying bills on time. Bronstein explains, "This leads to the same kind of drama that was in the script, but it unfolds with much more subtlety."[9]

In the case of Dore Mann, the experience of acting in *Frownland* became so intense that Bronstein indicated it pushed into psychological territory that he likens to psychodrama. When asked whether Mann had done any acting since the film, Bronstein was very forthright about the impact it had on their relationship:

> My relationship with him is really complicated, and in a way, it's really possible that I cannot separate my personal relationship with him with my working relationship with him. They can't exist independently. We just got so deep into it . . . Oh God, it's almost like we accidentally stumbled into the field of psychodrama without the therapeutic knowledge of how to deal with it. But he's moved into kind of a different line of work. He's not doing acting. He's doing social work.[10]

Bronstein has not made another film of his own since *Frownland* either, but he has subsequently collaborated with Josh and Benny Safdie as an actor, cowriter, and coeditor on *Daddy Longlegs*, aka *Go Get Some Rosemary* (2010), then as cowriter and coeditor on their own high-wire venture into psychodrama, *Heaven Knows What*, and as cowriter on *Good Time* (2017).

Unlike other filmmakers associated with improvisation, Bronstein has little interest in realism. In fact, he takes issue with the basic assumptions behind it:

> This idea of realism that all you have to do is sort of capture the external world as it is, as it unfolds, and this is enough to capture how reality makes you feel. And it doesn't require any sort of heightening and prodding, and getting underneath with the crow bar. I just don't have a relationship with that, you know what I mean? Because I know how the world makes me feel doesn't necessarily show up on my face.[11]

When he suggests that you have to get "underneath it with a crowbar," Bronstein really seems to imply that a technique like psychodrama is somehow necessary to achieve the kind of heightened realism he sought in *Frownland*.

The film begins with Keith watching a monster movie on TV as he eats eggs and popcorn, but he is interrupted by a call on the intercom from a female comics artist named Laura (Mary Wall), who cries uncontrollably. She turns out to be equally dysfunctional. As the two of them drive in her car through the New York City streets, Keith tries to find something to say, but he is incapable of constructing a coherent sentence. After Laura temporarily disappears from the car, the camera moves closer as Keith contorts his eyes and groans like a monster, eventually causing tears to well up in his eyes—a shot that is emblematic of the whole movie.

The scenes with Laura, which take up over fifteen minutes, would seem to suggest that this romantic plotline will be at the heart of Keith's story, but this proves not to be the case. Laura, in fact, largely disappears from the film. Only much later do we learn that Keith believes that Laura, a self-mutilator, has taken money he left on the table. After we view Keith's naked body as he takes a shower, *Frownland* veers in unexpected directions from the initial setup. The film is organized into episodic sequences involving: Laura, Keith's door-to-door job hawking coupons for charity, encounters with his boss, tribulations with his arrogant musician roommate, Charles (Paul Grimstad), and his attempts to inflict himself on a male friend named Sandy (David Sandholm). One structural oddity is the fact that, at roughly sixty-five minutes, the film takes an inexplicable detour to follow Charles for an extended period.

Eventually Keith confronts Charles about not paying the electric bill. He begins with a self-deprecating monologue, "I know what I must be like. One of those ghostly-like servants in the turn-of-the century manor houses in England, where you never really know they're around until you hear a spoon drop." Charles responds, "Who drops the spoon? You dropped the spoon. You're a servant? I'm confused." When Keith tries to explain the anxiety the unpaid bill causes him, Charles answers, "Has it ever occurred to you that your ridiculous, disjointed, splutterings might inspire me to want to malign you? That I might deliberately not pay the bill just to punish you for your pathologies?"

We see another side of Charles in the digressive sequence where he applies for a job at a restaurant; takes an LSAT test, presumably in hopes of training others for the exam; and ends up getting his Walkman stolen by a fellow test-taker. Already without electricity and faced with being evicted from the apartment, Charles now demands to talk about the situation with Keith, who no longer wants to discuss it. The power dynamic has been reversed temporarily, but Charles still insults Keith about his "mangled syntax" and refers to him as "a burbling troll in his underwear." As they argue, Charles suddenly punches Keith in the mouth.

The violence escalates when Keith manages to find his way into Sandy's building. Keith insists on explaining himself, but the two get into a tussle, leaving Keith with a bloody ear. Keith shows up at a party, where, to the sounds of "Jailhouse Rock," a couple of drunks place a lampshade on his head, like a dunce cap, causing him to freak out. Keith stumbles through the halls. He presses his hands to his face and cries and groans loudly as snot drips from his nose. The next morning, Keith appears on the graffiti-covered roof. He eventually urinates in the corner as credits appear over the scene, which ends with a close-up shot of Keith's head buried in his hands as sunlight from behind nearly obliterates his image.

Shot on 16 mm, *Frownland* has the overall feel and texture of an underground comic—dark and extremely hellish. Bronstein favors long takes, lots of close-ups, frontal shots, and grainy images. Dore Mann's performance as Keith is crucial to the success of *Frownland*.

There is one scene in the film where Keith grows agitated at his so-called friend, Sandy, causing Mann's dialogue to become an explosion of incoherent sentence fragments and utterances. While watching the scene, one cannot help but wonder how something like that could possibly be written. It wasn't exactly, but Bronstein describes how he was able to achieve the effect:

> Yeah, he's a complete maniac in it. The rehearsals for that particular scene involved making him prepare enough dialogue for like 10 scenes, then loading him up with a disgusting amount of caffeine, spinning him around, making him sprint down the block until he was dizzy and hyperventilating, and then sort of letting him go so that he was totally incapable of relaying this prepared information linearly or coherently. What came out was this berserk jumble of disparate sentiments that rendered him absolutely senseless.[12]

Bronstein's technique worked because there is something very genuine about his portrait of an inveterate loser.

JOSH AND BENNY SAFDIE: *HEAVEN KNOWS WHAT*

The genesis of Josh and Benny Safdie's third narrative feature, *Heaven Knows What* (2014), involved serendipity. While researching a new film project, entitled *Uncut Gems*, set in the Diamond District of Manhattan, Josh Safdie spied a young woman, Arielle Holmes, who he felt had screen presence and wanted to cast her in a film. Once Safdie got to know her, however, it became apparent that Holmes was a drug addict who was part of a much larger underground subculture in New York City. She and her friends hustled on the Upper West Side and often slept in Central Park. Holmes was also madly in love with another heavy drug user named Ilya Leontyev. After she disappeared for two months and attempted to commit suicide, Safdie decided to pay her to write down her story. The resulting memoir, *Mad Love in New York City*, consisted of hundreds of pages written on computers at various Apple stores and became the basis for the screenplay, which Safdie cowrote with Bronstein.

FIGURE 10.1   Harley (Arielle Holmes) hanging out on the street, *Heaven Knows What*

Arielle Holmes had an interesting backstory. As a teenager, she fled nearby Bayonne, New Jersey, for Manhattan, where she became involved in the drug scene. It was the section that Holmes wrote about her obsessive love for Ilya, however, that most fascinated the Safdies, especially because his self-destructive and sadistic behavior suggested the perfect villain. Josh Safdie describes Ilya after he finally met him: "He was such a mystery to me, and that was what Ronnie [Bronstein] and I were really intrigued by, his mystery. He was an evil, evil mystery beautiful super villain."[13] The decision to make a film involving junkies posed risks for the production. The Safdies not only wanted to cast Holmes, who had never acted in a film before, but also a number of her drug-user friends.

In an interview, Josh Safdie argues that Holmes was already an actor by the time he first met her. He takes the Goffman position that all social interactions involve a level of performance, but insists that street people often have much more at stake:

> Do you know what kind of actor she was before I met her? She was working at Pandora's playing characters every single day. Before that she was working for some weird guy in the financial district doing the dominatrix thing except as a house call girl. And she was 17 years old, an underage

girl doing it. And even beyond that, many times in her writing, I read about how she hustled someone off the street, pretending to be someone that she wasn't. She was an actress. I mean, a lot of people from the street are usually great actors because they have to act. In that case, the failure isn't a bad review in a movie, it's a punch in the face.[14]

Josh Safdie was convinced that Holmes had "star" quality—enough to play the lead role in a film based on her own personal life. What was it about her that convinced him? According to Safdie:

I think with Arielle, it was the way she carried herself. It was the way there was insanity around her, and she was just calmly leaving the Diamond District for the day, and swiping her Metro card. And the way she carried herself down the stairs. There was just something to her that reeked of composure, but mixed with this complete instability, so that there was a conundrum there, which really is acting, if you think about it. Acting is controlled chaos, because you're talking about being somebody, but having order to that being.[15]

Safdie actually used psychodrama as an inducement for her to be in the film: "I told her, I was like, look, I wanna make a movie out of these pages and she was game and I talked to her about the power of psychodrama and how she could work a lot of her suppressed inner demons out through performance and she was down."[16]

In various interviews about the film, it is not surprising that the term "psychodrama" crops up numerous times. At one point Josh Safdie states, "We were interested in psychodrama, allowing Arielle to act out her feelings without real consequence."[17] In an interview in *Film Comment*, Safdie discusses the nature of the brothers' collaboration with Bronstein. According to Josh Safdie, "Here, it's all about his intellectual and personal interests. The melodrama of the mind, the psychodrama—he was interested in that, and he really liked Arielle as well, so our collaboration was based on figuring out what makes her tick."[18]

In order to be in the film, Holmes agreed to stop using drugs. The Safdies also promised to pay for her to go to a rehabilitation center in Florida after shooting was completed. The brothers also wanted to cast Leontyev, but his volatility and self-destructive behavior ultimately made this impossible. The fantasy that he would be able to perform ended abruptly when he overdosed in a McDonald's restaurant toward the end of rehearsals. After shooting up in the bathroom, he finally emerged, only to collapse on the floor and stop breathing—a scene which Josh Safdie describes in some detail to Scott Macaulay in *Filmmaker*. Although they administered CPR and were able to revive Leontyev before the ambulance arrived, the experience left its mark on the production. Josh Safdie started to have serious misgivings about the film. He told Macaulay, "It was so dark. It was the first time where I was really confronted with the way [the drug addicts] fetishize death head-on. They talk about it all the time—murder, suicide. I said to Benny, 'I don't want to make this movie.' "[19] His brother and the other producers managed to convince Josh that it was important, especially at this late stage, to go ahead with the project.

Despite not wanting to appear in the film, the real-life Ilya continued to have an impact on the production. Leontyev had the uncanny knack of turning up and wreaking havoc at shoots. According to Josh Safdie, "All of a sudden he would just show up, and literally we would have to stop filming because he said he'd just beat the shit out of somebody. He was like a tornado."[20] Not coincidentally, much of his anger was directed toward Holmes. The risks of production, however, went far beyond the interruption of shooting by Leontyev, who continued to hang out with them when they were not filming. The Safdies also cast another friend of Holmes named Buddy Duress, a first-time performer as well, to play one of the main characters. The fact that there were already warrants for Duress's arrest on drug-related charges posed an even greater threat because, were he to be caught, the production would have to shut down. Josh Safdie explains, "I knew that he was on the run while we were making the movie, I knew that he had warrants out for his arrest, and that was why we had to make the movie when we did. Because I knew that after a year they come after you really hard, and I really wanted to work with Buddy. He was kind of a main inspiration for the movie just as Ari was."[21]

Heaven Knows What uses Holmes's addictive love for Leontyev as a frame to capture the subterranean lifestyle of junkies living in New York City. Shot with telephoto lenses by cinematographer Sean Price Williams, often from a block away, the film depicts a subculture that unobtrusively blends into the bustle of street life in Manhattan. The effect of the technique is to be simultaneously close yet distant from the performers, isolating

FIGURE 10.2 Harley and Mike, a relationship of convenience, *Heaven Knows What*

them within the shallow space of the frame, while weaving them into the tapestry of daily life on the streets. The approach had an additional benefit. It allowed the first-time actors to be less self-conscious because the camera was not in close proximity (though, of course, crew members had to be close to record sound). The Safdies were interested in mining the subtle blend between nonfiction and fiction. Although they were aware of the precedents to the kind of film they were making, such as Lionel Rogosin's *On the Bowery*, Josh Safdie claims that their reference was less to other films, including those dealing specifically with addiction like *The Panic in Needle Park* (1971), than to what they themselves directly observed on the streets of New York City. In a position that echoes that of Rogosin, he told an interviewer, "If we were looking for any inspiration or any way to be guided, we looked to the world and the characters themselves."[22]

Heaven Knows What begins with an extreme close-up of a passionate embrace between Holmes, who has been renamed Harley, and Ilya (Caleb Landry Jones) as they writhe ecstatically on the ground. After sounds of crying, the scene cuts to a shot of Harley as she cries on the street curb. At the library, Ilya ignores her, as she plaintively asks, "What could I do for you to forgive me?" Harley repeats her question, and then adds, "Would you forgive me if I die." Ilya later goads her to kill herself as a declaration of love. She slits her wrist in front of him, which sends her in an ambulance to Bellevue Hospital, where Ilya abandons her. The opening credits roll a good twelve minutes into the film over a tour-de-force, continuous Steadicam shot that lasts over four minutes and covers Harley's nightmarish stay in the psych ward.

A slow-witted guy named Skully (played by the rapper Necro) is waiting for her when she is released, but Harley soon ditches him for a drug dealer friend named Mike (Buddy Duress) who wears a ragged sock hat, gray hoodie, and a black jacket that has "success through partnership" written on the back. Harley's relationship with Mike inadvertently creates a romantic triangle, as she drifts into a relationship with him—less out of desire than friendship and a pragmatic need for a steady supply of drugs. Harley's time with Buddy, which forms the central part of the film (or nearly forty-four minutes of the film's ninety-four-minute running time), shows their daily struggles to survive on the city streets. Yet Ilya is always a lurking presence nearby. In one inspired scene, they congregate in the park with other drug addicts as day turns to night and some of them dance euphorically to "The Power of the Mind" by Headhunterz. The scene ends with Harley and Mike shooting up and making out on the ground, a spectacle that Ilya observes as he leaves the park.

As Harley sits on the street panhandling behind her usual hand-written sign, Ilya shows up and harasses her. Clearly jealous, he threatens to kill Mike and arranges a drug deal with him. Following a fight between the two, in which Mike gets injured by a handmade throwing star, Harley gets a phone call that Ilya has overdosed. As he lies motionless on the bathroom floor of a fast-food joint—his skin color now blue—Harley administers CPR. After great effort, she somehow manages to revive him. Afterward, she splits from Mike to be with Ilya again. Following a crime spree in which they steal energy drinks to obtain cash, Harley and Ilya kiss each other intensely and make love on the street to the sounds of Isao Tomita's "The Engulfed Cathedral." We hear Harley's voiceover, as she talks about what a sweet boy he was, his darkness, and her need for him. She concludes, "Everything I am today came from you."

The two buy more drugs and impulsively get on a bus headed to Florida. As Harley sleeps, Ilya forces the driver to let him off and hitchhikes back to Manhattan. He climbs a fence and enters a makeshift pad in a vacant, boarded-up building, where he falls asleep on the bed while

FIGURE 10.3 Harley with Ilya after shoplifting energy drinks, *Heaven Knows What*

smoking a cigarette. A fire erupts, engulfing Ilya in flames as he flails about, before the skin on his face begins to sizzle, which is underscored by the frenetic music of James Dashow's "Oedipus Orca (Titoli)." The film cuts from this horrific image to Harley, who wakes up on the bus and realizes that Ilya is gone. When the driver refuses to stop, she breaks the window with her elbow and gets thrown off the bus. She enters a Dunkin' Donuts restaurant, where Mike is holding court with a couple of junkies. Harley initially takes seat in a nearby booth, but, in the film's final shot, she has rejoined the group. As the credits begin to scroll over black, the dedication reads: "In Loving Memory of Ilya Leontyev 1989–2015."

The film's dedication comes as a shock and shifts the extratextual elements to the textual. Even for those viewers who might not know anything about the film's unusual backstory, this information indicates that the real Ilya died shortly after the production. The dedication naturally raises speculation about him. Leontyev had seen the film that was based on his actual life with Holmes. He walked the red carpet at the New York Film Festival and, according to the filmmakers, appeared happy to see himself portrayed on the screen. According to Benny Safdie, "Yeah, he loved it. He was at the New York Film Festival premiere and it was really something special. He sat in front of Jim Jarmusch at the premiere.

Jim said Ilya spoke full volume the entire time, and was just like on cloud nine: 'That's me, motherfucker!' It didn't matter how he looked at the time. It was like, 'I don't care that's me!' " Safdie added, "He felt the movie. I wish I got to talk to him more about it, but I remember I had a very brief probably like ten-minute conversation with him a few days after the premiere. He just talked to me about how the movie nailed the feeling of the life. That meant a lot to me."[23] In the same interview, however, Holmes counters, "He never talked to me about the movie."[24]

On April 12, 2015, six months after the film had its U.S. premiere at the festival, Leontyev was found dead of an apparent overdose in Central Park. Was his death a coincidence, or was it somehow related to the film? Although it is impossible to ever know how seeing his life depicted in *Heaven Knows What* affected him, Ilya's death, which was first fictionalized in the film, relates to its psychodramatic premise. Many biographical elements are contained in the film, including the scene where Leontyev nearly died from an overdose during rehearsals. The fire was also based on an incident that happened. Leontyev, of course, did not actually die in the fire that occurred in an apartment that he and Holmes shared in Jersey City, but he ended up in the hospital. According to Holmes, who not present at the time of the blaze, "His hands got burned. He had skin grafts. All his hair burned off."[25] The two of them subsequently spent two more years together in Manhattan before Holmes became involved with someone else, which is the point at which *Heaven Knows What* begins.

In terms of psychodrama, Holmes was forced to relive her drug addiction in *Heaven Knows What*, as well as her compulsive and abusive relationship with Leontyev. At the film's beginning, Harley tries to kill herself to prove her love for Ilya, which was the real-life event that helped set the entire film in motion. By basing the film on the lives of Holmes and Leontyev, as initially written by Holmes, the Safdies blend nonfiction and fiction. As Josh told an interviewer, "Ari says the film feels exactly like what her life felt like then. We tried to stick to the facts as much as possible. It's a true psychodrama in that regard."[26] While Holmes had to re-experience her suicide attempt during filming, Leontyev, for whatever reason, was incapable or unwilling to participate in the production, even though he played the role of the ghost who haunted not only the making of it but also the final film. Did Leontyev's near fatal overdose prior to shooting represent an unconscious attempt on his part to sabotage the production?

Was his subsequent death intended to be a coda to the film, or was it merely an inevitable consequence of his out-of-control lifestyle?

Holmes and Leontyev were on decidedly different paths by the time of production. Holmes's engagement with the film posed a distinct threat to the power that Leontyev held over her. She was paid to write her memoir, which was now being made into an independent feature film. Holmes had already stopped using drugs and was planning to go to rehab after shooting ended. Her life was changing for the better, whereas Leontyev remained in a downward spiral. He might have enjoyed the attention of being depicted in the film, but the portrait of him is not a flattering one. As the filmmakers recognized in reading Holmes's autobiographical account, Ilya clearly serves as Harley's malevolent antagonist. He goads her to commit suicide and leaves her at the hospital; he threatens to kill her subsequent boyfriend, Mike; he injures Mike with a homemade weapon after losing their fight; and he abandons Harley on the bus to Florida.

In addition, the incident of his being injured in a fire is transformed into a horrific scene in which Ilya catches fire and his flesh sizzles to the bone. Leontyev's subsequent death adds an additional psychodramatic layer to the film. Asked by a journalist "if his death complicates her relationship to the movie," Holmes responded, "He dies in the movie. I just . . . yeah. I don't really know what I think about that."[27] Throughout the film, Caleb Landry Jones is, in Moreno's terms, mirroring Leontyev. For Leontyev to watch his own callous behavior and subsequent demise in the film had to be a traumatic experience. Yet it did not prove to be a wake-up call for him in the same way that Holmes's suicide attempt was for her.

By the time Leontyev saw the film, Holmes was already on her way to developing a successful career. In an article in *Vulture* that appeared a mere five weeks after Leontyev's death, Amy Larocca writes:

The movie has also had the somewhat surprising effect of turning Holmes into a fledgling indie-film actress. She has an agent at ICM and a manager, and she shaved off most of her hair for a part in a science-fiction movie. She was photographed for a beauty story in *W* magazine. . . . On my way to meet Holmes at a coffee shop in L.A., I ran into Andy Spade, who is excited by Holmes as an actress. "She's amazing," he tells me. "We're doing some short films for Sleepy Jones, and I'm hoping she can be in one." A girl who has slept many nights on the street could soon be hawking $300 pajamas.[28]

Holmes subsequently played a minor role as the Darth Vader-obsessed Pagan, a member of a cult-like group of young people traveling around the American Midwest selling magazine subscriptions in Andrea Arnold's heavily improvised *American Honey* (2016).

It appears that Holmes has managed to turn her life around. She was able confront her demons successfully—thus far, at least—and *Heaven Knows What* largely became the vehicle for her to accomplish this. In the terms of psychodrama, Holmes was able to achieve what Moreno termed "actor's catharsis." John Nolte, a Moreno-trained psychodramatist, explains, "More than by seeing roles enacted and emotions expressed by others, it is by acting out roles that touch one deeply, roles that involve feelings to which one relates most meaningfully, that one masters those feelings and those roles."[29]

It is clear from interviews that Holmes has a deeper understanding of addiction. In objecting to the use of the term "addict," she argues that it is merely an "excuse," nothing more than a simple label for other problems that are not fully understood. As she puts it, "It's not the drug you're addicted to. It's something else. It's other issues."[30] In an online profile of her, Holmes elaborates, "In the past, I used drugs a lot and I became very detached, and it's something I still have. Even though all this crazy shit is going on in my life—don't get me wrong, I have severe depression and anxiety a lot—it didn't happen to the person I am right this second. But the stem of depression and all that, those things are still inside me. It doesn't really leave me."[31]

For Holmes, her addiction was also inextricably bound up with her compulsive love for Leontyev, despite the fact that the abusive relationship with him nearly killed her. We do not get backstory about either character because the film concentrates on the present moment, which is how these characters choose to live their lives. If we were to probe their pasts, the "other issues" would no doubt become obvious, but the film is less concerned with explanation than with conveying to viewers the experience of how it feels to be these characters whose lives play out on the streets.

While Jones does an admirable job of portraying Ilya, the two performances by Holmes and Duress somehow seem more genuine. Sarah Salovaara hints at this in a review of *Heaven Knows What* in *Filmmaker* when she writes, "If Ilya and Harley's elliptical relationship is the supposed centerpiece, I'm far more intrigued by the sideshow of Harley and Mike, where *Heaven* often assumes its most brutally honest stance."[32] One possible explanation of why the dynamic between these two first-time actors feels so authentic is that both performers were high on drugs during production. According to Josh Safdie, "Ari was on methadone while we were making the movie and I later found out that Buddy was using throughout the whole film."[33] That might account for their uncanny ability to block out the rest of the world while they were acting for the camera. Duress seems to talk as if he is in a slight fog. His eyes convey a glassy faraway look, even though he tends to stare at the other person as he speaks. Holmes, on the other hand, is often filmed at a slight angle. As she processes what is being said, her eyes dart quickly and she talks in short bursts that suggest the quick jabs of a scrappy prizefighter.

Yet there is another reason why their scenes stand out, which relates to the narrative and issues of characterization. The daily interactions between Mike and Harley create more dramatic friction through their arguments than her abusive relationship with Ilya, who tends to dominate and rob Harley of her independence. Harley and Mike operate more as equals, which turns out to be far more interesting in terms of their characters. Their exchanges often escalate into arguments over her failure to make the rent at the cheap place where they crash. Mike wants her to carry her weight, but Harley easily gets distracted from panhandling by wanting to get high instead. At the place where they crash, for instance, Harley wants Mike to front her two bags of dope, but he wants the money. When Mike finally gives in to her, she shoots up on the top bunk bed, but then tries to get the additional two bags he promised to give her as a "wake-up" in the morning. They proceed to get into a lengthy argument. He insists quite logically that it is night and not morning, whereas she claims he would still be giving her an equal number of bags. Harley yells, "Do you know how to do math?" Offended, Mike responds, "Yeah, I'm not fucking retarded, all right?"

The Safdie brothers used improvisation in rehearsals to make the dialogue feel more natural. As Benny Safdie explains, "We use improvisation as a form of getting the people's language right. We use it as a tool to get the dialogue perfect. It always sounds better when it's coming from someone's own voice as opposed to from above, from us. If somebody doesn't feel comfortable saying it a certain way we change it, and then that makes that person more comfortable."[34] But Josh Safdie indicates that he was looking beyond what we understand as standard improvisation in *Heaven Knows What*, given the highly personal nature of the material:

> Yes, I use improvisation as a major tool in this movie, but we always did really extensive rehearsals to kind of push away from the improv nature and arrive at something a little deeper than that. You always try to find people that are very present. In this milieu of people, everyone in that world and lifestyle is very present all the time, which just helps lead to performance, people like Arielle and Buddy. I'm looking back on the way I worked with him and Arielle. Caleb was really interesting because Caleb was coming from a trained and professional world, and I was constantly trying to surround him with stuff that would beat that out of him.[35]

The notion of pushing past improvisation into something deeper points toward his use of psychodrama as a means to get beneath the surface in terms of characterization.

Holmes initially struggled during rehearsals because she was too self-conscious about playing herself. The Safdies wanted her to play a more exaggerated version of herself, which is why they decided to change her name to Harley. Duress, who had never acted before but was something of a street legend like Ilya, intuitively knew how to create conflict with her. According to Josh Safdie, "[Duress] would probe her emotionally and he would get at psychodrama, almost. He would get her."[36] Benny Safdie goes on to explain, "There's a scene they filmed. Josh told them, 'Buddy, probe her this way.' 'Ari, don't resist in that way.' And it kind of devolved into this weird emotional argument. They weren't arguing about what they were talking about; they were arguing about something else completely different."[37]

Psychodrama does not focus on the past but on the present moment, which was something that fascinated the filmmakers about the drug users, whose lives they were intent on documenting. Benny Safdie responds to the way Holmes, Duress, and Leontyev experienced time. He told an interviewer, "There's something very intriguing to being completely unshackled. I can live in the now, but my grandmother and her friend said they were very struck by how frightening it was that these people didn't have any past or any future. I can relate to that in a way, because to me, it's frightening to live with the idea of not having that. That fear is also baked into the film."[38]

Although psychodrama can be an extremely powerful form of acting, especially for spontaneously living in the moment, there are inherent dangers in employing the technique. Early in his career, J. L. Moreno experienced the suicides of two of his patients—George and Robert— as a direct result of psychodramas, which profoundly disturbed him. According to Marineau:

> Soon after having worked with Moreno the couple separated, and five years later George killed himself. This incident always troubled Moreno, but it was the earlier suicide of another member of the group that made him question the nature and limits of his work. He was carrying out 'stage therapy' with another couple, Robert and Diora; everything seemed to be going well, but one day Diora left her partner and Robert killed himself the next morning.[39]

Despite these early setbacks, Moreno was nevertheless convinced of the efficacy of his therapeutic brand of theater.

As has already been indicated, many stage and film actors and directors attended Moreno's psychodrama sessions in the 1960s. Moreno, however, was trained as a psychiatrist, whereas others in the performing arts have often used a form of psychodrama to create greater dramatic conflict and deepen the level of performance. John Nolte addresses the responsibility of the director of a psychodrama, warning that the biggest risk is retraumatizing the subject.[40] According to Nolte, "The most successful psychodramas occur when protagonists achieve the spontaneity state," which involves great trust in the abilities of the director:

> Then, as in hypnosis, the protagonist turns over some degree of intellectual or ego functioning to the director, allowing the fullest arousal and the most complete expression to his/her emotions. This requires great confidence in the director's expertise. Once asked what the most important personal characteristic was that one needed in order to be a director, Moreno replied without a pause, "Courage." It is courage that is needed to go with the protagonist into the deepest, darkest areas of the protagonist's private world in order to attain release from the monsters and ghosts that may be lucking there.[41]

In tackling such abject subject matter under extraordinarily difficult conditions, the Safdies proved that they certainly do not lack courage.

In making the film, Josh Safdie was keenly aware of the fact that, as he put it, "Death was around the corner at any moment."[42] Yet the Safdies were willing to risk everything to have Holmes confront her addiction to both drugs and Leontyev by participating in the film. Duress was an additional and unexpected success story. He was arrested twelve hours after the film wrapped. Duress spent a year in jail and wound up missing the film's New York City premiere but now wants to be an actor.[43] He has since appeared in Dustin Guy Defa's *Person to Person* (2017) and opposite Robert Pattinson in the Safdies' latest film, *Good Time*.

There is some irony in the fact that Leontyev refused to be in the film and wound up being a casualty. Josh Safdie understood that for Holmes, acting in *Heaven Knows What* became a form of therapy. He told an interviewer, "I think that she was able to get out a lot of her demons. So what you're seeing on screen is greater than a performance that wins Oscars, it's something that should win the attention of psychiatrists and anyone that is trying to figure their own shit out."[44]

NATHAN SILVER: *STINKING HEAVEN*

Nathan Silver has explored the use of psychodrama in five consecutive films: *Exit Elena* (2012), *Soft in the Head* (2013), *Uncertain Terms* (2014), *Stinking Heaven* (2015), and *Actor Martinez* (2016). In the first four of them, Silver explores the concept of family—both the nuclear family as well as communal groups that mimic the family. Silver explains, "There's also this sense that you can't force family. At first people are very happy to be part of another family, but then it slowly gets ruptured and to watch that happen fascinates me."[45]

Like many other recent indie filmmakers, such as Swanberg, Porterfied, and Aaron Katz, Silver has forsaken traditional written scripts for outlines and improvisation. He told an interviewer, "A script should be something you use to wipe your ass. It's just to get people involved and some sort of insurance."[46] Silver's process is to develop his characters rather than the story: "I have ideas for their character and I sit down for months and talk things through and eventually I get to the point where I have the characters but I don't really have the story yet. I'm banging my head against the wall and then I bring my collaborators in and we start writing the outline together."[47]

During filming, Silver has an outline for various scenes, and apparently even certain turning points that he wants his actors to hit.[48] Yet, due to the chemistry of the performers involved, the director has no idea what will eventually occur once the cameras start rolling. For Silver, making the film becomes a way for him to find out.[49] Like Warhol, Silver has faith that, given the passage of time, something interesting will materialize out of a given situation. He told an interviewer: "If you allow improv, there will eventually be conflict if you let the cameras just run and run and run. Eventually some character will act out and that will spark something else, and then after a few takes you discover where the tensions are and you can then get coverage to make those tensions pop on screen."[50] Unlike Warhol, editing for Silver becomes a crucial means to shape the material.

Much of Silver's working method derives from creating certain psychologically charged situations. These usually involve an outsider entering an established family or communal group. In *Exit Elena*, a live-in nurse finds herself subsumed into the dynamic of a tension-filled family. An alcoholic young woman in *Soft in the Head* intrudes on her roommate's Orthodox Jewish family and also becomes part of an urban shelter for emotionally disturbed and homeless men to disastrous effect. In *Uncertain Terms*, the married nephew of the head of a small group home for unwed mothers falls in love with one of the pregnant young women. In *Stinking Heaven*, a disturbed young woman follows her ex-lover and upsets the delicate balance in a house of recovering addicts run by a duplicitous young guru obsessed with rules.

Silver has described his interest in spontaneity and improvisation in numerous interviews. He told *Filmmaker*: "Folks always talk about how they want human beings on screen yet so many friggin' movies squeeze them into hermetically sealed story lines and compositions. I say, let some air in and film it!"[51] Silver shares with Moreno a distrust for the scripted because he is more interested in what is occurring in the present moment during the process of filming. He explains:

Even though the story elements are always necessary—like in *Exit Elena* when the grandmother falls down, or the arrival of my character, those are inevitably elements of a story—when we were shooting I never wanted it to seem like the actors were telling the story. I just wanted them to live and for us to document them living. The actors know their characters, but they have no sense of what happens to those characters, because they have no context."[52]

Although less interested in the mechanics of plot per se, Silver is nonetheless obsessed with developing in-depth characters. In shooting *Soft in the Head*, a film about a young woman named Natalia (Sheila Etxeberría) who falls apart after breaking up with her abusive boyfriend, Silver went to extremes to develop her character. This included taping interviews and monologues as well as attending parties with Etxeberría in character.[53]

Because of the way Silver constructs his films, switching the emphasis from the story to the performers, his films are highly dependent on casting. Silver acknowledges some actors actually prefer the security of a written script. Yet, according to the filmmaker, "Others love it because it's a form of writing for them. They have more invested. It's about finding people who don't need heavy-handed direction."[54] Silver has expressed an interest in "real people" rather than actors: "For me, it comes down to this: let in people, keep out performers. I can't exactly explain that, but it's how I work."[55] What Silver seems to mean by this is that he is less interested in a performer playing a character than actually being a character.

Silver wants to minimize the degree of artifice. He initially used family and friends in *Exit Elena* and *Soft in the Head*, but in *Uncertain Terms* and *Stinking Heaven*, Silver cast well-known indie actors, such as Tallie Medel, Gina Piersanti, Deragh Campbell, Hannah Gross, and Keith Poulson. The distinction, however, between amateur and trained performers becomes blurred due to Silver's improvisational approach and lack of a traditional script:

When I'm shooting it's not scripted, the action is scripted but the dialogue is all improvised. So I guess even if the actors are playing characters who are completely different to who they are, I guess they are being themselves because they are in this documentary setting where they can do whatever they want, basically, within certain parameters.

Just like how in a documentary you have parameters. You understand that you can't just run off down the street because the camera can't catch up with you. You understand that you're being filmed, it has a documentary set up in that way. I want to capture the chaos, that's why I incorporate all these documentary elements and fictionalize them through putting these real people into these fake situations and mixing everything up and then in the edit everything shifts completely and adds another layer of fiction to it.[56]

Silver's blend of fictional and documentary elements is what gives his work a raw and unpredictable edge. For Silver, casting is largely an intuitive decision, but he is also looking for performers who, when thrown together, will create a combustible situation.

Silver's features seem to move in a progression toward greater emphasis on psychodrama. Set in a house for recovering addicts and shot with a 1980s Ikegami TV camera that creates colorful abstract patterns in the images, *Stinking Heaven* (2015) does not employ a script. The story is credited to Silver and Jack Dunphy, with credit for additional material shared by three of the main actors: Campbell, Gross, and Poulson. The film begins with a precredit sequence of two young women, Betty (Eleonore Hendricks) and Ann (Hannah Gross) smoking crack. After the credits, we get close-up shots of the two women walking together blissfully. A title indicates the setting: Passaic, New Jersey, 1990. There is a cut to a wedding ceremony between Betty and an older man named Kevin (Henri Douvry) in the communal house, with the camera focusing on their clasped hands.

The wedding is presided over by the head of a drug rehabilitation house, Jim (Keith Poulson), who recites clichéd platitudes about the two participants. We see Jim's wife, Lucy (Deragh Campbell), while three other members of the household play music, including Kevin's young daughter, Courtney (Tallie Medel). The group members sustain themselves by selling a fermented tea—a questionable concoction which they brew in the bathtub. As the house members sit around the table, underlying tensions are revealed.

In the first of what will be several reenactments by house members of traumatic low points in their lives, Kevin reimagines a degrading experience in which people urinated on him and beat him. Courtney consoles

him, as the camera captures Betty's embarrassed reaction. It is in the reenactments that *Stinking Heaven* transforms into psychodrama, blurring the
divide between fiction and actuality. One interviewer commented that
they were so "crazy intense" that she wondered whether what was transpiring was "really happening." Silver's response explicitly connects the
reenactments to psychodrama: "We realized, what if this could be some
form of therapy? And one of the other actors, Henri Douvry knew about
psychodrama therapy, and it kind of borders on what happens in these
scenes, actually. I think it was the production designer, Britney, who suggested we have them film it, during the shoot."[57]

In one scene, Gene (Lawrence Novak), an older hippie with long gray
hair and a beard, reenacts an experience of going down on a young guy for
twenty dollars. As he pretends to perform fellatio on Jim, the house leader
suddenly knees him, causing Gene to fall backwards, hit his head on the
floor, and have an epileptic seizure. His body shakes and tightens before
coming to rest. In voiceover, Gene adds other humiliating details. A woman's voice asks, "Was that your first time, Gene?" Al (Jason Giampietro)
questions whether he ever got the money, but someone slaps him. The others clap lethargically. In a subsequent reenactment by Al—an example of
Moreno's technique of role reversal—he performs the role of the young
man receiving a blow job from a guy near Penn Station, while Gene smiles
quizzically. He adds that the guy made loud groaning sounds and describes
the oral sex act as awful. He talks about kneeing the guy, causing him to
hit his head on the pavement and go into convulsions. Is Al ridiculing the
older man? Or, in Moreno's terms, is he "mirroring" him by serving as an
auxiliary ego for Gene? Whatever his motivation, the reenactment con-
founds our sense of how to read the intention behind his role playing.

As the group sings about the healing power of love—a refrain that is
heard throughout the film—Al attacks the others for their "weak" music
playing, which turns the singing into psychodrama, as an older woman
named Marie (Eileen Kearney) begins to screech the words like a mad-
woman. Shortly after this, while discussing Kevin's banishment from the
house, Eileen and Lucy get into a heated argument. When Eileen characterizes Lucy and Jim as a unit and refers to Lucy as a "we," the tension escalates. Lucy suddenly grabs Eileen around the throat and then
slaps her hard across her face. As Eileen physically retaliates, we hear loud
screaming. Ann violently slams a wooden chair against the ground until

it breaks. She then screams at Lucy that she will never leave her, runs into the kitchen and returns with a knife, causing mayhem to break out, as she proceeds to attack Lucy before bursting out in laughter on the floor. The scene ends with weak clapping, but Jim's worried expression is more telling, as both Hannah and Lucy sit on the floor exhaustedly and Hannah strokes Lucy's hair—a prelude to ditching her later on.

Jim embodies the worst attributes of those who set themselves up as self-appointed "gurus" of communal living groups. Yet it is really Ann who has the most toxic effect on the group. She observes the various members with a kind of indifference and initially refuses to participate in any reenactments. Her evil smirk suggests that drug addiction is only a symptom or a veneer of her deeper-rooted psychological problems, which is also true for the other members of the communal house. Ann has poisonous relationships with Betty and Tina prior to joining the cult-like group. The fury she unleashes at Lucy during the reenactment appears to come out of nowhere but in fact has been simmering underneath the surface for quite a while and, because it has been repressed, it explodes with a frightening velocity.

In many ways, *Stinking Heaven* most successfully accomplishes the type of psychodrama that Silver strives for in his films. In an interview, he seemed pleased and took it as a compliment when someone suggested that watching *Soft in the Head* felt like the person was "constantly going through a panic attack."[58] In the same interview, he expresses a desire to capture extreme psychological states on camera: "I keep thinking about how to capture a person's nervous breakdown in the way that [Lucien Castaing-Taylor and Véréna Paravel's documentary] *Leviathan* captures fishing. That would be my ideal. I have no idea what that would look like."[59] For Silver, people are most themselves when faced with a chaotic situation, so his goal becomes to create those types of situations for his performers. The scene where Ann explodes and attacks Lucy is a case in point. Silver speculates:

> But why do I keep coming back to chaos? I think because I don't have any fucking ideas, I don't have any ideas about the world. I have notions that I want to put into play and I want to see what people do with them. The only thing that interests me is watching insanity unfold because people are people then. I keep shying away from it and then returning to it, so it's

obviously something I have to stick with and accept that it's going to be hectic while making and doing it but there's something I love about that as well and can stand behind."[60]

For Silver, the process of making his films often becomes its own form of psychodrama.

William Greaves achieved this in *Symbiopsychotaxiplasm: Take One* by pretending to be an inept director. While Greaves exhibited caution about probing his performers' boundaries, Silver often achieves his effects by pushing his performers to the breaking point. His mother, Cindy Silver, who had major roles in *Exit Elena* and *Uncertain Terms*, talks about her own exasperation at performing in his movies. In discussing her son as a film director, she comments, "As in everything he does, he is driven by this amazing creative force and energy, and that can exhaust those of us being directed in his films. We do not stop being filmed or rehearsing until someone starts crying—usually me—after 18-hour shoots with no air conditioning in the middle of a Massachusetts summer."[61]

11

THE LINE BETWEEN REALITY AND STAGING

Actor Martinez, *Actress*, and *The Witness*

Although fiction films and documentaries are typically viewed as separate traditions in the history of cinema, there has always been considerable crossover between the two modes. As demonstrated in the early chapters, indie cinema has often looked to everyday life for inspiration, evidenced by the work of Lionel Rogosin, Kent Mackenzie, and Barbara Loden. Since staging and fabrication play a heavy role in Hollywood films, indie filmmakers have been drawn to the opposite tendency: using real locations, nonprofessional actors, and alternative scripting methods.

The line between the staged and the real is a slippery one. The whole aim of improvisation is to achieve something that appears natural and created in the moment. As we have seen, psychodrama occurs when the material becomes so deeply personal that it reflects some aspect of a performer's own life that merges with the fictional character that he or she is playing. A number of recent indie films have explored the divide between fiction and documentary and the staged and the real. *Actor Martinez*, *Actress*, and *The Witness* brilliantly interrogate the boundaries between fiction and nonfiction by showing the richness of their hybridity.

NATHAN SILVER AND MIKE OTT:
ACTOR MARTINEZ

A concern with filmmaking as a form of therapy continues in Nathan Silver's sixth feature, *Actor Martinez* (2016), which he codirected with Mike Ott. The idea for the film was hatched at the Denver Film Festival when a part-time actor, Arthur Martinez, approached Ott about casting him in one of his projects. Ott decided to build a film that centers on Martinez's life and talked Silver into becoming involved in the project. Like Silver's other films, *Actor Martinez* does not employ a traditional script. According to Lindsay Burdge, the female lead, it uses a brief outline containing three scenes that ended up in the final film. Burdge gives a sense of the details:

> It was like, "They decide to hire an actress, Lindsay Burdge, from New York. Arthur's worried that she's not Hollywood enough. She arrives, they meet each other, and they discuss that neither of them knows what's going on. They do some scenes where they walk around, they kiss, they bring home groceries. She looks at the camera. They tell her not to. She quits the movie. Arthur sits in his house as his house is taken down around him." That's basically how it was written.[1]

As the outline indicates, Silver and Ott had an actor, but they seem to be in search of a movie. Like Warhol, Mailer, Greaves or Swanberg, the filmmakers were more or less concocting the movie as they went along. Ott suggests, "We knew we wanted multiple layers of fiction and documentary elements in the mix, but just what we would do with these layers, we had to deal with in post."[2]

Although they were using a bare-bones outline, Silver explains their working method, "Most days we sketched in what we were going to do, then out of those sketches, we would develop scenes that we wanted to shoot. We allowed ourselves a lot of freedom in the schedule. It wasn't like we have to do this, that and the other thing to make our day. It was more about how are we going to find a movie in all of this?"[3] The filmmakers shoot scenes involving Martinez using a documentary style, and what

FIGURE 11.1 Arthur, after Trish leaves the film, *Actor Martinez*

becomes apparent is that the subject proves not very open to revealing himself. The film becomes an effort to break through his protective shield of defenses as he is placed under the scrutiny of the camera. As a result, a small semblance of plot develops. Similar to what occurred in Shirley Clarke's *Portrait of Jason*, the dramatic conflict of the film develops into a battle between the directors and their lead actor.

To the two filmmakers, it is understandable why Arthur—at least as he presents himself in the film—would appear to be something of an enigma. In many ways, he is an indie filmmaker's worst nightmare. Arthur conceives of acting as merely a job, while his conception of what makes a good movie is completely audience-based. Even as he complains about the emotional strain of making the film with Mike and Nathan, Arthur remains optimistic about what they are producing, even when the filmmakers are not. Silver has indicated that they originally planned to make a fictional film, but that plan was quickly scrapped. Instead the film became a dramatization of Martinez's life and personality. Silver explains, "You can't script a person. We didn't try to script a character—he was the character and we decided to make the movie around him, if that makes any sense."[4] Ott adds, "What we thought was interesting about him and would be in the movie didn't end up in there, and all this other stuff did."[5]

In some ways, *Actor Martinez* mirrors Abel Ferrara's *Dangerous Game* in being a multi-layered film within a film. Ott and Silver perform the role of two directors shooting a film about Arthur Martinez, who plays the eponymous lead character. But there is another layer involving the filmmakers' attempt—whether real or fictional—to create a dramatization based on elements from Arthur's life. Daniel Kasman comments about the film's labyrinthine structure: "So we now have four layers of conceptual drama: Martinez's life, the film about him, the film about the production of that film, and the film about the production of the film about the production."[6] The film deliberately confuses the boundary between fiction and nonfiction, the staged and improvised, actor and role. In the end, however, the film hinges on its lead actor who, in playing a character resembling himself, presents a mask. To the consternation of the filmmakers, any time the mask gets pulled away, another one appears.

Actor Martinez begins in media res with an out-of-focus shot of the two codirectors, Nathan and Mike. In voiceover, one of them asks Arthur whether he has any concerns about the movie thus far. Arthur deflects the question by replying that it is the directors who are supposed to have the concerns. Arthur conceives of making a film as merely a job. Mike replies, "My worry is that you're not going to come off as sympathetic." Arthur complains that he has yet to receive any real direction from them. He eventually walks into the frame and sits down with his back facing the camera. In the film's very first scene, the battle lines are already drawn.

Arthur works as a computer repair technician. He is also involved in a film-related networking group called Film Grind. The group is a collection of wannabes—an aspiring actor named Kenny Potrykus (Kenneth Berba), a construction worker, a stunt guy with a military background—hoping to make connections in whatever sliver of a film industry exists in the Denver area. Arthur, the last person to introduce himself, promotes film events. Arthur later arranges to get Kenny a job as an actor on an emergency training film. Kenny's acting is predictably atrocious, but Arthur exhibits a positive attitude as he coaches the novice about how to play a scene in which he is supposed to act disoriented. Arthur's directing tips are decidedly off the mark—in fact, they are downright misleading. "Your goal," he tells Kenny "is to help them."

The filmmakers conspire to get Arthur out of his comfort zone. Because Arthur has been emotionally impenetrable, they decide to find someone like his ex-wife to be in the film, which introduces the element of psycho-drama. A series of casting sessions with various female performers follow in an attempt to find him a girlfriend. The filmmakers bring up a number of issues to the actors they claim would be a deal breaker for Arthur—a dog, STDs, or lack of compassion. The audition scene involves a mono-logue about the final breakup of a relationship, which references Arthur's divorce. One actor stands out in the thin talent pool. In an awkward try-out scene afterward, Arthur attempts to kiss her. She grouses about his indiscretion to the filmmakers, but it does not matter because Arthur rejects her for being too similar to his wife. As a result, Mike and Nathan announce that they have hired indie actor Lindsay Burdge from New York to play his fictional girlfriend. Arthur is excited at this prospect because he believes that her previous acting credits will make the film more mar-ketable. He describes her as "beautiful" but "not his type."

In real life, Burdge is from Los Angeles rather than New York, which—at least for her—enables her to fictionalize the part. As she explains:

> At first, it was really a big challenge and I had to find a character of myself that I could play rather than feeling like it was a documentary about me, which it wasn't. Initially, I was pitched a narrative movie, then maybe a month before we started shooting, I got an outline that was this com-pletely other movie, without warning or discussion, so I had to find the edge of myself that I was willing to put into the movie and that took a second. Once I did, it was really fun.[7]

Burdge was brought into the movie by the two directors, presumably to bring out Arthur's character, but it was initially hard for the two actors to find their bearings. According to Burdge, "We didn't have anything really to hold onto at first. There's no script, there's no character, and so we weren't working on a scene together."[8]

The fact that they were not working from a fixed script, but rather trying to improvise the story, generated a certain tension between the actors. Burdge describes Ott and Silver's approach: "Yeah, it was sort of like Arthur was this animal in a cage and then they would take this other animal—me—out of this other cage, and they would whisper in my ear and then throw me into the cage with him. Occasionally, I wouldn't know that they'd also whispered in his ear."[9] After her first scenes with Arthur—one probes his previous marriage, while in a second one they swim in a large pool at night—Burdge, whose character is named Trish, raises concerns about Arthur being exploited by the filmmakers. Mike does not deny any of her accusations.

Burdge explains in an interview that she initially felt very uncomfortable on set, claiming she had a meltdown off camera. The situation changed afterward:

> Then, I had an opportunity to talk to Arthur off-camera, and I got a sense of what was actually going on with him: he was uncomfortable but he was willing. He was a completely willing participant, but he didn't want to know what was happening to him. I also started to realize that maybe he was acting more than he was letting on. Then I felt safer. I felt like I wasn't just fucking with some guy but that we were doing something together, even if we had different understandings of what we were doing. That was my hump that I had to get over.[10]

The actors' differing attitudes toward the film, however, will become an important part of the contrasting dynamic between them.

The introduction of Trish shifts the film from comedy to drama. The dynamic between Arthur and Trish manifests itself in three key scenes: one where Arthur is asked to cry, an argument between the two of them, and an intimate sex scene. Arthur and Trish spend an evening having dinner with Kenny, which ends with a shot in the mirror of her isolated and unhappy. The next day, as the two directors sit withthe characters, Mike brings up a conflict between them. Arthur talks about the difficulty of opening up to Trish and reveals that he never really cried during the breakup of his marriage. This sets up the next scene, in which Arthur is asked to cry in front of Trish, but his face remains immobile and he is unable to muster any tears. After a long time in which nothing occurs, Arthur insists that this is how he cries. The directors cut the scene. As the crew members appear, Trish suddenly begins to cry. While the cast and crew later stand around and get stoned, Arthur starts to apologize for being unable to cry but again claims that his noncrying is how he cries. When pressed by Mike, Arthur indicates that he would have to resort to tricks or need more prep time in order to get tears to flow. Burge's ability, as an actor and person, to cry provides a stark contrast to Arthur's inability to be vulnerable.

The next day Mike instructs Trish to "poke" Arthur because he is being resistant. In terms of motivation for Trish in the scene, Nathan describes Arthur as having been emotionally cut off for months. Mike chimes in that she needs "to push his buttons." Trish responds, "Okay, I'll try." The scene begins with Arthur asking Trish for a hug. She refuses and then goes on the attack. Arthur retaliates, suggesting he knew they should not have cast her. He vents that she was only cast because she was a "name" and that someone else was better suited to play the part. Trish calls him a "shell of a person" and proceeds to dump a bowl of pot on his head. As Arthur cleans up the pot, he remarks in voiceover, "This was some really good stuff, by the way. It wasn't easy to get."

It seems inevitable that the two actors would be asked to film a sex scene. After Arthur confesses, "My brain is scrambled," and Trish likens the experience to tripping on LSD, the film cuts to the two of them in the bedroom. Nathan announces they are going to do a sex scene. Trish wishes that she had been informed about this beforehand and thinks they should discuss the specifics, namely whether she has to be topless or can wear a bra, which would be her preference. The attempt at a sex scene follows. As the Arthur and Trish kiss, he removes her blouse. The two fall back on the bed with him on top of her. We hear a few curt directions. After two minutes, in which we watch the two entwined bodies and hear sounds of kissing, Arthur abruptly stops. He asks Trish, "Do you want a break?" Trish appears to be crying. Arthur tells her, "If you want to stop, we will." He turns and asks, "Guys, do we really need this scene?" The directors call a five-minute break, mercifully ending the scene.

The sex scene appears to be a staged contrivance. It is doubtful that the directors would be so insensitive as to spring this on their actors, especially Burdge. It is at this point that *Actor Martinez* might be viewed in a similar vein to faux documentaries made in the 1960s, such as Jim McBride's *David Holtzman's Diary* (1967) or Milton Moses Ginsberg's *Coming Apart* (1969). It also bears resemblance to certain films by Swanberg, especially *The Zone*. The film is playing with the idea of psychodrama, but—due to its staged nature—not exactly following through on the inherent premise. Martinez appears to be the main obstacle preventing the film from moving to a deeper level. In J. L. Moreno's terms, he fails to respond to events spontaneously or to express a full range of emotions. As a result, Martinez does not achieve catharsis.

For Aristotle, the notion of catharsis involved emotion that is passively experienced by the audience. Moreno, however, was more concerned with catharsis as experienced by the actor during a performance or by the protagonist in a psychodrama. John Nolte explains the difference between the need for an actor to access spontaneity while performing in order to keep the role alive and fresh and someone engaged in a psychodrama:

> The situation in psychodrama is quite different. Here, instead of an actor in a symbolic role on the conventional stage, we have private individuals with their private tragedies on the psychodrama stage. There is no script and no rehearsal. Everything happens for the first time. Protagonists must, with their own spontaneity, create both roles and action. The drama is created and produced simultaneously. There is only one performance of a psychodrama.[11]

Nolte goes as far to say that "Moreno's preoccupation with the actor's catharsis became the foundation of psychodrama."[12]

Actor Martinez represents an attempt at psychodrama in which the lead character turns out to be blocked. Silver suspects as much because in an interview he talks about films being "experiments" that should entail the risk of failure:

> I find it problematic in filmmaking these days that you can't experiment; it has to be a product. With every project, you have to have something in the end that you can present to [the] world, that you can sell, because movies cost money and we all know this. What fascinates me more is when you're playing. There should be movies that are playing around, that are trying things. I think we should fail more. We're a failure.[13]

In Ferrara's *Dangerous Game*, the Madonna character, Sarah, raises the point that acting involves feeling, and she argues that for the scene with Frank to be successful he needs to love her. The same issue is true here. Is Martinez playing a character who is incapable of emotional feeling, or is Martinez himself emotionally stunted?

Actor Martinez is, on some level, a brutally honest portrayal of Martinez. Are the filmmakers exploiting him? If so, there is simply no gauge by which to judge his performance. Subsequent interviews—either those filmed or in print—show someone very much like the person we see in the film. His answers are evasive. In one interview, he describes his performance as "fighting in the dark."[14] The problem with his metaphor is that it implies that we never actually had a chance to see it. When asked whether Martinez was playing himself in the film, Ott remarks, "maybe it was him," and adds, "I don't know Arthur any better now than I knew him before we started shooting."[15] His attempt at crying is a failure. Even worse is the sex scene, which fails to generate any sort of chemistry between the performers.

Burdge cries in the film because she can act and has the ability to access her emotions, whereas we are not so sure about Martinez's acting skills. In discussing the film's documentary-like style, Silver suggests, "You lose some of the control because you're relying on this person to give you some emotional pull."[16] Yet that is precisely what is sorely missing from the lead actor. For *Actor Martinez* to work either as a film or as a successful psychodrama, Martinez would have to confront his issues with intimacy, especially the sense of loss he experiences as a result of his divorce. Instead, he sadly holds on to his defenses, including that his costar, Lindsay Burge, is beautiful but not his type.

ROBERT GREENE: *ACTRESS*

In making a film, Abel Ferrara insisted, "The point is, you gotta make something happen up there: something's gotta go down or there's no sense in turning on the camera. How can I put this? There's gotta be an *event*, that you're gonna turn the camera on *for*, and if the event isn't there, then what's the point? What're you shooting?"[17] Ferrara's sense of urgency rests on the filmmaker's ability to generate something worth filming. It would make equal sense that—Arthur Martinez aside—an actor might feel similar pressures, especially in an observational documentary about her or his life. This proved to be the case when documentary filmmaker Robert Greene decided to make a film, entitled *Actress*, about his friend and next-door neighbor, Brandy Burre, who appeared in fifteen episodes of the third and fourth seasons of the acclaimed TV show, *The Wire* (2002–2008).

Burre became pregnant during the shooting of the TV series and subsequently decided to forego her acting career for motherhood and relocating to Beacon, New York, a town on the Hudson River. Coincidentally, Beacon is where J. L. Moreno established psychodrama in America. Burre has two young children, Henry and Stella, and lives with her boyfriend, Tim Reinke, who owns a couple of bar-restaurants. Greene's film grew from an idea about the travails of a female actor attempting to restart her professional career after a long hiatus. *Actress* deals with the obvious difficulties this poses for a woman in her late thirties, when lead roles routinely go to younger performers, a subject Swanberg dealt with in *All the Light in the Sky*. The film also explores Burre's struggle to balance the conflicting roles of career and family. As *Actress* unfolds, however, it transforms into something more provocative when Burre decides to upend her family life for the sake of the movie, causing the film to veer into a form of self-created psychodrama.

Due to his background in nonfiction filmmaking, Greene takes a position similar to Erving Goffman that we are performers in everyday social interactions. Greene insists, "Anyone who's on a stage in some way conceives of a camera when they're there. Even a bartender does that. When he's at work, he's performing—he's performing his job. Documentaries can get in trouble when there isn't that recognition by the people in them; it makes the films feel sort of off."[18] Actors are even more acutely aware of their own self-presentation. Greene explains, "When someone performs, they're revealing insecurity, a sense of themselves that they've worked on—how they speak, how they do their hair, how they work on their body, all in service to presenting a certain self. With the camera there, that's pushed even further since no one is ever in a totally relaxed state when a camera's around."[19]

Because Burre is an actor, she always seems cognizant of the camera and her relation to it. Unlike Arthur Martinez, Burre relishes the opportunity to play to the camera, even when she is not exactly in the mood. *Actress* is based on a premise similar to that of Jason Holliday in Clarke's *Portrait of Jason*. Greene explains, "From the beginning, my interest in Brandy as a subject grew before the story became so dramatic. She's a theatrical human being. The basic premise was, 'What happens if you make an observational documentary about an actor?' What is the effect that has?"[20] By using an actor as his subject, Greene attempts to turn the observational documentary on its head. Like Holliday, Burre proceeds to perform her life for the camera, but, as happened with the gay hustler in Clarke's film, this inevitably raises a number of perplexing questions.

The opening of *Actress* features a heavily stylized, slow motion shot from behind Burre, who wears a bright red dress while she washes dishes in the kitchen—an image that suggests a domestic melodrama in the tradition of Douglas Sirk. It is notable that her costume sharply clashes with the setting. In voiceover, Burre comments, "I was thinking the other day about that scene, where I say, 'I'm a type A, and I tend to break things.' It just occurred to me, it wasn't just the character, it's . . . it's me." The scene to which she is alluding is a line said by her fictional character, Theresa D'Agostino, in *The Wire*. By applying the line of dialogue to her own personal life, Burre suggests the divide between fiction and reality that *Actress* so deftly explores when she is cast to play herself. This conflation of the two, which has become fashionable lately, has always fascinated Greene who claims, "This is all I've ever cared about in movies, is that line between reality and staging. That's what I think is exciting about movies."[21]

Burre comes across as a harried parent. In dealing with her children, she seems to be playing the role of mother—almost as an afterthought. We see her grocery shopping, unclogging the kitchen drain, sitting and putting on makeup in the left foreground of a shot while her partner, Tim, glides through the background in slow motion. Greene uses slow motion in a number of sequences to highlight a sense of melodrama. He explains, "The slow motion segments are there because I realized this was melodrama, particularly because of Brandy's persona and her ability to be melodramatic in any and all situations."[22] As Burre sits on a large green beanbag in the children's room, she says the line, "I moved to Beacon. I'm not acting. So this is my creative outlet." The dialogue is repeated twice with slight variation—as if she is saying it in rehearsal. In the next scene, which appears equally staged and crosses the line into fiction, Burre reaches for something on the top shelf and causes two tin boxes to come crashing down, as she groans and exclaims theatrically, "Death."

It is apparent that Burre feels alienated in her current domestic situation. She confesses that her relationship with Tim is on the skids. She has twice suggested that he move out of the house, but their lives are so

FIGURE 11.2 With her family out of town, Brandy Burre prepares to go to New York City, *Actress*

intertwined that separation would be very complicated. We see her meet a guy in New York City, but the shot is framed so as not to reveal the person's identity. The question arises: Is she being unfaithful? Burre also attempts to get back into performing and muses she will probably get typecast: "I will play the bitchy over-the-hill girlfriend or wife."

At thirty-seven minutes into the film, Burre sits down and speaks directly to the camera. She announces that Tim has found out about the affair she had while he was gone, and he has decided to terminate their relationship. Burre discusses the difficulties this will entail. She considers the breakup to be inevitable, even though the process is going to be extremely painful, which causes her to cry. The film cuts to the very first shot of her in the red dress at the kitchen sink again, as somber music plays on the soundtrack. She admits that she and Tim were playing roles in their domestic relationship. According to her, they have not been friends for a long time, which results in more tears. Burre confesses that the two of them only knew each for three months prior to her getting pregnant and admits, "It wasn't properly thought out."

Although Greene did not try to provoke the drama stemming from the dissolution of Burre's relationship with Tim, the question remains:

Would it have ended if she wasn't the subject of the film? Presumably, Burre would have had the affair and separated from her current partner regardless. Yet, as an actor and the film's subject, her behavior cannot help but be influenced by the camera, especially by her newfound desire to be in front of it once again. Burre would have been keenly aware that a film about her life would need to have a dramatic arc in order to engage audiences. Did she—either consciously or unconsciously—manage to create one for the film? *Actress* would have been dramatically flat without her affair and the chaos that ensued from it. Although it is sometimes common for documentary filmmakers to stage reality for the sake of a film, the question arises whether the performer has adopted a similar strategy.

In discussing her relationship with Tim, Burre attempts to debunk the notion he is a nice guy and that she is the bad partner. The camera focuses on her face as she cries in an extreme close-up. In voiceover, Burre discusses some of the negative options available in her situation—feeling sad, cold, or miserable—and concludes, "I believe that my children deserve more than that." At a Valentine's Day party for the kids, her female friends do not appear sympathetic. When she visits Tim's apartment, neither he nor the kids pay much attention to her. As she starts to leave, she waits for some acknowledgement, but they continue to ignore her. Tim finally says, "Well, have fun in Manhattan." Is the scene staged or observed? It is a question that lingers throughout the film, especially in the final scenes.

In one of those scenes, Burre applies red lipstick while wearing sunglasses. The film cuts to a close-up of her face. One of her eyes is badly blackened. Burre stares directly at the camera, which begins to pull back as she slowly smiles and her children join and comfort her on the couch as the shot ends in a wide shot of the three of them. As she combs her hair in the bathroom mirror, Burre explains that most people thought someone had hit her. She then talks about beginning to play the role of the victim because of people's expectations. Burre indicates that this seemed to be a more socially acceptable or believable explanation than that she sustained the injury when she fell out of her car. She acknowledges, "I took the note from the universe," and goes on to add, "I'm not quite sure what it means, but I'm trying to listen to what it says." Burre takes a breath and stares at the camera, as the end credits begin to roll over shots of her in Los Angeles.

Greene has stated in interviews that he did not manipulate the events that occurred in the film. If anything, he tried to respect his subject and avoided anything that directly involved either Tim or the children. He told an interviewer, "I knew that a portrait of Brandy was never going to be a sweet, no-blemishes depiction, because that's not the type of human being she is. She's tough and prickly. I knew there was always going to be an edge to it. At the same time, I never put in fights that she and Tim had, and she appreciated it. It's all true, but like all documentaries, it's my version of the truth."[23] Burre certainly does not come across as especially likeable in the film. In fact, Tim's marginal role as a background player makes him seem like the more reasonable person because Burre proves to be unhappy in whatever situation she finds herself. She quit acting to be a homemaker, and yet she fled both roles, while turning herself into a victim. Choosing to appear at the end of the film with a black eye reinforces that perception. As Greene points out, "As a performer, she's always thinking about how you see her and what kind of power that gives her. She realizes that there's something dramatic and powerful in being the abused woman, and how fucked up that is."[24]

Burre had a lot at stake in the film personally. It is fair to say that *Actress* represents her comeback attempt as an actor. Much more than the audition tape she creates consisting of old scenes from *The Wire*, *Actress* is, in fact, her actual promo reel to showcase both her screen presence and acting skills. Although she is performing what Hilton Als calls "the narrative of the self" for the camera, to her credit, she does not attempt to create a flattering self-portrait.[25] Greene considers the film to be an active collaboration with her. Burre is not a passive subject but someone who is keenly aware that she is attempting to create an event worthy of being recorded. Greene remarks, "She really took the camera and said, 'OK, if we're going to do something then let's really do it, and I'm going to go there.' And going there meant baring her soul."[26] As Goffman makes clear in *The Presentation of Self in Everyday Life*, the performed self is perceived by others as an image. He writes, "While this image is entertained *concerning* the individual, so that a self is imputed to him, this self itself does not derive from its possessor, but from the whole scene of his action, being generated by that attribute of local events which renders them interpretable by witnesses."[27]

As a result, Burre inadvertently opens herself up to criticism by those who think "she's sacrificing the feelings and futures of her loved ones on the altar of self-interest."[28] Yet Greene is also aware of the element of exploitation: "I want the viewer to think about exploitation but also about Brandy exploiting herself, the camera exploiting her and all these levels of intricacy. Hopefully the experience is complex enough that it goes into spaces that are sometimes troubling and upsetting and moving."[29] Like *Portrait of Jason*, *Actress* is all those things and operates on many different levels. The film continually raises questions regarding what is real and what is performed and how the viewer might be able to distinguish between the two. In *Actor Martinez*, Arthur Martinez provides a series of masks, while Burre gives a series of "performed" roles. A. O. Scott's review in the *New York Times* hints at this ambiguity when he writes, "After an hour and a half in her company, you might feel as if you know her very well, even as you have no idea who she really is. That might be the result of her existential condition, or it might just be her job."[30]

Burre staged herself for the camera at great personal risk by inviting judgment. Many viewers will side with Tim and view Burre's behavior as reckless, but her tears seem real, no matter how calculated her choices. As Greene observes, "These gestures of fragility that she makes are more devastating to me than watching someone totally unaware of what she's doing. She's authentically in pain, but she's also demonstrating pain very consciously and dramatically. The combination of the real and the display is mind-boggling to me. You don't know where one begins and the other ends."[31]

In his review of *Actress*, Bilge Ebiri attempts to differentiate between the role playing that we all do in life and what an actor does. He notes, "A performer is different, to be sure—someone uniquely conscious of the various roles they must inhabit, and trained to do so—but in degree, not in kind."[32] The "degree," that Ebiri references involves artifice, which Burre deliberately employs to the hilt in every situation. It is the opposite of what Martinez does but equally as relentless. Yet in the confusing hall of mirrors that *Actress* creates, it proves difficult not to think of Freddie and Alice in Greaves's *Symbiopsychotaxiplasm: Take One*. We wait for Greene or Tim or someone to tell Burre, "Come on, Brandy, stop acting!" Either she can't or won't—which is at least part of the tragedy of the character she is intent on playing.

JAMES SOLOMON: *THE WITNESS*

Both *Actor Martinez* and *Actress* straddle the fine line between fiction and documentary, and they raise intriguing questions in the process. James Solomon's *The Witness* began as a scripted film idea that over the course of fifteen years turned into a documentary. The film explores the famous case of Kitty Genovese, a twenty-eight-year-old bar manager who was brutally stabbed to death in Kew Gardens, Queens in 1964. The killing became a symbol of urban indifference because—although thirty-eight neighbors reportedly heard her screams—no one came to her aid. That was the version of the event promulgated by A. M. (Abe) Rosenthal, an editor at the *New York Times*, who later wrote a book on the subject, *Thirty-Eight Witnesses*.[33]

The story of Kitty's death and her apathetic neighbors became a sociological phenomenon that captured the public imagination at the time and continues to hold fascination even today. This is the story that Solomon, a screenwriter, along with Joe Berlinger and Alfred Uhry, pitched to be an HBO fictional movie in 1999.[34] According to Solomon, "The HBO project didn't happen, largely because our script wasn't nearly as compelling as the people who had actually lived this story."[35] In researching the script, Solomon met Kitty's younger brother, Bill Genovese, who was sixteen at the time of her murder and the family member closest to her. He is the reason the fiction film became a documentary. *The Witness*, which took over ten years to complete, represents Bill Genovese's personal odyssey to discover what actually happened to his sister on that fateful night and come to terms with the personal trauma of the event.

An amputee who lost both his legs in Vietnam, Bill is obsessed with his sister's murder. Like a tireless detective, he systematically tracks down leads. He visits the scene of the crime and calculates the sightlines from windows of nearby apartments. He talks to the prosecutor in the case. As he interviews neighbors, a different picture begins to emerge. Remarkably, Bill learns that Kitty actually did not die alone. He speaks with Michael Farrar, the son of a woman who claims she came to Kitty's aid. One neighbor is shocked by the misinformation in the police report; another insists she called the police when she heard the screams but was told they had already received a call about it. When Bill checks the police log, there is only one call, but it occurred much later. Bill starts to wonder: Did the police fail to log the calls? Or did the neighbor invent the story in order to soothe her conscience? Whatever the case, the truth is elusive, and the quest for it becomes a *Rashomon*-like mystery. As Bill muses, "How can anything be believed about this story?"

Throughout Bill's search for the truth, it becomes clear that his sister's death has cast a pall over his entire personal life. It was the reason he enlisted in the marines at nineteen to fight in Vietnam—he did not want to be like one of those do-nothing bystanders who refused to come to Kitty's aid. Kitty's murder affected not only Bill but the entire family. According to Solomon, "Moreover, Bill understands other people's trauma because he embodies it. In the span of five years—from 16 to 21—Bill's sister was murdered, his mother had a stroke and nearly died, he lost both of his legs, and his father died of a stroke at age 59."[36] Bill's two brothers—Vincent, the oldest, and Frank, the youngest—were also traumatized by the event. After a sigh, Vincent comments on camera, "It never goes away." He describes his parents as "basket cases" and later admits that as a defense mechanism, "we almost erased her from our lives." He also adds that Kitty had a special fondness for Bill. Of Bill's obsessive investigation into his sister's murder, his wife, Dale, remarks, "I think he's looking for the ultimate inner peace. The choices that he made in his life were all related to the fact that no one helped his sister. And if he knows the truth, that's peacefulness. I mean, I'm hoping for Bill that there'll be closure."

As Bill indicates, Kitty's murderer, Winston Moseley, totally destroyed his family. A short, slightly built man who had a high IQ as well as a wife and children, he was apprehended five days after Kitty's murder for stealing a television. Moseley was a dangerous psychopath and serial killer. The film follows Bill's attempts to arrange a face-to-face meeting with Moseley. At the Department of Correctional Services in Albany, he talks with two people—one from the Office of Dispute Resolution, and another from the Office of Victim Services. When the woman from Victim Services queries Bill about what his reaction might be if Moseley is not willing to participate, Bill shifts his eyes and body, as the camera moves in closer. He stares penetratingly at the woman, before he finally says, "Well, I'd think it'd be unfortunate . . . on one level." Bill removes his glasses, and continues, "And then on another level, I think, well that's a relief."

At a family dinner, Bill talks about the fact that this whole situation is like a Rorschach test. He tells his brothers that he has contacted Moseley. His voice cracking with emotion, Frank asks, "Bill, what's the question you want answered? At what point are you going to be satisfied?" For Bill, however, one question only leads to another question ad infinitum. Frank counters that the family has been talking about Kitty for fifty years, and he needs to bury it. After Moseley refuses Bill's request, he arranges to interview Moseley's son, Steven, who is a minister. When Bill brings up the fact that his father won't talk to him and about his need for forgiveness, Steven asks Bill how he would feel about parole, and emphasizes that the event occurred fifty years ago.

Despite his profession, Moseley's son somehow views himself as an equal victim, citing the fact that he was called names in school. He offers a racialized explanation for his father's rape and murder of Kitty and claims to know nothing about the same crime committed by his father involving an African American woman two weeks before Kitty's murder. The minister asks whether Bill is connected to the Genovese crime family, and he suggests that this made him reluctant to speak to him initially. Steven talks about the need to move on from the past. A month later, Bill receives a letter from Winston Moseley that offers a bizarre and delusional account of what occurred that night—the actual murderer was a mobster

FIGURE 11.3 Bill Genovese meets Winston Moseley's son, *The Witness*

and Moseley was only the getaway driver. After reading the letter, Bill and his wife, Dale, are incredulous.

Bill tries to fathom what it felt like to be one of the bystanders—or Kitty. Only once, he claims, was he able to fathom what it must have been like for her that night. He recounts the time in Vietnam when he was lying there badly injured following the fateful explosion and thought of Kitty. He asks, "What was it like for her when she realized no one was going to save her? But Marines carried me to safety and I lived to tell the story." The film cuts from an image of a military helicopter flying off to a shot of the street signs of Austin Street and Mowbray Drive in Kew Gardens, where the infamous crime occurred. As Bill pulls into a parking space, he says in voiceover, "After 50 years, I felt there was one more thing I had to do." Inside a restaurant, he meets a female actor named Shannon Beeby. He calls Michael Farrar and explains that he is with the actor and they need to know how loud Kitty's screams were that night. We hear Farrar's voice on the phone say, "The scream was so loud that it woke me up from a dead sleep. I've never heard anything in my life that loud."

The film cuts to Bill putting up a resident notification flyer indicating that they will be filming there. He propels his wheelchair into position on the street, as we watch Beeby walking quickly down the street, panting slightly. Bill stares, as she suddenly lets out loud bloodcurdling screams and yells, "Help me! Help me. Oh, my God, please help me. Please help me!" Beeby looks up and cries again, "Help me!" As she continues to sob loudly, Bill covers his face with his hands. In a shot taken from above, Beeby staggers down the street. The camera is closer as she struggles to open the door and collapses in the vestibule, as we hear her whimpers. A shot of a desolate apartment window is blurred by a passing train. Beeby comes out of the building and hugs Bill.

The jaw-dropping scene—in which Bill restages Kitty's murder in order to observe it—is both gruesome and shocking. Richard Brody writes, "This brief, brilliant, harrowing restaging is a directorial invention of analytical brilliance. It's a sort of forensic *reductio ad absurdum*, a cinematic experiment in social science. Though the sequence is awkwardly filmed and punitively edited, its idea and its effect come through powerfully. It's a magnificent object lesson in cinema as an art of ideas."[37] A film critic in the *Village Voice* writes, "That scene [involving Steven Moseley] unsettles, as does a climactic street-art performance piece staged by William and an actress: In the same place and at the same time that

Genovese was attacked, the hired hand screams in the night, outside mostly unlit buildings."[38]

What reviewers fail to note and most viewers do not quite realize is that Bill has not created a "cinematic experiment" or a "street-art performance," but a pure instance of psychodrama on camera. Instead of enacting it in a clinical setting, using other members of a group as auxiliary egos to play the necessary roles, Bill has managed to turn the entire film into an extended psychodrama in which this staged scene serves as its culmination. As the final credits indicate, the reenactment of Kitty's death was an elaborate production. It was shot with multiple cameras from various apartments overlooking the two different locations that were visible.[39] According to Bill Genovese, "I thought of the reenactment as too self-indulgent, but I wanted to know what it was like on that very street, if we could duplicate the scream."[40]

In an effort to understand the mindset of the bystanders that night, Bill positions himself as one of them. As Solomon notes, "He chose to be there with her on the street."[41] He observes, but does not intervene, even though his personal odyssey has suggested an alternative view of the original event. He apparently still remains psychically tied to the original story, even as he debunks it in the film. By staging the scene, Bill Genovese makes the viewer a bystander as well. We watch Kitty's terrible ordeal with a sense of utter helplessness. Since she is already dead, we cannot save Kitty any more than Bill can, but in recreating it for the camera he forces us to listen to those harrowing screams and to experience the initial trauma firsthand. In effect, we are made to bear witness to the chilling tragedy of Kitty's death and to feel the power of the original event, regardless of its veracity. Factual or not—that part does not matter to a trauma victim—this is the version that Bill has lived with all these years. As his wife, Dale, said early in the film, all his life decisions were based on the single premise that no one came to the aid of his sister.

Solomon shot three hundred hours of footage, which was eventually cut down to eighty-nine minutes in the two-and-a-half years it took to edit it.[42] Given the filmmaker's background as a screenwriter, the film utilizes the traditional narrative structure of a police procedural. In *Heaven Knows What*, Josh and Benny Safdie had Arielle Holmes write down her story and then play the lead role. In a strange way, Solomon does something similar in *The Witness*. Genovese did not write the film, but, as the subject of the documentary or the protagonist, he was given

FIGURE 11.4 Bill looks out the window at his sister's murder scene, *The Witness*

the liberty to track down which subjects he felt compelled to interview—Farrar, Rosenthal, Mary Ann Zielonko (Kitty's lover), and Steven Moseley, among others—even if he had no idea what they might reveal to him. Bill also serves as the film's narrator, which further personalizes the story and provides its unique point of view.

Solomon believes the resulting film was superior to anything he could have written. As he observes, "There are so many unexpected characters, plot twists, and lines of dialogue in the film that I could never have imagined putting to paper as a screenwriter. Every time I thought I knew where this story was headed, it surprised me—and, I suspect, the viewer will be surprised as well."[43] In explaining the difference between narrative and documentary, Solomon notes, "As a screenwriter turned documentarian, I had to learn patience and trust. On the page, control is paramount and instantaneous over when to enter and exit a scene or to introduce a plot turn. In making a documentary, I had to allow it to unfold on its own terms—and hope."[44] Yet that sense of unpredictability is what distinguishes *The Witness*. Like so many other filmmakers chronicled in this study, Solomon laments the fact that his own imagination pales in comparison to what occurs in reality. He readily concedes, "If only I could write characters, plot twists and dialogue as well as real life."[45]

CONCLUSION

Blending Fiction and Documentary

Although improvisation in music and theater (where it is mainly associated with comedy rather than drama) has been written about extensively by scholars, surprisingly little attention has been paid to the subject within cinema studies. Improvisation, of course, is not the exclusive domain of American indie cinema. The technique has been used in Hollywood films—often as part of the rehearsal process—and can also be found in international art cinema. Forms of psychodrama occasionally surface as well.

In Kenneth Lonergan's *Manchester by the Sea* (2016), the highly acclaimed scene in which Lee (Casey Affleck) runs into his ex-wife, Randi (Michelle Williams), now remarried and pushing a baby carriage, provides a profoundly moving example in recent cinema. Although the scene was scripted, the performers added improvised elements in terms of stammering, line delivery, pauses, and stepped-on lines. Yet the scene's power stems from its extratextual element. Randi's attempt to beg Lee's forgiveness for the terrible things she has said to him in the past suggests that the raw emotion of the scene derives from the situation's relationship to Williams's own personal tragedy involving Heath Ledger.

Graham Fuller discusses psychodrama in cinema history in an article, entitled, "Nicholas Ray's *In a Lonely Place* as Psychodrama." He writes:

> Cinema is peppered with personal psychodramas, films in which directors or stars participate, knowingly or not, in alternative versions of their own lives: Louise Brooks in *Pandora's Box*, François Truffaut in the Antoine Doinel series, Jean-Luc Godard in *Pierrot le fou*, Ingrid Bergman in *Autumn Sonata*, Jodie Foster in *Nell*, Nicole Kidman and Tom Cruise in *Eyes Wide Shut*. *In a Lonely Place* is one of the most bitter and disturbing examples.[1]

Although we might find other examples outside indie cinema, improvisation and psychodrama have been used so extensively within American indie cinema that J. L. Moreno's theoretical legacy helps to define it—at least in two major periods of its history.

As we have seen in the preceding chapters, an interest conflating documentary and fiction, as well as actor and role, has been the goal of one important strain of indie cinema from the start of the New American Cinema. Moving from written screenplays to spontaneous performance pushed indie fiction filmmakers toward a realist aesthetic, and, in a sense, toward documentary film. Improvisation and psychodrama share a certain affinity with documentary in their focus on capturing the immediate moment.

Some of the films discussed in this study are typically categorized as documentaries: *On the Bowery*, *Portrait of Jason*, *Actress*, and *The Witness*. Others are considered hybrid forms, such as *Come Back, Africa*, *Symbiopsychotaxiplasm: Take One* and *Take 2 ½*, and *Actor Martinez*. Many of the films discussed, such as *Faces*, *Maidstone*, *Wanda*, *Heaven Knows What*, and *Stinking Heaven* are shot in a documentary style. Yet I argue that all the films have fictional elements, including James Solomon's *The Witness*—the only one that I would classify as a documentary—which contains a pivotal scene that the director staged at the subject's request. In the case of *Portrait of Jason* and *Actress*, creating a documentary portrait of an actor or performer invariably leads to a kind of fiction. Nathan Silver and Mike Ott attempted to do something similar with *Actor Martinez*, but, given the lead performer's limited skillset and protective armor, the results confuse the categories of documentary and fiction.

John Cassavetes spent long hours observing and taking notes on Gena Rowlands and even tape-recorded her extensively before writing *A Woman Under the Influence*.[2] Cassavetes was intent on creating a cinema that reflected what he considered to be actual human behavior. Although he worked as an actor in Hollywood, Cassavetes vented against the kind of cinema the industry produced. Speaking about *A Woman Under the Influence*, he contended, "Films today show only a dream world and have lost touch with the way people really are. For me the Longhetti family is the first real family I've ever seen on screen. Idealized screen families generally don't interest me because they have nothing to say to me about my own life."[3]

It was not only the fiction filmmakers of the New American Cinema who rebelled against staged and scripted cinema. Documentary filmmakers, such as Ricky Leacock, made similar attacks against the scripted Hollywood film. In an article that appeared in *Film Culture* in 1961, entitled, "For An Uncontrolled Cinema," Leacock argued that the fiction film was still too allied with conventional theater and staging:

> Ever since the invention of the "talking picture" it has been blithely assumed that films are an extension of the theatre, a marvelous gadget that allows you to change scenes in an instant, yet retains the fundamental aspect of theatre in that you cause a story to be acted out before an audience (the camera) under controlled conditions. Control is of the essence. The lines are written down and learned by the actors, the actions are rehearsed on carefully selected or constructed sets and these rehearsals are repeated over and over again until the resulting scene conforms with the preconceived conceptions of the director. What horror . . . None of this activity has any life of its own.[4]

Claiming to be bored by studio-produced films, Leacock proposed an alternative form of cinema that would be reality-based—a cinema that would not attempt to control events occurring in front of the camera. He writes, "Tolstoy envisioned the film-maker as an observer and perhaps as a participant capturing the essence of what takes place around him, selecting, arranging but never controlling the event. Here it would be possible for the significance of what is taking place to transcend the conceptions of the film-maker because essentially he is observing that ultimate mystery, the reality."[5]

This proposal served as the basis and rationale for the "observational" documentary that Leacock and his cohorts in direct cinema pioneered, which, by being "uncontrolled"—unscripted and unrehearsed—had a similar goal of creating a new cinematic realism. Leacock's sense of horror at the staged quality of the industrial fiction film is not much different from Jonas Mekas's hyperbole in wanting to "shoot all scriptwriters," his hatred of actors, or attack on those film directors who attempt to control the actors' performances.[6] It is also the approach that Robert Greene claimed to be using in shooting a documentary portrait of his neighbor, Brandy Burre, in *Actress*. Documentary filmmakers attempt to create compelling dramatic stories based on actuality, while many indie fiction filmmakers aspire to a cinematic realism that seeks to mimic aspects of the documentary. Greene's entire filmmaking career straddles the fine line between the two. Many of the other films discussed and analyzed in this study attempt a similar balancing act.

In the current digital era, many indie filmmakers, in a manner similar to Greene, are mining the intersection between documentary and fiction. As Winston, Vanstone, and Chi argue in *The Act of Documenting*, the status of documentary has changed radically over the years. They contend, "The documentary is no longer merely *comme un reste*—an afterthought—to fiction. It is its equal."[7] The increasing proliferation of reality-based TV, internet shows, and YouTube videos stands as a testament to this phenomenon. One reason for the new fascination with reality-based film stems from the fact that digital culture has destabilized the distinction between mediated experience and our own lives; and no doubt the division between the two threatens to disappear entirely in the future. This might explain Joe Swanberg's attempt to turn the process of making a film into a form of social interaction with his performers, including the ensuing questions he probed regarding the line between the staged and the real, and of simulated versus actual sex in cinema.

Many indie fiction filmmakers share the belief with documentary filmmakers that everyday reality is inherently more compelling than anything scripted, as Solomon demonstrated in his decision to abandon the written screenplay in favor of shooting *The Witness* as a straightforward documentary. It is a startling admission by a screenwriter that Bill Genovese's real-life quest to come to terms with his sister Kitty's death surpassed anything Solomon believed he could conceive on the page.

Although his films are often associated with Cassavetes's improvised work, Joe Swanberg uses a more spontaneous approach that is almost the polar opposite of Cassavetes's method of intensive rehearsal to discover believable characters. Like Warhol, Cassavetes shot an enormous amount of footage in ways that were more like a documentary filmmaker. Their approach to filming anticipated the advent of digital cinema because the price of film stock and processing are no longer prohibitive factors in shooting footage for fiction films. More than ever before, this under-cuts the need for precise planning and control, especially in terms of performance.

In moving away from the screenplay, indie filmmakers turned to meth-ods of improvisation and psychodrama as a way of differentiating their films from the industrial model in two major historical periods. The first occurred during the mid-1950s and extended through the 1960s, though Cassavetes continued to improvise his films in the following two decades, during which Charles Burnett also made *Killer of Sheep*. The filmmak-ers associated with the New American Cinema were experimenting with different strategies of alternative scripting, more or less out of necessity. Some early filmmakers—Rogosin, Mackenzie, Warhol, and Mailer—tried to do away with screenplays entirely, as did Swanberg and Porterfield in the new century.

The filmmakers from the first period, such as Mekas, who filmed The Living Theatre's production of *The Brig*, Warhol in numerous films, Clarke with *Portrait of Jason*, Mailer in *Maidstone*, and Greaves in *Sym-biopsychotaxiplasm: Take One*, also experimented with psychodrama. Regarding the new trend of therapeutic theatre, the drama critic Eric Bentley admitted:

> But gradually I found myself seeing shows less and Moreno's "psychodra-mas" more. If one wanted therapy in the theatre, why not go the whole hog? At the Moreno Institute, therapy was the acknowledged and sole aim in view, yet the sessions there were emotionally affecting and intel-lectually interesting to a much greater degree than the New York theatres. What more did I want?[8]

Psychodrama no doubt held a fascination for certain filmmakers who wanted to create deeply arresting dramas that bridged fiction and the real lives of their performers, as Warhol, Mailer and Greaves succeeded in accomplishing and Clarke tried to do with Jason Holliday in *Portrait of Jason*.

With the advent of digital cinema in the new century, improvisation and psychodrama were rediscovered and employed by a new generation of indie filmmakers. Ronald Bronstein was fully aware of Moreno's work when he made *Frownland*, and he, in turn, influenced the Safdies to use it in having Arielle Holmes write and enact her own life story in *Heaven Knows What*. Nathan Silver's work also delves into psychodrama, especially in *Stinking Heaven*. He and Mike Ott attempted to create a psychodrama by casting Arthur Martinez in *Actor Martinez*. Prior to releasing the film, Silver told an interviewer: "We basically put all these fictional elements into his life and turned it into this real mind fuck."[9]

Many contemporary filmmakers employ more minimal forms of scripting, such as the pared-down scripts used by Gus Van Sant, the one or two-page outlines created by Swanberg, or the five-page treatment that served as the basis for Matthew Porterfield's *Putty Hill*. The approaches employed by these filmmakers were as varied as in the earlier period, but there is no denying that the new technology of digital cinema served to democratize production. It allowed anyone to pick up a camera and make a film, using found locations and their friends as actors. This was much more difficult during the earlier period of the New American Cinema, when filmmakers used the amateur gauge of 16 mm film, which was still very costly for the average person.

What virtues result from dispensing with a conventional screenplay—whether for the filmmaking process or the finished work? The question is a complicated one. Not using a conventional screenplay changes the process of making a film. In employing improvisation or psychodrama, the emphasis automatically shifts from prewritten scripted lines to the performer or performers. It also makes the production process less hierarchical and more collaborative—not only between the director and actor but also between and among the actors themselves. In many films, such as those of Swanberg and Silver, the actors are credited as screenwriters. In the new equation, acting essentially becomes a form of writing, with the human body as its instrument. Using these techniques also reduces authorial control by shifting the emphasis from the writer and director to the process of making the film itself.

Cassavetes insisted that the experience of people collaborating trumped the efforts of a single person, which is why he developed intensive rehearsals with his actors as a means of fleshing out character and story. In a similar manner, Swanberg relies heavily on his performers to generate the film, which automatically opens up the production of the film to forces other than the director. Through the process of improvisation, the control Leacock railed against is ceded by the director, who must depend on the creativity of his or her performers. This is also true of psychodrama.

Of the filmmakers discussed, Van Sant is the one who created a more formal structure in *Gerry*, *Last Days*, *Elephant*, and *Paranoid Park*, but he counterbalanced it with improvised performances, allowing his actors and nonactors the flexibility to improvise and invent dialogue within the long tracking shots he employed. Cassavetes created an actor-centric cinema, which is the situation of most of the films featured in this study. Like in a documentary film, Cassavetes privileged performance over other elements. His cinematographer was tasked with following the movements of his actors rather than having the action conform to preset framing. Cassavetes claimed that the action was actually easier to follow because the cameraperson is able to follow the natural rhythms of the interaction of his actors. Speaking of actors, he told Ray Carney, "In fact, when you try it, you find that natural movement is easier to follow than rehearsed movement since it has a natural rhythm. Whereas when they rehearse something according to a technical mark, they begin to be jerky and unnatural, and no matter how talented they are, the camera has a difficult time following them."[10]

Looking at indie cinema through the lens of alternative forms of scripting helps us to view its history in a new light. Alternative scripting—a desire to abandon the written screenplay—was there from the start. In fact, improvisation in its various forms (the spontaneous, the planned, and the rehearsed), and later psychodrama, helped to define the New American Cinema. For reasons having to do largely with financing, the screenplay returned and dominated indie cinema for nearly thirty years before digital technology, in effect, democratized the medium, allowing young filmmakers to revive cinematic realism precisely at a time when indie cinema was at risk of losing its identity. In the new century, the use of improvisation and psychodrama provided a sense of continuity with indie cinema's roots.

Among filmmakers working on smaller budget films these days, it has become commonplace to forgo screenplays in favor of improvisation, structured improvisation, or even psychodrama. Acting itself has changed in the interim. Like filmmaking, it has also become democratized, echoing Moreno's and Viola Spolin's contention that everyone can act, which is one of the basic tenets of both improvisation and psychodrama. In fact, if the goal is "being" as opposed to "acting" in an attempt to get closer to everyday life, it makes sense that indie filmmakers would not use professional performers as evidenced by the contempt Mekas had for traditional actors or Silver wanting to keep them out of his films.

Most of the films analyzed and examined in the study have shied away from using professional performers. Sam Fleischner used a neophyte to play the lead role in *Stand Clear of the Closing Doors*. Sean Baker has consistently worked with first-time actors in his films, including *Tangerine* and his commercially successful new film, *The Florida Project* (2017), in which he also cast veteran performer Willem Dafoe. Cassavetes used Gena Rowlands, Peter Falk, Ben Gazzara, and Joan Blondell, but he also used nonprofessionals, such as Lynn Carlin, Elsie Ames, Jenny Runacre, John Kullers, and Leola Harlow. Barbara Loden cast herself and the male lead actor, Michael Higgins, but otherwise depended on nonprofessionals. Van Sant had the benefit of working with Casey Affleck and Matt Damon in *Gerry*, but otherwise relied on nonactors in films such as *Elephant* and *Paranoid Park*. Swanberg, Bronstein, the Safdies, and Silver have done the same.

The use of nonactors has become so prevalent in indie cinema today that it is not a minor tradition anymore. After immersing himself in the setting for *Ballast* (2008) and doing extensive interviews with local residents, Lance Hammer abandoned the initial screenplay he wrote because he felt it was "too overt" or "untruthful" to the experience of the people who lived in the Delta. He eventually wrote a new version, which was based on a series of photographs and very extensive notes, over the course of two years. Hammer then cast African Americans who lived there to play the parts rather than hire professional actors. To find local participants, Hammer talked to the pastors of local black churches and held open casting sessions. He was looking for "temperament" and certain physical qualities in performers.[11] Lena Dunham cast herself in the lead role as well as her own mother and sister to play her family in her semi-autobiographical debut feature *Tiny Furniture* (2010), which launched her career.

This trend continues with Chloé Zhao's acclaimed second feature, *The Rider* (2017). Upon returning to the Pine Ridge Reservation in South Dakota after making her first feature there, she met Brady Jandreau and thought he would make a great subject for a film. Zhao made several attempts to base scripts around him, but it was only after he became injured that she found a story about a young bronco rider named Brady Blackburn who suffers an identity crisis following an accident that fractures his skull. Zhao cast Jandreau's father and sister to play Brady's family and several of his pals, including Lane Scott, a former rodeo star who is now partially paralyzed and unable to speak.

Using "more of a skeleton of a script," the director worked closely with her cast in suggesting situations and dialogue.[12] She would give the actors a scene and have them rework the dialogue while making sure to have adequate coverage. What they improvised was usually better than what might be scripted.[13] This stemmed from the fact that her first-time performers are playing roles close to their actual lives, even though Zhao is clearly fictionalizing events. She suggests that the reason Brady appears to be playing himself is because "even though I liked him as an actor first, I came up with a story that is written specifically for him."[14] Zhao elsewhere observes, "With non-actors, you have to be in the moment. You have to actually allow them to be. People love to go to the theater to see this kind of acting."[15]

Eleonore Hendricks, who has acted in a number of major indie films and works as a casting director, has become a master of what is known as "streetcasting." Most recently, Hendricks served in this capacity for Andrea Arnold's *American Honey* (2016) as well as Tim Sutton's film on the Aurora massacre, *Dark Night* (2016). For Sutton's film, Hendricks scoured places in Sarasota, such as the beaches and bars, looking for interesting people to cast. She found the lead actor who plays Jumper (Robert Jumper) by following a vintage white Mercedes. When Hendricks's car pulled up next to it she was struck by the driver's piercing blue eyes.[16] Sutton, however, added a twist to her streetcasting. He gave Hendricks the leeway to suggest potential performers for roles that were not in the script but somehow might be incorporated into the film. Sutton sees the process as extending from writing to casting to shooting. As he explains, "It's all part of this organic process of finding things. It doesn't always work, but when it does work, you find these people who can live and be themselves on the screen, and they become different versions of themselves because you're pairing them in a fiction."[17]

Sean Baker has also relied heavily on streetcasting in making his films. For *The Florida Project*, he found one of the child performers, Valeria Cotto, who plays Jancey, at a Target store. Baker discovered Lithuanian-born Bria Vinaite, who plays Moonee's mom, Halley, not on the street, but on Instagram. The clothing designer had no previous acting experience prior to being cast largely on the basis of her striking tattoos, penchant for pot, and unfiltered behavior. In one video that Vinaite posted on the social media platform, she dances around the backyard wearing a yellow feather headdress and pink boa. In effect, her look and childlike energy helped land her the part. In some ways, the whole notion of casting appears to be changing as a result of social media. Baker comments, "In the past, an actor would have to move to LA, get a manager and an agent, and get in that database. But now, you can see people from all over the world, if you take the time."[18]

For acting in most indie films, there is no rigorous training required; in fact, it can even prove to be an impediment to a performer's spontaneity. The career of Greta Gerwig serves as a case in point. A. O. Scott, the film critic for the *New York Times*, writes of Gerwig, who had no professional training prior to appearing in Swanberg's films and Noah Baumbach's *Greenberg* (2010), that she "most likely without intending to be anything of the kind, may well be the definitive screen actress of her generation . . . redefining just what it is we talk about when we talk about acting."[19] He elaborates:

> When she takes off her clothes—which is not infrequently—it does not seem teasing or exhibitionistic but disarmingly matter-of-fact. Her diction is more like what you hear at the next table in the local coffee bar than at the movies. She tends to trail off in midsentence, turn statements into questions or sometimes tangle herself up in a rush of words. She comes across as pretty, smart, hesitant, insecure, confused, determined— all at once or in no particular order. Which is to say that she is bracingly, winningly and sometimes gratingly real.[20]

This is a generation that has grown up onscreen—they seem completely at ease in front of cameras—which helps to explain how performance has changed in the intervening years since the New American Cinema.

Why has performance changed in the interim? The answer no doubt has to do with the impact of digital culture, where people's identities are intimately bound up with how they interact with social media. Not only have younger people grown up being photographed, but they express themselves and their behavior becomes validated by what they post about themselves on social media. Everyday experience becomes an opportunity for a selfie or a short video. Cell phones have become so much an extension of people that everything becomes fodder for documentation. Streetcasting works because media culture has become exhibitionistic. Young people have become highly adept at performing themselves. As in the case of Bria Vinaite, piercings and tattoos allow people to wear their personalities on their skin. The phenomenon has its origins in Warhol's Factory. Warhol believed he didn't need a script because the look and behavior of his superstars proved endlessly fascinating for the camera. Swanberg adopted a similar strategy with his peers, which is why he didn't feel he needed a screenplay either.

By focusing on the shifting role of the screenplay throughout history we are able to see the continuity of alternative forms of scripting. Initially, forsaking the script and experimenting with forms of improvisation and psychodrama became a way for the New American Cinema to break with Hollywood conventions by seeking to create a cinematic realism that bridged the gap between art and life. In this century, a return to these strategies can be viewed as a sign of indie cinema's resistance to the scripted and staged. In some ways, these strategies—both practically and discursively—served to revitalize American indie cinema at a moment of crisis by keeping it from becoming either marginalized or absorbed by the dominant industry. Indie and documentary filmmakers are allies in their shared belief that the drama inherent in everyday life has the potential to be more engaging than what might otherwise be imagined.

NOTES

INTRODUCTION

1. Norman Mailer, "A Course in Film-Making," *New American Review*, no. 12 (1971): 205.
2. Steven Maras, *Screenwriting: History, Theory and Practice* (London: Wallflower, 2009), 5.
3. Anthony Frost and Ralph Yarrow, *Improvisation in Drama, Theatre and Performance: History, Practice, Theory*, 3rd ed. (London: Palgrave, 2016), xv.
4. Virginia Wright Wexman, "The Rhetoric of Cinematic Improvisation," *Cinema Journal* 20, no. 1 (Fall 1980): 29.
5. Steven Price, *A History of the Screenplay* (New York: Palgrave Macmillan, 2013), 221.
6. For a discussion of improvisation in international cinema, see Gilles Mouëllic, *Improvising Cinema* (Amsterdam: Amsterdam University Press, 2013).
7. Viola Spolin, *Improvisation for the Theater: A Handbook of Teaching and Directing Techniques*, 3rd ed. (Evanston, IL: Northwestern University Press, 1999), 19.
8. Spolin, *Improvisation for the Theater*, 3.
9. R. Keith Sawyer, *Improvised Dialogues: Emergence and Creativity in Conversation* (Westport, CT: Ablex, 2003), 15–16.
10. James Naremore, *Acting in the Cinema* (Berkeley: University of California Press, 1988), 2.
11. See Colin Counsell, *Signs of Performance: An Introduction to Twentieth-Century Theatre* (New York: Routledge, 1996), 55.
12. According to Moreno, "The conventional theatre is, at its best, dedicated to the worship of the dead, of dead events—a sort of resurrection-cult." See J. L. Moreno, *The Theatre of Spontaneity*, 2nd ed. (Beacon, NY: Beacon House, 1973), 18.
13. Moreno, *Theatre of Spontaneity*, 18.
14. Sawyer, *Improvised Dialogues*, 17.
15. See Moreno, *Theatre of Spontaneity*.
16. Moreno, *Theatre of Spontaneity*, 5.

17. Moreno, *Theatre of Spontaneity*, 42.

18. Jonathan D. Moreno, *Impromptu Man: J. L. Moreno and the Origins of Psychodrama, Encounter Culture, and the Social Network* (New York: Bellevue Literary Press, 2014), 103–104.

19. See René F. Marineau, *Jacob Levy Moreno 1889–1974: Father of Psychodrama, Sociometry, and Group Psychotherapy* (New York: Tavistock/Routledge, 1989), 74–79. See also A. Paul Hare & June Rabson Hare, *J. L. Moreno* (Thousand Oaks, CA: Sage, 1996), 13–14.

20. John Nolte, *The Philosophy, Theory and Methods of J. L. Moreno: The Man Who Tried to Become God* (New York: Routledge, 2014), 180.

21. See P. Adams Sitney, *Visionary Film: The American Avant-Garde*, (New York: Oxford University Press, 1974).

22. Peter Felix Kellermann, *Focus on Psychodrama: The Therapeutic Aspects of Psychodrama* (Philadelphia: Jessica Kingsley Publishers, 1992), 20.

23. Zerka Moreno, quoted in "Introduction," *Psychodrama in Action*, The Zerka T. Moreno Series (Mill Valley, CA: psychotherapy.net, 2007), DVD.

24. Moreno, *Theatre of Spontaneity*, 126.

25. Moreno, *Theatre of Spontaneity*, 126.

26. Moreno, *Theatre of Spontaneity*, 126.

27. Moreno, *Theatre of Spontaneity*, 127.

28. Kathryn Millard, *Screenwriting in a Digital Era* (New York: Palgrave Macmillan, 2014), 99.

29. Spolin, *Improvisation for the Theater*, 4.

30. Kathryn Millard, "The Universe Is Expanding: Keynote at Screenwriting Research Network Conference, London, 3 September 2015," *Journal of Screenwriting* 7, no. 3 (September 2016): 281.

31. Daniel Belgrad, *The Culture of Spontaneity: Improvisation and the Arts in Postwar America* (Chicago: The University of Chicago Press, 1998), 1.

32. Belgrad, *Culture of Spontaneity*, 15–16.

33. See Gerald Peary, "Sundance: What Happened When Robert Redford Brought the Hollywood Cattlemen and Independent Sheepherders Together?," *American Film*, October 1981, 46–51.

34. See Ellin Stein, "Quality Time," *American Film*, January–February 1986, 46–51.

35. Stein, "Quality Time," 48. See also David Housham, "American Playhouse: Channel for Quality Drama," *Broadcast*, March 29, 1985, 24.

36. Jon Jost, "End of the Indies: Death of the Sayles Men," *Film Comment*, January/February 1989, 42–45.

37. See Ted Hope, "Indie Film Is Dead," *Filmmaker Magazine*, Fall 1995, 18, 54–58.

38. Counsell, *Signs of Performance*, 53.

39. See Mouëllic, *Improvising Cinema*, 121–141.

40. The term "scriptment" has been used by other filmmakers, such as James Cameron and Kriv Stenders. See Alex Munt, "'Am I Crazy to Make a Film for Only $100,000 or Am I Crazy Not to?' Kriv Stenders Goes Micro-budget Digital for *Boxing Day*," *Senses of Cinema*, no. 46 (March 2008), http://sensesofcinema.com/2008/australian-cinema-46/kriv-stenders-boxing-day/.

41. Millard, *Screenwriting in a Digital Era*, 116.

42. Dave Kehr, "Out of the Bowery's Shadows (Then Back In)," *New York Times*, February 26, 2012, AR22.

43. Sam Fleischner, quoted in interview with the author, November 19, 2016.

1. AND I HATE ACTORS: THE NEW AMERICAN CINEMA

1. Daniel Belgrad, *The Culture of Spontaneity: Improvisation and the Arts in Postwar America* (Chicago: University of Chicago Press, 1998), 1.

2. Belgrad, *Culture of Spontaneity*, 15.

3. Jonas Mekas, "New York Letter: Towards a Spontaneous Cinema," *Monthly Film Bulletin*, Summer/Autumn 1959, 119.

4. Jonas Mekas, "Cinema of the New Generation," *Film Culture*, no. 21 (Summer 1960): 17.

5. Mekas, "Cinema of the New Generation," 19.

6. Jonas Mekas, "Movie Journal," *Village Voice*, November 25, 1959, 6.

7. Jonas Mekas, "From the Diaries," in *The American New Wave: 1958–1967*, ed. Melinda Ward and Bruce Jenkins (Minneapolis: Walker Art Center, 1982), 5.

8. Jonas Mekas, "Movie Journal," *Village Voice*, March 2, 1961, 11.

9. Mekas, "Movie Journal," 12.

10. James Agee, quoted in Jonas Mekas, "Notes on the New American Cinema," *Film Culture*, no. 24 (Spring 1962): 7.

11. Mekas, "Notes on New American Cinema," 7.

12. Mekas, "Notes on New American Cinema," 8.

13. Arthur Knight, "SR Goes to the Movies: The Venturesome Camera," *Saturday Review*, November 7, 1953, 36.

14. Alain Bergala, "Foreword: Never Mind," in *Morris Engel and Ruth Orkin: Outside: From Street Photography to Filmmaking*, ed. Stefan Cornic, trans. William Snow (Paris: Carlotta Films, 2014), 11.

15. André Bazin, "Film Through a Telephoto Lens: Ray Ashley, Morris Engel, and Ruth Orkin's *The Little Fugitive*," in André Bazin, *Bazin on Global Cinema: 1948–1958*, trans. and ed. Burt Cardullo (Austin: University of Texas Press, 2014), 149. The article originally appeared in *Cahiers du cinéma*, January 1954.

16. Cornic, *Morris Engel and Ruth Orkin*, 113.

17. Eric Ferrara, *The Bowery: A History of Grit, Graft and Grandeur* (Charleston, SC: The History Press, 2011), 43.

18. Lionel Rogosin interviewed in *The Perfect Team: The Making of "On the Bowery*," directed by Michael Rogosin (2009), Disc 1, *On the Bowery*, directed by Lionel Rogosin (1956; Harrington Park, NJ: Milestone Film & Video, 2012), Blu-ray.

19. Mark Sufrin, "Filming a Skid Row," *Monthly Film Bulletin*, Winter 1956, 135.

20. Lionel Rogosin, "Interpreting Reality (Notes on the Esthetics and Practices of Improvisational Acting)," *Film Culture*, no. 21 (Summer 1960): 22.

21. Rogosin, "Interpreting Reality," 27–28.

22. Lionel Rogosin interviewed in *The Perfect Team.*

23. Rogosin, "Interpreting Reality," 28.

24. Sufrin, "Filming a Skid Row," 139.

25. Milek [Emil] Knebel, "Notes on the Making of *Come Back, Africa,*" in *Come Back, Africa: Lionel Rogosin—A Man Possessed,* ed. Peter Davis (Johannesburg: STE Publishers, 2004), 140.

26. Lionel Rogosin, quoted in Davis, *Come Back, Africa,* 54.

27. Lionel Rogosin, quoted in Davis, *Come Back, Africa,* 54.

28. Rogosin, "Interpreting Reality," 27.

29. Lionel Rogosin, quoted in Davis, *Come Back, Africa,* 54.

30. Allen Ginsberg, quoted in Philip Brookman, "A Conversation with Allen Ginsberg," in *Frank Films: The Film and Video Work of Robert Frank,* ed. Brigitta Burger-Utzer and Stefan Grissemann (Zurich: Scalo, 2003), 74.

31. Allen Ginsberg, quoted in Philip Brookman, "A Conversation with Allen Ginsberg," 74.

32. Allen Ginsberg, quoted in Philip Brookman, "A Conversation with Allen Ginsberg," 76.

33. Mekas was very critical of the constrictions of conventional plot-oriented narrative cinema and praised a type of "plotless cinema" instead. On this basis, he considered Jean Renoir's films to be superior to those by Ingmar Bergman. He writes, "Whereas Bergman sustains his scenes through the dramatic climaxes, the theatrical stuff, Renoir avoids any such dramatizations. There is no Aristotle in Renoir. Renoir's people look like people, act like people, and, again, are confused like people, and vague, and unclear. They are moved not by the plot, not by theatrical dramatic climaxes, but by something that one could even call the stream of life itself, by their own irrationality, their sporadic, unpredictable behavior." See Jonas Mekas, "Movie Journal," *Village Voice,* January 26, 1961, 11–12.

34. Taylor Mead, "Acting: 1958–1965," in *The American New Wave: 1958–1967,* ed. Melinda Ward and Bruce Jenkins (Minneapolis: Walker Art Center, 1982), 14.

35. Ron Rice, "Foundation for the Invention and Creation of Absurd Movies," *Film Culture,* no. 24 (Spring 1962): 19.

36. Taylor Mead, quoted in Jack Sargeant, *Naked Lens: Beat Cinema* (London: Creation Books, 1997), 81.

37. Taylor Mead, quoted in Sargeant, *Naked Lens,* 82.

38. Parker Tyler, "For *Shadows,* Against *Pull My Daisy,*" *Film Culture,* no. 24 (Spring 1962): 31.

39. Manny Farber, "White Elephant Art Versus Termite Art," *Film Culture,* no. 27 (Winter 1962–63): 13.

40. See Ron Rice, "DAZENDADA WORKS," *Film Culture,* no. 39 (Winter 1965): 118–119.

41. John Cassavetes, quoted in Ray Carney, *Cassavetes on Cassavetes* (London: Faber and Faber, 2001), 63.

42. John Cassavetes, quoted in Carney, *Cassavetes on Cassavetes,* 65.

43. See Ray Carney, *Shadows* (London: BFI Publishing, 2001), 33–34.

44. John Cassavetes, quoted in Carney, *Cassavetes on Cassavetes,* 68.

45. John Cassavetes, quoted in Carney, *Cassavetes on Cassavetes,* 71.

46. Carney, *Cassavetes on Cassavetes,* 72.

47. John Cassavetes, quoted in Carney, *Cassavetes on Cassavetes*, 67.

48. Jonas Mekas, "Movie Journal," *Village Voice*, January 27, 1960, 10.

49. Carney, *Shadows*, 49.

50. Carney, *Cassavetes on Cassavetes*, 82.

51. See Ray Carney, "No Exit: John Cassavetes' *Shadows*," in *Beat Culture and the New America: 1950–1965*, ed. Lisa Phillips (New York: Whitney Museum of American Art, 1995), 238.

52. Marshall Fine, *Accidental Genius: How John Cassavetes Invented American Independent Film* (New York: Miramax Books/Hyperion, 2005), 85.

2. LET'S NOT PHONY IT UP ANYMORE:
THE FILMS OF JOHN CASSAVETES

1. John Cassavetes, quoted in Ray Carney, *Cassavetes on Cassavetes* (London: Faber and Faber, 2001), 341.

2. Carney, *Cassavetes on Cassavetes*, 216.

3. Carney, *Cassavetes on Cassavetes*, 216.

4. Carney, *Cassavetes on Cassavetes.*, 217.

5. Gilles Mouëllic, *Improvising Cinema* (Amsterdam: Amsterdam University Press, 2013), 34.

6. Steven Maras, *Screenwriting: History, Theory and Practice* (London: Wallflower Press, 2009), 2.

7. Carney, *Cassavetes on Cassavetes*, 149.

8. John Cassavetes, quoted in Joseph Gelmis, *The Film Director as Superstar* (Garden City, NY: Doubleday, 1970), 80.

9. See Carney, *Cassavetes on Cassavetes*, 170.

10. Tom Charity, *John Cassavetes: Lifeworks* (London: Omnibus, 2001), 67.

11. J. L. Moreno distinguishes the "moment" from the "present." He writes, "The present is a *formal* category in contradistinction from the moment which is dynamic and a *creative* category; it is through a spontaneous-creative process that the formal category of the present attains dynamic meaning, when it turns into a moment." See J. L. Moreno, *The Theatre of Spontaneity*, 2nd ed. (Beacon, NY: Beacon House, 1973, 125.

12. John Cassavetes, quoted in Gelmis, *Film Director as Superstar*, 83.

13. See Gelmis, *Film Director as Superstar*, 84.

14. John Cassavetes, *Faces* (New York: Signet, 1970). For additional commentary on the screenplay for *Faces*, see Steven Price, *A History of the Screenplay* (New York: Palgrave Macmillan, 2013), 222.

15. See Gelmis, *Film Director as Superstar*, 81.

16. John Cassavetes, quoted in Carney, *Cassavetes on Cassavetes*, 170.

17. John Cassavetes, quoted in Gelmis, *Film Director as Superstar*, 80.

18. Charity, *John Cassavetes*, 22.

19. Carney, *Cassavetes on Cassavetes* 217.

20. Marshall Fine, *Accidental Genius: How John Cassavetes Invented American Independent Film* (New York: Miramax Books/Hyperion, 2005), 214–215.

21. Jenny Runacre, quoted in Charity, *John Cassavetes*, 82. For a discussion of Runacre's improvised acting, see 82–83.

22. John Cassavetes, quoted in Fine, *Accidental Genius*, 292.

23. Jeremy Kagan, quoted in Charity, *John Cassavetes*, 83.

24. Victor Kemper, quoted in Fine, *Accidental Genius*, 215.

25. See Ray Carney, *John Cassavetes: The Adventure of Insecurity*, 2nd rev. ed. (Walpole, MA: Company C Publishing, 2000), 26.

26. Jenny Runacre, quoted in Charity, *John Cassavetes*, 82.

27. Ray Carney, *Shadows* (London: BFI Publishing, 2001), 35.

28. See Fine, *Accidental Genius*, 164.

29. John Cassavetes, quoted in Carney, *Cassavetes on Cassavetes*, 283.

30. See Carney, *Cassavetes on Cassavetes*, 283–287.

31. Gena Rowlands, quoted in Carney, *Cassavetes on Cassavetes*, 287.

32. See John Cassavetes, Original Screenplay: *Minnie and Moskowitz*, (Los Angeles: Black Sparrow Press, 1973).

33. John Cassavetes, Shooting Script: *Minnie and Moskowitz*, revised March 23, 1971 (Faces Music Inc., Universal Release), 27, http://cinearchive.org/post/89468144695/minnie-and-moskowitz-isnt-much-like-anything.

34. Michael Ventura, *Cassavetes Directs: John Cassavetes and the Making of Love Streams* (Harpenden, UK: Kamera Books, 2007), 100.

35. Ventura, *Cassavetes Directs*, 100.

36. Ventura, *Cassavetes Directs*, 101.

37. "Gena Rowlands and Ben Gazzara," Special Features, *Opening Night*, directed by John Cassavetes (1977) in *John Cassavetes: Five Films* (New York: The Criterion Collection, 2004), DVD.

38. Zohra Lampert, quoted in Charity, *John Cassavetes*, 163.

39. Zohra Lampert, quoted in Charity, *John Cassavetes*, 164.

40. Carney, *Cassavetes on Cassavetes*, 420–421.

41. "Gena Rowlands and Ben Gazzara," *Opening Night*.

42. John Cassavetes, quoted in Carney, *Cassavetes on Cassavetes*, 411.

43. See, for instance, Jessica Winter, *The Rough Guide to American Independent Film* (London: Rough Guides, 2006). Winter lists *A Woman Under the Influence* as #1 in her list of "The Top Ten Indie Films," 32.

44. John Cassavetes, quoted in Carney, *Cassavetes on Cassavetes*, 341.

45. John Cassavetes, quoted in Carney, *Cassavetes on Cassavetes*, 312.

46. John Cassavetes, quoted in Carney, *Cassavetes on Cassavetes*, 336.

47. John Cassavetes, quoted in Carney, *Cassavetes on Cassavetes*, 311.

48. See Carney, *Cassavetes on Cassavetes*, 344.

49. John Cassavetes originally quoted in *Filmmakers Newsletter*, January 1975. See Charity, *John Cassavetes*, 122.

50. Charity, *John Cassavetes*, 126.

3. PLACE-BASED REALISM:
MACKENZIE, LODEN, AND BURNETT

1. Ross Lipman compares Kent Mackenzie's *The Exiles* to Robert Frank's *The Americans*. See Ross Lipman, "Kent Mackenzie's *The Exiles*: Reinventing the Real of Cinema," in *Alternative Projections: Experimental Film in Los Angeles, 1945–1980*, ed. David E. James and Adam Hyman (New Barnet, UK: John Libbey Publishing, 2015), 166.

2. Jack Kerouac, "Introduction," *The Americans*, by Robert Frank (New York: Pantheon Books, 1959), 8.

3. Thom Andersen, quoted in Evan Kindley, "An Interview with Thom Andersen," *Not Coming to a Theater Near You*, November 16, 2009, http://www.notcoming.com /features/thomandersoninterview/.

4. Dennis Lim, "Displaced and Adrift in Los Angeles," *New York Times*, July 6, 2008, AR8.

5. Kent Robert Mackenzie, *A Description and Examination of the Production of "The Exiles": A Film of the Actual Lives of Young American Indians*, (MA Thesis, University of Southern California, 1964), 8–9. Included on Special Features, *The Exiles*, directed by Mackenzie (1961; Harrington, Park, NJ: Milestone Film & Video, 2009), DVD.

6. Mackenzie, *Production of "The Exiles,"* 53.

7. Mackenzie, 32.

8. Mackenzie, 35.

9. Mackenzie, 73.

10. Mackenzie, 43.

11. Mackenzie, 37.

12. Mackenzie, 50–51.

13. Mackenzie, 17.

14. Mackenzie, 46.

15. Mackenzie, 124.

16. Mackenzie, 125.

17. Mackenzie, 130.

18. Sherman Alexie, quoted in Lim, "Displaced and Adrift."

19. Charles Burnett, quoted in Eric Kohn, "indieWIRE Interview: *The Exiles* Presenters, Charles Burnett and Sherman Alexie," *indieWIRE*, July 10, 2008, http://www.indiewire .com/2008/07/indiewire-interview-the-exiles-presenters-charles-burnett-and-sherman -alexie-72076/.

20. Ruby Melton, "Barbara Loden on *Wanda*: 'An Environment That Is Overwhelmingly Ugly and Destructive,'" *Film Journal*, Summer 1971, 12.

21. Barbara Loden, quoted in Melton "Barbara Loden," 13.

22. Kate McCourt, "Who Was Barbara Loden? *Wanda* and the Life of an Actual Woman," *Propeller Magazine*, Fall 2012, http://www.propellermag.com/Fall2012/McCourtLoden-Fall12.html.

23. Barbara Loden, quoted in Melton "Barbara Loden," 12.

24. See Gilles Mouëllic, *Improvising Cinema* (Amsterdam: Amsterdam University Press, 2013), 121–129.

25. Barbara Loden, quoted in Kevin Thomas, "Miss Loden's *Wanda*—'It's Very Much Me,'" *Los Angeles Times*, April 8, 1971, 17.
26. Barbara Loden, quoted in Melton "Barbara Loden," 11.
27. See Nathalie Léger, *Suite for Barbara Loden*, trans. Natasha Lehrer and Cécile Menon (St. Louis, MO: Dorothy, a publishing project, 2016), 72–76. Léger identified the woman in the newspaper article as Alma Malone and includes biographical details about her life.
28. Barbara Loden, quoted in Madison Women's Media Collective, "Barbara Loden Revisited," *Women and Film* 1, no. 5–6 (1974): 68.
29. Barbara Loden, quoted in Melton "Barbara Loden," 11.
30. Barbara Loden, quoted in Madison Women's Media Collective, "Barbara Loden Revisited," 68.
31. Elia Kazan, *Elia Kazan: A Life* (New York: Alfred A. Knopf, 1988), 793.
32. Kazan, *Elia Kazan*, 794.
33. Barbara Loden, quoted in Thomas, "Miss Loden's *Wanda*," 17.
34. Barbara Loden, quoted in Thomas, "Miss Loden's *Wanda*," 17.
35. Kazan, *Elia Kazan*, 668–669.
36. Elia Kazan, quoted in Marguerite Duras and Elia Kazan, "Conversation on *Wanda* by Barbara Loden," *Cinema Comparat/ive Cinema* 4, no. 8 (2016): 12.
37. Marguerite Duras, quoted in Duras and Kazan, "Conversation on *Wanda*," 12.
38. Cristina Álvarez López and Adrian Martin, "Nothing of the Sort: Barbara Loden's *Wanda* (1970)," *Cinema Comparat/ive Cinema* 4, no. 8 (2016): 47.
39. López and Martin, "Nothing of the Sort," 48.
40. Barbara Loden, quoted in Melton "Barbara Loden," 11.
41. Barbara Loden, quoted in Melton 13.
42. Barbara Loden, quoted in McCandlish Phillips, "Barbara Loden Speaks of the World of *Wanda*," *New York Times*, March 11, 1971, 32.
43. Charles Burnett, quoted in Catherine Arnaud and Yann Lardau, "An Artisan of Daily Life: Charles Burnett," in *Charles Burnett Interviews*, ed. Robert E. Kapsis (Jackson: University Press of Mississippi, 2011), 9.
44. Charles Burnett, quoted in Arnaud and Lardau, "Artisan of Daily Life," 8.
45. Charles Burnett, quoted in Arnaud and Lardau, 8–9.
46. Charles Burnett, quoted in Arnaud and Lardau, 9.
47. Charles Burnett and Richard Peña, Commentary Track, Disc 1, *Killer of Sheep*, directed by Charles Burnett (1977; Harrington Park, NJ: Milestone Film & Video, 2007), DVD.
48. Charles Burnett, quoted in *Killer of Sheep* Press Kit (Harrington Park, NJ: Milestone Film & Video, 2007), 19, http://www.killerofsheep.com/images/KOSfinalPK.pdf.
49. The dialogue quoted is transcribed from the film, which differs from the dialogue in the screenplay. See Charles Burnett, "*Killer of Sheep* Screenplay," in *Screenplays of the African American Experience*, ed. Phyllis Rauch Klotman (Bloomington: Indiana University Press, 1991), 105.
50. Charles Burnett, quoted in Burnett and Peña, Commentary Track.
51. Charles Burnett, quoted in James Ponsoldt, "This Bitter Earth: After 30 years Charles Burnett's lullaby for America, *Killer of Sheep*, finally gets its due," *Filmmaker Magazine*, Spring 2007, 50–51.

52. Charles Burnett, quoted in Ponsoldt, "This Bitter Earth," 91.

53. See Burnett, "*Killer of Sheep* Screenplay," 99–116. Burnett's reproduced screenplay is seventeen pages long, but it is formatted for a book. In order to determine its actual length, I reformatted the script using Celtx screenwriting software and Courier font.

54. Paula J. Massood, "An Aesthetic Appropriate to Conditions: *Killer of Sheep*, (Neo)Realism, and the Documentary Impulse," *Wide Angle* 21, no. 4 (October 1999): 30.

4. EXPERIMENTS IN PSYCHODRAMA: MEKAS, WARHOL, CLARKE, AND MAILER

1. John Nolte, *The Philosophy, Theory and Methods of J. L. Moreno: The Man Who Tried to Become God* (London: Routledge, 2014), 189. The dating and frequency of the public psychodrama sessions appear to be a matter of dispute. Jonathan Moreno writes: "From the late 1940s through the early 1970s, six nights a week, anyone could go to Manhattan's Moreno Institute (first near Grand Central Station and then on the Upper West Side), and participate in a psychodrama session for about the price of a movie ticket." See, Jonathan D. Moreno, *Impromptu Man: J. L. Moreno and the Origins of Psychodrama, Encounter Culture, and the Social Network* (New York: Bellevue Literary Press, 2014), 234.

2. Moreno, *Impromptu Man*, 234.

3. Moreno, *Impromptu Man*, 235.

4. Zerka T. Moreno, *To Dream Again: A Memoir*, ed. Edward Schreiber (Catskill, NY: Mental Health Resources, 2012), 373.

5. Marcia Karp, Skype interview with the author, May 29, 2016.

6. Marcia Karp, foreword to *To Dream Again*, by Moreno, 25.

7. Eric Bentley, *Thinking about the Playwright: Comments from Four Decades* (Evanston, IL: Northwestern University Press, 1987), 322.

8. Bentley, *Thinking about the Playwright*, 332.

9. Bentley, *Thinking about the Playwright*, 322.

10. John Tytell, *The Living Theatre: Art, Exile, and Outrage* (New York: Grove Press, 1995), 180.

11. Tytell, *Living Theatre*, 182.

12. See J. J. Murphy, *The Black Hole of the Camera: The Films of Andy Warhol* (Berkeley: University of California Press, 2012).

13. Shirley Clarke, quoted in Melinda Ward, "Shirley Clarke: An Interview," in *The American New Wave: 1958–1967*, ed. Melinda Ward and Bruce Jenkins (Minneapolis: Walker Art Center, 1982), 21.

14. *Portrait of Jason* Press Kit (Harrington Park, NJ: Milestone Films, 2012), 6, https://cdn .shopify.com/s/files/1/0150/7896/files/PortraitOfJasonPressKitFinal.pdf.

15. J. Hoberman, "Studies in Decay and Flamboyance: *The Picture of Dorian Gray* and *Portrait of Jason* on Blu-ray," *New York Times*, December 28, 2014, AR 12.

16. See Lauren Rabinovitz, "Choreography of Cinema: An Interview with Shirley Clarke," *Afterimage*, December 1983, 10.

17. Shirley Clarke, quoted in Mekas, "Movie Journal," *Village Voice*, August 24, 1967, 23.

18. Shirley Clarke, quoted in Mekas, "Movie Journal," 23.

19. Shirley Clarke, quoted in Mekas, 23.

20. Shirley Clarke, quoted in Mekas, 23.

21. Shirley Clarke, quoted in Mekas, 23.

22. Shirley Clarke, quoted in Mekas, 23.

23. Shirley Clarke, quoted in Will Jones, "Her Role Was Not to Keep Out of Way," *The Minneapolis Tribune*, November 26, 1967, 12.

24. Shirley Clarke, quoted in Mekas, "Movie Journal," 23.

25. Shirley Clarke, quoted in Rabinovitz, "Choreography of Cinema," 11.

26. Shirley Clarke, quoted in Rabinovitz, "Choreography of Cinema," 11.

27. Robert Fiore, quoted in Michel Martin, "*Portrait of Jason*: '60s Counterculture Restored," *Tell Me More*, NPR News, April 18, 2013, http://www.npr.org/2013/04/18/177765545/portrait-of-jason-60s-counterculture-restored.

28. See "The Lost Confrontation," Bonus Features, *Portrait of Jason*, directed by Shirley Clarke (1967; Harrington Park, NJ: Milestone Film & Video, 2014), DVD. What Jason did that so angered Clarke is still not obvious, but her venom toward Jason is apparent. In the deleted segment, we hear a voice recording and see outtakes. As Clarke recalls, "It was a moment before Carl actually starts to attack Jason where I remind Jason of something really horrendous that he once did to me, you know, probably one of the most evil things ever done to me in my life. And he starts to cry." In the audio, she tells him, "You almost had me kill myself, Jason." Jason cries and admits, "I was jealous of you." Based on the remnants of the discarded scene, I agree with Clarke that it lacks dramatic impact and is not very believable.

29. Shirley Clarke, quoted in Rabinovitz, "Choreography of Cinema," 11.

30. See Jones, "Her Role," 12. Clarke says something quite different in the Rabinovitz interview: "I gave Jason some money, and I made a deal with him that any money I got from the film, half would go to him. To this day, he still gets bits of money." Shirley Clarke, quoted in Rabinovitz, "Choreography of Cinema," 10.

31. James Baldwin, quoted in "James Baldwin: The Price of the Ticket," YouTube video, posted by "California Newsreel," October 27, 2009, https://www.youtube.com/watch?v=4_hYraYI2J8.

32. Jones, "Her Role," 12.

33. Lauren Rabinovitz, for instance, writes, "Its raw material is a single stationary camera view from one continuous twelve-hour take edited down to ninety minutes." See Lauren Rabinovitz, *Points of Resistance: Women, Power & Politics in the New York Avant-garde Cinema, 1943–71* (Urbana, IL: University of Illinois Press, 1991), 136.

34. Shirley Clarke, quoted in Jones, "Her Role," 12.

35. Shirley Clarke, quoted in Jones, "Her Role," 12.

36. Shirley Clarke, quoted in Rabinovitz, "Choreography of Cinema," 11.

37. Marshall Fine, *Accidental Genius: How John Cassavetes Invented American Independent Film* (New York: Miramax Books/Hyperion, 2005), 73.

38. Norman Mailer, quoted in Michael Chaiken, "Author, *Auteur*: A Conversation with Norman Mailer," *Mailer Review* 2, no. 1 (Fall 2008): 410.

39. See Vincent Canby, "When Irish Eyes Are Smiling, It's Norman Mailer," *New York Times*, October 27, 1968, D15.

40. See Norman Mailer, "Some Dirt in the Talk: A Candid History of an Existential Movie Called *Wild 90*," *Esquire*, December 1967, 190–194, 261–269.

41. See Norman Mailer, "A Course in Film-Making," *New American Review*, no. 12 (1971): 200–241. Reprinted in Norman Mailer, *Maidstone: A Mystery* (New York: Signet, 1971), 137–180.

42. Norman Mailer, quoted in Joseph Gelmis, *The Film Director as Superstar* (Garden City, NY: Doubleday, 1970), 58.

43. Mailer, "Some Dirt in the Talk," 194.

44. Mailer, "A Course in Film-Making," 202.

45. Mailer, "A Course in Film-Making," 204.

46. See Kathryn Millard, "Writing for the Screen: Beyond the Gospel of Story," *Scan: Journal of Media Arts Culture*, 2006, http://scan.net.au/scan/journal/display.php?journal_id =77.

47. Mailer, "A Course in Film-Making," 239–240.

48. Norman Mailer, *The Spooky Art: Some Thoughts on Writing* (New York: Random House, 2003), 89.

49. Norman Mailer, quoted in Gelmis, *Film Director as Superstar*, 48.

50. See Carl Rollyson, *The Lives of Norman Mailer: A Biography* (New York: Paragon House, 1991), 208.

51. Norman Mailer, quoted in Gelmis, *Film Director as Superstar*, 50.

52. Daniel Kramer, "Norman, *Maidstone* and Me," *Mailer Review* 3, no. 1 (Fall 2009): 534.

53. See Canby, "Irish Eyes," D15.

54. Rip Torn interviewed in Griselda Steiner, "*Maidstone*: A Sign of Our Times," *Mailer Review* 3, no. 1 (Fall 2009): 560.

55. Norman Mailer, quoted in Chaiken, "Author, *Auteur*," 419.

5. HUMAN LIFE ISN'T NECESSARILY WELL-WRITTEN: WILLIAM GREAVES'S *SYMBIOPSYCHOTAXIPLASM: TAKE ONE* AND *TAKE 2½*

1. *Symbiopsychotaxiplasm: Take One* underwent numerous revisions over the years. According to Scott MacDonald, in 1994 Greaves added "four minutes of material . . . in order to provide contemporary viewers with a clearer sense of the original project." The version discussed here is the one eventually released on home video by the Criterion Collection. See "William Greaves," *A Critical Cinema 3: Interviews with Independent Filmmakers*, ed. Scott MacDonald (Berkeley: University of California Press, 1998), 42.

2. See Maria San Filippo, "What a Long, Strange Trip It's Been—William Greaves' *Symbiopsychotaxiplasm: Take One*," *Film History* 13, no. 2 (2001): 216–217.

3. For a more detailed description of the film, see Vincent Canby, "Why, Even You and I Can Be Stars," *New York Times*, April 27, 1969, D1, D11.

4. Biographical information about Jonathan Gordon from a Skype interview with Gordon by the author, June 1, 2016.

5. Amy Taubin, "*Symbiopsychotaxiplasm*: Still No Answers," *Criterion Collection*, December 4, 2006, https://www.criterion.com/current/posts/460-symbiopsychotaxiplasm-still-no -answers.

6. William Greaves, "*Symbiopsychotaxiplasm: Take One*: Director's Early Notes Prior to and During Production in the Spring of 1968," in *Screen Writings: Scripts and Texts by Independent Filmmakers*, ed. Scott MacDonald (Berkeley: University of California Press, 1995), 34.

7. William Greaves, "*Symbiopsychotaxiplasm*," 34.

8. William Greaves, quoted in MacDonald, *A Critical Cinema 3*, 60.

9. MacDonald, "William Greaves," in *Screen Writings*, 32.

10. J. L. Moreno, *The Theatre of Spontaneity*, 2nd ed. (Beacon, NY: Beacon House, 1973), 127.

11. William Greaves, "Program Notes for *Symbiopsychotaxiplasm: Take One*," in MacDonald, *Screen Writings*, 48.

12. William Greaves, quoted in MacDonald, *A Critical Cinema 3*, 51.

13. William Greaves, quoted in MacDonald, *A Critical Cinema 3*, 49.

14. Richard Brody, "The Daring, Original, And Overlooked *Symbiopsychotaxiplasm: Take One*," *New Yorker*, February 5, 2015, http://www.newyorker.com/culture/richard-brody /daring-original-overlooked-symbiopsychotaxiplasm-take-one.

15. See William Greaves, "*Symbiopsychotaxiplasm*," 35.

16. Joe Dallesandro, quoted in Dan Sullivan, "Interview: Joe Dallesandro," *Film Comment*, May 24, 2016, http://www.filmcomment.com/blog/interview-joe-dallesandro/.

17. Jonathan Gordon, quoted in Skype interview with the author, June 2, 2016.

18. Joe Dallesandro, quoted in Sullivan, "Interview: Joe Dallesandro."

19. William Greaves, quoted in *Discovering William Greaves*, produced by Debra McClutchy, Disc 1, *Symbiopsychotaxiplasm: Two Takes by William Greaves* (New York: Criterion Collection, 2006), DVD.

20. William Greaves, quoted in John Gaspard, "William Greaves and Steven Soderbergh on *Symbiopsychotaxiplasm*," *Fast, Cheap Movie Thoughts*, May 6, 2010, http://fastcheap moviethoughts.blogspot.com/2010/05/william-greaves-and-steven-soderbergh.html. The blog is no longer accessible online.

21. See John Gaspard, "William Greaves and Steven Soderbergh on *Symbiopsychotaxiplasm*."

22. Biographical information provided by Louise Archambault in personal interview with the author, May 15, 2016.

23. William Greaves, quoted in MacDonald, *A Critical Cinema 3*, 61.

24. Marcia Karp expressed this interpretation of her lines in a Skype interview with the author, May 29, 2016.

25. Karp, Skype interview.

26. Karp, Skype interview.

27. Peter Felix Kellermann, *Focus on Psychodrama: The Therapeutic Aspects of Psychodrama* (Philadelphia: Jessica Kingsley Publishers, 1992), 147.

28. Tian Dayton, *The Living Stage: A Step-by-Step Guide to Psychodrama, Sociometry and Experiential Group Therapy* (Deerfield Beach, FL: Health Communications, Inc., 2005), 36–37.

29. Dayton, *Living Stage*, 37.

30. Karp, Skype interview.

31. Louise Archambault, personal interview with the author, May 15, 2016.

32. This information is based on interviews with the two actors: Shannon Baker, personal interview with the author, May 15, 2016; and Audrey Henningham, personal interview with the author, May 17, 2016.

33. William Greaves, quoted in *Discovering William Greaves.*

34. Archambault, interview.

6. BEYOND THE METHOD:
ABEL FERRARA AND HARVEY KEITEL

1. William Greaves, "*Symbiopsychotaxiplasm: Take One*: Director's Early Notes Prior to and During Production in the Spring of 1968," in *Screen Writings: Scripts and Texts by Independent Filmmakers*, ed. Scott MacDonald (Berkeley: University of California Press, 1995), 35.

2. See J. L. Moreno, *The Theatre of Spontaneity*, 2nd ed. (Beacon, NY: Beacon House, 1973), 101.

3. René F. Marineau, *Jacob Levy Moreno 1889–1974: Father of Psychodrama, Sociometry, and Group Psychotherapy* (New York: Tavistock/Routledge, 1989), 124.

4. Jonathan D. Moreno, *Impromptu Man: J. L. Moreno and the Origins of Psychodrama, Encounter Culture, and the Social Network* (New York: Bellevue Literary Press, 2014), 107.

5. Cynthia Baron and Sharon Marie Carnicke, *Reframing Screen Performance* (Ann Arbor: University of Michigan Press, 2008), 26.

6. See Anthony Frost and Ralph Yarrow, *Improvisation in Drama, Theatre and Performance: History, Practice, Theory*, 3rd ed. (London: Palgrave, 2016), 42.

7. Richard Hornby, *The End of Acting: A Radical View* (New York: Applause Books, 1992), 5.

8. Hornby, *End of Acting*, 6.

9. Shonni Enelow, *Method Acting and Its Discontents: On American Psycho-Drama* (Evanston, IL: Northwestern University Press, 2015), 33.

10. Abel Ferrara, quoted in Catherine Shoard, "Abel Ferrara at Cannes: 'You Gotta Be Careful What You Say . . . but I'm Not,'" *The Guardian*, May 23, 2014, http://www.theguardian.com/film/2014/may/23/abel-ferrara-interview.

11. Harvey Keitel, quoted in Julian Schnabel, "Harvey Keitel, Zoë Lund, and Abel Ferrara: The Unholy Trinity that Makes *Bad Lieutenant* a Religious Experience," *Interview*, December 1992, 140.

12. Cory Reynolds, "Abel Ferrara, 2002," *Index Magazine*, 2008, http://www.indexmagazine.com/interviews/abel_ferrara.shtml.

13.   Marshall Fine, *Harvey Keitel: The Art of Darkness* (London: Harper Collins, 1997), 199.

14.   Shonni Enelow, "The Great Recession: Restrained but Resilient, A Style of Acting Has Taken Hold That Speaks To an Era's Anxieties," *Film Comment*, September/October 2016, 60.

15.   Fine, *Harvey Keitel*, 183.

16.   Fine, *Harvey Keitel*, 202.

17.   Zöe Lund, quoted in Scott Macaulay, "Vice Squad: Shaking Down the Bad Lieutenant," *Filmmaker Magazine*, Winter 1992/93, 20.

18.   Roger Ebert, "Harvey Keitel on the Edge," *Roger Ebert Interviews*, January 17, 1993, http://www.rogerebert.com/interviews/harvey-keitel-on-the-edge.

19.   Not only does Ferrara claim that the scene was shot in a single take, but he also suggests that Keitel actually exposed himself during it. Ferrara told Reynolds: "Yeah, [Keitel] just whipped it out. And that was his live-in babysitter in the car! I said, 'You sure you want to do this with your babysitter?' He says, 'Yeah, I want to try something.' [laughs]." See Reynolds, "Abel Ferrara," 2002. Hunter, however, emphatically denies that this occurred. Bianca Hunter, Skype interview with the author, July 11, 2016.

20.   Biographical information about the shooting of the scene provided by Bianca Hunter, Skype interview with the author.

21.   Hunter, Skype interview with the author.

22.   Hunter, Skype interview.

23.   Lawrence Cohn, "Cannes Fest: *Bad Lieutenant*," *Variety*, May 4, 1992, 284.

24.   Gavin Smith, "New Faces," *Film Comment*, January/February 1993, 23.

25.   Abel Ferrara, quoted in Gavin Smith, "The Gambler: From *The Driller Killer* and *Ms. 45* to *Bad Lieutenant*, Abel Ferrara's Low-Budget, Hardboiled, and Brutal Films Have Looked for Trouble," *Sight and Sound* 3, no. 2 (1993): 21.

26.   Donald Lyons, "Scumbags," *Film Comment*, November/December 1992, 7.

27.   Kent Jones, "Abel Ferrara: The Man: Who Cares?," *Lingo*, no. 4 (1995): 36.

28.   Jake Cole, "Dangerous Game," *Slant Magazine*, November 25, 2015, http://www.slantmagazine.com/dvd/review/dangerous-game.

29.   Brad Stevens, *Abel Ferrara: The Moral Vision* (Surrey, England: FAB Press, 2004), 187.

30.   Abel Ferrara, quoted in Scott Tobias, "Abel Ferrara," *A.V. Club*, November 27, 2002, http://www.avclub.com/article/abel-ferrara-13793.

31.   Andrew Morton, *Madonna* (New York: St. Martin's Press, 2001), 260.

32.   Morton, *Madonna*, 261.

33.   Janet Maslin: "A Movie Within a Movie, With a Demure Madonna," *New York Times*, November 19, 1993, C14.

34.   See Fine, *Harvey Keitel*, 181–183.

35.   Jonathan D. Moreno, *Impromptu Man*, 34.

36.   Xavier Mendik, "'Performative Hysteria': Gestures of Male Masochism in *Dangerous Game*," in *Harvey Keitel: Movie Top Ten*, ed. Jack Hunter (London: Creation Books, 1999), 94.

37.   Mendik, "Performative Hysteria," 94.

38.   Stevens, *Abel Ferrara*, 192.

39.   Stevens, *Abel Ferrara*, 194.

40.   Nancy Ferrara, quoted in Morton, *Madonna*, 263.

41.   Morton, Madonna, 259.

42.   Madonna, quoted in Morton, *Madonna*, 262.

7. TIED TO A MACHINE:
THE FILMS OF GUS VAN SANT

1.   Gus Van Sant, quoted in Jeffrey M. Anderson, "Interview with Gus Van Sant: *Last Days*," *Combustible Celluloid*, June 27, 2005, http://www.combustiblecelluloid.com/interviews /vansant2.shtml.

2.   Gus Van Sant, quoted in Mario Falsetto, *Conversations with Gus Van Sant* (New York: Rowman & Littlefield, 2015), 87.

3.   Gus Van Sant, quoted in Scott Macaulay "Sands of Time," *Filmmaker Magazine*, Winter 2002, 88–89.

4.   Gus Van Sant, quoted in Macaulay "Sands of Time," 89.

5.   Gus Van Sant, quoted in Macaulay "Sands of Time," 90.

6.   See Rob Blackwelder, "Desert Dare: Gus Van Sant Returns To His Off-the-Wall Indie Roots with Experimental, Existential *Gerry*," *SPLICEDwire*, February 12, 2003, http:// www.splicedwire.com/03features/gvansant.html.

7.   Gus Van Sant, quoted in Macaulay, "Sands of Time," 89.

8.   Gus Van Sant, quoted in Blackwelder, "Desert Dare."

9.   Gus Van Sant, quoted in Fred Beldin, "Last Days," *Paste*, July 26, 2005, https://www .pastemagazine.com/articles/2005/07/last-days.html.

10.   Gus Van Sant, quoted in Falsetto, *Conversations*, 87.

11.   Gus Van Sant, quoted in Blackwelder, "Desert Dare."

12.   See Falsetto, *Conversations*, 86.

13.   Gus Van Sant, quoted in Falsetto, *Conversations*, 83.

14.   See Falsetto, *Conversations*, 83.

15.   Gus Van Sant, quoted in Jason Guerrasio, "Waxing Improvisational: Why Directors Work Without Scripts, *Independent Film & Video Monthly*, December 2003, 43.

16.   Gus Van Sant, Screenplay: *Elephant*, first draft: July 24, 2002 (American Film Scripts Online, Alexander Street Press), https://alexanderstreet.com/products/film-scripts-online-series.

17.   Gus Van Sant, Screenplay: *Last Days*, first draft: June 8, 2002 (American Film Scripts Online, Alexander Street Press), https://alexanderstreet.com/products/film-scripts -online-series.

18.   Gus Van Sant, quoted in Falsetto, *Conversations*, 112.

19.   Lukas Haas, "The Making of Gus Van Sant's *Last Days*," Bonus Features, *Last Days*, directed by Gus Van Sant (2005; New York: HBO Video, 2005), DVD.

20.   Gus Van Sant, quoted in Falsetto, *Conversations*, 112.

21.   Falsetto, *Conversations*, 100.

22.   Falsetto, *Conversations*, 100.

23.   Gus Van Sant, quoted in "Back in Portland, The Latest Outsider Has a Skateboard," *New York Times*, March 2, 2008, AR15.

24.   Dennis Lim, "Fleshing Out the Lives of Others," *New York Times*, July 11, 2010, AR10.

25.   Lim, "Fleshing Out," AR10.

26.   Lim, "Fleshing Out," AR10.

27.   Dustin Lance Black, *Milk* (New York: Newmarket Press, 2008), 117.

28.   Black, *Milk*, 117.

29.   Black, *Milk*, 117.

30.   David Geffner, "A Place Called Hope," *ICG Magazine*, November 2008, 37.

31.   Black, *Milk*, 107.

32.   Gus Van Sant, quoted in Black, *Milk*, 18.

33.   Harry Savides, quoted in Geffner, "A Place Called Hope," 37.

34.   Geffner, "A Place Called Hope," 38.

35.   Black, *Milk*, 105.

36.   Black, *Milk*, 105.

37.   "iW Critics Poll '08: The Complete Results," *IndieWire*, December 24, 2008, http://www
.indiewire.com/2008/12/iw-critics-poll-08-the-complete-results-71052/.

38.   "Final Cut 2008: The Editors and Contributors Look Back on the Year in Movies," *Film Comment*, January/February 2009, 36.

39.   Manohla Dargis, "In the Big Picture, Big-Screen Hopes," *New York Times*, December 21, 2008, AR9.

40.   Dargis, "Big Picture," AR9, AR16.

41.   Blake Nelson, *Paranoid Park* (New York: Speak, 2008), 93.

42.   See Bob Davis, "Death in Portland," *American Cinematographer*, April 2008, 22.

43.   See Kathryn Millard, "After the Typewriter: The Screenplay in a Digital Era," *Journal of Screenwriting* 1, no. 1 (2010): 11–15.

44.   Andrew Bujalski, quoted in Livia Bloom, "None of Your Beeswax: A Conversation with Andrew Bujalski," *Cinema Scope*, Spring 2009, 33.

45.   Black, *Milk*, 3.

46.   Black, *Milk*, 57.

47.   J. Hoberman, "Adaptive Behavior," *Village Voice*, June 16–22, 2010, 44.

48.   Fyodor Dostoevsky, quoted in epigraph to Nelson, *Paranoid Park*.

49.   Amy Taubin, "Portrait of the Artist?: Amy Taubin On Gus Van Sant's *Paranoid Park*," *Artforum International*, March 2008, 107.

50.   See Millard, "After the Typewriter," 12.

51.   Millard, "After the Typewriter," 15.

8. I LIKE HOW YOU TALK:
THE FILMS OF JOE SWANBERG

1.   For a detailed discussion of mumblecore, see Geoff King, *Indie 2.0: Change and Continuity in Contemporary American Indie Film* (New York: Columbia University Press, 2014),

122–168. See also J. J. Murphy, "Looking through a Rearview Mirror: Mumblecore as Past Tense," in *A Companion to American Indie Film*, ed. Geoff King (Malden, MA: Wiley Blackwell, 2017), 279–299.

2. Joe Swanberg, quoted in Richard Brody, "The Lessons of Film School, Distilled in One Speech," *New Yorker*, March 25, 2016, http://www.newyorker.com/culture/cultural-comment /the-lessons-of-film-school-distilled-in-one-speech.

3. Joe Swanberg, quoted in Brigitta Wagner, "Accidental Cinema and the YouTube Sublime: An Interview with Joe Swanberg," *Senses of Cinema*, no. 59 (June 2011), http:// sensesofcinema.com/2011/feature-articles/accidental-cinema-and-the-youtube-sublime -an-interview-with-joe-swanberg/.

4. Joe Swanberg, quoted in Wagner, "Accidental Cinema."

5. See "Interview with Kate," Special Features, *Kissing on the Mouth*, directed by Joe Swanberg (2005; Park City, UT: Heretic Films, 2006), DVD.

6. Joe Swanberg, quoted in "Rehearsal Footage," Special Features, *Kissing on the Mouth*, DVD.

7. Joe Swanberg, quoted in Miriam Bale, "Swanberg's Way: An Interview with the Prolific Filmmaker Joe Swanberg for his Moving Image Retrospective," *Moving Image Source*, February 27, 2014, http://www.movingimagesource.us/articles/swanbergs-way-20140227.

8. "About the Production," *Hannah Takes the Stairs* Press Kit (Brooklyn, NY: Visit Films, 2007), 4, http://visitfilms.com/media/product/sj_product_65_6_947_530.pdf.

9. Joe Swanberg, quoted in Bale, "Swanberg's Way."

10. Dan Sallitt, "*Nights and Weekends*: IFC Center, through October 16, 2008," *Thanks for the Use of the Hall–Archive*, October 15, 2008, http://sallitt-archive.blogspot.com/2008/10 /nights-and-weekends-ifc-center-through.html.

11. Greta Gerwig, quoted in Sara Cardace, "Mumblecore Muse Greta Gerwig on *Nights and Weekends* and the Ugly Side of Movie Sex," *Vulture*, October 10, 2008, http://www .vulture.com/2008/10/mumblecore_muse_greta_gerwig_0.html.

12. Joe Swanberg, quoted in Wagner, "Accidental Cinema."

13. Joe Swanberg, quoted in Bale, "Swanberg's Way."

14. Joe Swanberg, quoted in Wagner, "Accidental Cinema."

15. Joe Swanberg, "Director's Statement," *Art History* Press Kit (www.joeswanberg.com, 2011), 2, http://www.joeswanberg.com/arthistory/ArtHistoryPressKit.pdf.

16. Joe Swanberg, quoted in Wagner, "Accidental Cinema."

17. Dan Sallitt, "Improvisation in Joe Swanberg's Silver Bullets," *Thanks for the Use of the Hall*, October 23, 2011, http://sallitt.blogspot.com/2011/10/improvisation-in-joe-swanbergs -silver.html.

18. Joe Swanberg, quoted in Bale, "Swanberg's Way."

19. Lawrence Michael Levine, quoted in phone interview with the author, September 8, 2015.

20. Levine, phone interview.

21. Joe Swanberg, quoted in Gary Kramer, "Interview: Joe Swanberg on *Drinking Buddies*, Bigger Budgets, and More," *Slant Magazine*, August 2, 2013, http://www.slantmagazine .com/features/article/interview-joe-swanberg-2013.

22.   Jane Adams, quoted in Clark Collis, "Jane Adams Talks *All the Light in the Sky*," *Entertainment Weekly*, December 16, 2013, http://www.ew.com/article/2013/12/16/all -the-light-in-the-sky-jane-adams-joe-swanberg.

23.   Jane Adams, quoted in Steve Rickinson, "Interview: Jane Adams (Co-Writer/Actress) & Sophia Takal (Actress)—*All the Light in the Sky*," *Indiewood Hollywoodn't*, December 18, 2013, http://indienyc.com/interview-jane-adams-co-writeractress-sophia -takal-actress-all-the-light-in-the-sky/.

24.   Jane Adams, quoted in Tara Aquino, "Interview: Jane Adams and Sophia Takal Talk Joe Swanberg's Latest Film *All the Light in the Sky*," *Complex*, December 19, 2013, http:// amp.au.complex.com/pop-culture/2013/12/all-the-light-in-the-sky-jane-adams-sophia -takal-joe-swanberg-interview.

25.   Jane Adams, quoted in Aquino, "Interview."

26.   Jane Adams, quoted in Rickinson, "Interview."

27.   Sophia Takal, quoted in Aquino, "Interview."

28.   Joe Swanberg, quoted in Stephen Saito, "Interview: Joe Swanberg on His Roxie Retrospective, *All the Light in the Sky*, and Career Benchmarks," *The Moveable Fest*, February 20, 2013, http://moveablefest.com/joe-swanberg-retrospective-roxie-interview/.

29.   Joe Swanberg, quoted in Kramer, "Interview."

30.   Joe Swanberg, quoted in Saito, "Interview."

9. IMPROVISATION AND PLACE:
PUTTY HILL, STAND CLEAR OF THE CLOSING DOORS, AND THE FILMS OF SEAN BAKER

1.   Nicole Elmer, quoted in John Yost, "The Microbudget Conversation: Script vs. Story," *Filmmaker Magazine*, August 3, 2011, http://www.filmmakermagazine.com/news /2011/08/the-microbudget-conversation-script-v-story/.

2.   Matthew Porterfield, quoted in "SXSW '10: *Putty Hill* Director Matt Porterfield's Circuitous Journey to SXSW," *IndieWire*, March 9, 2010, http://www.indiewire.com/2010 /03/sxsw-10-putty-hill-director-matt-porterfields-circuitous-journey-to-sxsw-245662/.

3.   Matthew Porterfield, Original Treatment, *Putty Hill*, 1–5, accessed September 25, 2018, http://puttyhillmovie.com/site/wp-content/uploads/2010/05/PuttyHill_v5.pdf.

4.   Matthew Porterfield, quoted in Ricky D'Ambrose, "Interview: Matthew Porterfield Talks *Putty Hill*, Pasolini, and More," *Slant Magazine*, February 17, 2011, http://www .slantmagazine.com/film/feature/interview-matthew-porterfield/252.

5.   Porterfield, Original Treatment, 1.

6.   Matthew Porterfield, quoted in D'Ambrose, "Interview."

7.   Porterfield, Original Treatment, 5.

8.   Matthew Porterfield, quoted in Don Simpson, "Matt Porterfield (*Putty Hill*): SXSW 2010 Interview," *Smells Like Screen Spirit*, April 2, 2010, http://smellslikescreenspirit .com/2010/04/matt-porterfield-putty-hill-interview-sxsw-2010/.

9. Matthew Porterfield, quoted in D'Ambrose, "Interview."

10. Amy Seimetz, quoted in "Shooting and Editing the Non-Scripted Feature @ SXSW, 3/12/12," *The Film Panel Notetaker*, April 26, 2012, http://thefilmpanelnotetaker.com /shooting-and-editing-the-non-scripted-feature-sxsw-31212 (site discontinued).

11. Porterfield, Original Treatment, 1.

12. Matthew Porterfield, quoted in Pamela Cohn, "Matthew Porterfield," *BOMB Magazine*, June 9, 2010, http://bombmagazine.org/article/4391/.

13. Matthew Porterfield, quoted in Cohn, "Matthew Porterfield."

14. Mark Ruffalo, quoted in Rebecca Mead, "Lost Time: After Years Spent Battling Hollywood Producers, Kenneth Lonergan returns with *Manchester by the Sea*," *New Yorker*, November 7, 2016, 46.

15. Mark Ruffalo, quoted in Mead, "Lost Time," 46.

16. Sam Fleischner, quoted in personal interview with the author, November 19, 2016.

17. For an account of the actual event, see Kirk Semple, "Scared and Silent, Runaway, 13, Spent 11 Days in the Subways," *New York Times*, November 24, 2009, A1, A30.

18. Sam Fleischner, quoted in personal interview with the author.

19. Sam Fleischner, quoted in Karen Kemmerle, "*Stand Clear of the Closing Doors*' Director Sam Fleischner on Storytelling and Happy Accidents," *Tribeca Film*, May 22, 2014, https://www.tribecafilm.com/stories/stand-clear-director-sam-fleischner.

20. Sam Fleischner, quoted in Kemmerle, "Director Sam Fleischner on Storytelling."

21. Sam Fleischner, quoted in "Sam Fleischner on *Stand Clear of the Closing Doors*," *Indie Outlook*, July 15, 2014, https://indie-outlook.com/2014/07/15/sam-fleischner-on -stand-clear-of-the-closing-doors/.

22. Sam Fleischner, quoted in Brandon Harris, "Underground: Sam Fleischner on *Stand Clear of the Closing Doors*," *Filmmaker Magazine*, May 23, 2014, http://filmmaker magazine.com/86065-underground-sam-fleischner-on-stand-clear-of-the-closing -doors/#.WCf8v8no6YE.

23. Sam Fleischner, quoted in Oakley Anderson-Moore, "The Quintessential New York Movie: Sam Fleischner on Making *Stand Clear of the Closing Doors*," *No Film School*, May 23, 2014, http://nofilmschool.com/2014/05/new-york-movie-sam-fleischner-making -stand-clear-of-the-closing-doors.

24. Sam Fleischner, quoted in Kemmerle, "Director Sam Fleischner on Storytelling."

25. See Kemmerle, "Director Sam Fleischner on Storytelling."

26. Sam Fleischner, quoted in Anderson-Moore, "Quintessential New York Movie."

27. Sam Fleischner, quoted in Anderson-Moore, "Quintessential New York Movie."

28. Stephen Saito, "Interview: Sam Fleischner, Andrea Suarez Paz & Jesus Sanchez-Velez on Opening Up *Stand Clear of the Closing Doors*," *The Moveable Fest*, April 25, 2013, http:// moveablefest.com/stand-clear-of-the-closing-doors-tribeca-interview/.

29. Sean Baker, quoted in "indieWIRE Interview: *Take Out* Co-Director Sean Baker," *indieWIRE*, June 3, 2008, http://www.indiewire.com/2008/06/indiewire-interview-take -out-co-director-sean-baker-72270/.

30. Sean Baker, quoted in "indieWIRE Interview."

31. Shih-Ching Tsou, quoted in Jennifer M. Wood, "Sean Baker and Shih-Ching Tsou Order $3,000 *Take Out*," *MovieMaker*, November 18, 2009, https://www.moviemaker.com /archives/series/how_they_did_it/shih-ching-tsou-sean-baker-take-out-20091112/.

32. Sean Baker, quoted in Carolina Francesca, "Filmmaker Sean Baker Talks Chinese *Take Out*, Crif Dogs, And 3 a.m. Karaoke Nights in Flushing," *Guest of a Guest*, October 15, 2008, http://guestofaguest.com/nyc-interviews/filmmaker-sean-baker-talks-chinese -take-out-crif-dogs-and-3am-karaoke-nights-in-flushing.

33. Sean Baker, quoted in interview with the author, October 24, 2015.

34. Baker, quoted in interview.

35. Sean Baker, quoted in "indieWIRE Interview."

36. Baker, quoted in interview.

37. See David Bordwell, *The Way Hollywood Tells It: Story and Style in Modern Movies* (Berkeley: University of California Press, 2006), 121–138.

38. Angela Watercutter, "*Tangerine* Is Amazing—But Not Because of How They Shot It," *Wired*, July 7, 2015, https://www.wired.com/2015/07/tangerine-iphone/.

39. Baker, quoted in interview. All subsequent quotes from Baker are from this interview, unless otherwise noted.

10. REDISCOVERING PSYCHODRAMA: *FROWNLAND, HEAVEN KNOWS WHAT,* AND *STINKING HEAVEN*

1. Ronald Bronstein, quoted in David Lowery, "Bleak Moments: Ronald Bronstein on *Frownland*," *Filmmaker Magazine*, February 27, 2017 (originally posted on August 29, 2007), http://filmmakermagazine.com/4843-bleak-moments-by-david-lowery/# .WVUqYiGQxaQ.

2. Ronald Bronstein, quoted in Jeremiah Kipp, "Notes from Underground: An Interview with *Frownland* Writer-Director Ronald Bronstein," *The House Next Door*, March 7, 2008, http://www.slantmagazine.com/house/article/notes-from-underground-an-interview -with-frownland-writerdirector-ronald-bronstein.

3. Ronald Bronstein, quoted in Kipp, "Notes from Underground."

4. Mike Leigh, quoted in *Mike Leigh on Mike Leigh*, ed. Amy Raphael (London and New York: Faber and Faber, 2008), 23.

5. Mike Leigh, quoted in Raphael, *Mike Leigh*, 26.

6. Howie Movshovitz, "Introduction," *Mike Leigh Interviews*, ed. Howie Movshovitz (Jackson: University Press of Mississippi, 2000), IX.

7. Mike Leigh, quoted in Judy Bloch, "A Conversation with Mike Leigh and Alison Steadman," in Movshovitz, *Mike Leigh Interviews*, 20.

8. Ronald Bronstein, quoted in Kipp, "Notes from Underground."

9. Ronald Bronstein, quoted in Kipp, "Notes from Underground."

10. Ronald Bronstein, quoted in "Ronnie Bronstein," *Cinemad*, April 2009, http://www .cinemad.iblamesociety.com/2009/04/ronnie-bronstein.html.

11. Ronald Bronstein, quoted in "Ronnie Bronstein."

12. Ronald Bronstein, quoted in Lowery, "Bleak Moments."

13. Josh Safdie, quoted in Scott Macaulay, "I Want to Take You Higher," *Filmmaker Magazine*, Spring 2015, 51.

14. Josh Safdie, quoted in Brandon Harris, "The Safdie Brothers' *Heaven Knows What* Is the Most Powerful Movie About the Life of Addicts in a Long, Long Time," *Vice*, June 2, 2015, http://www.vice.com/read/vice-exclusive-clip-of-heaven-knows-what-and-an-interview-with-the-safdie-brothers-and-actress-arielle-holmes-555.

15. Josh Safdie, quoted in Scott Tobias, "The Safdie Brothers on the Heightened Reality of *Heaven Knows What*," *The Dissolve*, May 29, 2015, https://thedissolve.com/features/interview/1047-safdies-interview/.

16. Josh Safdie, quoted in Riley Ceder, "*Heaven Knows What*: Josh Safdie of the Safdie Brothers," *American Apparel*, accessed January 12, 2016, http://www.747warehouse.net/safdie-brothers/ (site discontinued).

17. Josh Safdie, quoted in Macaulay, "I Want to Take You Higher," 52.

18. Josh Safdie, quoted in Dan Sullivan, "Interview: Josh & Benny Safdie," *Film Comment*, May 26, 2015, http://www.filmcomment.com/blog/interview-josh-and-benny-safdie/.

19. Josh Safdie, quoted in Macaulay, "I Want to Take You Higher," 82.

20. Josh Safdie, quoted in Sullivan, "Interview: Josh & Benny Safdie."

21. Josh Sadie, quoted in Robin Nierynck, "Love and Heroin Addiction in NYC Laid Bare in *Heaven Knows What*: Director Q & A," *Huck*, June 25, 2015, http://www.huckmagazine.com/art-and-culture/film-2/heaven-knows-what/.

22. Josh Safdie, quoted in Carlos Aguilar, "Interview: *Heaven Knows What* Directors Josh and Benny Safdie Are Addicted to the Truth," *IndieWire*, May 29, 2015, http://www.indiewire.com/2015/05/interview-heaven-knows-what-directors-josh-and-benny-safdie-are-addicted-to-the-truth-171185/.

23. Benny Safdie, quoted in Harris, "The Safdie Brothers' *Heaven Knows What*."

24. Arielle Holmes, quoted in Harris, "The Safdie Brothers' *Heaven Knows What*."

25. Arielle Holmes, quoted in Stephen Applebaum, "Drugs, Destruction and Movie Glory: How Arielle Holmes Rose from the Streets," *Guardian*, July 6, 2015, 12.

26. Josh Safdie, quoted in Henry Stewart, "Tales of Two Cities: Talking to the Safdie Brothers about *Heaven Knows What* and Privilege and Struggle in Modern NYC," *The L Magazine*, May 26, 2015, http://www.thelmagazine.com/2015/05/tales-two-cities-talking-safdie-brothers-heaven-knows-privilege-struggle-modern-nyc/.

27. Arielle Holmes, quoted in Rich Juzwiak, "Who Gets To Tell Homeless Junkies' Stories?: *Heaven Knows What*," *Defamer*, May 29, 2015, http://defamer.gawker.com/who-gets-to-tell-homeless-junkies-stories-heaven-know-1707711632.

28. Amy Larocca, "The Star on the Sidewalk: How Arielle Holmes Went from Homeless Addict to Hollywood Actress," *Vulture*, May 21, 2015, http://www.vulture.com/2015/05/arielle-holmes-heaven-knows-what.html.

29. John Nolte, *The Philosophy, Theory and Methods of J. L. Moreno: The Man Who Tried to Become God* (New York: Routledge, 2014), 221.

30. Arielle Holmes, quoted in Harris, "The Safdie Brothers' *Heaven Knows What*."

31.   Arielle Holmes, quoted in Larocca, "The Star on the Sidewalk."

32.   Sarah Salovaara, "NYFF'14: *Heaven Knows What, Eden, The Look of Silence*," *Filmmaker Magazine*, September 30, 2014, http://filmmakermagazine.com/87642-nyff-14-heaven-knows-what-the-look-of-silence-eden/#.WVVSi1GQxaQ.

33.   Josh Sadie, quoted in Nierynck, "Love and Heroin."

34.   Benny Safdie, quoted in Aguilar, "Interview."

35.   Josh Safdie, quoted in Ceder, "*Heaven Knows What.*"

36.   Josh Safdie, quoted in Macaulay, "I Want to Take You Higher," 53.

37.   Benny Safdie, quoted in Macaulay, "I Want to Take You Higher," 53.

38.   Benny Safdie, quoted in Tobias, "The Safdie Brothers."

39.   René F. Marineau, *Jacob Levy Moreno 1889–1974: Father of Psychodrama, Sociometry, and Group Psychotherapy* (London: Tavistock/Routledge, 1989), 77.

40.   Nolte, *Philosophy, Theory and Methods*, 186.

41.   Nolte, *Philosophy, Theory and Methods*, 186.

42.   Josh Safdie, quoted in Larocca, "The Star on the Sidewalk."

43.   See Kerry O'Conor, "The Brothers Grit: An Interview with *Heaven Knows What* Directors Ben and Josh Safdie," *MovieMaker*, June 4, 2015, http://www.moviemaker.com/archives/interviews/the-brothers-grit-an-interview-with-heaven-knows-what-directors-ben-and-josh-safdie/.

44.   Josh Safdie, quoted in Ceder, "*Heaven Knows What.*"

45.   Nathan Silver, quoted in Mark Lukenbill, "*Soft in the Head* Interview with Nathan Silver," *The House Next Door*, April 19, 2014, http://www.slantmagazine.com/house/article/soft-in-the-head-interview-with-nathan-silver.

46.   Nathan Silver, quoted in Whitney Mallett, "Nathan Silver's New Film *Stinking Heaven* Reeks of Cynicism and Kombucha," *Vice*, January 26, 2015, http://www.vice.com/read/nate-silvers-new-feature-film-stinking-heaven-reeks-of-cynicism-and-kombucha-456.

47.   Nathan Silver, quoted in David Loius Zuckerman, "Nathan Silver," *BOMB Magazine*, June 5, 2014, http://bombmagazine.org/article/1000164/nathan-silver.

48.   See Sarah Salovaara, "Behaving Badly in Nathan Silver's *Stinking Heaven*," *Filmmaker Magazine*, July 25, 2014, http://filmmakermagazine.com/86869-behaving-badly-in-stinking-heaven/#.WVaDIVGQxaQ.

49.   See Zuckerman, "Nathan Silver."

50.   Nathan Silver, quoted in Lukenbill, "*Soft in the Head* Interview."

51.   Nathan Silver, quoted in Sarah Salovaara, "'Let Some Air In!': Nathan Silver on Directing Improvisation," *Filmmaker Magazine*, April 18, 2014, https://filmmakermagazine.com/85465-let-some-air-in-nathan-silver-on-directing-improvisation/#.W61smC-ZNZI.

52.   Nathan Silver, quoted in Zuckerman, "Nathan Silver."

53.   See Nicolas Rapold, "A Freewheeling Pursuit of Spontaneity on Film," *New York Times*, April 13, 2014, AR22.

54.   Nathan Silver, quoted in Nigel M. Smith, "The Indiewire Springboard: How *Uncertain Terms* Director Nathan Silver Stays Inspired," *IndieWire*, June 20, 2014, http://www.indiewire.com/2014/06/the-indiewire-springboard-how-uncertain-terms-director-nathan-silver-stays-inspired-25089/.

55. Nathan Silver, quoted in Nick Dawson, "Five Questions with *Soft in the Head* Director Nathan Silver," *Filmmaker Magazine*, April 10, 2013, http://filmmakermagazine.com /68440-five-questions-with-soft-in-the-head-director-nathan-silver/#.WVaFiFGQxaQ.

56. Nathan Silver, quoted in Ottilie Wilford, "Nathan Silver Talks About His Latest Film *Soft in the Head*," *Berlin Film Journal*, February 2014, http://berlinfilmjournal .com/2014/02/nathan-silverwe-all-know-there-is-no-fiction-or-non-fiction-really -when-youre-making-a-movie/.

57. Nathan Silver, quoted in Nicole Disser, "Brooklyn Filmmaker Nathan Silver Talks His Latest, *Stinking Heaven*," *Bedford + Bowery*, December 21, 2015, http://bedfordandbowery .com/2015/12/brooklyn-filmmaker-nathan-silver-talks-his-latest-stinking-heaven-a -dizzying-display-of-sober-living/.

58. Nathan Silver, quoted in Hannah Gross, "Nathan Silver," *morning to morning*, August 2013, http://nicolasnorena.wixsite.com/morningtomorning/nathan-silver-interview.

59. Nathan Silver, quoted in Gross, "Nathan Silver."

60. Nathan Silver, quoted in Gross, "Nathan Silver."

61. Cindy Silver, quoted in Valentina I. Valentini, "LA Film Fest 2014 Interview: *Uncertain Terms* Actress Cindy Silver on Her Son, Director Nathan Silver," *Screen Anarchy*, June 21, 2014, http://screenanarchy.com/2014/06/la-film-fest-2014-interview-uncertain-terms -director-nathan-silvers-mom.html.

11. THE LINE BETWEEN REALITY AND STAGING: *ACTOR MARTINEZ*, *ACTRESS*, AND *THE WITNESS*

1. Lindsay Burdge, quoted in Emily Buder, "Why Shooting Reality–Fiction Blur *Actor Martinez* was 'Like Being on LSD,' " *No Film School*, April 26, 2016, http://nofilmschool .com/2016/04/actor-martinez-interview-art-life-tribeca-lindsay-burdge-nate-silver -mike-ott.

2. Mike Ott, quoted in "The AFI Fest Interview: *Actor Martinez* Directors Mike Ott and Nathan Silver," *American Film*, October 23, 2016, http://blog.afi.com/the-afi -fest-interview-actor-martinez-directors-mike-ott-and-nathan-silver/.

3. Nathan Silver, quoted in Stephen Saito, "Interview: Nathan Silver, Arthur Martinez & Lindsay Burdge on Art Imitating Life in *Actor Martinez*," *Moveable Fest*, April 27 2016, http://moveablefest.com/nathan-silver-actor-martinez/.

4. Nathan Silver, quoted in Irina Trocan, "Indie Filmmaking Plays Itself: *Actor Martinez*," *Fandor Keyframe*, April 12, 2016, https://www.fandor.com/keyframe/indie-filmmaking -plays-itself-actor-martinez (section of site discontinued).

5. Mike Ott, quoted in Trocan, "Indie Filmmaking Plays Itself."

6. Daniel Kasman, "Rotterdam 2016. Acting Out: Spain's Crisis in Discussion, 'A Fictitious Report on the Architecture of the Brain,' and a Collaboration between Two Indie Directors," *MUBI Notebook*, February 1, 2016, https://mubi.com/notebook/posts /rotterdam-2016-acting-out.

7. Lindsay Burdge, quoted in Saito, "Interview."

8. Lindsay Burdge, quoted in Zachary Shevich, "Lindsay Burdge and Arthur Martinez on Blurring the Lines of Fiction and Documentary in *Actor Martinez*," *Way Too Indie*, April 18, 2016, http://waytooindie.com/interview/lindsay-burdge-and-arthur-martinez -on-blurring-the-lines-of-fiction-and-documentary-in-actor-martinez/.

9. Lindsay Burdge, quoted in Buder, "Shooting Reality–Fiction Blur."

10. Lindsay Burdge, quoted in Buder, "Shooting Reality–Fiction Blur."

11. John Nolte, *The Philosophy, Theory and Methods of J. L. Moreno: The Man Who Tried to Become God* (New York: Routledge, 2014), 221.

12. Nolte, *Philosophy, Theory and Methods*, 221.

13. Nathan Silver, quoted in Buder, "Shooting Reality–Fiction Blur."

14. Dogg Souljah, Groovey.TV, "Actor Martinez Interview," YouTube Video, 11:37, June 7, 2016, https://www.youtube.com/watch?v=dSZPafoN1wE.

15. Mike Ott, quoted in Trocan, "Indie Filmmaking Plays Itself."

16. Nathan Silver, quoted in Trocan, "Indie Filmmaking Plays Itself."

17. Abel Ferrara, quoted in Kent Jones, "Abel Ferrara: *The Man: Who Cares?*," *Lingo*, no.4 (1995): 36.

18. Robert Greene, quoted in Adam Nayman, "Diary of a Mad Housewife: Robert Greene's *Actress*," *Cinema Scope*, Summer 2014, 14.

19. Robert Greene, quoted in Pamela Cohn, "Robert Greene: Exploring Performance in Documentary Film," *BOMB Magazine*, November 4, 2014, https://bombmagazine.org /articles/robert-greene/.

20. Robert Greene, quoted in Steven Erickson, "Walking Toward the Flame: An Interview with Robert Greene about *Actress*," *IndieWire*, November 5, 2014, http://www.indiewire .com/2014/11/walking-toward-the-flame-an-interview-with-robert-greene-about -actress-133265/.

21. Robert Greene, quoted in Vadim Rizov, " 'You Might as Well be Selling Drugs': Robert Greene on *Actress*," *Filmmaker Magazine*, November 6, 2014, http://filmmakermagazine .com/88201-you-might-as-well-be-selling-drugs-robert-greene-on-actress/.

22. Robert Greene, quoted in Cohn, "Robert Greene."

23. Robert Greene, quoted in Erickson, "Walking Toward the Flame."

24. Robert Greene, quoted in Matthew Caron, "Real Life Turned Up to 11: *Actress* and the Documentaries of Robert Greene," *Vice*, March 5, 2015, http://www.vice.com/read /real-life-turned-up-to-11-actress-and-the-documentaries-of-robert-greene-167.

25. Hilton Als, "Dark Rooms: Revisiting Nan Goldin's *The Ballad of Sexual Dependency*," *New Yorker*, July 4, 2016, 26.

26. Robert Greene, quoted in Caron, "Real Life Turned Up to 11."

27. Erving Goffman, *The Presentation of Self in Everyday Life* (New York: Anchor Books, 1959), 252.

28. Nayman, "Diary of a Mad Housewife," 13.

29. Robert Greene, quoted in Erickson, "Walking Toward the Flame."

30. A. O. Scott, "Reality, or Artful Dodge?," *New York Times*, November 7, 2014, C6.

31. Greene, quoted in Cohn, "Robert Greene."

32. Bilge Ebiri, "*Actress* Is a Great Documentary—Fast, Alive, Ever-Changing," *Vulture*, November 7, 2014, http://www.vulture.com/2014/11/movie-review-actress-documentary .html.

33. See A. M. Rosenthal, *Thirty-Eight Witnesses* (New York: McGraw-Hill, 1964).

34. See James Solomon in Chris O'Falt, "How *The Witness* Evolved From HBO-Scripted Series to a Doc Revealing the Truth Behind a Shocking Murder," *IndieWire*, June 3, 2016, http://www.indiewire.com/2016/06/the-witness-james-solomon-hbo-kitty-genovese -murder-documentary-1201684033/.

35. James Solomon, quoted in O'Falt, "How *The Witness* Evolved."

36. James Solomon, quoted in Paula Bernstein, "Five Questions with *The Witness* Director James Solomon," *Filmmaker Magazine*, June 2, 2016, http://filmmakermagazine .com/98679-five-questions-with-witness-director-james-solomon/#.WVfHk1GQxaQ.

37. Richard Brody, "Kitty Genovese's Brother Reëxamines Her Famous Murder," *New Yorker*, October 6, 2015, http://www.newyorker.com/culture/richard-brody/kitty-genoveses -brother-reexamines-her-famous-murder.

38. Alan Scherstuhl, "Kitty Genovese's Brother Asks Whether New Yorkers Truly Ignored Her Murder," *Village Voice*, May 31, 2016, https://www.villagevoice.com/2016/05/31 /kitty-genoveses-brother-asks-whether-new-yorkers-truly-ignored-her-murder/.

39. See Maria Garcia, "*The Witness*: Kitty Genovese's Brother Unravels the Truth Behind Her Infamous Murder," *Biography*, June 2, 2016, http://www.biography.com/news/kitty -genovese-the-witness-movie.

40. Bill Genovese, quoted in Garcia, "*The Witness*."

41. James Solomon, quoted in Skype interview with the author, December 14, 2016.

42. See James Solomon in O'Falt, "How *The Witness* Evolved."

43. James Solomon, quoted in Bernstein, "Five Questions."

44. James Solomon, quoted in O'Falt, "How *The Witness* Evolved."

45. James Solomon, quoted in O'Falt, "How *The Witness* Evolved."

CONCLUSION: BLENDING FICTION AND DOCUMENTARY

1. Graham Fuller, "Nicholas Ray's *In a Lonely Place* as Psychodrama," *Cineaste*, Fall 2016, https://www.cineaste.com/fall2016/nicholas-ray-lonely-place-psychodrama/.

2. See Ray Carney, *Cassavetes on Cassavetes* (London: Faber and Faber, 2001), 311.

3. John Cassavetes, quoted in Carney, *Cassavetes on Cassavetes*, 314.

4. Richard Leacock, "For an Uncontrolled Cinema, *Film Culture*, no. 22–23 (Summer 1961): 24.

5. Leacock, "For an Uncontrolled Cinema," 25.

6. Jonas Mekas writes, "There is no doubt that most of the dullness of our movies is concocted in advance in the so-called heads of the so-called scriptwriters. Not only the dullness: they also perpetuate the standardized film constructions, dialogues, plots. They follow closely their textbooks of 'good' screen-writing. Shoot all scriptwriters, and we may yet have a rebirth of American cinema." See Jonas Mekas, "Movie Journal," *Village Voice*, November 25, 1959, 6.

7. Brian Winston, Gail Vanstone, and Wang Chi, *The Art of Documenting: Documentary Film in the 21st Century* (New York: Bloomsbury Academic, 2017), 4–5.

8. Eric Bentley, *Thinking about the Playwright: Comments from Four Decades* (Evanston, IL: Northwestern University Press, 1987), 322.

9. Nathan Silver, quoted in Nicole Disser, "Brooklyn Filmmaker Nathan Silver Talks His Latest, *Stinking Heaven*," *Bedford + Bowery*, December 21, 2015, http://bedfordandbowery .com/2015/12/brooklyn-filmmaker-nathan-silver-talks-his-latest-stinking-heaven-a-dizzying -display-of-sober-living/.

10. John Cassavetes, quoted in Carney, *Cassavetes on Cassavetes*, 72.

11. See Robert Koehler, "Listening to Silence: An Interview with Lance Hammer," *Cineaste*, Winter 2008, 8–13.

12. Chloé Zhao, quoted in Devika Girish, "*The Rider* & Chloé Zhao Interview," *Reverse Shot*, April 12, 2018, http://reverseshot.org/reviews/entry/2373/rider_chloe.

13. Chloé Zhao, quoted in Girish, "*The Rider* & Chloé Zhao Interview."

14. Chloé Zhao, quoted in James Ponsoldt, "Rodeo Dream," *Filmmaker*, Spring 2018, 30.

15. Chloé Zhao, quoted in Emily Buder, "How Werner Herzog-Approved *The Rider* Director 'Got Creative' Financing Her Exquisite Cannes Premiere," *No Film School*, May 23, 2017, https://nofilmschool.com/2017/05/rider-chloe-zhao.

16. Emily Buder, " 'I Didn't Want a Shoot-Out': *Dark Night* Director on Depicting a Massacre Without Violence," *No Film School*, February 9, 2017, http://nofilmschool.com/2017/02 /dark-night-director-tim-sutton-interview.

17. Tim Sutton, quoted in Buder, " 'I Didn't Want a Shoot-Out.' "

18. Sean Baker, quoted in Brian Raftery, "How Instagram Helped Discover One of This Year's Breakout Movie Stars," *Wired*, October 16, 2017, https://www.wired.com/story /florida-project-breakout-star-instagram/.

19. A. O. Scott, "No Method to Her Method: Greta Gerwig Is What We Talk About When We Talk About Acting," *New York Times*, March 28, 2010, AR1.

20. Scott, "No Method to Her Method," AR9.

BIBLIOGRAPHY

Baron, Cynthia, Diane Carson, and Frank P. Tomasulo, eds. *More Than A Method: Trends and Traditions in Contemporary Film Performance*. Detroit, MI: Wayne State University Press, 2004.

Baron, Cynthia, and Sharon Marie Carnicke. *Reframing Screen Performance*. Ann Arbor: University of Michigan Press, 2008.

Bazin, André. "Film through a Telephoto Lens: Ray Ashley, Morris Engel, and Ruth Orkin's *The Little Fugitive*." In *Bazin on Global Cinema 1948–1958*, translated and edited by Burt Cardullo, 145–49. Austin: University of Texas Press, 2014.

Belgrad, Daniel. *The Culture of Spontaneity: Improvisation and the Arts in Postwar America*. Chicago: The University of Chicago Press, 1998.

Bentley, Eric. *Thinking about the Playwright: Comments from Four Decades*. Evanston, IL: Northwestern University Press, 1987.

Biner, Pierre. *The Living Theatre*. New York: Horizon Press, 1972.

Black, Dustin Lance. *Milk*. New York: Newmarket Press, 2008.

Bordwell, David. *The Way Hollywood Tells It: Story and Style in Modern Movies*. Berkeley: University of California Press, 2006.

Bozung, Justin, ed. *The Cinema of Norman Mailer: Film Is Like Death*. New York: Bloomsbury, 2017.

Burger-Utzer, Brigitta, and Stefan Grissemann, eds. *Frank Films: The Film and Video Work of Robert Frank*. New York: Scalo, 2003.

Burnett, Charles. "*Killer of Sheep* Screenplay." In *Screenplays of the African American Experience*, edited by Phyllis Rauch Klotman. Bloomington: Indiana University Press, 1991.

Carney, Ray. *American Dreaming: The Films of John Cassavetes and the American Experience*. Berkeley: University of California Press, 1985.

——. *Cassavetes on Cassavetes*. New York: Faber and Faber, 2001.

——. *John Cassavetes: The Adventure of Insecurity*. 2nd rev. ed. Walpole, MA: Company C Publishing, 2000.

——. *Shadows*. London: BFI Publishing, 2001.

Cassavetes, John. *Faces*. New York: Signet, 1970.

——. Original Screenplay: *Minnie and Moskowitz*. Los Angeles: Black Sparrow Press, 1973.

Charity, Tom. *John Cassavetes: Lifeworks*. London: Omnibus, 2001.

Coleman, Janet. *The Compass*. New York: Alfred A. Knopf, 1990.

Cornic, Stefan, ed. *Morris Engel and Ruth Orkin: Outside: From Street Photography to Filmmaking*. Translated by William Snow. Paris: Carlotta Films, 2014.

Counsell, Colin. *Signs of Performance: An Introduction to Twentieth-Century Theatre*. New York: Routledge, 1996.

Davis, Peter, ed. *Come Back, Africa: Lionel Rogosin—A Man Possessed*. Johannesburg: STE Publishers, 2004.

Dayton, Tian. *The Living Stage: A Step-by-Step Guide to Psychodrama, Sociometry and Experiential Group Therapy*. Deerfield Beach, FL: Health Communications, Inc., 2005.

Enelow, Shonni. *Method Acting and Its Discontents: On American Psycho-Drama*. Evanston, IL: Northwestern University Press, 2015.

Falsetto, Mario. *Conversations with Gus Van Sant*. New York: Rowman & Littlefield, 2015.

Ferrara, Eric. *The Bowery: A History of Grit, Graft and Grandeur*. Charleston, SC: History Press, 2011.

Field, Allyson Nadia, Jan-Christopher Horak, and Jacqueline Najuma Stewart, eds. *LA Rebellion: Creating a New Black Cinema*. Oakland: University of California Press, 2015.

Fine, Marshall. *Accidental Genius: How John Cassavetes Invented American Independent Film*. New York: Miramax Books/Hyperion, 2005.

——. *Harvey Keitel: The Art of Darkness*. London: Harper Collins, 1997.

Frost, Anthony, and Ralph Yarrow. *Improvisation in Drama, Theatre and Performance: History, Practice, Theory*. 3rd ed. London: Palgrave, 2016.

Gelmis, Joseph. *The Film Director as Superstar*. Garden City, NY: Doubleday, 1970.

Glick, Joshua. *Los Angeles Documentary and the Production of Public History, 1958–1977*. Oakland: University of California Press, 2018.

Goffman, Erving. *The Presentation of Self in Everyday Life*. New York: Anchor Books, 1959.

Hare, A. Paul & June Rabson Hare, *J. L. Moreno*. London, Thousand Oaks, and New Delhi: Sage, 1996.

Hornby, Richard. *The End of Acting: A Radical View*. New York: Applause Books, 1992.

James, David E. *Allegories of Cinema: American Film in the Sixties*. Princeton, NJ: Princeton University Press, 1989.

——, ed. *To Free the Cinema: Jonas Mekas and the New York Underground*. Princeton, NJ: Princeton University Press, 1992.

Kapsis, Robert E., ed. *Charles Burnett Interviews*. Jackson: University Press of Mississippi, 2011.

Kazan, Elia. *Elia Kazan: A Life*. New York: Alfred A. Knopf, 1988.

Kellermann, Peter Felix. *Focus on Psychodrama: The Therapeutic Aspects of Psychodrama*. Philadelphia: Jessica Kingsley Publishers, 1992.

King, Geoff. *American Independent Cinema*. Bloomington: Indiana University Press, 2005.

——, ed. *A Companion to American Indie Film*. Malden, MA: Wiley Blackwell, 2017.

——. *Indie 2.0: Change and Continuity in Contemporary American Indie Film*. New York: Columbia University Press, 2014.

Kouvaros, George. *Awakening the Eye: Robert Frank's American Cinema*. Minneapolis: University of Minnesota Press, 2015.

Léger, Nathalie. *Suite for Barbara Loden*. Translated by Natasha Lehrer and Cécile Menon. St. Louis, MO: Dorothy, a publishing project, 2016.

Lipman, Ross. "Kent Mackenzie's *The Exiles*: Reinventing the Real of Cinema." In *Alternative Projections: Experimental Film in Los Angeles, 1945–1980*, edited by David E. James and Adam Hyman, 163–174. New Barnet, UK: John Libbey Publishing, 2015.

MacDonald, Scott, ed. *A Critical Cinema 3: Interviews with Independent Filmmakers*. Berkeley: University of California Press, 1998.

——, ed. *Screen Writings: Scripts and Texts by Independent Filmmakers*. Berkeley: University of California Press, 1995.

Mackenzie, Kent Robert. "A Description and Examination of the Production of *The Exiles*: A Film of the Actual Lives of Young American Indians." Master's Thesis, University of Southern California, 1964.

Mailer, Norman. *Maidstone: A Mystery*. New York: Signet, 1971.

——. *The Spooky Art: Some Thoughts on Writing*. New York: Random House, 2003.

Maras, Steven. *Screenwriting: History, Theory and Practice*. New York: Wallflower Press, 2009.

Marineau, René F. *Jacob Levy Moreno 1889–1974: Father of Psychodrama, Sociometry, and Group Psychotherapy*. New York: Tavistock/Routledge, 1989.

Mendik, Xavier. " 'Performative Hysteria': Gestures of Male Masochism in *Dangerous Game*." In *Harvey Keitel: Movie Top Ten*, edited by Jack Hunter, 93–111. London: Creation Books, 1999.

Millard, Kathryn. *Screenwriting in a Digital Era*. New York: Palgrave Macmillan, 2014.

Moreno, J. L. *The Theatre of Spontaneity*. 2nd ed. Beacon, NY: Beacon House, 1973.

Moreno, Jonathan D. *Impromptu Man: J. L. Moreno and the Origins of Psychodrama, Encounter Culture, and the Social Network*. New York: Bellevue Literary Press, 2014.

Moreno, Zerka T. *To Dream Again: A Memoir*. Edited by Edward Schreiber. Catskill, NY: Mental Health Resources, 2012.

Morton, Andrew. *Madonna*. New York: St. Martin's Press, 2001.

Mouëllic, Gilles. *Improvising Cinema*. Amsterdam: Amsterdam University Press, 2013.

Movshovitz, Howie, ed. *Mike Leigh Interviews*. Jackson: University Press of Mississippi, 2000.

Murphy, J. J. *The Black Hole of the Camera: The Films of Andy Warhol*. Berkeley: University of California Press, 2012.

——. "Looking through a Rearview Mirror: Mumblecore as Past Tense." In *A Companion to American Indie Film*, edited by Geoff King, 279–299. Malden, MA: Wiley Blackwell, 2017.

——. *Me and You and* Memento *and* Fargo: *How Independent Screenplays Work*. New York: Continuum, 2007.

Naremore, James. *Acting in the Cinema*. Berkeley: University of California Press, 1988.

Nelson, Blake. *Paranoid Park*. New York: Speak, 2008.

Nolte, John. *The Philosophy, Theory and Methods of J. L. Moreno: The Man Who Tried to Become God*. New York: Routledge, 2014.

Phillips, Lisa. *Beat Culture and the New America: 1950–1965*. New York: Whitney Museum of American Art, 1995.

Price, Steven. *A History of the Screenplay*. New York: Palgrave Macmillan, 2013.

Rabinovitz, Lauren. *Points of Resistance: Women, Power & Politics in the New York Avant-garde Cinema, 1943–71*. Chicago: University of Illinois Press, 1991.

Raphael, Amy, ed. *Mike Leigh on Mike Leigh*. New York: Faber and Faber, 2008.

Rollyson, Carl. *The Lives of Norman Mailer: A Biography*. New York: Paragon House, 1991.

Rosenthal, A. M. *Thirty-Eight Witnesses*. New York: McGraw-Hill, 1964.

Sargeant, Jack. *Naked Lens: Beat Cinema*. London: Creation Books, 1997.

Sawyer, R. Keith. *Improvised Dialogues: Emergence and Creativity in Conversation*. Westport, CT: Ablex Publishing, 2003.

Sitney, P. Adams. *Visionary Film: The American Avant-Garde*. New York: Oxford University Press, 1974.

Smith, Wendy. *Real Life Drama: The Group Theatre and America, 1931–1940*. New York: Alfred A. Knopf, 1990.

Spolin, Viola. *Improvisation for the Theater: A Handbook of Teaching and Directing Techniques*. 3rd ed. Evanston, IL: Northwestern University Press, 1999.

Sweet, Jeffrey. *Something Wonderful Right Away*. New York: Avon Books, 1978.

Stevens, Brad. *Abel Ferrara: The Moral Vision*. Surrey, England: FAB Press, 2004.

Tytell, John. *The Living Theatre: Art, Exile, and Outrage*. New York: Grove Press, 1995.

Ventura, Michael. *Cassavetes Directs: John Cassavetes and the Making of Love Streams*. Harpenden, UK: Kamera Books, 2007.

Ward, Melinda, and Bruce Jenkins, eds. *The American New Wave 1958–1967*. Minneapolis: Walker Art Center, 1982.

Winston, Brian, Gail Vanstone, and Wang Chi. *The Art of Documenting: Documentary Film in the 21st Century*. New York: Bloomsbury Academic, 2017.

Winter, Jessica. *The Rough Guide to American Independent Film*. New York: Rough Guides, 2006.

INDEX

Brody, Richard, 128, 278
Brolin, Josh, 179, 180
Bronstein, Ronald, 3, 20, 187, 234, 286; Safdie
brothers' collaboration with, 241, 242;
workshop approach to rehearsals, 235–37,
240. See also *Frownland*
Brooks, Louise, 282
Brown, Kenneth, 98
Buice, Susan, 187
Bujalski, Andrew, 16, 47, 185, 187, 193
Bunker Hill (1956), 71
Burdge, Lindsay, 261, 264–65, 266, 268
Burnett, Charles, 14, 18, 70, 211, 285; L.A.
Rebellion movement and, 86–87; on
situation of black people in America, 91.
See also *Killer of Sheep; To Sleep with
Anger*
Burre, Brandy, 268–74, 271, 284
Burroughs, William, 154
Burtynsky, Edward, 81
Buscemi, Steve, 129, 131, 133, 134, 135

cameras: Ikegami TV camera, 256; iPhone
5s, 13, 228; portable 16-mm cameras, 12;
portable 35-mm cameras, 28
Campbell, Deragh, 255, 256
Cannes Film Festival, 15, 127–28
Carlin, Lynn, 49, 52, 56, 288
Carmen Jones (1954), 106
Carney, Ray, 41, 53, 56, 65, 287
Carnicke, Sharon Marie, 145
Carruthers, Ben, 42
Cassady, Carolyn, 37
Cassady, Neal, 37
Cassavetes, John, 3, 79, 109–10, 128, 210;
as actor/director, 54, 65, 80; ad-libbing
opposed by, 9, 48, 232; Best Director
nomination, 69; commercial trajectory
of, 16–17; dialogue and, 64–65; digital
cinema anticipated by, 285; as early
promoter of improvisation, 17; on
emotion as improvisation in *Faces*, 50;
ethical issues of directorial power and,
204; on experience of collaboration, 287;
improvisation and, 10, 11, 23, 40, 41, 47,
48, 156, 233; influence of, 18, 47, 78, 110,

227; manipulation of actors by, 56; New
American Cinema and, 24, 70, 120; as
professional actor, 12, 55, 283; rehearsal
process and, 11, 18, 48, 50, 51, 61, 110,
232, 236, 287; on script rewriting, 46–47;
"Slackavetes" filmmakers and, 16; on story
and characters in *Shadows*, 40. See also
*Faces; Husbands; Love Streams; Minnie
and Moskowitz; Opening Night; Shadows;
Woman Under the Influence, A*
Cassavetes Directs (Ventura), 61
Cassel, Seymour, 52, 56, 59
Castaing-Taylor, Lucien, 258
Charity, Tom, 53, 54–55, 56, 69
Chelsea Girls, The (1966), 100, 112, 118
Chopra, Joyce, 15
Cinema 16, 42
cinéma vérité, 100, 101
Clarke, Shirley, 3, 19, 21, 79, 128; American
"underground" cinema and, 82; ethical
issues of directorial power and, 204;
making of *Portrait of Jason*, 101–8,
302n28, 302n30; New American Cinema
and, 100, 120; psychodrama peak (1960s)
and, 234; Warhol's influence on, 100–101.
See also *Connection, The; Cool World,
The; Portrait of Jason; Robert Frost: A
Lover's Quarrel with the World*
class, social, 105, 109
Clurman, Harold, 144
Cobain, Kurt, 172, 179
Cohn, Lawrence, 153
Cole, Jake, 156
Come Back, Africa (1959), 26, 29, 32–35, 34,
282
comedy, 4, 40, 105
Coming Apart (1969), 266
commedia dell'arte, 5, 97
Compass, The, 5
Connection, The (1961), 100
Cool World, The (1963), 100
Copeau, Jacques, 5
Corso, Gregory, 35, 39
Cotto, Valeria, 290
Counsell, Colin, 18
counterculture, 13

FILM AND CULTURE

A series of Columbia University Press

Edited by John Belton